Indian Military Domestic Deployment

Armed Forces Special Powers Act and Human Rights

Indian Military
Domestic Deployment
Armed Forces Special Powers Act and Human Rights

Wg Cdr (Dr) U C Jha (Retd)

Vij Books India Pvt Ltd

New Delhi (India)

Published by

Vij Books India Pvt Ltd
(Publishers, Distributors & Importers)
2/19, Ansari Road
Delhi – 110 002
Phones: 91-11-43596460, 91-11-47340674
Fax: 91-11-47340674
e-mail: vijbooks@rediffmail.com

Copyright © 2017, *U C Jha*

ISBN: 978-93-86457-42-4

ebook : 978-93-86457-43-1

In the Memory of *Didi* (Vijay Laxmi Jha)

Contents

Preface

Every country in the world maintains armed forces to reduce external threat, and in a world that is growing more dangerous and less stable, to contribute to domestic security. The armed forces have four distinct advantages over the civilian set-up: they have superior quality of organization, well-defined command structure, professionalism in functioning, and monopoly of arms. In democratic states, the armed forces have another unique characteristic, they obey civilian superiors.

There is an increasing international trend towards the domestic deployment of the armed forces. The US and Canada have already established separate military commands to tackle internal security operations, and there are political demands to make domestic security a core mission of the armed forces in several countries. In India, the armed forces have been deployed in internal security operations for the last five decades to deal with situations that go by various names such as terrorism, insurgency, militancy, proxy war and armed rebellion. While deployed in aid to civil power, the armed forces function under a clear legal and constitutional framework, defining the basic relationship between the state, the armed forces and the society. They are governed by Acts of Parliament and their functioning is overseen by independent judicial forums, the Armed Forces Tribunal and the Supreme Court of India.

This enlarged and updated version of the text published under the title, "The Armed Forces Special Powers Act: A Draconian Law" takes a close look at the role of the armed forces in aid to civil power. The revised edition has been necessitated by the developments in this sphere since the book was published in 2015. Some of these are the use of lethal force by the armed forces, judicial intervention in the protection available to military personnel, and the use of law as a weapon against the armed forces.

The book contains seven chapters. Chapter I is introductory and discusses the constitutional provisions relating to the armed forces and their deployment in the aid of civil power. It briefly covers the role of the armed and central paramilitary forces; different kinds of conflicts and the laws applicable to these conflicts; the deployment of the armed forces in disturbed areas and the use of force; and the concept of martial law. Chapter II contains an analysis of the special legislation, the Armed Forces Special Powers Act. Besides discussing the findings and recommendations of the judicial commissions and the verdicts of the higher judiciary on the legality of the various provisions of the AFSPA, the chapter also discusses how the law has been successfully used as a weapon against the armed forces engaged in non-international armed conflict.

Allegations of torture, enforced disappearance, offences against women, extrajudicial killings and fake encounters made against the armed forces have been discussed in Chapter III, which also analyses the adequacy of the military legal system in punishing a military person accused of such offences. The 2006 sub-conventional doctrine of the Indian Army states that since the centre of gravity for counter-insurgency operations is the populace, operations have to be undertaken with full respect to human rights and in accordance with the laws of the land. The doctrine further provides for expeditious investigation in cases of allegations of human rights violations and punishment of defaulting military personnel. Five prominent cases of alleged human rights violations in Jammu and Kashmir and Manipur have been covered in Chapter IV. These cases highlight the roles played by non-governmental organizations, human rights activists, the legal fraternity and the public in disturbed areas.

Article 21 of the Constitution of India guarantees the right to a life with dignity to everyone living in the country. The members of the armed forces serve under harsh or extreme conditions and certain of their fundamental rights have been curtailed. In Chapter V, the issue of the rights of military and paramilitary personnel has been discussed.

Mobilizing military for the domestic use has become a norm after the 'war on terror' was declared by the US government and its allies since 2001. This has caused blurring of line between police and military functions; giving soldiers "shoot to kill" powers on domestic soil and affording legal immunities to them. Chapter VI analyses the practice of employing the armed forces for internal security duties in Australia, Canada, Germany, Japan, Nigeria, the UK, and the USA. Chapter VII concludes the study and makes certain recommendations that require to be implemented by the Government of India and the armed forces.

I thank Vij Books India Pvt. Ltd., New Delhi for their cooperation in bringing out this edition.

Noida   U C Jha

August 2017

1

Introduction

Every State in the world maintains armed forces. They are one of the most powerful institutions in any country. In some, they are inseparably linked with the existence of the State and even the State's primary decision-making organ. In a democracy, the armed forces are established by the fundamental laws of the country, embodied its constitution or legal code. Their role is defined by laws enforceable by courts of law and enshrined in the ethos of the armed forces.[1] Most democracies have evolved a set of practices and procedures that ensure that the armed forces play a positive role, are not involved in political activity, and are directed and overseen by other organizations of the government as well as observed closely by institutions such as a free media and other non-international organizations. Citizens of a democracy expect their armed forces to be capable of deterring and defeating threats to their national interest; whether internal or external. They hold members of their armed forces in high esteem for their perceived high standard of professional and personal integrity, which is much higher than that of other government officials.[2]

---

1   For instance, the Indian Army draws its strength from its ethos, traditions and culture that have shaped the organisation's thinking over centuries. The essence of these manifests amongst all ranks in the form of a spirit of self-denial, moderation, tolerance, respect for women and elderly members of society and an ability to live in peace and harmony in a multi-ethnic and multi-religious environment. See: Indian Army's Doctrine on 'Sub Conventional Operations', Headquarters Army Training Command, 31 December 2006, p. 38.

2   The armed forces have three massive political advantages over civilian organizations: a marked superiority in organization, a highly emotionalized symbolic status, and a monopoly of arms. In practically every country in the world the armed forces are marked by superior quality of its organization. Even the most poorly organized or maintained of such armed forces is far more highly and tightly structured than any

Indian Constitution and the Armed Forces

The Constitution is the basic law and founding document of both the State and its system of government. A written constitution lays down a body of coherent provisions under which its government shall be established and conducted.[3] India has the longest written constitution in the world.[4] The Indian constitutional philosophy has three strands: protecting and enhancing national unity and integrity; establishing democratic institutions and the spirit of democracy; and fostering a social revolution to better the lot of the masses.[5] The powers and responsibilities of the union and the states are demarcated in the Constitution of India. Article 246 of the Constitution distributes legislative powers between the parliament and the state legislative assemblies.[6]

The Union Parliament has exclusive power to make laws with respect to any of the matters enumerated in List 1 in the Seventh Schedule (Union List). Entry 1 of List 1 provides for the defence of the country, while Entry 2 provides for the naval, military, air forces and other armed forces of the Union. Entry 2A deals with the deployment of any armed force of the Union or any other force subject to the control of the Union in any State in aid of civil power; and powers, jurisdiction, privileges and liabilities of

---

civilian group. Finer, S.E. 1962 (2006 reprint), *The Man on Horseback: The Role of the Military in Politics,* London: Transaction Publishers, p. 6.

3   Bryce, J. 1905. *Constitution,* Oxford University Press, New York.

4   India, with an area of 32,87,782 sqkm and a population of 1.20 billion, is a union of 28 states and 7 union territories. The states are: Andhra Pradesh, Arunachal Pradesh, Assam, Bihar, Chhattisgarh, Goa, Gujarat, Haryana, Himachal Pradesh, Jammu & Kashmir, Jharkand, Karnataka, Kerala, Madhya Pradesh, Maharastra, Manipur, Meghalaya, Mizoram, Nagaland, Orissa, Punjab, Rajasthan, Sikkim, Tamilnadu, Tripura, Uttar Pradesh, Uttaranchal and West Bengal. Union Territories are areas, which do not form part of states' jurisdiction and are under the control of the central government. These are Andaman and Nicobar Islands, Chandigarh, Dadra & Nagar Haveli, Daman & Diu, Delhi, Lakshadweep Islands and Pondicherry.

5   For greater details see: Austin Granville. 1999. *Working a Democratic Constitution: A History of the Indian Experience,* New Delhi: Oxford University Press.

6   Article 246 of the Indian Constitution refers to three lists of subjects given in the Seventh Schedule of the Constitution: List 1: Union List -includes subjects in respect of which the Parliament has the sole power to make laws. List 2: State List -includes subjects in respect of which the State legislature has exclusive powers to make laws. List 3: Concurrent List -consists of subjects on which both the Parliament and the State Legislatures can make laws.

the members of such forces while on such deployment.[7] Thus the Central Government is empowered to deploy the Army, Navy, Air Force, Assam Rifles and any other central armed police force in any state in aid of civil power.

Article 53 makes the President the supreme commander of the defence forces of the Union and states that the exercise of this command is to be regulated by law.[8] Article 74 (1) states that the President has to act on the advice of the Council of Ministers. It is the duty of the Union to protect every state against external aggression and internal disturbance.[9] However, it must be remembered that in a federal State, internal security becomes the responsibility of the police, and the function of protection against external aggression is performed by the Centre through its armed forces. The armed forces may assist the civil power, but their sole function in a democracy is to fight and win wars.[10] The Indian Armed Forces, which are apolitical, have always functioned in accordance with the Constitution. They have protected the sovereignty of the nation in international armed conflicts and countered violent internal threats and armed rebellion.[11]

---

7 Article 246, Seventh Schedule: List I—Union List: 1. Defence of India and every part thereof including preparation for defence and all such acts as may be conducive in times of war to its prosecution and after its termination to effective demobilisation. 2. Naval, military and air forces; any other armed forces of the Union. 2A. Deployment of any armed force of the Union or any other force subject to the control of the Union or any contingent or unit thereof in any State in aid of the civil power; powers, jurisdiction, privileges and liabilities of the members of such forces while on such deployment.

8 Article 53, Constitution of India.

9 The Union Government has a duty and, therefore, the responsibility expressly imposed on it to protect every state against external aggression and internal disturbance under Article 355 of the Constitution. In substance, this duty is to maintain the unity and integrity of India. The Union Government is expected to use its armed forces for the discharge of this responsibility and, if the situation so demands, may do so *suo motu*, even if there is no request from the State Government concerned. It is clear from Entry 2A of List I that deployment of Union's armed forces in aid of the civil power is a matter entirely for the Union Government. If the consent of the State Government for such deployment were to be made a pre-condition, the Union Government would not be able to discharge its duty under Article 355. In practice, the Union forces are deployed in aid of the civil power at the request of the State Government. But this practice cannot be construed as a legal requirement, nor can it detract in any way from the Union's responsibility under Article 355 and powers to discharge the same.

10 Finer, S.E. 1962 (Reprint 2006). *The Man on Horseback: The Role of the Military in Politics,* London: Transaction Publishers, p. 7.

11 For more details see Ganguly Sumit and David P. Filler (ed). 2009. *India and Counterinsurgency: Lessons Learned,* London: Routledge.

Role of the Armed Forces

The Armed Forces serve as the ultimate instrument for maintaining the unity and the integrity of India in the face of external threats and internal unrest and disturbances. The two major roles of the Indian Armed Forces are to: (a) Safeguard sovereignty, territorial integrity and unity of the country and preserve national interests against any threat in the entire spectrum of conflict by possessing and projecting a robust deterrence capability or by application of force, as required; and (b) Assist civil authorities to cope with internal threats/contingencies and provide necessary aid, when requested.[12] The Regulations for the Army provides that the troops may be called upon to aid civil authorities and perform duties relating to the maintenance of law and order; maintenance of essential services; assistance during natural calamities and industrial accidents; and any other type of duties which may be needed.[13] These duties encompass counterterrorism, detecting and monitoring aerial or maritime transit of illegal drugs; integrating command, control, communications, computer and intelligence assets that are dedicated to interdicting the movement of illegal drugs; supporting drug interdiction and enforcement agencies; and humanitarian aid.[14]

Apart from a border dispute with China which led to a war in 1962, the Indian armed forces have fought wars with Pakistan in 1947, 65, 71 and 99. Exercise Brass-tacks in 1987, the nuclear crisis in 1990-91 and Operation Parakram in 2001, were other instances of military mobilization which led to high tension between the Indian and Pakistani military. India is also facing an ongoing proxy war with Pakistan. The international

---

12 The other three roles are (i) Participate in peacekeeping operations and protect the global commons under UN charter; (ii) Render military assistance to friendly foreign countries, when requested; and (iii) Progress military diplomacy to constructively engage with defence forces of friendly foreign countries. Joint Doctrine: Indian Armed Forces, Directorate of Doctrine, Headquarters Integrated Defence Staff, Ministry of Defence, April 2017, p.18-19.

13 Defence Services Regulations, Regulations for the Army, Volume I, 1987, paragraph 301. These duties may relate to the road and infrastructure construction, assistance to public administration in case of a major industrial incident; or a sanitary crisis following a major disaster. The tasks can also include search and rescue operations; law enforcement; environmental protection; medical support for poor communities; support of training opportunities for disadvantaged youth; border surveillance; provision of security for supplies (food, energy, transport, storage, distribution networks and information systems); security provision during major public events (international sport events or major global conferences); and the replacement of vital services during labour strikes.

14 Schnabel Albrecht and Marc Krupanski. 2012. *Mapping Evolving Internal Roles of the Armed Forces*, SSR Paper 7, The Geneva Centre for the Democratic Control of Armed Forces.

border with Pakistan and in the Northeast is required to be manned on a permanent basis to counter infiltration, drug-trafficking, gun-running and to control the movement of trained terrorists.[15] The armed forces have also supported the civil system in times of civil disorder and unrest, such as riots, communal violence, strikes and rebellions. India has moved to a pro-active and pragmatic philosophy to counter various conflict situations. The response to terror provocations could be in the form of 'surgical strikes'. In recent years the Indian Army has launched two surgical strikes; the first against militant outfits in Myanmar and the second against terror launch pads in Pakistan Occupied Kashmir.[16] This is true to other countries as well. For instance the Canadian Army was deployed against a Mohawk uprising known as the "Oka Crisis" in 1990;[17] the British armed forces were actively involved in Northern Ireland, including the notorious "Bloody Sunday" incident of 1972; [18] and the French military was deployed for domestic security in 1996. [19]

---

15 Kasturi Bhashyam, 'The State of War with Pakistan', in Marston Daniel P. And Chander S. Sundaram (ed.). 2007. *A Military History of India and South Asia: From the East India Company to the Nuclear Era*, London: Praeger Security International, p. 139-156.

16 The surgical strikes took place inside the Myanmar border against militant outfits on 9 June 2015 in retaliation for their previous ambush on an army convoy and in Pakistan-occupied Kashmir (POK) Uri sector on 29 September 2016.

17 The 1990 Oka Crisis was a land dispute between the Mohawk indigenous community of Kanesatake and the town of Oka, Quebec, particularly centering around the question of indigenous land rights and historical burial grounds. The dispute escalated to an armed conflict along with massive land and road blockades by protesting members of the Mohawk community. After the deployment of provincial police, followed by the Royal Canadian Mounted Police (RCMP), the Quebec premier invoked the National Defence Act section 275 to requisition military support in "aid of the civil power". Schnabel Albrecht and Marc Krupanski, *Mapping Evolving Internal Roles of the Armed Forces*, SSR Paper 7, (2012), The Geneva Centre for the Democratic Control of Armed Forces.

18 The British troops were officially deployed between 1969 and 2007 under the mandate of securing law and order in response to violent tensions between Irish republican and British unionist communities and paramilitary forces during a period known as "the Troubles". The British Army was deployed in support of the Royal Ulster Constabulary and later the Police Service of Northern Ireland, and became a lightning rod for republican forces. Legally, much of the deployment fell under the Northern Ireland (Emergency Provisions) Act 1973, which followed the imposition of direct rule of Northern Ireland by the British government. Additionally, in 2002 when the UK firefighters union took industrial action by going on strike, the British armed forces were called into service to provide emergency cover. Schnabel Albrecht and Marc Krupanski, *Mapping Evolving Internal Roles of the Armed Forces*, SSR Paper 7, (2012), The Geneva Centre for the Democratic Control of Armed Forces.

19 In 1996, over 200,000 French soldiers were deployed in domestic security as part of Operation Vigipirate. The land, air and sea forces participated in the operation alongside

The domestic counterterrorism roles of the armed forces have expanded greatly across the world. The domestic deployment of the armed forces of some countries has been discussed in Chapter VI of this book. The internal disturbances in the South and West Asia have had an impact on India; which shares borders with six countries. South Asia has emerged as the epicentre of global terrorism; and the vast and porous nature of Indian borders continues to be exploited by hostile elements for gun running, illegal immigration, drug-trafficking, circulation of counterfeit currency, money laundering, etc. These activities undermine India's internal security environment.[20]

The Central Paramilitary and Armed Police Forces

In India, the central paramilitary and armed police forces play a significant role in ensuring border security and maintaining the domestic law and order situation.[21] A paramilitary is a militarized force whose function and organization are similar to those of a professional military, but which is not considered part of a State's formal armed forces. The Crown Representative's Police Force was raised in 1939 as a reserve force to aid the former Princely States in maintaining law and order in times of emergency. After independence, it was renamed as the Central Reserve Police Force (CRPF) under the Central Reserve Police Force Act, 1949. The Assam Rifles was initially raised as a police force mainly to guard the plains of Assam from the tribes inhabiting the surrounding hill tracts,

---

gendarmerie and police, with the purpose of enhancing security and patrols in stations, airports, ports and other key spots; airspace patrol to intercept suspect aircraft; and monitoring maritime activities. Schnabel Albrecht and Marc Krupanski, *Mapping Evolving Internal Roles of the Armed Forces*, SSR Paper 7, (2012), The Geneva Centre for the Democratic Control of Armed Forces.

20 For more details see: Katzman Kenneth and Thomas Clayton, Afghanistan: Post-Taliban Governance, Security and US Policy, Congressional Research Service, July 24, 2017, pp.78.

21 There are six central armed police forces (CAPFs), namely, Border Security Force (BSF), Central Industrial Security Force (CISF), Central Reserve Police Force (CRPF), Indo-Tibetan Border Police (ITBP), Sashastra Seema Bal (SSB) and National Security Guards (NSG) and one central paramilitary force (CPMF), namely, Assam Rifles (AR) governed by the Ministry of Home Affairs (MHA). Out of these seven paramilitary/armed police forces, the AR, BSF, ITBP and SSB are entrusted with guarding the border, while the CRPF assists the states/Union territories in the maintenance of public order. The CRPF is also trained and equipped to perform counter-insurgency duties. The Rapid Action Force (RAF) and Commando Battalion for Resolute Action (CoBRA) are specialized wings of the CRPF to deal with riots and extremism/insurgency.

but it became an armed force when the Assam Rifles Act, 1941, a Central Act, came into force. This Act has been replaced by the Assam Rifles Act 2006. The Assam Rifles has been assigned certain special functions in the north-eastern region, *viz.* the security of international borders in certain sectors, counter-insurgency operations and assistance to civil authorities in maintaining law and order in sensitive areas. Three other paramilitary forces were raised after the CRPF and the Assam Rifles. These are the Indo-Tibetan Border Police (ITBP) in 1962, the Border Security Force (BSF) in 1965, and the Central Industrial Security Force (CISF) in 1969. The Railway Protection Force was made an armed force in 1985. Like the CRPF and the Assam Rifles, these too are armed forces of the Union. Their names broadly describe their functions.

Under Section 139 of the BSF Act, 1968 members of the Force exercise powers and discharge duties under Union Acts like the Passport (Entry into India) Act, 1920 and Registration of Foreigners Act, 1939, as also the Criminal Procedure Code, 1973 (Cr PC) when they function within the local limits of specified areas adjoining the borders. The purpose of their being so empowered is to prevent cognizable offences under these Acts and to apprehend offenders. The members of the CRPF when deployed in a state, have certain powers of arrest, search, pursuit of offender, seize, and dispersal of unlawful assembly by use of civil force, etc., under the Cr PC.

When a request is received from a state government for the assistance of armed forces, the Union Government, after reviewing the availability of the state government's own armed police, tries to meet the requirement by deploying central paramilitary/ armed police forces. The mushrooming of organized transnational crime groups and their nexus with terrorists and the exploitation of the resulting situation by Pakistani Inter-Services Intelligence (ISI) to wage a proxy war against India have also kept the central paramilitary/armed police forces busy.[22]

Armed Conflict

Before discussing the role of the armed forces in domestic deployment, it is important to look at how international law defines the term 'armed

---

22 Mallick, P. K., Role of the Armed Forces in Internal Security: Time for Review, *CLAWS Journal*, Winter 2007, p. 68-120.

conflict'.[23] The four Geneva Conventions of 1949[24] provides no definitive definition of the term, though the term is specifically used in Common Article 2 and Common Article 3 of the Geneva Conventions.[25] International law recognizes at least four different types of conflict situations, each of which is governed by a different set of legal norms. These are (i) international armed conflicts; (ii) wars of national liberation; (iii) internal armed conflicts; and (iv) situations of tension and disturbance.[26] The term "international armed conflict" refers to situations that involve two or more States engaged in armed conflict. In such situations, the central provisions of international humanitarian law (IHL)[27] become operative, particularly those contained in the four Geneva Conventions of 1949 and the 1977 Additional Protocol I (AP I) to the Geneva Conventions. In addition, most human rights guarantees remain applicable in such situations, albeit subject to the same types of derogations and limitations permitted to governments in situations of internal tension and disturbance. The term "wars of national liberation" refers to armed conflicts in which "peoples are fighting against colonial domination and alien occupation and against racist regimes in the exercise of their right to self-determination". Generally,

---

23 Recent events have led to a debate about what constitutes armed conflict in international law. The emergence of non-State groups as a major threat to international peace and security and the assertions of few States that the "war on terror" is an armed conflict under international law have been at the centre of the controversy. Currently, there is no authoritative definition of armed conflict in international law and the debate focuses almost solely on how the term "armed conflict" is used in the Geneva Conventions of 1949 and their Additional Protocols of 1977, which form the core of international humanitarian law (IHL). Balendra Natasha, Defining Armed Conflict, *Cordazo Law Review*, Vol. 29 (6), 2008, p. 2461-2516.

24 The four Geneva Conventions of 1949 are: I Amelioration of the condition of the wounded and sick in armed forces in the field; II Amelioration of the condition of wounded, sick and shipwrecked members of armed forces at sea; III Treatment of prisoners of war; and IV Protection of civilian persons in time of war.

25 Graham, David E., 'Defining Non-International Armed Conflict: A Historically Difficult Task', in Watkin Kenneth and Andrew J. Norris (eds.). 2011. *Non-International Armed Conflict in the Twenty-first Century*, International Law Series, Vol. 88, the US Naval War College, p. 43-56.

26 Freeman Mark, International Law and Internal Armed Conflict: Clarifying the Interplay between Human Rights and Humanitarian Protections, available at: http://sites.tufts.edu/jha/archives/152, accessed 23 October 2014.

27 International humanitarian law (IHL) is a set of rules which seek, for humanitarian reasons, to limit the effects of armed conflict. It protects persons who are not or are no longer participating in the hostilities and restricts the means and methods of warfare. IHL is also known as the law of war or the law of armed conflict.

the same provisions of IHL and international human rights laws (IHRL) that apply in the context of international armed conflict apply equally in the context of wars of national liberation.

The term "internal armed conflict" refers to all armed conflicts that cannot be characterized as either international armed conflicts or wars of national liberation. The 1977 Additional Protocol II (AP II) to the Geneva Conventions of 1949 provides that internal armed conflicts "must take place in the territory of a High Contracting Party between its armed forces and dissident armed forces or other organized armed groups which, under responsible command, exercise such control over a part of its territory as to enable them to carry out sustained and concerted military operations and to implement the Protocol".[28] The term "internal tensions and disturbances" refers to situations that fall short of armed conflict, but involve the use of force and other repressive measures by a government to maintain or restore public order or public safety. Only IHRL applies in such situations, and the governments may derogate from or limit a restricted set of obligations under IHRL in the context of tensions and disturbances.

Kinds of Internal Armed Conflicts

Countries that have deployed their armed forces in the aid of civil power are generally reluctant to use the term 'internal or non-international armed conflict' to describe the situation prevailing in their territory. One of the main reasons for this is that terrorism or militancy is a new form of threat, from a new kind of combatants who are supported by actors across the international border. Several terms such as 'low intensity conflict', 'counter-revolutionary war', 'military operations other than war', 'sub-conventional operations', 'asymmetrical war', 'fourth generation war', 'hybrid war', 'small wars', and 'war on terror' have been used to describe internal or non-international armed conflict.

Low intensity conflict (LIC) operation is a politico-military confrontation between contending States or groups, below conventional war and above routine peaceful competition among States. Proxy war is

---

28 According to Fleck, "A non-international or internal armed conflict is a confrontation between the existing government authority and group of persons subordinate to this authority or between different groups none of which acts on behalf of the government, which is carried out by force of arms within national territory and reaches the magnitude of an armed confrontation or a civil war". Fleck Dieter (ed.). 2008. *The Handbook of International Humanitarian Law*, Oxford: Oxford University Press, p. 54.

being waged against India, by an inimical adversary, engineered through hybrid elements. Counter Proxy war is being waged through a number of means *viz* political, economic, social, cultural, psychological, informational and military. In combating LIC, the military dimension is not dominant, as in conventional war, but supportive - it is low profile, restrained and people-friendly nature. At the tactical level, military operations in LIC may include direct actions such as raids, cordon and search, show of force etc. At operational and strategic level, these operations are conducted for creating a situation conducive for implementation of political, economic and psychological actions.[29]

Military analysts in India have been cautious about the use of the term 'non-international or internal armed conflict'. Only in one book, written by a former Indian military officer, has the term 'internal armed conflict' been used. [30] According to one military analyst, low intensity conflict (LIC) has certain essential features. These are: (i) the nature of the conflict is both political and military; (ii) the conflict could be for the achievement of political, social, economic or psychological objectives; (iii) the conflict is often protracted; (iv) the conflict is generally restricted to a specific geographical area; (v) there are constraints on the uses of 'means and methods of warfare'; and (vi) the intensity of the conflict is below the level of conventional armed conflict. [31]

The term "proxy war" is used when an armed conflict is conducted between nations utilizing non-state actors. At least one of the States must employ a third party to fight on its behalf for a conflict to be termed as a proxy war. The extent and type of support provided by the States to the non-State actors may vary, but financial and logistical support are normally provided. According to Grasser (1983), such conflicts could be also termed as 'internationalized non-international armed conflicts', as they are characterized by the intervention of the armed forces of a foreign power.[32]

---

29 Joint Doctrine: Indian Armed Forces, Directorate of Doctrine, Headquarters Integrated Defence Staff, Ministry of Defence, New Delhi, April 2017, p. 20.

30 Nanavatty Rostum K. 2013. *Internal Armed Conflict in India*, New Delhi: Pentagon Press.

31 Chadha Vivek. 2005. *Low Intensity Conflicts in India*, New Delhi: Sage, p. 24. Also see: Krishna Rao VK. 1997. *The Genesis of Insurgency in Jammu & Kashmir, and in the Northeast, and Future Prospects*, New Delhi: United Service Institution of India.

32 Intervention by the armed forces of a foreign country is not a clear and well-defined phenomenon. The participation of entire military units in hostilities taking place on

'Insurgency' is an organized armed struggle by a section of the local population against the State, usually with foreign support.[33] The possible causes of an insurgency include ideological, ethnic or linguistic differences; politico-socio-economic reasons and fundamentalism/extremism. Interference by external forces or inept handling of the situation may act as a catalyst to provide impetus to the movement. 'Counterinsurgency' is comprehensive civilian and military efforts designed to simultaneously defeat and contain insurgency and address its root causes. It includes all measures taken by the government to combat insurgency, such as operations by the military, economic development, political reforms and perception management aimed at winning the hearts and minds of the people.

'Terrorism' is the unlawful use or threatened use of force or violence against people or property to terrorize, coerce or intimidate governments or societies.[34] It is most often resorted to with the aim of achieving political, religious, or ideological objectives. Terrorism thrives on a fear psychosis and could be employed as a part of an insurrectionist movement or independently. The term 'counter-terrorism' covers all offensive measures taken to respond to terrorist acts and could include actions taken by all government agencies, including the security forces of a nation. The measures could be of bringing terrorists to justice or their elimination by direct action, isolation and application of pressure on States that sponsor terrorism.

---

foreign soil is military intervention; yet difficulties arise in cases such as logistical assistance and the presence of military advisers. The problems frequently remain unsolved. Gasser Hans-Peter, Internalized Non-International Armed Conflict, Case Studies of Afghanistan, Kampuchea and Lebanon, *The American University Law Review*, Vol 33, 1983, p. 145-161.

33 Insurgency describes the actions of a minority group within a State with the intention of forcing political change by means of a mixture of subversion, propaganda and military pressure. The intent is to persuade or intimidate the broad mass of the people to accept such change. Insurgent forces may have help from outside.

34 The lack of a universally recognized definition of the term 'terrorism' is to some extent predetermined by its highly politicized nature and origin. This allows for different interpretations depending on the purpose of the interpreter and on the political demands of the moment. The term has been defined in UN Security Council resolution as "....criminal acts, including against civilians, committed with the intent to cause death or serious bodily injury, or taking of hostages, with the purpose to provoke a state of terror in the general public or in a group of persons or particular persons, intimidate a population or compel a government or an international organization to do or to abstain from doing any act...". United Nations, S/RES/1566 (2004).

The term 'asymmetric warfare' is used to describe a military situation in which two belligerents of unequal power or capacity of action, take advantage of their strengths and the weaknesses of their adversaries.[35] It often involves strategies and tactics outside the bounds of conventional warfare and may include the use of cyber and informational warfare, and/or chemical, biological, radiological or nuclear technologies.[36]

Internal or non-international armed conflicts are, thus, the armed confrontations occurring within the territory of a single State and in which the 'armed forces' of no other State are engaged. Even when a foreign State extends its military support to the government of a State within which a non-international armed conflict is taking place, the conflict remains non-international in character. Internal disturbances and tensions (such as riots, isolated and sporadic acts of violence, or other acts of a similar nature) do not amount to a non-international armed conflict.

Law Applicable in Internal Armed Conflict

The international legal instruments governing non-international armed conflict are limited. They includes (i) Common Article 3 of the 1949 Geneva Conventions; (ii) the 1977 Additional Protocol II to the Geneva Conventions; and (iii) the 1998 Rome Statute of the International Criminal Court. The term 'non-international armed conflict' also finds mention in the treaties like the 1980 Convention on Certain Conventional Weapons, as amended, and its Protocols; the 1997 Ottawa Convention banning anti-personnel land mines; the 1993 Chemical Weapons Convention; and the 1954 Hague Convention for the Protection of Cultural Property and its 1999 Second Protocol. In addition to treaty law, there is a growing body of customary law applicable in non-international armed conflict. The International Court of Justice has recognized Common Article 3 as

---

35 Pfanner Toni, Asymmetrical warfare from the perspective of humanitarian law and humanitarian action, *International Review of the Red Cross*, Vol. 87, No. 857, March 2005, p. 149-174.

36 In asymmetric warfare a weaker party to armed conflict may choose means and methods that are not in conformity with IHL. This is very effective for non-State actors, because opponent States are unable to deviate from the rules in the same manner without facing the risk of serious consequences both in terms of responsibility and reputation. A term that sometimes is used as a synonym to asymmetric warfare is fourth generation warfare. Frida Lindstrom, Asymmetric warfare and challenges for international humanitarian law: Civilian direct participation in hostilities and state response, Unpublished Master's Thesis, 2012, UPPSALA University.

customary international law.[37] Common Article 3, to which India is a party, and customary laws of war[38] govern non-international armed conflict in India.

Common Article 3 provides that parties to "armed conflict(s) not of an international character" (i.e., internal armed conflicts) must apply certain minimum standards to "persons taking no active part in the hostilities". In particular, Common Article 3 establishes an affirmative obligation to collect and care for the wounded and sick, and expressly prohibits four specific categories of acts: (i) violence to life and person, in particular murder of all kinds, mutilation, cruel treatment and torture; (ii) taking of hostages; (iii) outrages upon personal dignity, in particular humiliating and degrading treatment; and (iv) the passing of sentences and the carrying out of executions without previous judgment pronounced by a regularly constituted court, affording all the judicial guarantees which are recognized as indispensable by civilized peoples.

The original text of Common Article 3, before the 1949 Diplomatic Conference stated: "In all cases of armed conflict not of an international character which may occur in the territory of one or more of the High Contracting Parties, each of the Parties to the conflict shall be bound to implement the provisions of the present Convention, subject to the adverse Party likewise acting in adherence thereto. The Convention shall be applicable in those circumstances, whatever the legal status of the Parties to the conflict and without prejudice thereto."

The draft article was considered by some countries as being too wide in its application and failing to protect the rights of States adequately in

---

37 The Court has held that Common Article 3 represents customary international law in both international and non-international armed conflict; Military and Paramilitary Activities in and against Nicaragua (*Nicaragua v. US*), 1986, ICJ Rep. 4 (June 27), at paragraphs 118-120.

38 A recent comprehensive study undertaken under the auspices of the International Committee of the Red Cross (ICRC) has uncovered a large body of customary rules, the majority of which are claimed to apply to both international and non-international armed conflicts. However the study has neither clarified the distinction between international and non-international armed conflicts - in particular in cases where a conflict with a non-state actor extends beyond the borders of one state ☒ nor has it defined the lower threshold at which violence amounts to an armed conflict (for non-international armed conflicts).

favour of individual rights.[39] It was felt that the Article in this form would cover all forms of insurrections, rebellion and civil disorder, compelling a government to grant belligerent status to insurgents who may be no more than a small group of rebels. It was also feared that criminals might form themselves into organizations in order to claim protection under the Convention, and hamper a government's legitimate measures of repression. There were other opinions[40] which saw the draft article as being less than perfect, but supported its attempt to make humanitarian protection as complete as possible during internal armed conflict. It was also felt that the proposal may prevent a legitimate government from taking measures under its own laws for the repression of acts considered illegal or dangerous to the security of the State. It was, therefore, suggested that a sub-committee be constituted to deal with the definition of armed conflict and suggest a draft that would meet the requirements of the divergent opinions.[41]

The full text of the Common Article 3 is as follows.

> In the case of armed conflict not of an international character occurring in the territory of one of the High Contracting Parties, each Party to the conflict shall be bound to apply, as a minimum, the following provisions:
>
> (1)   Persons taking no active part in the hostilities, including members of armed forces who have laid down their arms and those placed *hors de combat* by sickness, wounds, detention, or any other cause, shall in all circumstances be treated humanely, without any adverse distinction founded on race, colour, religion or faith, sex, birth or wealth, or any other similar criteria. To this end, the following acts are and shall remain prohibited at any time and in any place whatsoever with respect to the above-mentioned persons:

---

39 Australia, Canada, China, France, Greece, Italy, Spain, the United Kingdom and the United States.

40 Denmark, Hungary, Mexico, Norway, Romania and the USSR.

41 A special committee was constituted comprising of Australia, the Soviet Union, Switzerland, the UK, the United States and Uruguay.

(a)   violence to life and person, in particular murder of all kinds, mutilation, cruel treatment and torture;

(b)   taking of hostages;

(c)   outrages upon personal dignity, in particular humiliating and degrading treatment;

(d)   the passing of sentences and the carrying out of executions without previous judgement pronounced by a regularly constituted court, affording all the judicial guarantees which are recognized as indispensable by civilized peoples.

(2)   The wounded and sick shall be collected and cared for. An impartial humanitarian body, such as the International Committee of the Red Cross, may offer its services to the Parties to the conflict.

The Parties to the conflict should further endeavour to bring into force, by means of special agreements, all or part of the other provisions of the present Convention.

The application of the preceding provisions shall not affect the legal status of the Parties to the conflict.

Additional Protocol II (AP II) improves upon the "minimum" protections afforded by Common Article 3, although its coverage is not as broad in scope as the Geneva Conventions or AP I. The important components of AP II are Part II (provisions concerning humane treatment of persons who do not take a direct part in or who have ceased to take part in hostilities), Part III (provisions concerning the wounded, sick, and shipwrecked, and medical and religious personnel) and Part IV (provisions concerning the civilian population). Under Part II, Article 4(2) supplements the prohibitions contained in Common Article 3 by adding prohibitions against, *inter alia*, collective punishment, terrorism, slavery, pillage, and threats to carry out the same acts. Part II also provides for detailed special protections for children [Art. 4(3)] and persons whose liberty has been restricted (Art. 5), as well as setting out a fairly rigorous set of standards regarding the prosecution and punishment of criminal offences related to the conflict (Art. 6). In Part IV, the most relevant provisions are Articles 13(2) (prohibiting attacks or violent threats against civilians), 14 (prohibiting starvation of civilians), 15 (protecting works containing dangerous forces) and 17 (prohibiting forced displacements of civilians). However, India is not a party to AP II.[42]

The principle of distinction is one of the fundamental tenets of the laws of war and applies in the context of non-international as well as international armed conflicts. This principle mandates that "the Parties to the conflict shall at all times distinguish between the civilian population and combatants....and accordingly shall direct their operations only against military objects."[43] Indiscriminate attacks violate the principle of distinction and are prohibited in international and non-international armed conflicts.[44] Indiscriminate attacks are:

(a)   those which are not directed at a specific military objective;

(b)   those which employ a method or means of combat which cannot be directed at a specific military objective; or

(c)   those which employ a method or means of combat the effects of which cannot be limited as required....; and consequently, in each such case, are of a nature to strike military objectives and civilians or civilian objects without distinction.

Besides the obligations under IHL, international human right law (IHRL) establishes a range of fundamental and universal civil, political, economic, social and cultural rights that individuals are entitled to invoke as claims upon the State. IHRL aims to prevent as well as punish breaches of its provisions. However, in contrast to parts of IHL (the "grave breaches" provisions of the Geneva Conventions), the rules of IHRL generally do not create obligations for non-State actors. On the other hand, unlike IHL,

---

42 For more details see: Burra Srinivas, India and the Additional Protocols of 1977, *Indian Journal of International Law*, Volume 53, No. 3, July-Sep 3013, p. 422-450.

43 The principle of distinction applies to conflict in India as customary law of war or international humanitarian law (IHL). See; International Committee of the Red Cross (ICRC), *Customary International Humanitarian Law*, Cambridge, UK: Cambridge University Press, 2009, Rule 1 dealing with the Principle of Distinction between Civilians and Combatants.

44 The 1977 Additional Protocol I, Article 51(4). This prohibition applies to non-international armed conflict as customary international law; see ICRC, Customary International Humanitarian Law, Rule 11 dealing with indiscriminate attacks.

the rules of IHRL apply both in times of peace and war, subject to certain limitations.

The primary IHRL instruments are the UN Charter, and the 1948 Universal Declaration of Human Rights, the 1966 International Covenant on Economic, Social and Cultural Rights, the 1966 International Covenant on Civil and Political Rights (ICCPR), and the Optional Protocol to the ICCPR. In addition to these instruments, there are many other relevant instruments including, the 1926 Slavery Convention, the 1948 Genocide Convention, the 1951 Refugee Convention, the 1966 Convention on the Elimination of all Forms of Racial Discrimination, the 1979 Convention on the Elimination of All Forms of Discrimination Against Women (CEDAW), the 1984 Convention Against Torture, the 1989 Convention on the Rights of Child, and the 2006 Convention Against Enforced Disappearances. During an internal armed conflict, governments are entitled to restrict or suspend the exercise of many of the rights established under these IHRL instruments. Some of the IHRL rights are not established as absolute entitlements, but rather as rights subject to reasonable restrictions in order to protect, *inter alia*, public safety. Governments may temporarily suspend certain rights altogether in cases where a treaty contains a separate "derogation clause". Fortunately, most derogation clauses provide that certain rights, like the right to life, and the prohibitions against torture, slavery, and retroactive application of penal law cannot be made the subject of derogation.[45]

Aid to Civil Power

Article 355 of the Constitution casts a duty on the Union to protect every State against external aggression and internal disturbances, and also to ensure that the Government of every State is carried on in accordance with the provisions of the Constitution. In case it appears to the Central Government that a state government is unable or unwilling to suppress an internal disturbance and may even refuse to seek the aid of the armed forces of the Union, the Union Government, in view of its constitutional obligation, may deploy its armed forces *suo motu* to deal with the disturbance and restore public order.

---

45 Article 4(2) of the ICCPR states that no derogation from articles 6, 7, 8 (paragraphs 1and 2), 11, 15, 16 and 18 may be made under this Article. All such derogation clauses, including Article 4 of the ICCPR, stipulate that that the derogating States may not adopt measures that would be "inconsistent with their other obligations under international law".

The expression "in aid of the civil power" in Entry 1 of the State List and in Entry 2-A of the Union List of the Seventh Schedule to the Constitution[46] implies that deployment of the armed forces of the Union shall be for the purpose of enabling the civil power in the State to deal with the situation affecting maintenance of public order which has necessitated the deployment of the armed forces in the State.[47] The word "aid" postulates the continued existence of the authority to be aided. This would mean that even after deployment of the armed forces the civil power will continue to function. The power to make a law providing for deployment of the armed forces of the Union in aid of the civil power in the State does not comprehend the power to enact a law which would enable the armed forces of the Union to supplant or act as a substitute for the civil power in the State. What is contemplated by Entry 2-A of the Union List and Entry 1 of the State List is that in the event of deployment of the armed forces of the Union in aid of the civil power in a State, the said forces shall operate in the State concerned in cooperation with the civil administration so that the situation which has necessitated the deployment of the armed forces is effectively dealt with and normalcy is restored. The armed forces of the Union could be deployed for situations of law and order as also for humanitarian aid such as in the event of an earthquake or floods, should it be necessary, in aid of the civil power. This is because Entry 2A of List I does not limit the deployment of the armed forces to any particular situation. The view of the Supreme Court has always been that legislative entries must not be read in a narrow or restricted sense and that each general word should be held to extend to all ancillary or subsidiary matters which can fairly and reasonably be comprehended in it.

---

46 Entry 2A of List I of the Seventh Schedule of the Constitution (the Union List) relating to the deployment of armed forces of the Union in any State in aid of the civil power: 2-A. Deployment of any armed force of the Union or any other force subject to the control of the Union or any contingent or unit thereof in any State in aid of the civil power; powers, jurisdiction, privileges and liabilities of the members of such forces while on such deployment.

47 The use of the armed forces of the Union in the maintenance of public order (Entry I of List II) has always been outside the purview of the states. Even before the insertion of Entry 2A in List I by the 42nd Amendment, the Union Government did have, by virtue of Entry 2 in List I, exclusive control over its armed forces and had the power to deploy them in aid of the civil power whether for maintaining public order or quelling an internal disturbance.

Amongst all the duties generally performed by the armed forces in aid to civil authority, maintenance of law and order is the most important and sensitive one. The levels of violence encountered in such commitments have been progressively escalating. Under such conditions, deployment and conduct of the armed forces has to be thought through and planned meticulously bearing in mind prevailing sensitivities. The armed forces work on the well established principles of good faith, use of minimum force and prior warning to the people whenever they are compelled to take action.[48]

The Use of Force in Internal Armed Conflict

The armed forces have to be careful against the use of force while being deployed in internal armed conflict. Proportionality is an obligation under international law as also under the Indian Constitution, domestic laws and military manual. The Regulations for the Army states that before opening fire, the troops must warn the unlawful assembly using the 'most effective measures' that the fire will be effective. It also lays down the principle of the use of minimum force and incapacitation rather than killing a violator.[49] The use of force in the dispersal of unlawful assemblies is governed by the following principles as explained in the Manual of Military Law.

    (a)   Necessity: (i) There must be justification for each separate act; (ii) Action should not be taken in one place with the object of creating effect in another place; (iii) There should be no reprisals; and (iv) Action should be preventive and not punitive.

    (b)   Minimum force: No more force is to be used than is necessary to achieve the immediate object. This refers to the actual amount of force used and not to the number of troops employed.

    (c)   Impartiality: Officers and other persons must be impartial in communal disturbances or labour strikes. They should not accept gifts or show favours.

---

48 Joint Doctrine: Indian Armed Forces, Directorate of Doctrine, Headquarters Integrated Defence Staff, Ministry of Defence, New Delhi, April 2017, p. 21.

49 Defence Services Regulations, Regulations for the Army, Volume I (1987), paragraph 306.

(d)   Good faith: Officers and other persons must act in good faith. [50]

The actual use of troops for the dispersal of an unlawful assembly is the most difficult of all military operations in aid of civil power. It is, therefore, imperative that all ranks fully understand its implications. The Manual of Military Law prohibits the use of police methods or being armed with police weapons like lathies and truncheons during such operations. It states that the troops will use their own weapons and military tactics to deal with the situation. While opening fire on an unlawful mob, the following procedure must be followed.

(a) **Before firing**: If possible, the crowd should be warned that unless the unlawful assembly disperses, fire is to be opened and that it will be effective. The magistrate present should give this warning in the vernacular, if he is able to do so. Attention of the crowd can be attracted by sounding a bugle or whistle. A warning notice in the appropriate vernacular, where possible, should be carried and exposed to the mob at the required moment. The police force present at the spot does not come under the command of the officer commanding the body of troops. Troops should be kept out of sight of the mob, until they are to be actively used.

(b) **During firing**: Firing will be controlled strictly. If the officer commanding the body of troops considers that firing by a single or a few individuals is likely to prove sufficient, he will issue orders to one person of a few specified individuals. If more fire is required, he will issue orders to specified section commanders. While giving fire orders, he will indicate definite targets and state the number of rounds to be fired. The most effective targets are usually the ring leaders. Troops should shoot for effect. They should normally direct their fire low in order to injure and incapacitate rather than to kill. Rapid fire should never be necessary except in self-defence. Pauses in firing will give the crowd an opportunity to disperse. Firing should be stopped immediately when the crowd begins to disperse. It should be ensured that the mob does not get so close

---

50 Manual of Military Law, Volume I, 2010, chapter VII, paragraph 8.

to the troops as to hamper their tactical handling of weapons or to get involved in hand-to-hand fighting.

(c) **After firing:** Immediate steps should be taken to provide succor to the injured. Arrangements should be made for first-aid, medical attention, and evacuation of injured rioters to the hospital. All empty cases should be recovered and the number of rounds fired counted and recorded in a diary. Important witnesses to the incident should be detained with the help of the executive magistrate. All arrested rioters should be handed over to the civil authority for being dealt with in accordance with the law. It is absolutely essential that a minute to minute and item by item diary of events be maintained by the officer commanding the body of troops. The importance of this record cannot be over-emphasized, since in case of an inquiry about the firing, such a diary would be most useful.[51]

The troops, while using force against militants/terrorists, must observe the principle of distinction. The use of force should be judicious and governed by explicit rules of engagement that must hinge on the principle of 'minimum force', besides taking into account the political, legal and moral stipulations. The endeavour should be to neutralize the militants/terrorists rather than to seek their elimination. To obviate collateral damage, it is imperative that operations are well planned, coordinated and carried out with precision. All ranks must guard against any provocations that may be induced by the terrorists or their sympathizers. It must be remembered that any unsavoury incident can act as a retrograde step to our initiatives for creating a secure environment. Such situations demand extremely mature handling.[52]

The 'Sub-Conventional Operations Doctrine' for the Army emphasises a humane and people-centric approach. It underscores the need for scrupulous upholding of the laws of the land, deep respect for human rights and the minimum use of kinetic means, to create a secure environment, without causing any collateral damage. It propagates the use of overwhelming force against foreign and hardcore terrorists, while

---

51 Manual of Military Law (2011), Volume I, Chapter VII, paragraph 9.

52 Indian Army's Doctrine on 'Sub Conventional Operations', Headquarters Army Training Command, 31 December 2006, p. 33-34.

affording a fair chance to indigenous inimical elements to shun violence, surrender and join the mainstream as per the laws of the land. Wilful killings of civilians violate the principle of distinction and are prohibited in international and non-international armed conflict.[53] When committed in the context of a non-international armed conflict, the wilful killing of civilians would amount to an offence of murder triable under the military legal system.[54]

Deployment of the Armed Forces

In India, a state government has the sole responsibility for maintaining public order.[55] The Cr PC, 1973 contemplates that an unlawful assembly should normally be dispersed by an executive magistrate or, in his absence, a police officer by commanding the persons forming the assembly to disperse. If this fails, he should disperse them by use of civil force, i.e., by using the state police with the assistance, if required, of other male persons who do not belong to an armed force of the Union. If these efforts too do not succeed, the executive magistrate of the highest rank who is present; may require an officer of the armed forces of the Union to disperse the assembly with the help of the forces under his command and to arrest and confine members of the assembly. The officer of the armed forces so called

---

53 Civilians are protected from attack "unless and for such time as they take a direct part in hostilities"; See Additional Protocol (AP) I Article 48; AP II, Article 13(3). To constitute direct participation in hostilities, "(1) the act (of a civilian) must be likely to adversely affect the military operations or military capacity of a party to an armed conflict or, alternatively, to inflict death, injury, or destruction on persons or objects protected against direct attack (threshold of harm), and (2) there must be a direct causal link between the act and the harm likely to result either from that act, or from a coordinated military operation of which that act constitutes an integral part (direct causation), and (3) the act must be specifically designed to directly cause the required threshold of harm in support of a party to the conflict and to the detriment of another (belligerent nexus)." In non-international armed conflict, all persons who are not members of the armed forces of the government or an organized non-state group are civilians. Members of the armed forces of organized non-state groups are those individuals whose continuous function it is to take a direct part in hostilities (continuous combat function). See: ICRC, *Interpretive Guidance on the Notion of Direct Participation in Hostilities Under International Humanitarian Law* (2009).

54 The Army Act, 1950, section 69 and 70.

55 Public order, which connotes public peace, safety and tranquillity, is primarily the responsibility of a State Government (Constitution of India, Seventh Schedule: Entry 1 of List II), which has the necessary infrastructure for the purpose, *viz.*, the police, the magistracy, the judiciary, etc.

upon has to obey the requisition 'in such manner as he thinks fit'.[56]The officer of the armed forces while complying with the requisition made by an executive magistrate will decide, on his own, the manner in which the unlawful assembly has to be dispersed by forces under his command.

The Regulations provide that when the services of troops are required by the civil authorities, the local military commander will first obtain, through the authorised channels, the approval of the Central Government to their employment. In cases of emergency, when reference to Central Government would entail delay, hazardous to life or property, the local military authorities will comply immediately, as far as possible with the demand, reporting their action at once through the authorised channels for confirmation. Further, the strength and composition of the force, the amount of ammunition, arms and equipment to be taken and the manner of carrying out the task are matters for the decision of the military authorities alone.[57]

In a situation where the measures described above are neither feasible nor appropriate, the State Government may request the Union Government to make available Union armed forces to help restore public order. Even where the public disorder is not serious enough to fall in the category of an internal disturbance as contemplated in Article 355 of the Constitution, the Union Government may accede to the request, unless it finds that the state police force should, on its own, be able to deal with the disorder.

In addition, Section 131 of the Cr PC provides for an initiative being taken by armed forces of the Union, including the central paramilitary forces. In a public disorder situation, when a commissioned officer of the armed forces finds that he is unable to communicate with an executive magistrate, he may, with the help of the men under his command, disperse an unlawful assembly in the interest of public security and arrest and confine persons forming part of it. He should then communicate with an executive magistrate, if it becomes practicable to do so, and thereafter obey his instructions.

---

56 The Criminal Procedure Code, 1973 section 129 and 130.

57 Defence Services Regulations, Regulations for the Army, Volume I, 1987, Paragraphs 303 and 305.

Declaration of Disturbed Area

The Armed Forces (Special Powers) Act, 1958 and the Armed Forces (Jammu and Kashmir) Special Powers Act, 1990 are Union enactments which primarily relate to Entries 2 and 2A of List I, as well as to Entry 2, List III. The former Act applies in a few parts of the seven states in the north-eastern region and the latter in certain territories of Jammu and Kashmir. These Acts confer on the Governor of the particular state and on the President the power to declare an area in any of these states as a "disturbed area" if, in the opinion of that authority, the area is in such a disturbed or dangerous condition that it is necessary to use the armed forces of the Union in aid of the civil power. Specified categories of officers in the Union armed forces who are deployed in an area declared as a 'disturbed area' can exercise, by virtue of the provisions of these Acts, certain enhanced powers, e.g., to fire upon or otherwise use force even to the extent of causing death and to destroy arms dumps. The power to declare an area as a disturbed area has been used by the Union Government in a state troubled by insurgency or violent public disturbances.

Functioning of the State Machinery in Disturbed Areas

The maintenance of public order involves a whole range of functions starting with the cognizance of offences, search, seizure and arrest, and followed by registration of reports of offences (FIRs), investigation, prosecution, trial and, in the event of conviction, execution of sentences. The Union's armed forces, where their members have been invested with powers under the Cr PC, are responsible only for search, seizure and arrests. The remaining functions have to be undertaken by the state criminal justice machinery, i.e., the police, the magistrates, the prosecuting agency, the courts, the jails, etc. The purpose of deployment of the armed forces, which is to restore public order and ensure that effective follow-up action is taken in order to prevent the recurrence of disturbances, cannot be achieved without the active assistance and cooperation of the entire law enforcing machinery of the state government. The Supreme Court has held that the use of the term 'aid' shows continued existence of the state authority to be aided. This means that even after the deployment of the armed forces, the state machinery will continue to function. [58]

---

58 *Naga People's Movement of Human Rights v Union of India* (1998) 2 SCC 109, AIR 1998 SC 431, para 24 and 74.

Martial Law

In conditions of extreme disorder, when the civil authorities, even with the aid of the armed forces, are unable to bring the situation under control, 'martial law'[59] may be imposed in a disturbed area by a military commander. Martial law may also be imposed by a military commander when there is a complete breakdown of civil administration, e.g., during an insurrection against the government. Martial law is thus, the exercise of the right of private defence by repelling force by force.[60]

During the 1857 Mutiny, martial law was proclaimed in divisions of Varanasi (Benares) and Allahabad. While the forces were engaged in fighting, everyone who appeared to belong to or to be siding with the rebels was dealt with as an enemy. After the fighting was over, civilians were attached to the army for the purpose of trial. The State Offences Act, 1857 empowered the Executive to proclaim any district which was, or had been, in a state of rebellion and to issue a commission for the trial of the rebels for any offence against the State or for murder, arson, robbery or any other serious crime against person or property. The proceedings were summary and without any appeal. On 14 April 1919, the Martial Law Ordinance was promulgated by the Governor-General bringing Lahore and Amritsar under martial law regime from the midnight of 15 and 16 April on the grounds of existence of a state of open rebellion against the authority of the government in certain parts of the province of Punjab. There were a number of other occasions when martial law was proclaimed in India during the British rule.

The expression 'martial law' has been used in different contexts by various authors at different times. In earlier times, 'martial law' was

---

59 The term 'martial law' was originally applied to the law administered by the court of the Marshal and the Constable of England. According to Dicey, martial law is the power of the government or of loyal citizens to maintain public order, at whatever cost of blood or property may be necessary. See: Dicey A.V., *Law of the Constitution*, 1915, p. 286. In our close vicinity Bangladesh and Pakistan have faced a few martial law regimes. These martial law regimes were subsequently validated by the Constitution. See: Minattur Joseph. 1962. *Martial Law in India, Pakistan and Ceylon*, The Hague: Martinus Nijhoff.

60 Martial law is not statutory in character. It is the law of emergencies and arises out of strict military necessity. Martial law means the suppression of the civil authority, by military authority, and its sole object is to restore conditions, as expeditiously as possible, to enable the civil authority to resume charge.

used to denote the law regulating the discipline and governance of the armed forces. Later the term was used to mean 'military government' in occupied foreign territory and signified the law administered by a military commander in occupied foreign territory in times of war. In international law, the term 'martial law' refers to the powers of a military commander in wartime in enemy territory. The term martial law as applied to England has been described as the action of the military when, in order to deal with an emergency amounting to a state of war, they impose restrictions and regulations upon civilians in their own country. A partial martial law would include the situation wherein the ordinary law as applied by the ordinary courts is suspended in whole or in part and civilians are tried by court martial. It has been held that 'martial law arises from the State necessity.'[61]

By imposing martial law, a military commander assumes the appointment of Martial Law Administrator (MLA) and takes control of the affected area. He may, however, require the civil authorities to discharge their normal functions under such conditions as may be prescribed by him. Being an extreme step, the decision to declare martial law has to be taken at the highest level possible. Before imposing martial law, as far as practicable, the military commander should obtain the approval of the Central Government. Where the situation is grave, and the circumstances are such that it is not possible to obtain the prior approval, of the Central Government the military commander may, on his own, assume supreme authority for the maintenance of law and order. However, such situations should be extremely rare. The military commander should, in any case, inform the Central Government as soon as possible after martial law is proclaimed. He should also issue a proclamation for the information of the inhabitants that martial law has been declared.

Since the main object of the imposition of martial law is to restore law and order and the functioning of essential services vital to the community, the military commander should issue Martial Law Regulations, specifying therein the martial law offences, punishments for such offences, and constitute military courts for the trial of offenders against martial law. Military courts under martial law are convened under the orders of the MLA to deal with all offences including breaches of Martial Law Regulations. One civil member having judicial experience should, if possible, be appointed to each court.

61 Cyril Dodd, *The Case of Marais*, (1902), 18 LQR, 143, at p. 145.

After law and order has been restored, and the civil authority resumes charge, civil courts may inquire into the legality of the acts of military authorities while martial law was in force. In order to protect persons who have been administering martial law, an 'Act of Indemnity' is to be passed by Parliament under Article 34 of the Constitution.[62] Such an Act make ordinarily illegal transactions legal; free the individuals concerned from legal liability, and make the judgment of military courts valid, without which sentences passed by them would automatically cease on the withdrawal of martial law. Protection afforded under the Act of Indemnity would be only for those acts which were bonafide and performed in the honest belief that they were part of the duty.[63] Martial law has never been imposed in independent India.

Hazards

Frequent use of the armed forces in aid of the civil power undermines the prestige and authority of the state police. The deterrent effect of the armed forces on anti-social and criminal elements fomenting trouble also tends to diminish rapidly when they are deployed time and again. Also, frequent and long use of army troops in civil duties adversely affects their operational training and undermines their morale. Another hazard of granting the armed forces a more prominent internal role may include the loss of civilian control over the forces and the military establishment's potential assertion of a greater role and influence in society and politics, thus eroding the principle of separation of civilian and military authority. There are also fears of potential misconduct and abuse by the armed forces due to improper training for internal deployment and inadequate understanding of applicable civil and criminal law and procedures.[64]

---

62 Constitution of India, Article 34 provides: "Parliament may by law indemnify any person in the service of the Union or of a State or any other person in respect of any act done by him in connection with the maintenance or restoration of order in any area within the territory of India where martial law was in force or validate any sentence passed, punishment inflicted, forfeiture ordered or other act done under martial law in such area." This Article empowers Parliament to make an Act of Indemnity to cover illegalities committed during the operation of martial law. However, the Constitution does not specify by whom and in what circumstances martial law may be proclaimed.

63 Manual of Military Law, Volume I, Chapter VII, paragraphs 15 to 19.

64 Schnabel Albrecht and Marc Krupanski, *Mapping Evolving Internal Roles of the Armed Forces*, SSR Paper 7, 2012, The Geneva Centre for the Democratic Control of Armed Forces.

In India, the prolonged use of armed forces in disturbed areas has resulted in allegations of atrocities/excesses against the armed forces. The media, members of the civil society and nongovernmental organizations (NGOs) have been severely critical of the special legislation giving enhanced powers to the members of the armed and paramilitary forces. They have claimed that the special legislation is an unjustified legal shield that protects the members of the armed forces when they commit atrocities. The provisions of the special legislations, i.e., Armed Forces (Special Powers) Act (AFSPA) have been discussed in the next chapter of the book.

2

Special Legislation
AFSPA: An Analysis

Background

In order to deal with the disorder in certain parts of India on account of the partition of the country in 1947, the Government of India issued four ordinances; the Bengal Disturbed Areas (Special Powers of Armed Forces) Ordinance, 1947 (Act 11 of 1947); the Assam Disturbed Areas (Special Powers of Armed Forces) Ordinance, 1947 (Act 14 of 1947); the East Punjab and Delhi Disturbed Areas (Special Powers of Armed Forces) Ordinance, 1947 (Act 17 of 1947); and the United Provinces Disturbed Areas (Special Powers of Armed Forces) Ordinance, 1947 (Act 22 of 1947). These ordinances were based on the Armed Forces (Special Powers) Ordinance, 1942 (Ordinance No. XLI of 1942), a copy of which may be found in Appendix A.

The Armed Forces (Special Powers) Ordinance was promulgated by the British on 15 August 1942 to suppress the Quit India movement. It bestowed 'special powers' on officers not below the rank of Captain or equivalent ranks in the Air Force and the Navy to deal with an 'emergency'. The said officer or the personnel under his command were empowered to arrest and take into custody any person who did not stop when challenged by a sentry or attempted to damage or was engaged in damaging property. The said officer or personnel under his command were empowered to use such force as may be necessary, even if it caused death. The arrested person was required to be handed over to the appropriate authority for further action. The Ordinance provided some immunity to the officers in that

~ 29 ~

they could be prosecuted for their alleged acts in court only with the prior approval of the Central Government.[1]

The four Ordinances of 1947 were replaced by the Armed Forces (Special Powers) Act, 1948 (Act 3 of 1948). Act 3 of 1948 was a temporary statute, enacted for a period of one year, though it continued till it was repealed by Act 36 of 1957, only to be resurrected a year later in 1958. The reason for the introduction of the Act of 1958 was the deteriorating situation with respect to internal security in the 'unified Assam'.[2] The Nagas, who inhabited the Naga Hills of Assam and Manipur, had opposed the merger of their area with the rest of India on the ground that they were racially and socio-politically different from the Indians.[3] They had voted in favour of a referendum declared independence in 1951 and raised the banner of revolt. The Nagas boycotted the first general election of 1952, demonstrating their non-acceptance of the Indian Constitution, and engaged in acts of violence against the Indian state.[4] In order to deal with the difficult situation, the Assam Government imposed the Assam Maintenance of Public Order (Autonomous District) Act in the Naga Hills in 1953 and intensified police action against the rebels. When the

---

1   Section 4 of the Ordinance of 1942 dealing with the protection to persons provided: "No prosecution, suit or other legal proceedings for any order purporting to be made under this ordinance or for any act purporting to be done in obedience to any such order shall be instituted in any Court except with the previous sanction of the Central Government, and notwithstanding anything contained in any other law for the time being in force, no person purporting in good faith to make such an order or to do any act in obedience thereto shall, whatever consequences ensure, be liable therefor."

2   Before Independence, the Naga and Mizo Hills were not properly administered by the British, so the independent Indian government inherited little authority in those areas. Prior to the outbreak of armed violence, the degree of governance in both the Naga and Mizo Hills was insignificant. Governance in the state of Assam was marked by corruption, economic weakness and administrative neglect. The insurgency movements in these areas were also rife with internal tensions. There were competing sources of power, and disagreements about strategy and tactics. For more details see: Walter C Ladwig III, 'Insights from the Northeast: Counterinsurgency in Nagaland and Mizoram', in Ganguly Sumit and David P. Fidler (ed.). 2009. *India and Counterinsurgency: Lessons Learned*, London: Routledge, p. 45-62.

3   The Naga movement for an independent unified homeland for Naga inhabitants has a long history. Its roots can be traced back to the British colonial period. For more details see: Goswami Namrata, The Naga Narrative of Conflict: Envisioning a Resolution Roadmap, *Strategic Analysis*, Vol. 31, No. 2, March 2007, p. 287-313.

4   Das Pushpita, 'The History of Armed Forces Special Powers Act', in Chadha Vivek (ed.), *Armed Forces Special Powers Act: The Debate*, IDSA Monograph Series No. 7, 2012, New Delhi: IDSA, p.12.

situation worsened, the state government deployed the Assam Rifles in the Naga Hills and enacted the Assam Disturbed Areas Act, 1955 (ADAA), to provide a legal framework for the paramilitary forces as well as the armed state police to contain insurgency.[5] However, the Assam Rifles and the state armed police were not successful in containing the Naga rebellion and the rebel Naga Nationalists Council (NNC) formed a parallel government 'The Federal Government of Nagaland', on 22 March 1956.

This intensified the widespread violence in the Naga Hills. The state administration could not handle the situation effectively and it asked for Central assistance. In response the Central government sent the army to quell the rebellion and restore normalcy in the region. The President of India promulgated the Armed Forces (Assam and Manipur) Special Powers Ordinance on 22 May 1958 to confer 'special powers' on the armed forces, as well as provide them with a legal framework to function within the 'disturbed areas' of Assam and the Union Territory of Manipur. A Bill seeking to replace the ordinance was subsequently introduced in the monsoon session of Parliament on 18 August 1958. While introducing the Bill, the Union Home Minister, G B Pant, said: "This is a very simple measure. It only seeks to protect the steps the armed forces might have to take in the disturbed areas... It will be applied only to such parts as have been declared by the administrations concerned as being disturbed.... After such a declaration has been made, then alone the provisions of this Bill will be applicable to that particular area. I do not think it is necessary for me to say more in this connection. It is a simple measure."

Several members of Parliament, however, argued that giving such sweeping powers to the armed forces would lead to the violation of the fundamental rights of the people. They felt that it would allow the government to circumvent the Constitution to impose an emergency, without actually declaring it and the armed forces would usurp all the powers of the civilian government. Further, they feared that it would allow the armed forces to commit excesses with impunity. After a brief discussion, the Bill was passed by both the houses of the Parliament with retrospective effect from 22 May 1958. It received the President's assent on

---

5   The ADAA was a copy of the Armed Forces Special Powers Ordinance of 1942. It gave 'special powers' to the armed forces engaged in counterinsurgency operations. For more details see: Kotwal Dinesh, The Naga Insurgency: the Past and the Future, *Strategic Analysis*, Volume 24, No 4, July 2000, p 751.

11 September 1958 and finally the 1942 Ordinance was reincarnated in the name of the Armed Forces (Special Powers) Act, 1958.

In the decade that followed, the northeast was divided into separate states to accommodate the ethnic claims of various tribal and other ethnic groups. In 1972, the Armed Forces (Special Powers) Act was amended to cover the states of Assam, Manipur, Meghalaya, Nagaland and Tripura and the Union Territory of Arunachal Pradesh. In 1986, the Act was further amended to additionally cover Arunachal Pradesh and Mizoram. The Armed Forces (Special Powers) Act 1958 now extends to certain parts of the State of Arunachal Pradesh, Assam, Manipur, Meghalaya, Mizoram, Nagaland and Tripura.[6]

In November 2015, a full bench of the Meghalaya High Court issued a *suo moto* order, directing the Government of India to consider promulgation of the AFSPA in the Garo Hills region of the State. The order was issued in the context of the Court's negative perception of the internal security situation in the southern parts of the State, particularly in the South-West, South, West and East Garo Hills districts, and regions bordering Bangladesh. The High Court cited various recent instances of widespread lawlessness in the region including extortions and kidnappings by Garo National Liberation Army (GNLA) insurgents. The court said that even the police and civil administrative stealthily fulfil the illegal demands of the insurgents.[7] However, the officials of the Central Government were

---

6   The Armed Forces (Special Powers) Act, 1958, section 1. The AFSPA is not applicable in the entire northeastern part of India. For example, in Arunachal Pradesh the Act is applicable only to the two eastern districts of Tirap and Changlang, which have been declared as 'disturbed areas'. In Meghalaya, the Act is applicable only in a 20-Kilometer belt along the Assam border. Similar is the case with other States.

7   The Court Order particularly cited the abduction of 25 civilians, 27 businessmen, 25 private sector employees, five government engineers, five teachers and a Block Development Officer between January and October 2015. An assistant central intelligence officer was also abducted and killed in the last week of September 2015. The Court Order also mentioned that the judges have also received veiled threats. , the Bench reminded the Union Government of its constitutional obligation to protect the State against internal disturbance under Article 355 and the fundamental rights of the citizens under Article 21. To ensure an environment that sustains normal civic life and the basic rights of the people in the State, the High Court observed that it has no option but to direct the Central Government to consider invoking the AFSPA in the Garo Hills area and the deployment of armed and para-military forces in the aid, but certainly not under the control, of civil and police authorities. In other words, the Court has expressed its exasperation at the ineffectiveness of the State administration in curbing these insurgent groups despite the presence of the Central Armed Police Forces

of the view that situation in Garo Hills was not serious enough to warrant deployment of the army and the local government was competent to manage the situation with the help of central police forces.

The Armed Forces (Special Powers) Act, 1958

The Armed Forces (Special Powers) Act, 1958 (or AFSPA) defines the 'armed forces' as 'the military forces and the air forces of the Union so operating'.[8] Under the Act, the term 'disturbed area' means an area which has for the time being been declared by notification to be a disturbed area. The Delhi High Court has held that the lack of precision in the definition is not an issue since the government and the people of India understand its meaning. According to the Court, "The term 'disturbed area' defies any definition—it has to be adjudged according to the location, situation and circumstances of a particular case."[9] The Act provides that all the words and expressions used in the AFSPA, but not defined in it shall have meanings assigned to them in the Air Force Act 1950, or the Army Act 1950.[10]

Power to Declare Areas as Disturbed Areas

The AFSPA provides that if the Governor of a state or the Central Government is of the opinion that the whole or any part of the state is in such a disturbed or dangerous condition that the use of the armed forces in aid of the civil powers is necessary, the said Governor or the Central Government may, by notification in the Official Gazette, declare the whole or such part of the state or Union territory to be a disturbed area.[11] The expression 'in aid of civil power' implies that the deployment of the armed forces of the Union shall be for the purposes of enabling the civil power in the state to deal with the situation (affecting the maintenance of public order) which has necessitated the deployment of the armed forces in the state. The word 'aid' implies the continued existence of the authority to

---

in Meghalaya. Sen Gautam, Meghalaya High Court Calls for Invoking Armed Forces Special Powers Act in Garo Hills, IDSA Comment, 17 November 2015.

8   The Armed Forces (Jammu and Kashmir) Special Powers Act, 1990, defines the term 'armed forces', as 'the military forces and the air forces operating as land forces and includes any other armed forces of the Union so operating.'

9   *Indrajit Barua v State of Assam* AIR 1983 Del 54.

10 The Armed Forces (Special Powers) Act 1958 section 2(c).

11 The Armed Forces (Special Powers) Act 1958 section 3.

be aided, i.e., the civil authority will continue to function even after the deployment of the armed forces.[12]

The power to declare an area as a disturbed area cannot be construed as conferring the power to issue such a declaration without any time limit. There should be a periodic review of the declaration before the expiry of six months. Although a declaration under this provision can be made by the Central Government *suo moto* without consulting the concerned state government, it is desirable that the state government be consulted. The conferment of the power to make such a declaration on the Central Government is not violative of the federal scheme as envisaged by the Constitution.[13]

Special powers of the armed forces

Section 4 of the AFSPA confers special powers on commissioned officers, warrant officers and non-commissioned officers (NCOs) or any other persons of equivalent rank in the armed forces. These officers, acting in a disturbed area, for the maintenance of public order, may after giving due warning, fire upon or otherwise use force against, even to cause the death of, any person who acts in contravention of any law in the disturbed area or is carries weapons or things capable of being used as weapons or ammunition or explosive substances. The armed forces personnel under the power conferred by section 4 of the AFSPA, cannot kill a person without any reason, as alleged by various human rights activists. The pre-conditions, *inter alia*, are:

(a) There has to be a **declaration of disturbed area** by a high level authority as mentioned in the Act.

(b) The concerned officer has to be of the opinion that it is **necessary to do for the maintenance of public order**.

(c) He has to **give such due warning** as he may consider necessary.

---

12 *Naga People's Movement of Human Rights v Union of India* (1998) 2 SCC 109, AIR 1998 SC 431, para 24 and 74.

13 *Naga People's Movement of Human Rights v Union of India* (1998) 2 SCC 109, AIR 1998 SC 431.

(d)   The person against whom action is being taken by armed forces must be "**acting in contravention of any law or order** for the time being in force in the disturbed area".

(e)   Such law or order **must relate to prohibiting** the assembly of five or more persons or the carrying of weapons or of things capable of being used as weapons or of fire-arms, ammunition or explosive substances.

The designated members of the armed forces are also empowered to destroy any arms dump or fortified position or shelter from which armed attacks are made or are likely to be made or any structure used as a training camp for armed volunteers or utilized as a hide-out by armed gangs or absconders wanted for any offence. They can arrest, without warrant, any person who has committed a cognizable offence or against whom a reasonable suspicion exists that he has committed or is about to commit a cognizable offence and may use such force as may be necessary to effect the arrest.[14] They are also empowered to enter and search, without warrant, any premises to make any arrest or to recover any person believed to be wrongfully restrained or any arms, ammunition or explosive substances believed to be unlawfully kept in such premises and may for that purpose use necessary force.[15]

The power to enter and search must be exercised in accordance with the provisions relating to search and seizure contained in the Cr PC 1973 and the property or the arms, ammunitions, etc., that is seized during the course of the search must be handed over to the officer in charge of the nearest police station with the least possible delay, together with a report of the circumstances occasioning the search and seizure.

---

14 Section 4 (c), the Armed Forces (Special Powers) Act 1958. The power conferred under this provision read with the Section 5 of the AFSPA has to be exercised in consonance with the overriding requirements of Article 22 clauses (1) and (2) of the Constitution which means that the person who is arrested by an officer has to be made over to the officer in charge of the nearest police station together with a report of the circumstances occasioning the arrest with the least possible delay so that the person arrested can be produced before the nearest magistrate within a period of 24 hours of such arrest excluding the time necessary for the journey from the place of arrest to the court of the magistrate and no such person can be detained in custody beyond the said period without the authority of a magistrate. *Naga People's Movement of Human Rights v Union of India* (1998) 2 SCC 109.

15 The Armed Forces (Special Powers) Act 1958 section 4.

A number of human rights activists, both in India and abroad, have claimed that the powers of arrest and search available to military persons under Section 4 of the AFSPA are draconian and excessive. In fact, a police officer exercises similar powers under the Cr PC 1973. Any police officer may, without an order from a magistrate and without a warrant, arrest any person against whom a reasonable complaint has been made or a reasonable suspicion exists that he has committed a cognizable offence punishable with imprisonment for a term which may be less than seven years if certain conditions mentioned in Section 41 of the Cr PC are satisfied.[16] The provisions under the Arms Act and Explosives Act also confer such powers on police officers. The Cr PC gives every private person the power to arrest a person who in his presence commits a non-bailable and cognizable offence or is a proclaimed offender.[17] In making an arrest, a police officer or a private person may use the necessary force and if the person being arrested forcibly resists the endeavour to arrest him, or attempts to evade arrest, the police officer or private person may use all means necessary to effect the arrest.[18]

If an offender has taken shelter in a place to which a police officer is not allowed free ingress, it is lawful for the officer to enter such place and search. He can break open any outer or inner door or window to enter or exit from a house or place where the alleged offender is thought to be present. The only condition is that if such place is in the actual occupancy of a female, the police officer shall, before entry, give notice to the female to withdraw.[19] The civil police are also empowered to search an arrested person in order to seize any weapon.[20] If a person in lawful custody escapes or is rescued, the person in whose custody he was may pursue and arrest him in any place in India. The person pursuing may enter any place to search and may break open any outer or inner door for ingress or egress.[21]

---

16 Incidentally any police officer may arrest without warrant any person reasonably believed to subject to the Army, Navy or Air Force Acts and to be a deserter or to be travelling without authority. The Army Act 1950 section 105 (2) and the Cr PC, 1973 section 41 (f).

17 The Criminal Procedure Code, 1973 section 43.

18 The Criminal Procedure Code, 1973 section 46 (2).

19 The Criminal Procedure Code, 1973 section 47.

20 The Criminal Procedure Code, 1973 section 51 and 52.

21 The Criminal Procedure Code, 1973 section 60.

The power to open fire in a disturbed area is necessary for the functioning of the armed forces against actions of militants/ terrorists that could be described as perfidy.[22] Militants posing as civilians have attacked the military convoys, tossed grenades on military personnel and fired at them. They have taken refuge in houses occupied by civilians or in places of worship. They have also employed or forced women and children to carry arms for them and act as shields. The armed forces deployed in disturbed areas, therefore, have to use force to eliminate those who violate the general principles of laws of armed conflict.

The 'special powers' conferred upon the armed forces to open fire, even causing death, is not unfettered. It may be used in a disturbed area, where the assembly of five or more persons or the carrying of weapons is forbidden, only if a person is seen as violating such a law. In keeping with this, the armed forces deployed in disturbed areas do not open fire unless it becomes absolutely necessary to do so for self-defence or for the defence of comrades or the civilian population. The Supreme Court has held that the powers conferred on the officers of the armed forces, including a NCO under the AFSPA are not arbitrary and unreasonable and are not violative of the provisions of Articles 14, 19 or 21 of the Constitution.[23] However, there are views contrary to this.[24]

Arrested persons to be made over to the police

Section 5 of the AFSPA stipulates that any person arrested and taken into custody under the AFSPA shall be made over to the officer-in-charge of the

---

22 Perfidy has been prohibited under international law. Article 37 of the 1977 Additional Protocol I states: It is prohibited to kill, injure or capture an adversary by resort to perfidy. Acts inviting the confidence of an adversary to lead him to believe that he is entitled to, or is obliged to accord, protection under the rules of international law applicable in armed conflict, with intent to betray that confidence, shall constitute perfidy. Killing or wounding treacherously a combatant adversary in non-international armed conflicts amounts to war crime under the Rome Statute Article 8 (2)(e)(ix). For more details see: Jackson, Richard B., Perfidy in Non-International Armed Conflicts, in Watkin Kenneth and Andrew J. Norris (eds.). 2011. *Non-International Armed Conflict in the Twenty-first Century*, International Law Series, Vol. 88, the US Naval War College, p. 237-259.

23 Conferment of power on non-commissioned officer like a havildar cannot be said to be bad and unjustified. *Indrajit Barua v State of Assam* AIR 1983 Del 54; *Naga People's Movement of Human Rights v Union of India* (1998) 2 SCC 109; *Luithukia v Rishang Keishing* (1988) 2 Gau LR 159.

24 The AFSPA can be held to be actually in violation of Article 21 of the Constitution, the right to life, basic to the Fundamental Rights. Habibullah Wajahat, 'Armed Forces Special Powers Act, Jammu & Kashmir' in Chadha Vivek (ed.), *Armed Forces Special Powers Act: The Debate*, IDSA Monograph Series No. 7, 2012, New Delhi: IDSA, p. 25.

nearest police station with the least possible delay, together with a report of the circumstances occasioning the arrest. It has been held that the words 'least possible delay' means 'within the shortest possible time' though no arbitrary time limit can be set down as it may not be possible in many cases to precisely quantify the period of time by reference to hours, days or months. Therefore, whenever the question of 'least possible delay' arises for decision in computing the period of time the court has to have regard to the particular circumstances of the case, for example, physical impossibility or otherwise to make over the arrested person to the nearest police station, and how, where and in what circumstances the arrest was effected.[25] The provision does not permit the arresting personnel of the armed force to keep the arrested person in custody for the purpose of interrogation, or to be fully satisfied whether the concerned person was really involved in the matter which led to his (her) arrest. This satisfaction has to precede the arrest, and not to follow it.

Protection of persons acting under AFSPA

Section 6 of the AFSPA provides limited immunity to the members of the armed forces operating in disturbed areas.[26] This provision prevents the filing of frivolous claims[27] and protects armed forces personnel engaged in a difficult task and risking their lives to prevent destruction of life and property. Since the order of the Central Government refusing or granting the sanction under Section 6 of the AFSPA is subject to judicial review, the Central Government must give reasons while passing such an order. The Supreme Court has recently held that the words 'no' and 'shall' in Section 6 denotes the mandatory requirement of obtaining the sanction of the Central Government before the institution of prosecution, suit or legal proceedings.[28]

---

25 *Bacha Bora v. State of Assam* (1991) 2 GLR 119.

26 The Armed Forces (Special Powers) Act 1958 s 6 states: "No prosecution, suit or other legal proceeding shall be instituted, except with the previous sanction of the Central Government against any person in respect of anything done or purported to be done in exercise of the powers conferred by the Armed Forces (Special Powers) Act 1958.

27 *Naga People's Movement of Human Rights v Union of India* (1998) 2 SCC 109; *Indrajit Barua v State of Assam* AIR 1983 Del 54.

28 *General Officer Commanding v Central Bureau of Investigation* AIR 2012 SC 1890.

Incidentally, the protection from unnecessary and unwarranted prosecution is not exclusive to the armed forces. The civil police also enjoy similar protection under Section 197 of the Cr PC. The following case amply illustrates this. In a complaint before the Deputy Commissioner of Police, a lady had claimed that her husband, a social worker, was beaten to death by few members of the Calcutta police. On 28 May 2001, she filed a complaint in the court of the Chief Judicial Magistrate, Alipore, in respect of offences, punishable according to her, under Sections 302, 201, 109 read with Section 120-B of the Indian Penal Code. In the complaint, she stated that her husband, a law-abiding citizen with no criminal background was severely assaulted by the police staff, instigated by the officer-in-charge of Police Station; and later succumbed to his injuries. She demanded stern punishment for the murderer of her husband.

The Chief Judicial Magistrate took cognizance of the offence and issued a warrant for the arrest of Assistant Commissioner of Police (ACP) and his application for anticipatory bail was rejected by the Calcutta High Court. The ACP, meanwhile, filed a Petition under Section 482 of the Cr PC before the High Court for the quashing of the complaint on the ground that the Chief Judicial Magistrate had no jurisdiction to entertain the complaint since the condition precedent for entertaining the complaint, a sanction under section 197(1) of the Cr PC had not been obtained. The High Court (by an order dated 11 July 2003) dismissed the application. It overruled the contention of the accused and held: "In its considered view section 197 Cr PC has got no manner of application in the present case. Under section 197 sanction is required only if the public servant was, at the time of commission of offence, 'employed in connection with the affairs of the Union or of a state' and he was 'not removable from his office save by or with the sanction of the Government'. The bar under section 197 Cr PC cannot be raised by a public servant if he is removable by some authority without the sanction of the Government." The High Court further held: "Committing an offence can never be a part of an official duty. Where there is no necessary connection between the act and the performance of the duties of a public servant, section 197 Cr PC will not be attracted. Beating a person to death by a police officer cannot be regarded as having been committed by a public servant within the scope of his official duties"

On appeal, the Supreme Court to referred the Constitution Bench decision on the scope of Section 197 of the Cr PC in *Matajog Dobey v HC*

Bhari[29] wherein it was held that section 197 of the Cr PC was not violative of the fundamental rights conferred on a citizen under Article 14 of the Constitution of India. The Supreme Court had observed: "Public servants have to be protected from harassment in the discharge of official duties while ordinary citizens not so engaged do not require this safeguard." The Court also referred to its earlier decision in the case of *Bakhshish Singh Brar v Gurmej Kaur*[30], wherein it was held that it was necessary to protect public servants in the discharge of their duties. They must be made immune from being harassed in criminal proceedings and prosecution, and that is the rationale behind Sections 196 and 197 of the Cr PC. The Supreme Court set aside the order of the Calcutta High Court holding that for the prosecution of a public servant, sanction under Section 197(1) of the Cr PC was necessary.[31]

The Jammu and Kashmir Public Safety Act (PSA), enacted in 1978 and amended in 1987 and 1990, also allows for immunity from prosecution, stating: "No suit, prosecution or any other legal proceeding shall lie against any person for anything done or intended to be done in good faith in pursuance of the provisions of this Act."

The Armed Forces (Punjab and Chandigarh) Special Powers Act, 1983

The 1980s Punjab witnessed a decade-long militancy fuelled by failed attempts at procuring greater autonomy. Militants were responsible for numerous human rights abuses during the violent separatist struggle for an independent Khalistan, including the killings of civilians, assassinations of political leaders, and the indiscriminate use of bombs leading to a large number of civilian deaths in Punjab and other parts of India. Under the cover of militancy, criminals began to coerce businessmen and landowners, demanding protection money. In order to counter militancy in Punjab, the Government of India enacted the Armed Forces (Punjab and Chandigarh) Special Power Act 1983, which came into force from 15 October 1983. The Act enabled certain special powers to be conferred upon members of the armed forces in the disturbed areas of Punjab and the Union territory of

---

29 1955 (2) SCR 925.

30 (1987) 4 SCC 663.

31 *Sankaran Moitra v. Sadhna Das* (2006) 4 SCC 584: (2006) 2 SCC (Cri) 358: AIR 2006 SC 1599. Also see: *Om Prakash v State of Jharkhand*, Criminal Appeal No. 1491 of 2012, decided by the Supreme Court on 26 September 2012.

Chandigarh. This Act was allowed to lapse in Punjab once violence ended in 1997.

The Act was broadly the same as that of the Armed Forces (Assam and Manipur) Special Powers Act of 1972 except for two sections, which provided additional powers to the armed forces. Section 4 (e) of the Act provided that any vehicle could be stopped, searched and seized forcibly if it was suspected of carrying proclaimed offenders or ammunition or explosive substance.[32] Section 5 provided that a soldier had the power to break open any lock if the key thereof was withheld.[33]

The Armed Forces (Jammu and Kashmir) Special Powers Act, 1990

An armed separatist movement started in Kashmir in 1989 and was supported by Pakistan. Very soon Pakistan started sending its own Islamist jihadis and Afghan war veterans to support the insurgency in the state. As the situation deteriorated, the Central Government imposed Governor's rule in the state in January 1990. In September 1990, the governor invoked the Disturbed Areas Act and the state was declared 'disturbed'. The Disturbed Areas Act of 1990 was temporary in nature and remained in force till 18 July 1992. This was replaced by the Disturbed Areas Act of 1992 which was re-enacted as a Presidential Act. After the state assembly was restored in 1996, it enacted the Disturbed Areas Act of 1997 and declared the entire State a disturbed area. The Act was however allowed to lapse in 1998. In September 1990, the Central Government enacted the Armed Forces (Jammu and Kashmir) Special Powers Act and enforced it retrospectively from 5 July 1990.

---

32 The Armed Forces (Punjab and Chandigarh) Special Power Act, 1983 section 4 (e) provided: "Stop, search and seize any vehicle or vessel reasonably suspected to be carrying any person who is a proclaimed offender, or any person who has committed a non-cognizable offence, or against whom a reasonable suspicion exists that he has committed or is about to commit a non-cognizable offence, or any person who is carrying any arms, ammunition or explosive substance believed to be unlawfully held by him, and may, for that purpose, use such forces as may be necessary to effect such stoppage, search or seizure, as the case may be."

33 The Armed Forces (Punjab and Chandigarh) Special Power Act 1983 section 5 provided: "Every person making a search under the Armed Forces (Punjab and Chandigarh) Special Power Act 1983, shall have the power to break open the lock of any door, almirah, safe, box, cupboard, drawer, package or other thing, if the key thereof is withheld."

Section 3 of the Act, dealing with the power to declare areas to be disturbed areas provides:

If, in relation to the state of Jammu and Kashmir, the Governor of that state or the Central Government, is of opinion that the whole or any part of the state is in such a disturbed and dangerous condition that the use of armed forces in aid of the civil power is necessary to prevent:

(1)   activities involving terrorist acts directed towards overawing the Government as by law established or striking terror in the people or any section of the people or alienating any section of the people or adversely affecting the harmony amongst different sections of the people;

(2)   activities directed towards disclaiming, questioning or disrupting the sovereignty and territorial integrity of India or bringing about cession of a part of the territory of India or secession of a part of the territory of India front the Union or causing insult to the Indian National Flag, the Indian National Anthem and the Constitution of India;

the Governor of the state or the Central Government, may, by notification in the Official Gazette, declare the whole or any part of the state to be a disturbed area. Under this provision, 'terrorist act' has the same meaning as in explanation to Article 248 of the Constitution of India as applicable to the state of Jammu and Kashmir.[34]

Through a notification dated 7 July 1990, the Governor had declared only the 20 km belt along the line of control in the districts of Rajouri and Poonch of Jammu division and six districts, namely Srinagar, Budgam, Anantnag, Pulwama, Baramulla and Kupwara, of the valley as 'disturbed' under Section 3 of the Armed Forces (J&K) Special Powers Act 1990. After reviewing the matter in its totality, the Governor through another notification dated 10 August 2001, declared the whole of the Jammu division as disturbed, in addition to the six districts of the Kashmir division. Accordingly, the following areas now are notified as 'disturbed' under Section 3 of the Armed Forces (J&K) Special Powers Act, 1990: the Districts of Jammu, Kathua, Udhampur, Poonch, Rajouri, Doda, Srinagar,

---

34 The Armed Forces (Jammu and Kashmir) Special Powers Act 1990 section 3.

Budgam, Anantnag, Pulwama, Baramulla and Kupwara.[35] The Armed Forces (Jammu and Kashmir) Special Powers Act 1990 is similar in content to the Punjab and Chandigarh Special Powers Act of 1983.

Various human rights organizations in the country and abroad and the foreign and local media have questioned the effectiveness of Indian laws in dealing with the violation of human rights by armed forces personnel. They have also criticized the AFSPA, which gives enhanced powers to the armed forces for dealing effectively with disruptive activities in specific areas. The United Nations Human Rights Committee, in 1991, found Section 4 of the AFSPA to be incompatible with Articles 6, 9 and 14 of the International Covenant on Civil and Political Rights (ICCPR), 1966, which was ratified by India on 10 April 1979. In reality, there are safeguards relating to imposition of AFSPA to prevent the possibility of arbitrariness in the exercise of power under the Act. The provisions of the AFSPA can be applied only in the following special cases.

- The central government is satisfied that the normal law and order situation has deteriorated to the extent that it has created a disturbed or dangerous situation.

- The state police force is not in a position to stop infiltration or undesirable forces.

- The power conferred by the statute can be exercised only in the specified area and in no other state.

- The law has to be followed even in a disturbed area, for example, an order under Section 144 of the Cr PC must be in force before the powers under Section 4 of the Act can be exercised.

- The powers under the Act can be exercised only in respect of those who are violating law and order.

- Before exercising such power, a warning is required to be given to those who are violating the law in force.

---

35 The following outfits operating in Jammu & Kashmir, namely, Jaish-e-Mohhamd [JeM], Lashkar-e-Toiba [LeT], Hizbul-Mujahideen [HM], Harkat-ul-Mujahideen [HuM], Al-Umar-Mujahideen [AuM], Jammu & Kashmir Islamic Front [JKIF], Al-Badr , Jamiat-ul-Mjahideen [JuM] and Dukhtaran-e-Millat [DeM] were declared 'terrorist organizations' under the Prevention of Terrorism Act, 2002 [No.15 of 2002] (The Act now stands repealed). The outfits remain banned under the Unlawful Activities (Prevention) Act, 2004.

- The military person exercising the power is answerable to the organization for any breach in the policy directives issued by the organization.

The AFSPA also contemplates that in the event of the deployment of armed forces, the said forces will operate in the state concerned in cooperation with the civil administration so that the situation that has necessitated the deployment of the armed forces is effectively dealt with and normalcy is restored. Thus there are ample safeguards to prevent the wanton abuse of the power conferred by the AFSPA.

The Regulations for the Army are very specific as regards firing on unlawful assembly.

Firing on an Unlawful Assembly

When the officer commanding the troops is required by a magistrate under Sections 130 and 131 of the Cr PC to disperse an unlawful assembly by force, he will, before taking action, adopt the most effective measure possible to explain to the people concerned that the firing by the troop will be effective.

All orders to the troops will be given by their commanders. They will on no account fire except by the Commander's word of command. If it becomes necessary to order them to fire, he will exercise a humane discretion in deciding both the number of rounds and the object to be aimed at. If the commander is of the opinion that a slight effort will attain the object, he will command one or more selected soldiers to fire. If a greater effort be required, he will command one or more sections to fire. Each of the other sections will fire, if required, only on the regular word of command of the commander. If it is necessary for more sections than one to fire at a time, the commander will clearly indicate to the troops which subordinate commander is to order any of the section to fire. The order to any one or more selected soldiers or to a particular section will be given only by the commander indicated.

If it becomes necessary to fire, officers and soldiers have a serious duty, which they must perform with coolness and steadiness and in such a manner as to be able to ceasefire the instant it is no longer necessary.

Care will be taken to fire only on those persons who can be seen to be implicated in the disturbance. To fire over the heads of a crowd has the effect of favouring the most daring and guilty, and sacrificing the less daring, and even the innocent. Firing should be for effect and should be aimed low, the idea being to injure and incapacitate rather than to kill. It would be borne in mind that the amount of force, both as regards the number of rounds used as well as the damage done, should be the minimum required to disperse the unlawful assembly or to perform the task indicated. Officers should also bear in mind that they are legally protected if they act in good faith which is held to mean "with due care and attention".

Firing with blank ammunition is forbidden.[36]

There is a contention that drastic powers have been conferred on low-ranking officials like non-commissioned officers (NCO), without understanding that an NCO holds a responsible position. When troops are deployed, the sections/patrols, which go for search and patrolling operations are commanded by the NCO. In isolated places/ remote areas, while encountering insurgents, the NCO is expected to take a decision as regards the suitable use of force in the particular situation, for which he is trained. It is strange that we question his capability in such situations when we never do so in a war or natural calamity.

The government has constituted various committees and commissions for the review of the AFSPA. The details of the findings and recommendations of three such judicial committees/commissions has been discussed in the following section.

Judicial Committees for Review of AFSPA

Justice Jeevan Reddy Committee

There was an intense agitation in Manipur following the death of Ms Manorama Devi on 11 July 2004 while in the custody of the Assam Rifles. An indefinite fast was also undertaken by Ms Irom Sharmila in 2000 demanding repeal of the Armed Forces (Special Powers) Act, 1958

---

36 The Regulations for the Army, 1987, Volume I, Para 306.

(AFSPA).[37] The Home Minister visited Manipur in September 2004 and a number of delegations of the civil society raised a demand for the revocation of the AFSPA. Other groups demanded a review of the AFSPA, but favoured retaining the Army. In November 2004, during the visit of the Prime Minister to Manipur, several organizations and other individuals made similar pleas. On 19 November 2004, the Government of India set up the Jeevan Reddy Committee with the following terms of reference:[38]

> Keeping in view the legitimate concerns of the people of the North Eastern Region, the need to foster human rights, keeping in perspective the imperatives of security and maintenance of public order to review the provisions of the Armed Forces (Special Powers) Act, 1958 as amended in 1972 and to advise the Government of India whether:
>
> (a)   To amend the provisions of the Act to bring them in consonance with the obligations of the government towards protection of human rights; or
>
> (b)   To replace the Act by a more humane Act.

The Committee published a notice in all the national dailies and regional papers on 10 December 2004 and invited individuals, organizations, parties, institutions and NGOs interested in the issue to send their responses within 30 days. It visited Imphal (Manipur) from 27 to 30 December 2004. Though a section of Apunba Lup[39] had given a call to boycott the visit of the Committee; a large number of individuals,

---

37 Ersatz protest against AFSPA is not new. In November 2000, Irom Sharmila from Manipur started hunger strike for repeal of AFSPA from the State. In the due course she was designated as "Iron Lady" by selected group and media portrayed her as a person fighting for people of the State. On 26 July 2016, Sharmila announced that she would end her fast and contest forthcoming election in the State. The objective was to fight for removal of AFSPA, albeit politically. In the 2017 assembly election she received a total of 90 votes and lost her deposit. This was people's verdict and exposed her popularity in the state and the cause for which she was projected as the torch bearer.

38 The Central Government set up a 5-Member Committee (vide Ministry of Home Affairs Office Order No. 11011/97/2004-NE-III dated 19 November 2004) under the Chairmanship of Justice B P Jeevan Reddy, former Judge of the Supreme Court with the following four Members: (i) Dr S B Nakade, Former Vice Chancellor and Jurist, (ii) Shri P Shrivastav, Former Special Secretary, Ministry of Home affairs, (iii) Lt Gen (Retd) V R Raghavan, Former DGMO, and (iv) Shri Sanjoy Hazarika, Journalist.

39 Apunba Lup is a coalition of some 34 human rights NGOs fighting for repeal of AFSPA in Manipur.

groups, organizations and lawyers appeared before the Committee and expressed their views on the AFSPA. The general officer commanding of the Mountain Division, Imphal, also gave a presentation on the existence of various militant underground outfits and the role of the Army in containing the insurgency; justifying the powers and protection given to the members of the armed forces under the AFSPA. In the third week of April 2005, the Committee visited the hill districts of Manipur (Senapati and Churachandpur) and had discussions with representatives of Nagas, Kukis, Zomis, Paites, and other ethnic groups and received submissions. The Committee also visited the Agartala district of Tripura on 8 February 2005, and met a few groups. In Guwahati and Dibrugarh, a large number of lawyers, students, businessmen, individuals and some tribal groups appeared before the Committee. The Director-General of Assam Rifles also gave a presentation on the need for retaining the AFSPA. During its visit to Nagaland and Arunachal Pradesh, members of the civil society, officials of Assam Rifles and the state police gave representations to the Committee.

In the Churachandpur district of Manipur, the responses of the local population were diverse. One group was in favour of the replacement of the AFSPA by a more effective law so that peace and harmony could be restored. Others said that they did not want the Act to be revoked since the people were the major victims of the underground outfits, which were an impediment to the development work. A few were of the opinion that the Army should stay but the excesses committed by them should be checked. Only one organization desired the complete withdrawal of the AFSPA.

In January 2005, the Committee organized public hearings at Delhi. A large number of individuals, groups, NGOs and human rights organizations appeared before it and most of these demanded the repeal of the Act. The Committee was also briefed by the representatives of the Army, BSF and CRPF who favoured the retention of the Act. The governments of Assam, Arunachal Pradesh, Meghalaya and Mizoram also conveyed their views to the Committee. While the governments of Assam and Arunachal Pradesh favoured the retention of the AFSPA, the other two states felt that there was no further need for the Act.

The Committee found that the civil society was under the mistaken impression that the state police forces were also working under the powers conferred by the AFSPA. Hence, people were blaming the armed forces and the AFSPA for even the excesses committed by the state police personnel and police commandos. In fact, the National Human Rights Commission too has used the generic term 'security forces' and failed to distinguish between the actions of the Manipur police commandos and those of the Assam Rifles.

The Committee had specifically asked the people who appeared before it whether they wanted both the AFSPA and the Army to go, or whether they want only the Act to go but the Army to remain. The overwhelming response to this question was that while the AFSPA should be repealed, the Army should remain to fight the militants and guard the borders. A few elderly persons and associations wished both the AFSPA and the Army to remain for ensuring the safety of small ethnic groups and other minorities. According to the Committee's report, "when explained that the continuance of Army's operations would require a legal mechanism, quite a few of them agreed but suggested that such a mechanism should duly take into account the need to protect the rights and interests of citizens as also of the State."

The Committee submitted its report to the government in June 2005.[40] Though the report was not made public, some media persons managed to access it. Most human rights organizations and anti-AFSPA campaigners, chose to quote certain lines of the report which vindicated their stand: "The Act (AFSPA), for whatever reason, has become a symbol of oppression, an object of hate and an instrument of discrimination and high-handedness....It is highly desirable and advisable to repeal this Act altogether."[41] However, by quoting these lines out of context, they acted unethically. In fact, the report continued to say: "....without, of course, losing sight of the overwhelming desire of an overwhelming majority of the region that the Army should remain. For that purpose, an appropriate legal mechanism has to be devised."

---

40 In October 2006, the human rights community in India was surprised at the disclosure by *The Hindu* that it had managed to secure a copy of the Justice Reddy Committee Report. The report was not made public by the government, however, a copy of it was available on a few websites: <http://www.hinduonnet.com/nic/afa/afa-part-i.pdf> and <http://notorture.ahrchk.net/profile/india/ArmedForcesAct1958.pdf>

41 Baruah Sanjib, 'Routine Emergencies: India's Armed Forces Special Powers Act', in Sundar Aparna and Sundar Nandini (ed.). 2014. *Civil Wars in South Asia: State, Sovereignty, Development*, New Delhi: Sage, p. 189-211.

The Committee was of the opinion that there was a deliberate and carefully planned attempt by the militant organizations to damage the reputation and morale of the armed forces. In the view of the Committee, "The requirement therefore is to ensure that the powers of the army to conduct operations against militant organizations remain while at the same time, ensuring that these operations do not impinge upon the rights and the safety of the citizens". It recommended bringing amendments to the Unlawful Activities (Prevention) Act (UAPA), 1967 (as amended in 2004), to provide the armed forces with the protection that had been available under the AFSPA. The reasons advanced by the Committee were the following:

- The UAPA is a comprehensive law designed to (i) ban unlawful organizations; (ii) to curb terrorist activities and the funding of terrorism; and (iii) investigation, trial and punishment of persons indulging in terrorist acts, unlike the AFSPA which deals only with the operations of the armed forces of the Union in a disturbed area.

- The UAPA defines "terrorism" in terms which encompass and cover the activities of the nature carried on by several militant/ insurgent organizations in the North-east States. The Act also specifically lists some of the organizations engaged in militant / insurgent activity in Manipur, Tripura, Nagaland and Assam as terrorist organizations in the schedule appended to the Act.

- The UAPA does contemplate, by necessary implication, the use of armed forces of the Union as well as the other paramilitary forces under the control of the Union to fight and curb the terrorist activities in the country. It expressly prohibits (section 49), any suit, prosecution or other legal proceedings against "any serving or retired member of the armed forces or paramilitary forces in respect of any action taken or purported to be taken by him in good faith, in the course of any operation directed towards combating terrorism".

- Since the UAPA applies the whole of India including the north-eastern states; its amendment would erase the feeling of discrimination and alienation among the people of the north-eastern states.

- An accused would be entitled to the safeguard contained in Section 45 of the UAPA which provides that no court shall take cognizance of any offence under the Act unless previous sanction for the prosecution is granted by the appropriate government.

- The Committee also proposed the setting up of "grievance cells" in every district where the armed forces are deployed. These cells were to receive complaints regarding allegations of missing persons or abuse of law by security/armed forces, make prompt enquiries and furnish information to the complainant. They were to be composed of three persons; a senior member of the local administration as its chair, an officer of the armed forces of the rank of captain and a senior member of the local police as members. The cells were to be located within the premises of the sub divisional magistrate.

The Committee was of the view that after the proposed amendments, UAPA would be more comprehensive in the sense that it would expressly permit the deployment of armed forces and paramilitary forces of the Union to achieve its object i.e., curbing terrorism.

The recommendations of the Committee were viewed as "one step forward and two steps backward."[42] A few human rights lawyers were of the view that the repeal of the AFSPA in its proposed form would be a "fake repeal"[43] as the Committee, while recommending the repeal of the AFSPA, had also recommended the addition of a new chapter 'special powers' in the Unlawful Activities (Prevention) Act, 1967 (UAPA). In view of Amnesty International, if Justice Reddy's recommendations were adopted, it would result in many of the special powers granted to the armed forces under the AFSPA being maintained under the proposed amendment, and the strengthening of the UAPA, which itself already grants powers that are either inherently violative of human rights law or else widely open to abuse. Amnesty International was of the opinion that the Committee's recommendation would simply transfer draconian powers from one piece of legislation to another. It would not change the way the people living in those regions feel, since it was highly likely that the UAPA would be

---

42 Amnesty International, November 2006, AI Index: ASA 20/031/2006.

43 Gonsalves Colin, The Fake Repeal of AFSPA, *Combat Law*, Volume 5, Issue 5, November–December 2006.

applied more heavily in these areas, resulting in the same feeling of discrimination.[44]

The Justice Verma Committee (2013)

After the gang rape and murder of a 23-years-old-girl in the capital on 16 December 2012, a committee headed by Justice Verma was appointed by the government on 23 December 2012 to review laws against sexual assault.[45] The Committee submitted a 644-page report to the Prime Minister on 23 January 2013. The report included a section on sexual offences against women in border areas / conflict zones.[46] The Committee observed that impunity for systematic or isolated sexual violence in the process of internal security duties was being legitimized by the Armed Forces Special Powers Act, in force in large parts of our country. The Committee's observations on "systematic" sexual violence in conflict areas were, however, not supported by any documentary or oral evidence. Nonetheless, the Committee made the following recommendations for immediate implementation:

(i)   Sexual violence against women by members of the armed forces or uniformed personnel must be brought under the purview of ordinary criminal law.

(ii)   Special care must also be taken to ensure the safety of women who are complainants and witnesses in cases of sexual assault by armed personnel.

---

44 Amnesty International November 2006, AI Index: ASA 20/031/2006.

45 The Committee consisting of Justice J S Verma former Chief Justice of India as chairman, Justice (Smt) Leila Seth former Chief Justice of Himachal Pradesh and Sri Gopal Subramaniam former Solicitor General of India as members was formed by the Central Government in response to the country-wide public outcry of civil society, led by the youth, against the failure of governance to provide a safe and dignified environment for the women of India, who are constantly exposed to sexual violence. The committee was not formed for a review of AFSPA. The immediate cause was the brutal gang rape of a young woman in the heart of the nation's capital in a public transport vehicle in the late evening of 16 December 2012. Ministry of Home Affairs (UT Division) Notification SO 3003 (E) dated 23 December 2012 stated: "....in the light of the recent incident, the Government has given their anxious consideration to the need for reviewing the present Laws so as to provide for speedier justice and enhanced punishment in case of aggravated sexual assault....the Committee of eminent Jurists to look into possible amendments of the Criminal law so as to provide for quicker trials and enhanced punishment for criminals, accused of committing sexual assault of extreme nature against women."

46 Justice Verma Committee Report (2013), page 149-151.

(iii)   There should be special commissioners – who are either judicially or legislatively appointed –for women's safety and security in all areas of conflict in the country. These commissioners should be chosen from those who have experience with women's issues preferably in conflict areas. They should be vested with adequate powers to monitor and initiate action for redress and criminal prosecution in all cases of sexual violence against women by armed personnel.

(iv)   Care must be taken to ensure the safety and security of women detainees in police stations, and women at army or paramilitary check points, and this should be a subject under the regular monitoring of the special commissioners.

(v)   The general law relating to detention of women during specified hours of the day must be strictly followed.

(vi)   Training and monitoring of armed personnel must be reoriented to include and emphasize strict observance by the armed personnel of all orders issued in this behalf.

(vii)   There is an imminent need to review the continuance of AFSPA in internal conflict areas as soon as possible.

(viii)   Jurisdictional issues must be resolved immediately and simple procedural protocols put in place to avoid situations where the police refuse or refrain from registering cases against paramilitary personnel.

The Committee's observations that, "The brutalities of the armed forces faced by residents in the border areas have led to a deep disenchantment and the lack of mainstreaming of such persons into civil society", is indeed strange.[47] The Committee's conclusion that serious allegations of 'persistent sexual assault on the women' in border/conflict areas are causing more alienation appears superfluous.[48]

---

47   Kadyan Lt Gen Raj, The Armed Forces Special Powers Act—Need for review? *Journal of the United Service Institution of India*, Vol. CXLII, No. 591, January-March 2013, p. 124.

48   The Verma Report Report, conclusion, para 17, p. 414.

In commenting on the AFSPA, the Verma Committee strayed into areas that were not strictly within its charter. This was perhaps because the members had become swayed by populist sentiments. There is a general assumption that the armed forces let off their members found guilty of sexual misconduct. The truth, however, is that the actions taken in such cases are not publicized. The Verma Committee's comments must indeed sound like music to the ears of the detractors of the AFSPA.[49]

The Justice Hegde Commission, 2013

On 4 January 2013, the Supreme Court of India appointed a three-member commission headed by Justice Santosh Hegde,[50] in response to a writ petition seeking an investigation into alleged extrajudicial executions committed in the state of Manipur between 1978 and 2010.[51] The Commission was established to make a thorough investigation in the six cases detailed in the petition, with a further direction to the Commission to record a finding regarding the past antecedents of the victims and the circumstances in which they were killed. It was also mandated to evaluate the role of the security forces in Manipur. The Commission submitted its report to the Court on 30 March 2013.[52]

There have been recommendations for the revocation of the AFSPA from other Committees as well. These include the Veerappa Moily Second

---

49 Kadyan Lt Gen Raj, The Armed Forces Special Powers Act—Need for review? *Journal of the United Service Institution of India*, Vol. CXLII, No. 591, January-March 2013, p. 123-126.

50 The Supreme Court appointed a special 3-member Commission headed by Justice N. Santosh Hegde, a retired judge of the Supreme Court of India, the former Chief Election Commissioner, J.M. Lyngdoh, and the former DGP, Karnataka, Ajay Kumar Singh.

51 Writ Petition (Cri) No. 129 of 2912 filed in the case of *Extra-judicial Execution Victims Families Association Manipur (EEVFAM) v Union of India* and Writ Petition (C) No. 445 of 2012 in *Suresh Singh v Union of India*. The petitioners alleged that they had documented 1528 extra judicial executions carried out by the police and the security forces and the large majority of these were killings in custody and in cold blood after torturing the persons in custody. They also alleged that a large number of people had been eliminated by the security and police forces in joint or separate operations which were termed encounters.

52 The Commission, after having several sittings including public sittings at Imphal, Manipur, and having received many written submissions, documents, affidavits including personal appearances by witnesses for the petitioners and the respondents (Government of India, Ministry of Home Affairs, Assam Rifles, Home Department of Manipur, Manipur Police) submitted its report on 30 March 2013. More details about the findings of the Commission are covered in Chapter 5 of the book.

Administrative Reforms Committee Report 2007 and the Hamid Ansari Working Group Report 2007.

AFSPA: Legal Challenges

The constitutional validity of the AFSPA was challenged for the first time in 1997 in the Supreme Court of India in the *Naga People's Movement of Human Rights v Union of India* case.[53] The writ petitions and appeals submitted in the case raised questions relating to the validity of the Armed Forces (Special Powers) Act, 1958 (AFSPA) enacted by Parliament and the Assam Disturbed Areas Act, 1955 (ADAA) enacted by the state legislature of Assam.

The AFSPA was enacted in 1958 to enable certain special powers to be conferred upon the members of the armed forces in the disturbed areas in the State of Assam and the Union Territory of Manipur. By Act 7 of 1972 and Act 69 of 1986 the AFSPA was amended and it extends to the whole of the State of Arunachal Pradesh, Assam, Manipur, Meghalya, Mizoram, Nagaland and Tripura. Some of the important portions of the decision are as follows.

> The expression "disturbed area" has been defined in section 2(b) of the AFSPA to mean an area which is for the time being declared by notification under Section 3 to be a disturbed area. Section 3 makes provision for issuance of a notification declaring the whole or any part of State or Union Territory to which the AFSPA is applicable to be a disturbed area. In the AFSPA, as originally enacted, the power to issue the notification was only conferred on the Governor of the State or the Administrator of the Union Territory. By the Amendment Act of 1972 power to issue a notification under the said provision could also be exercised by the Central Government.

> In the UK, under section 23(1) of the Reserve Forces Act, 1980, power has been conferred on the Secretary of the State, at any time when occasion appears to require, to call out the whole or so many as he thinks necessary, of the members of the Army or Air Force Reserve to aid the civil power in the preservation of the public peace. In section 23 (2) of the said Act it is provided that for the same purpose, on the requisition in writing of a justice of the

---

53 *Naga People's Movement of Human Rights v Union of India*, 1998 AIR SC 459.

peace, any officer commanding her Majesty's forces or the regular air force in any town or district may call out the men of the Army Reserve or Air Force Reserve, as the case may be, who are there resident, or so many of them as he thinks necessary. Under the Queen's Regulations for the Army 1975, a service commander who received a request from the civil power for assistance in order to maintain peace and public order is under a duty at once to inform his immediately superior service authority and the Ministry of Defence, but if, in very exceptional circumstances, a grave and sudden emergency arises which, in the opinion of the commander present, demands his immediate intervention to protect life and property, he must act on his own responsibility, and report the matter as soon as possible to the chief officer of police and to the service authorities.

The State Legislature does not have any legislative power with respect to the use of the armed forces of the Union in aid of the civil power for the purpose of maintaining public order in the State and the competence to make a law in that regard vests exclusively in Parliament.

The expression "in aid of the civil power" in entry 1 of the State List and in Entry 2-A of the Union List implies that deployment of the armed forces of the Union shall be for the purpose of enabling the civil power in the State to deal with the situation affecting maintenance of public order which has necessitated the deployment of the armed forces in the State.

Entry 2-A of the Union List and Entry I of the State List contemplate that in the event of deployment of the armed forces of the Union in aid of the civil power in a State, the said forces shall operate in the State concerned in cooperation with the civil administration so that the situation which has necessitated the deployment of the armed forces is effectively dealt with and normalcy is restored.

The word "aid" postulates the continued existence of the authority to be aided. This would mean that even after deployment of the armed forces the civil power will continue to function.

The power conferred under section 4 (a) of AFSPA can be exercised only when any person is found acting in contravention of any law or order for the time being in force in the disturbed area prohibiting the assembly of five or more persons or the carrying of weapons or of things capable of being used as weapons or of fire arms, ammunition or explosive substances. The said powers under the AFSPA are conditional upon the existence of a prohibitory order issued under a law, e.g. Cr PC or the Arms Act, 1959. Such prohibitory orders can be issued only by the civil authorities of the State. In the absence of such a prohibitory order the power conferred under section 4 (a) of the AFSPA cannot be exercised.

Under section 5 of the AFSPA there is a requirement that any person who is arrested and taken into custody in exercise of the power conferred by section 4 (c)) of the AFSPA shall be made over to the officer in charge of the nearest police station with the least possible delay, together with a report of the circumstances occasioning the arrest.

The powers conferred under the AFSPA only provide for cognizance of offences, search, seizure and arrest and destruction of arms dumps and shelters and structures used as training camps or as hide-outs for armed gangs. The other functions (cognizance of offences, search and seizure, arrest followed by registration of FIRs, investigation, prosecution, trial and , in the event of conviction, execution of sentences) have to be attended by the State criminal justice machinery, viz., the police, the magistrates, the prosecuting agency, the courts, the jails, etc.

Under section 3 of the AFSPA, as amended in 1972, the Central Government has been empowered to declare an area to be a disturbed area. There is no requirement that it shall consult the State Government before making the declaration. As a consequence of such a declaration the power under section 4 can be exercised by the armed forces and such a declaration can only be revoked by the Central Government. The conferment of the said power on the Central Government regarding declaration of areas to be disturbed areas does not, however, result in taking over of the state administration by the Army or by other armed forces of the Union because after such declaration by the Central Government the powers under section 4 of the AFSPA can be exercised by the personnel of the armed forces only with the cooperation of the authorities of the State Government concerned. It is, therefore, desirable that the State Government should be consulted and its co-operation sought while making a declaration.

The primary task of the armed forces of the Union is to defend the country in the event of war or when it is face with external aggression. They are trained to defeat the hostile forces. A situation of internal disturbance involving the local population requires a different approach. Involvement of armed forces in handling such a situation brings them in confrontation with their countrymen. Prolonged or too frequent deployment of armed forces for handling such situations is likely to generate a feeling of alienation among the people against the armed forces who by their sacrifices in the defence of their country have earned a place in the hearts of the people. It also has an adverse effect on the morale and discipline of the personnel of the armed forces.

By virtue of Article 355 the Union owes a duty to protect the States against internal disturbance and since the deployment of armed forces in aid of civil power in a State is to be made by the Central Government in discharge of the said constitutional obligation, the conferment of the power to issue a declaration on the Central Government cannot be held to be violative of the federal scheme as envisaged by the Constitution.

The provisions contained in section 130 and 131 of Cr PC cannot be treated as comparable and adequate to deal with the situation requiring the continuous use of armed forces in aid of the civil power for certain period in a particular area as envisaged by the AFSPA.

The State Legislature in exercise of its power under Entry of List II of the Constitution was not competent to enact a law in relation to armed forces of the Union.

Any operation in a counter insurgency environment is normally under a commissioned officer/junior Commissioned officer, depending on the nature of the operation. However, during an operation the group is required to be further sub divided into teams which are commanded by Non Commissioned Officers (NCO). A Jawan is promoted to the rank of Naik (NCO) after approximately

8 to 10 years of service and to the rank of Havildar after 12 to 15 years of service and that a NCO exercising powers under section 4 of the AFSPA is a mature person with adequate experience and is reasonably well versed with the legal provisions.

The AFSPA cannot be regarded as a colourable legislation or a fraud on the Constitution. It is not a measure intended to achieve the same result as contemplated by a Proclamation of Emergency under Article 352 or a proclamation under Article 356 of the Constitution.

The Supreme Court also quoted a report sent by the Governor of Assam on the prevailing situation in certain districts of the State. It read: "Apart from killings, many people were kidnapped and released after the ransom was paid. The extortion, to begin with, was on a limited scale. The magnitude of loot and plunder, however, became colossal in due course of time, presumably in view of the State Government's failure to act." In the concluding part of his report the Governor stated; "The cumulative consequence of all this is that the entire State is gripped by fear psychosis. The holders of public offices have been rendered totally ineffective. The statutory authorities are in a state of panic incapable of discharging their function. The holders of constitutional offices stand totally emasculated so much so that the State Cabinet cannot even discuss the situation. The loss of faith in the efficacy and the credibility of the Government apparatus is so great that the thin distinction between ULFA, AASU and AGP which existed at some stage, stands totally obliterated. A gloom hangs over the whole state. By the fall of dusk, the people are huddled in their homes. Nobody's life, property or honour is safe. The basic attributes of a civilized and orderly society stand annihilated."

The Supreme Court, after hearing petitions challenging it, upheld the constitutional validity of the AFSPA, ruling that the powers given to the army were not "arbitrary" or "unreasonable." The Court held that powers conferred under section 4 (a) to (d) and 5 on the officers and NCOs are not arbitrary and unreasonable and are not violative of the provisions of Article 14, 19 and 21 of the Constitution. The Court further ruled that the declaration of an area as "disturbed" – a precondition for the application of the AFSPA - should be reviewed every six months. Concerning permission to prosecute, the Court ruled that the Central Government had to divulge reasons for denying sanction. The Court also ruled that safeguards issued by the Army in the form of a list of "Do's and Don'ts" - including one requiring army personnel to use 'minimum force' in all circumstances - were legally binding, and that soldiers violating them should be prosecuted and punished. Army officers while effecting the arrest of a woman or making a search of a woman or in searching a place in the actual occupancy of a woman shall follow the procedure meant for police officers as contemplated under the proviso to Sections 47 (2), section 51 (2), section 100 (3) and proviso to Section 160 (1) of the Cr PC.

The following Do's and Don'ts, formulated by the army as guidelines for operations, were also upheld by the Supreme Court.[54]

List of Do's and Don'ts while acting Under AFSPA (1978)[55]

Do's

1. Action before Operation

(a)   Act only in the area declared "Disturbed Area" under Section 3 of the Act.

(b)   Power to open fire using force or arrest is to be exercised under the AFSPA only by an officer/JCO/WO and NCO.

(c)   Before launching any raid/search, definite information about the activity to be obtained from the local civil authorities.

(d)   As far as possible co-opt representative of local civil administration during the raid.

---

54 The instructions in the form of "Do's and Don'ts" had to be treated as binding instructions which were required to be followed by the members of the armed forces exercising powers under the AFSPA and a serious note had to be taken of violation of the instructions and the persons found responsible for such violation had to be suitably punished under the Army Act, 1950. Ahmed Ali, Reconciling AFSPA with the Legal Spheres, *Journal of Defence Studies*, Vol. 5, No. 2, April 2011, p. 109-121.

55 These instructions provide an effective check against any misuse or abuse of the powers conferred under the AFSPA on an officer in the Army inasmuch as contravention of these instructions is punishable under sections 41, 42(e), 63 and 64(f) of the Army Act, 1950; see *Naga People's Movement of Human Rights v Union of India*, 1998 AIR SC 459.

2. Action during Operation

(a)   In case of necessity of opening fire and using any force against the suspect or any person acting in contravention to law and order, ascertain first that it is essential for maintenance of public order. Open fire only after due warning.

(b)   Arrest only those who have committed cognizable offence or who are about to commit cognizable offence or against whom a reasonable ground exists to prove that they have committed or are about to commit cognizable offence.

(c)   Ensure that troops under command do not harass innocent people, destroy property of the public or unnecessarily enter into the house/dwelling of people not connected with any unlawful activities.

(d)   Ensure that women are not searched / arrested without the presence of female police. Infact women should be searched by female police only.

3. Action after operation

(a)   After arrest prepare a list of the persons so arrested.

(b)   Hand over the arrested persons to the nearest police station with least possible delay.

(c)   While handing over to the police a report should accompany with detailed circumstances occasioning the arrest.

(d)   Every delay in handing over the suspects to the police must be justified and should be reasonable depending upon the place, time of arrest and the terrain in which such person has been arrested. Least possible delay may be 2-3 hours extendable to 24 hours or so depending upon particular case.

(e)   After raid make out a list of all arms, ammunition or any other incriminating material/document taken into possession.

(f) All such arms, ammunition, stores, etc. should be handed over to the police State along with the seizure memo.

(g) Obtain receipt of persons, arms/ammunition, stores etc. so handed over to the police.

(h) Make record of the area where operation is launched having the date and time and the persons participating in such raid.

(i) Make a record of the commander and other officers/JCOs/NCOs forming part of such force.

(k) Ensure medical relief to any person injured during the encounter, if any person dies in the encounter his dead body to be handed over immediately to the police along with the details leading to such death.

4. Dealing with civil court

(a) Directions of the High Court/Supreme Court should be promptly attended to.

(b) Whenever summoned by the courts, decorum of the court must be maintained and proper respect paid.

(c) Answer questions of the court politely and with dignity.

(d) Maintain detailed record of the entire operation correctly and explicitly.

Don'ts

1. Do not keep a person under custody for any period longer than the bare necessity for handing over to the nearest police station.

2. Do not use any force after having arrested a person except when he is trying to escape.

3. Do not use third degree methods to extract information or to extract confession or other involvement in unlawful activities.

4. After the arrest of a person by a member of the armed forces, he shall not be   interrogated by the member of the armed forces.

5. Do not release a person directly after apprehending on your own. If any person is   to be released, he must be released through civil authorities.

6. Do not tamper with official records.

7. The armed forces shall not take back person after he is handed over to civil police.

The instructions in the List of "Do's and Don'ts" which must be followed while providing aid to the civil authority are as under.

List of Do's and Don'ts while providing Aid to Civil Authority

Do's

1. Act in closest possible communication with civil authorities throughout.

2. Maintain inter-communication if possible by telephone/radio.

3. Get permission/requisition from the magistrate when present.

4. Use as little force and do as little injury to person and property as may be consistent with the attainment of objective in view.

5. In case you decide to open fire:-

    (a) Give warning in local language that fire will be effective.

    (b) Attract attention before firing by bugle or other means.

    (c) Distribute your men in fire units with specified commanders.

    (d) Control fire by issuing personal orders.

(e)   Note number of rounds fired.

(f)   Aim at the front of crowd actually rioting or inciting to riot or at conspicuous ring leaders, i.e., do not fire into the thick of the crowd at the back.

(g)   Aim low and shoot for effect.

(h)   Keep light machine gun and medium gun in reserve.

(i)   Cease firing immediately once the object has been attained.

(j)   Take immediate steps to secure wounded.

6.   Maintain cordial relations with civilian authorities and paramilitary forces.

7.   Ensure high standard of discipline.

Don'ts

8.   Do not use excessive force.

9.   Do not get involved in hand-to-hand struggle with the mob.

10.   Do not ill treat any one, in particular, women and children.

11.   No harassment of civilians.

12.   No torture.

13.   No meddling in civilian administration affairs

14.   No military disgrace by loss/surrender of weapons.

15.   Do not accept presents, donations and rewards

16.   Avoid indiscriminate firing.

Besides these do's and don'ts, the chief of the army staff has also issued "Ten Commandments" which are to be followed by all officers and men deployed in counterinsurgency role.[56]

---

56 The ten commandments of human rights which are to be followed in the Army are as follows: (i) Do not use excessive force, (ii) Avoid indiscriminate firing (iii) Do not ill-

In the case of *Masooda Parveen v Union of India*,[57] the petitioner, a widow, claimed that her husband, Ghulam Mohi-ud-din Regoo, was taken to the Lethapora army camp by the military personnel on 1 February 1998, where he was tortured leading to his death. It was only thereafter, in order to hide their crime; explosives were placed on his dead body and then detonated. She pointed out numerous subsequent acts of omission and commission which revealed that there been an attempt by the Army as well as the police to suppress the truth. Further, her husband was illegally kept in custody by the armed forces for at least 30 hours and thereafter died in their custody, making them liable for his death.

In June 1998, the petitioner had sent letters/petitions to the Chief Justice of India alleging that her husband had been killed in the illegal custody of the Army. Her writ petition, in the nature of habeas corpus, sought a direction to the central government to pay damages and compensation to her for causing the custodial death of her husband Ghulam Mohi-ud-din Regoo, as well as ex-gratia payment of rupees one lakh and appointment in a government job on compassionate grounds. The Supreme Court referred the matter to the Supreme Court Legal Services Committee, which advised her to approach the J&K High Court. The Petitioner replied that she did not wish to present her case before the J&K High Court under Article 226 as the J&K Bar Association was politicizing such cases and issues. The Supreme Court in June 1999 treated her writ petition under Article 32.

According to the Army, during interrogation Regoo had confessed that he was a Pakistan-trained militant and an ex-divisional commander of Al Barq militant outfit, and had agreed to lead the Army to the hideout of the said group in the general area of Wasterwan Heights. At about 3 am in the morning on 3 February 1998, while he was removing the stones at the hideout there was an explosion, probably a booby trap, in which he died. As proof of genuineness of their claim the Army stated that three members of its patrol party sustained splinter injuries in the explosion.

---

treat anyone, in particular women and children, (iv) Do not damage civilian property, (v) Do not torture anyone, (vi) No discrimination on any grounds while dealing with civilians, (vii) Ensure wounded and sick are collected and cared for, (viii) No meddling in civil administration, land disputes or quarrels, (ix) Ensure a high standard of discipline, and (x) Uphold *Dharma*.

57 *Masooda Parveen v Union of India* (2007) 4 SCC 548.

The Supreme Court pronounced its judgment on 2 May 2007, dismissing the writ petition on the ground that there was "not an iota of evidence to support the petitioners' plea". The Court held that the army and police record pertaining to the incident clearly showed that Regoo was indeed a militant and that the circumstances leading to his death were as per the circumstances put on record by the respondents". While dealing with the provisions of the AFSPA and the detailed directions given by a Constitution Bench of the Supreme Court in the *Naga Peoples case*, the Court observed that: "the guidelines referable to Section 6 and in the cited case cannot be mechanically applied and must of necessity relate to the facts of each case".[58] When a person had been detained (by the army authorities), and his interrogation had revealed the presence of arms and ammunition, the first priority would have been to recover the weapons, as to cause any delay could lead to a failure of the operation. Therefore, according to the Court, in the present case it was neither feasible nor practicable to first inform the nearest police station. The Court further commented: "We are also not un-mindful of the fact that prompt action by the army in such matters is the key to success and any delay can result in the leakage of information which would frustrate the very purpose of the army action."

In May 2012, the Supreme Court in *General Officer Commanding v CBI*[59] reviewed the applicability of Section 7 of the AFSPA, which mandates prior permission from the Central Government to prosecute a member of the security forces in areas where the AFSPA is in force. In this case, the Central Bureau of Investigation had conducted an investigation and filed charges against the military officers and a junior commissioned officer in 2006. The CBI contended that no sanction was necessary to prosecute in a civilian court as the accused could not be considered as having acted as part of their "official duty". The Army argued that sanction was required, as the accused soldiers' actions were done "in performance of their official duty". The Supreme Court re-affirmed the requirement for sanction to prosecute

---

58 Section 6 of the AFSPA 1990 states: Any person arrested and taken into custody under the Armed Forces (Jammu and Kashmir) Special Powers Act 1990 and every property, arms, ammunition or explosive substance or any vehicle or vessel seized under the aforesaid Act, shall be made over to the officer-in-charge of the nearest police station with the least possible delay, together with a report of the circumstances occasioning the arrest, or as the case may be, occasioning the seizure of such property, arms, ammunition or explosive substance or any vehicle or vessel, as the case may be.

59 *General Officer Commanding v CBI* [2012] 5 SCR 599.

in a civilian court, and gave the army the first option to try the accused in a military court stating, "the question as to whether the act complained of, is done in performance of duty or done in purported performance of duty, is to be determined by the (Central Government) and not the court." It held that the term "institution" contained in Section 7 means taking cognizance of the offence and not mere presentation of charge-sheet by the investigating agency.[60] Therefore, a charge-sheet against army personnel cannot be filed without prior sanction of the Central Government.[61] This protection is available only when the alleged act done by the army personnel is reasonably connected with the discharge of his official duty. Further, the Legislature has conferred "absolute power" on the statutory authority to accord sanction or withhold the same and the court has no role in this subject.

The Supreme Court also held that option to try an accused by a court martial rather than by a criminal court is exercised after filing of the charge-sheet and before taking cognizance and not mere framing of the charges. If the Army chooses, it can prosecute the accused through court-martial instead of going through the criminal court. Once the option is made that accused is to be tried by a court-martial, further proceedings would be in accordance with the provisions of Section 70 of the Army Act and for that purpose, the sanction of the Central Government is not required. The army chose to try its personnel by court martial.[62] However, a number of human rights activists and organizations, not being aware of the procedure followed by a court martial; expressed their disappointment with the ruling.

---

60 Section 7 of the AFSPA 1990 reads as: "No prosecution, suit or other legal proceeding shall be instituted, except with the previous sanction of the Central Government, against any person in respect of anything done or purported to be done in exercise of the powers conferred by the Armed Forces (Jammu and Kashmir) Special Powers Act 1990." The term 'institution' has to be ascertained taking into consideration the scheme of the Act/ Statute applicable as far as criminal proceedings are concerned, "institution" does not mean filing; presenting or initiating proceedings, it means taking cognizance as per the provisions contained in the Cr PC, 1973.

61 The conjoint reading of Section 197(2) Cr PC and Section 7 of the AFSPA 1990 shows that prior sanction is a condition precedent before institution of any legal proceedings.

62 For more details see Chapter IV of the book: "Pathribal Killing".

The Supreme Court, in a recent case,[63] has issued detailed guidelines to be followed in all cases of police encounters resulting in death or grievous injury. These norms must be strictly observed in all such cases by treating them as law under Article 141 of the Constitution.[64] The guidelines are as follows:

(1)   Whenever the police is in receipt of any intelligence or tip-off regarding criminal movements or activities pertaining to the commission of grave criminal offence, it shall be reduced into writing in some form (preferably into case diary) or in some electronic form. Such recording need not reveal details of the suspect or the location to which the party is headed. If such intelligence or tip-off is received by a higher authority, the same may be noted in some form without revealing details of the suspect or the location.

(2)   If pursuant to the tip-off or receipt of any intelligence, as above, an encounter takes place and firearm is used by the police party and as a result of that, death occurs, an FIR to that effect shall be registered and the same shall be forwarded to the court under Section 157 of the Cr PC without any delay. While forwarding the report under Section 157 of the Cr PC, the procedure prescribed under Section 158 of the Cr PC shall be followed.

(3)   An independent investigation into the incident/encounter shall be conducted by the CID or police team of another police station under the supervision of a senior officer (at least a level above the head of the police party engaged

---

63 *People's Union for Civil Liberties v State of Maharashtra*, Criminal Appeal No.1255 of 1999, judgment delivered by the Supreme Court on 23 September 2014.

64 Article 141 of the Constitution states: "The law declared by the Supreme Court shall be binding on all courts within the territory of India." What is binding in terms of Article 141 of the Constitution is the *ratio* of the judgment. The *ratio decendi* of a judgment is the reason assigned in support of the conclusion. If the reasons contained in a judgment do not appeal to a subsequent Bench, the matter may be referred to a larger bench but so long as the same is not done, the *ratio* can neither be watered down nor brushed aside; see: *State of West Bengal v Kesoram Industires Ltd.*, (2004) 10 SCC 201.

in the encounter). The team conducting inquiry/investigation shall, at a minimum, seek:

a. To identify the victim; colour photographs of the victim should be taken;

b. To recover and preserve evidentiary material, including blood-stained earth, hair, fibers and threads, etc., related to the death;

c. To identify scene witnesses with complete names, addresses and telephone numbers and obtain their statements (including the statements of police personnel involved) concerning the death;

d. To determine the cause, manner, location (including preparation of rough sketch of topography of the scene and, if possible, photo/video of the scene and any physical evidence) and time of death as well as any pattern or practice that may have brought about the death;

e. It must be ensured that intact fingerprints of the deceased are sent for chemical analysis. Any other fingerprints should be located, developed, lifted and sent for chemical analysis;

f. A post-mortem must be conducted by two doctors in the district hospital, one of them, as far as possible, should be in-charge/head of the district hospital. The post-mortem shall be video-graphed and the images preserved;

g. Any evidence of weapons, such as guns, projectiles, bullets and cartridge cases, should be taken and preserved. Wherever applicable, tests for gunshot residue and trace metal detection should be performed.

    h.   The cause of death should be determined, whether it was a natural death, accidental death, suicide or homicide.

(4)   A magisterial inquiry under Section 176 of the Code must invariably be held in all cases of death which occur in the course of police firing and a report thereof must be sent to judicial magistrate having jurisdiction under Section 190 of the Code.

(5)   The involvement of NHRC is not necessary unless there is serious doubt about independent and impartial nature of the investigation. However, the information of the incident without any delay must be sent to NHRC or the State Human Rights Commission, as the case may be.

(6)   The injured criminal/victim should be provided medical aid and his/her statement recorded by the magistrate or medical officer with certificate of fitness.

(7)   It should be ensured that there is no delay in sending FIR, diary entries, panchnamas, sketch, etc., to the concerned court.

(8)   After full investigation into the incident, the report should be sent to the competent court under Section 173 of the Code. The trial, pursuant to the charge-sheet submitted by the investigating officer, must be concluded expeditiously.

(9)   In the event of death, the next of kin of the alleged criminal/victim must be informed at the earliest.

(10)   Six monthly statements of all cases where deaths have occurred in police firing must be sent to the NHRC by DGPs. The statements may be sent in the format along with the post-mortem and inquest. The inquiry reports should contain the date and place of occurrence; police station and district; circumstances leading to deaths: self defence in encounter, in the course of dispersal of unlawful assembly, or in the course of affecting arrest; brief facts of the incident; investigating agency; and the findings of the

magisterial inquiry or inquiry by senior officers disclosing, in particular, names and designation of police officials, if found responsible for the death; and whether use of force was justified and action taken was lawful.

(11)   If on the conclusion of investigation the materials/evidence having come on record show that death had occurred by use of firearm amounting to offence under the IPC, disciplinary action against such officer must be promptly initiated and he must be placed under suspension.

(12)   As regards compensation to be granted to the dependants of the victim who suffered death in a police encounter, the scheme provided under Section 357-A of the Code must be applied.

(13)   The police officer(s) concerned must surrender his/her weapons for forensic and ballistic analysis, including any other material, as required by the investigating team, subject to the rights under Article 20 of the Constitution.

(14)   An intimation about the incident must also be sent to the police officer's family and should the family need the services of a lawyer/counselling, the same must be offered.

(15)   No out-of-turn promotion or instant gallantry rewards shall be bestowed on the concerned officers soon after the occurrence. It must be ensured at all costs that such rewards are given/ recommended only when the gallantry of the concerned officers is established beyond doubt.

(16)   If the family of the victim finds that the above procedure has not been followed or there exists a pattern of abuse or lack of independent investigation or impartiality by any of the functionaries as above mentioned, it may make a complaint to the Sessions Judge having territorial jurisdiction over the place of incident. Upon such complaint being made, the concerned Sessions Judge shall look into the merits of the complaint and address the grievances raised therein.

It has been held that the general principles of law laid down by the Supreme Court are applicable to every person including those who were not parties to that order.[65] However, it needs to be clarified whether the guidelines issued by the Supreme Court would be applicable in the event of a joint operation undertaken by the armed forces and the state police in disturbed areas where the AFSPA is applicable.

Not satisfied with the decisions of the Supreme Court in matters relating to the AFSPA, some have accused the higher judiciary of giving pro-State rulings in national security matters.[66] However, research/studies have shown that India's Supreme Court does not give pro-State rulings even when the country is facing war. It is more likely to focus on the facts of a case rather than on prior ideological or personal biases. A researcher reports: "Even in an atmosphere of increased concern about terrorism by Islamist jihadi groups led by the Al Qaeda and others after 2001, one did not find significantly different treatment of Muslim plaintiffs/defendants by the judges."[67]

International Response

The Universal Declaration of Human Rights, adopted by the General Assembly in 1948, provided the basis for the formulation of several covenants and conventions. Three documents—The Universal Declaration of Human Rights (UDHR), the International Covenant on Civil and Political Rights (ICCPR), 1966 and the International Covenant on Economic, Social and Cultural Rights (ICESCR),1966, along with two protocols– Optional Protocol to the ICCPR, and Second Optional Protocol to the ICCPR, constitute the International Bill of Human Rights. The Convention against Torture and other Cruel and Inhuman or Degrading Treatment or Punishment was adopted by the General Assembly on 10 December 1984 and came into force on 26 June 1987. The Convention on the Elimination of All Forms of Discrimination against Women was adopted by the General Assembly on 18 December 1979 and came into force on 3 September 1981. In addition, the Convention on the Rights of the Child was adopted by

---

65 *Union of India v Lalita S Rao* (2001) SCC 384.

66 *The Myth of Normalcy: Impunity and the Judiciary in Kashmir*, Allard K. Lowenstein International Human Rights Clinic Yale Law School, April 2009, p. 45.

67 Shankar Shylashri. 2009. *Scaling Justice: India's Supreme Court, Anti-terror Laws and Social Rights*, New Delhi: Oxford University Press, p. 111-115.

the UN General Assembly on 20 November 1989 and came into force on 2 September 1990. The UN Convention on Enforced Disappearance was adopted by the General Assembly on 22 December 2006.

It has been claimed by certain international bodies that the AFSPA, by its form and application, violates the UDHR, the ICCPR, the Convention Against Torture, the UN Code of Conduct for Law Enforcement Officials, the UN Body of Principles for Protection of All Persons Under any form of Detention, and the UN Principles on Effective Prevention and Investigation of Extra-Legal and Summary Executions. Specifically, the AFSPA violates the following Articles of the UDHR: (a) Free and Equal in Dignity and Rights; (b) Non-discrimination; (c) Right to Life, Liberty, Security of Person; (d) Right Against Torture; (e) Equality before the Law; (f) Effective Remedy; (g) Right Against Arbitrary Arrest; and (h) Right to Property.

India submitted its Second Periodic Report under the ICPPR to the UN Human Rights Committee in March 1991. The members of the Committee pointed out that the AFSPA violated certain rights contained in the ICCPR. In response, the Attorney General of India justified the AFSPA under Article 355 of the Indian Constitution, which makes it the duty of the Union to protect each state from external aggression. He said the AFSPA was necessary given the context of the north east where there is "infiltration of aliens into the territories mingling with the local public, and encouraging them towards this [secession]", and, "that the ICCPR does not encourage secession and governments are not encouraged to promote it."

Rashida Manjoo, the UN Special Rapporteur on violence against women, its causes and consequences, has recently alleged that the AFSPA has resulted in impunity for human rights violations broadly. She has called for the repeal of the law in Jammu and Kashmir and the northeastern states of India as it is affecting the rights to freedom of movement, association and peaceful assembly, safety and security, dignity and bodily integrity of women. Cristof Heyns, the UN Special Rapporteur on extrajudicial, summary or arbitrary executions, who visited India in March 2012, was of the view that the widespread deployment of the military creates an environment in which the exception becomes the rule, and the use of lethal force is seen as the primary response to conflict. During the review of human rights record at the United Nations Human Rights Council on 4 May 2017, India has been asked to revise the Armed Forces Special Powers

Act (AFSPA) to bring it into compliance with the obligations under the International Covenant on Civil and Political Rights (ICCPR), with a view to fighting impunity.[68]

Restrictions on Human Rights

One of the main characteristic of democracy is that all members of society are free to express their views, organize against the government without any fear of armed reprisal. However, unexpectedly emergency situations may place democratic governments in a dilemma by bringing about a conflict between its primary obligation to protect the integrity of the State and its equally important obligation to protect the human rights of its citizens and other persons within its jurisdiction. Many national constitutions permit the suspension of guaranteed fundamental rights during such emergencies and make provision for deploying armed forces to deal with the situation. During the domestic deployment of armed forces certain basic civil liberties and human rights are threatened. Such fundamental rights include freedom of speech, association, assembly and movement, and arbitrary detention.

The International Covenant on Civil and Political Rights of 1966 (ICCPR) provides for suspension of the human rights guaranteed by the Government in time of public emergency, which threatens the life of the nation. Article 4(1) of the ICCPR provides:

> In time of public emergency which threatens the life of the nation and the existence of which is officially proclaimed, the States Parties to the present Covenant may take measures derogating from their obligations under the present Covenant to the extent strictly required by the exigencies of the situation, provided that such measures are not inconsistent with their other obligations under international law and do not involve discrimination solely on the ground of race, colour, sex, language, religion or social origin.

At the same time it is also recognized that there are certain basic human rights, which cannot be suspended during any kind of emergency, be it war

---

68 UN General Assembly, Draft Report of the Working Groups on the Universal Periodic Review, UN Doc. A/HRC/WG.6/27/L.8 dated 8 May 2017.

or armed rebellion or civil insurrection. These rights, as contained in the ICCPR Article 4(2), are so basic that to suspend them destroys the basis of a civilized State and the Rule of Laws. Indeed, they are so fundamental to the human personality that without them human life is either not possible.[69] Human Rights Watch (World Report: 2017) maintains that the right to judicial remedies and especially the writ of habeas corpus must not only be guaranteed by the Constitution but should also be made non-suspendable during emergencies. This would ensure effective supervisory jurisdiction by a competent court of law to determine whether detention is legal and valid. It should also enable the production of detainees before the court, which will go a long away to prevent torture, degrading and inhuman treatment which detainees are usually subjected. In case production is detrimental to public interest the government must be obligated to inform the court about the condition of the detainee and place of his detention. According to Soli Sorabjee, a noted jurist and former Attorney-General of India, however grave the national emergency, it should always be remembered that an inseparable bond between legality, democratic institutions and the rule of law always exists.

International Humanitarian Law (IHL)

The four Geneva Conventions of 1949 along with three additional protocols, and weapons ban/ regulation treaties constitute international humanitarian law (IHL). The principles of IHL find fair mention in the Constitution of India. Part III (Fundamental Rights), Part IV (Directive Principles) and Part IVA (Fundamental Duties) of the Constitution, together ensure the basic human rights embodied in IHL. The rights mentioned in Part III are enforceable by the courts. The Directive Principles mentioned in Part IV are non-justiceable, but are fundamental in the governance of the country. Further, the Indian Parliament has been empowered by Article 253 of the Constitution to make laws to give effect to the treaties and conventions to which India is a signatory.

---

69 At present there are eleven rights, which are recognized as non-derogable in international human rights instruments. These are the right to life (ICCPR, Article 6); prohibition of torture (ICCPR, Article 7); prohibition of slavery or servitude (ICCPR, Article 8); prohibition of retroactive criminal laws (ICCPR, Article 15); right to recognition of legal personality (ICCPR, Article 16); freedom of conscience and religion (ICCPR, Article 18); and the prohibition of imprisonment for breach of contractual obligation (ICCPR, Article 11).

The significant provisions of the four Geneva Conventions can be summarized as (i) outlawing violation of right to life; (ii) prohibiting cruel treatment and torture; (iii) protecting personal dignity; (iv) providing for treatment of the wounded and sick during hostilities; and (v) prohibiting discrimination on the basis of race, colour, religion, nationality, etc. Article 3, common to all the four Geneva Conventions and applicable during non-international armed conflicts, also extends basic protection to persons not taking part in hostilities.[70] It provides for humane and non-discriminatory treatment of all such persons, in particular by prohibiting acts of violence to life and person (specifically murder, mutilation, cruel treatment and torture), the taking of hostages, and outrages upon personal dignity, in particular humiliating and degrading treatment. It also prohibits the passing of sentences and the carrying out of executions without judgment being pronounced by a regularly constituted court, providing all the judicial guarantees recognized as indispensable. Finally, it imposes an obligation on the parties to collect the wounded and sick and to care for them.[71]

Additional Protocol II (AP II) of June 1977 introduces more detailed rules in the case of armed conflicts of a non-international nature. The issues addressed are (i) fundamental guarantee to all persons not directly involved in hostilities; (ii) special provisions in respect of persons where liberty is restricted; (iii) general protection of the civilian population; (iv) prohibition of forced movement and starvation as a method of combat; (v) protection of objects indispensable to the survival of the civilian population, cultural objects and places of worship; (vi) prohibition of taking of hostages and outraging of personal dignity; and (vii) prohibition of violence to life and persons, in particular murder, mutilation, cruel treatment and torture. Additional Protocol II (AP II) sets out specific provisions and protections for certain categories of persons such as children, persons deprived of liberty for reasons related to the conflict, persons prosecuted for criminal

---

70 The International Court of Justice (ICJ) has affirmed in 1986 that the provisions of common Article 3 reflect customary international law and represent a minimum standard from which the parties to any type of armed conflict must not depart; see *Military and Paramilitary Activities In and Against Nicaragua*, 1986 ICJ Reports, p.114. Common Article 3 does not apply to situations of internal disturbances and tensions, such as riots and other isolated and sporadic acts of violence, which India is facing in some parts of Jammu and Kashmir and the northeast.

71 Michelle Mack and Jelena Pejic, *Increasing Respect for International Humanitarian Law in Non-International Armed Conflict*, Geneva: ICRC, 2008, p.7.

offences related to the conflict, persons who are wounded, sick and shipwrecked, medical and religious personnel, and the civilian population (attacks on civilian populations, starvation as a method of combat, and forced displacement are all prohibited).Though India is not a signatory to AP II, these fundamental guarantees are being observed by the forces deployed in non-international armed conflict.[72]

A number of other IHL treaties also apply to situations of non-international armed conflict. Among them are the following: the Protocol on Prohibitions or Restrictions on the Use of Mines, Booby-Traps and Other Devices, as amended on 3 May 1996 (amended Protocol II to the 1980 Convention on Prohibitions or Restrictions on the Use of Certain Conventional Weapons (CCW)); Protocols I, III, IV and V of the CCW, through paragraph 6 of Article 1 of the CCW, as adopted on 21 December 2001; the Convention for the Protection of Cultural Property in the Event of Armed Conflict, 14 May 1954; and the Second Protocol to the Hague Convention of 1954 for the Protection of Cultural Property in the Event of Armed Conflict, 26 March 1999.

The Indian armed forces have been a part of the UN Peacekeeping efforts since the UN intervention in Korea in 1950. India is one of the largest contributors to the UN peacekeeping missions with a deployment of about 200,000 troops for various UN missions in the last four decades. India has so far participated in nearly 50 UN peacekeeping missions and at present it has 7,676 troops engaged in peace-keeping operations. Indian troops have taken part in some of the most difficult operations, and their professional excellence has won them universal admiration. They have consistently won appreciation from the UN authorities for their efforts to help in the social development of the areas where they have been posted. In Lebanon, for instance, Indian Army doctors have set up medical

---

72 AP II applies only where it has been ratified by the State. Its scope is more restricted than that of common Article 3: it applies only to conflicts between a State's armed force and "dissident armed forces or other organized armed groups which, under responsible command, exercise such control over a part of its territory as to enable them to carry out sustained and concerted military operations and to implement this Protocol" (Article 1, paragraph 1, AP II). Though at a general level the Additional Protocols only strengthen the protection already provided in the Geneva Conventions, while doing so, at specific levels they create new obligations of the State parties. For more details on the issue see: Burra Srinivas, India and the Additional Protocols of 1977, *Indian Journal of International Law*, Vol. 53, No. 3, July-Sept 2013, p. 422-450.

camps, veterinary hospitals, and rehabilitation centres and have supplied amputees with the Jaipur foot, a prosthetic developed in India. In 1971, in particular, the Indian armed forces provided protection to about 20,000 civilians, including women and children and kept about 95,000 prisoners of war affording them humane treatment under the norms of the Geneva Convention. During the Kargil conflict in 1999, the armed forces again showed their adherence to IHL in the way they used force and treated captured Pakistani soldiers.

Secessionist groups in India have of late been provoking the armed forces into over-reaction and subsequently mobilizing public opinion against alleged excesses committed by the troops. In many so called non-international armed conflicts in India, the militants or non-state actors with little or no training in IHL are directly involved in the fighting. They have used human-shields, predominantly women to escape when confronted by the armed forces. This ruse enables them to allege misconduct on the part of the armed forces through a favourable media. The Indian armed forces, while engaging in counter-insurgency operations have been maintaining the principles of 'minimum force' and avoidance of collateral damage. Cordon and search operations are being conducted in accordance with the policy guidelines issued by the headquarters on the basis of intelligence, and in association with village elders.

Army's Point of View

There are strong arguments about the necessity and efficacy of AFSPA in handling militancy or insurgency. The military bureaucracy is of the view that the AFSPA is absolutely necessary to combat insurgency in the country and to protect the borders. According to Lt Gen Harwant Singh, former deputy chief of army staff, "In a virulent insurgency, security forces just cannot operate without the cover of the AFSPA. Without it, there would be much hesitation and caution which would work to the advantage of insurgents."[73] According to Maj Gen Bakshi, there is a concerted campaign on the part of some foreign-funded NGOs to demonize the Army and delegitimize its counter-insurgency and counter-terrorist operations.[74]

---

73 Lt. Gen. Harwant Singh, AFSPA in J&K: Selective withdrawal may be harmful, *Indian Defence Review*, 8 January 2013.

74 Bakshi, Major General G D, AFSPA debate: Disarming the state, *The Times of India*, 18 November 2011.

The Indian Army sees the AFSPA as a necessity of security management in terrorism-hit states. In November 1998, Lieutenant-General Vijay Uberoi, then head of the Army Training Command in Shimla, presented a concept paper titled "Management of Internal Conflict" to the Defence Minister. It outlined existing and emerging threats in various parts of the country, and argued that the Army needed special legal protections and powers in the areas where it operated. He felt it was imperative to use special legislation to boost the morale, maintain the operational efficiency of and protect the rights of soldiers.[75] The former chief of army staff, Gen V K Singh emphasized that the AFSPA, was a "functional requirement" of the army.[76]

Lt Gen Kadyan, in reaction to the observations of the Justice Verma Committee, states "….solving insurgency has never been and in a democracy can never be task of the Army….the continued involvement in a difficult and complicated environment is not of Army's volition; it is a national compulsion. Soldiers need legal cover to operate in these circumstances. AFSPA serves a very useful purpose and should not be misconstrued as a licence for sexual offences. Undeniably aberrations do occur but the army has always taken necessary punitive and preventive actions. There are and will always be anti-national elements out to defame, demoralize and finally drive out the army from the affected areas. Let us not contribute to their design by constantly throwing darts at the army."[77]

A former adjutant general of the Indian army is of the view that the fighting capability of the militants in the northeast and Jammu and Kashmir has improved considerably over the years. They possess sophisticated weapons, modern communication equipment and have moral and financial support from across the borders. Areas close to the international border witness trans-border movement of militants from their camps and hideouts in neighbouring countries. The armed forces

---

75 Swami Praveen, The Army and Special Powers, *Frontline*, Volume 21 - Issue 18, 28 August 28 – 10 September 2004, available at: http://www.flonnet.com/fl2118/stories/20040910006002200.htm, accessed 12 July 2014.

76 Singh, Gen V K, AFSPA required by armed forces in certain areas, *The Indian Express*, 16 April 2012, available at: http://www.indianexpress.com/news/afsparequired-by-armed-forces-in-certain-areas-gen-v-k-singh/937486/, accessed 24 September 2014.

77 Kadyan Lt Gen Raj, The Armed Forces Special Powers Act—Need for review? *South Asia Defence & Strategic Review*, March-April 2013, p. 29-30.

are required to operate in varied terrains such as thick forests, as well as built-up areas, such as villages, towns and cities, where the insurgents have established their training camps and support bases. The AFSPA assists the armed forces in dealing with these special situations.[78]

On the need for the AFSPA, the former Army Chief General Bikram Singh had stated that it is an enabling Act as it gives the Army additional powers to operate in an environment which is marked by a very high degree of uncertainty and complexity and an asymmetric environment where you cannot differentiate between a friend and a foe as the terrorist merges with the backdrop and hides amongst the locals.

Reacting to the comment of former Finance Minister P Chidambaram (PC) that the government would like to make the AFSPA "more humanitarian", but the army has been an obstacle to that proposal;[79] a former defence officer writes: [80]

> PC's remarks are grossly unfair to the army which cannot respond in the media to state its position on the AFSPA. Even though PC is well versed in law, the politician in him appears to have overcome his sense of justice to provide the "accused" opportunity to respond, knowing well that it cannot do so because of legal restraint. Accusing the army of wanting imposition of AFSPA is political chicanery to divert attention from and shift blame for decades of political and administrative failure and corruption through a toxic combination of mal-governance, mis-governance and non-governance in the northeast and Kashmir, that is the primary cause for social disaffection and unarmed and armed militancy in those states. The same irresponsible political-bureaucratic approach, independent of political ideology but surely centered on corruption and sell-out to corporate interests, exacerbates poverty and is responsible for growing militancy in other states of the Indian union.

78 Sabharwal Lt Gen Mukesh, The Armed Forces Special Powers Act (AFSPA), *Indian Defence Review*, Vol. 27 (2), April-June 2012, p. 134-139.

79 Army's stand makes it hard to amend AFSPA: Chidambaram, *The Hindu*, 7 February 2013.

80 Vombatkere S. G., AFSPA: Misconceptions and Ground Realities, available at: http://www.countercurrents.org/vombatkere120313.htm, accessed 15 September 2014.

Providing security and public order by the fair and just enforcement of extant laws, and maintenance of supplies and services essential to the public, is the primary task of the civil administration, which is the combination of the powers, roles and functions of people's elected representatives, bureaucrats and integral police forces. The disturbance of law and order usually happens because of conflicts of interest within civil society, caused by inappropriate laws and/ or unfair policies and/or poor or ill-motivated implementation – in short, mal-administration. When law and order, and peace in society is disturbed and is beyond political resolution, governance calls for using the force of the state and/or central police. When law and order breaks down despite deploying state and central police or because of their misuse, it can only be restored by the deployment of the army on internal security (IS) duties. The government has no other option.... Calling the army in aid to civil power (whether for internal security (IS), natural disaster, accident or even rescuing kids from bore-wells) is implicit admission of political-administrative failure and incompetence.

The military on IS duties is to civil society what an ICU is to a critically ill person. A patient cannot remain for years in a hospital ICU, because he/she would be effectively dead. The patient needs treatment for the disease and right nutrition to regain normal health. Likewise, the military remaining deployed on IS duties over decades makes civic and political life in society effectively dead, without assuring peace or security. India's societies need the "treatment" of honest political effort by transparent dialogue and engagement with people, and the "nutrition" of good governance for their growth. Society does not need the army, except to guard the country's borders against external aggression.

Echoing similar sentiments, another author comments: "It is the utterly corrupt, impotent and non-performing government of the state in the last two decades that is responsible for the persisting tragedy. It is the total failure of all parameters of governance in the state....."[81] Further,

---

81 Devasahayam M. G., Solution to Kashmir problem--War or basic governance? *The Hindu*, 04 June 2002.

"J&K administration must stop covering up for political failures by scapegoating the army..... Most people in Kashmir think that the AFSPA issue is only meant to distract attention...and the governance deficit is mainly responsible for it... Indian Army will happily quit Kashmir if the political establishment in Delhi and Srinagar are convinced that its services are not needed."[82]

Army's Response to Human Rights Violations

According to Sabharwal, the former adjutant general of the Indian Army, allegations of the army shielding soldiers accused of serious human rights violations are baseless.[83] The Army accords the highest importance to upholding human rights in its counter-insurgency operations which are conducted using minimum force, avoiding collateral damage, acting in good faith and maintaining high moral standards.[84]

According to a report made to the National Human Rights Commission by the Army's Command Headquarter, only 54 cases out of 1,517 received since 1994 have been found to be true, amounting to less than four per cent. Of the 129 persons who have been punished, there were 38 officers, 12 JCOs and 79 soldiers. Punishments awarded to the military accused have been strict and include life and rigorous imprisonments and dismissal for offences such as rape, murder, extortion and molestation. Further, in Jammu and Kashmir, where the AFSPA is applicable, 150 allegations were reported in 2002. These have progressively declined to 18 in 2010 and a few in 2011. Where violations have been proved, action against the perpetrators has been quick and the aggrieved persons have been accorded suitable reparations. During the period 2001-2010, 69 officers and men were been punished in the Northern and Eastern Commands, where 37 cases were investigated by the Army on own its own motion. Recently a general court martial has sentenced five military personnel, including two officers, to life

---

82 Kishwar, M. P., Playing a Dangerous Game, *The Times of India*, 18 November 2011.

83 After a court of inquiry found gross violation of rules of engagement by the soldiers, the Army has indicted nine soldiers, including a junior commissioned officer for killing two youths in Jammu and Kashmir's Budgam district on 3 November 2014.

84 Sabharwal, Lt Gen Mukesh, The Armed Forces Special Powers Act (AFSPA), *Indian Defence Review*, Vol. 27 (2), April-June 2012, p. 134-139.

imprisonment for killing of three civilians in a fake encounter and passing it off as an anti-militancy operation.[85]

---

85 On 13 November 2014 a general court martial (GCM) sentenced five Army personnel, including two officers, to life imprisonment for the staged killing of three civilians in a fake encounter in Jammu and Kashmir's Machil on 29 April 2010. The GCM proceedings were ordered against six persons in December 2013 and one of them was not found guilty. Three civilians were allegedly lured by a former special police officer and his accomplices to Machil on the pretext of offering a job. They were later handed over to the army for Rs. 50,000 each and shot dead by troops in a staged encounter. The Army described them as militants trying to sneak in from the Machil sector along the Line of Control. Their bodies were exhumed on 28 May 2010. The controversial killings triggered widespread protests and bloodshed in the Kashmir Valley in which 113 people were killed. The convicted person's appeal against the court martial verdict is pending at the principal bench of the Armed Forces Tribunal.

3

Human Rights Violations

The Armed Forces Special Powers Act (AFSPA) has been applicable in certain parts of Northeast India and Jammu and Kashmir since 1958 and 1990 respectively. In the last five decades or so, India has witnessed an escalation of violent conflicts in these territories. These conflicts, variously termed terrorism, insurgency and militancy aim to discredit the government's ability to protect the citizens. They feed on the people's discontent over political failure to fulfil promises, inefficiency of the civil administration and occasional failure of the judicial machinery. It is in such situations that the armed forces have been called upon to rein in the chaos and restore normalcy.

The armed forces, while operating under the powers vested in them by the AFSPA, have often been accused of extra-judicial execution of innocent civilians; illegal imposition of curfew; rape, molestation and sexual harassment of women; torture; forced labour; and large-scale looting of homes and granaries. It has been reported that between 2012 and 2016, a total of 186 complaints of human rights violations by armed forces personnel were received in states where the AFSPA is in force. The records maintained by the Ministry of Home Affairs show that J&K accounted for 49 per cent of the complaints, while a little over 31 per cent were from people from Assam, while remaining were from Manipur, Meghalaya, Tripura, Meghalaya and Arunachal Pradesh. Only one complaint was received from Nagaland during this period.[1]

---

1   The data given by the Ministry of Home Affairs segregates the complaints into 12 categories, ranging from "arbitrary use of power", to "custodial death", custodial torture", "death in army encounter", and "death in army firing". Banerjee Rumu, 198 rights violations cases filed in 4 years, *The Times of India*, New Delhi, July 15, 2017.

Various human rights organizations in the country and abroad and the foreign and local media have criticized the effectiveness of Indian laws in dealing with the violation of human rights by armed forces personnel. They have also criticized the AFSPA, which gives enhanced powers to the armed forces for dealing effectively with disruptive activities in specific areas. This chapter deals with allegations relating to human rights violations and analyses the adequacy of the legal system applicable to the armed forces in punishing a military accused, while the next chapter is devoted to four cases in which the armed forces were accused of mass rape, extra-judicial execution, and murder.

Torture

Torture is the intentional infliction of severe mental or physical pain or suffering by or with the consent of the state authorities for a specific purpose. The aim of torture is to break down the victim's personality and is often used to obtain information or a confession or create terror and fear within a population. Torture is distinguished from other forms of ill-treatment by the severe degree of suffering, which may be both physical and psychological. The most widely accepted definition of the term 'torture' is contained in Article 1 of the United Nations Convention Against Torture and other Cruel, Inhuman or Degrading Treatment or Punishment (UNCAT):

> An act by which severe pain or suffering, whether physical or mental, is intentionally inflicted on a person for such purposes as obtaining from him or a third person information or a confession, punishing him for an act he or a third person has committed or is suspected of having committed, or intimidating or coercing him or a third person, or for any reason based on discrimination of any kind, when such pain or suffering is inflicted by or at the instigation of or with the consent or acquiescence of a public official or other person acting in an official capacity.

This definition contains three cumulative elements: (i) the intentional infliction of severe mental or physical suffering; (ii) by a public official, who is directly or indirectly involved; and (iii) for a specific purpose. Torture is often used to punish, to obtain information or a confession. Torture can be physical or psychological. Some of the most common methods of physical torture include beating, electric shocks, stretching, submersion, suffocation, burns, rape and sexual assault. Psychological forms of torture, which may have long-lasting consequences for victims, commonly include: isolation, threats, humiliation, mock executions, mock amputations, and witnessing the torture of others.[2]

The National Human Rights Commission (NHRC) has recorded 12,727 custodial deaths in India from 2001 to 2010, i.e. nearly 4 deaths in police and judicial custody in India every day. A large number of these deaths are a direct consequence of custodial torture. The NHRC has issued detailed guidelines to the chief secretaries of all states to report custodial deaths and custodial rapes to the Commission within 24 hours of their occurrence.[3] Similarly, directives/guidelines have also been issued in matters relating among others, to post-mortem examinations in cases of deaths in custody and encounter deaths.[4] The NHRC, however, does not have jurisdiction over the armed forces under the Human Rights Act[5] and has no details of custodial torture not resulting in death. The NHRC has registered 25 cases of death in the custody of the military/ para-military forces from 2001-2010. According to The Asian Centre for Human Rights, torture remains endemic, institutionalized and central to the administration of justice and counter-terrorism measures; and the members of the military and paramilitary forces deployed in insurgency situations continue to be responsible for torture.[6] An individual narrates his experience in the custody of the armed forces:

---

2 Psychological torture is a new method and was developed more recently. Psychological torture is often more severe and long-lasting than physical torture. Psychological torture remains undetected as the medical professionals are often not sufficiently trained and the victim is reluctant to speak about his or her experiences. It creates a feeling of shame, guilt and disgrace leads to transformation of the personality, to a loss of self-esteem and self-worth; and is usually accompanied by symptoms of anxiety and loss of self-worth. Torture: Interview with Dr Abdel Hamid Afana, *International Review of the Red Cross*, Vol. 89, No. 867, September 2007, p. 505-509.

3 National Human Rights Commission letter to all Chief Secretaries on the reporting of custodial deaths within 24 hours, Letter No 66/SG/NHRC/93, dated 14 December 1993.

4 National Human Rights Commission letter to Chief Ministers/Administrators of all States/Union Territories with a request to adopt the Model Autopsy form and the additional procedure for inquest, Letter No NHRC/ID/PM/96/57, dated 27 March 1997.

5 The Protection of Human Rights Act, 1993.

6 *Torture in India 2001*, Asian Centre for Human Rights, New Delhi, p.1.

They kept on pouring water into my nostrils until the water came out in my ears; it felt warm inside my ears. Then they stamped on both my thighs while two persons held my feet while another man sat on my head….. They touched the wires' ends to my chest and gave me shocks three times. Each time I felt as if my whole body had contracted….. I keep remembering how they used to beat me and see everything that happened to me vividly.[7]

The military and paramilitary forces, while operating in a disturbed area have the power to arrest an individual under the AFSPA.[8] The arrested person is required to be handed over to the nearest police station with the least possible delay.[9] The provision thus allows the armed forces to 'question' a suspect while he/she is in their custody, as the term 'least possible delay' has not been defined in the Act. In the case of *Masooda Parveen v Union of India*,[10] it was admitted by the army that after the victim was apprehended, he was taken to the military camp and interrogated, on which he revealed that he was a Pakistan-trained militant and an ex-divisional commander of the Al-Barq terrorist group. His interrogation also revealed the presence of arms and ammunition kept at a hideout. The militant remained in military custody for about 6 hours. He was taken to the hideout to recover the arms and ammunitions, where he was killed in a grenade explosion. The Supreme Court held that the time lapse between the arrest and the death in this case[11] was clearly minimal and that the guidelines issued in the *Naga People's Movement of Human Rights* case[12] cannot be mechanically applied. Further, in this case, the first priority for the armed forces was to recover the weapons and any delay could lead to a failure of the operation.

---

7   Witness statement of arrest and torture in Manipur cited in Pinto L.A. and N. Thockchom, "Indigenous Children of North East India: the denial of childhood," Centre for Organisation Research and Education, Imphal, Manipur, 2000.

8   Section 4 of the AFSPA permits persons of specified rank to arrest without warrant in situations referred to therein.

9   Section 6 of the AFSPA: "Any person arrested and taken into custody under this Act and every property, arms, ammunition or explosive substance or any vehicle or vessel seized under this Act, shall be made over to the officer-in-charge of the nearest police station with the least possible delay, together with a report of the circumstances…."

10   *Masooda Parveen v. Union of India* AIR 2007 SC 1840.

11   Ibid.

12   *Naga People's Movement of Human Rights v Union of India* (1998) 2 SCC 109.

What has to be appreciated in such cases is that the armed forces are required to take prompt action and any delay can result in the leakage of information which would frustrate the very purpose of the action. The next issue is what techniques may be used during the questioning of a suspect to bring out information. Can physical force be used? Can the techniques of 'enhanced interrogation' authorized by the Bush administration after September 11 be employed or would they amount to torture.

Torture is considered a 'grave breach' of the 1949 Geneva Conventions; and the violator could be punished for committing a 'war crime'.[13] The 1948 Universal Declaration of Human Rights (UDHR) has outlawed the use of torture against any individual under any circumstances.[14] The binding human rights treaty, the 1966 International Covenant on Civil and Political Rights (ICCPR) also prohibits torture,[15] and the provision cannot be derogated even in times of public emergencies.[16] The prohibition on torture was reaffirmed and expanded in the 1984 Convention against Torture (CAT),[17] where parties took the additional step of delegating away a significant amount of national sovereignty through the principle of universal jurisdiction.[18] Universal jurisdiction allows any State to arrest and try an individual suspected of committing a violation, regardless of the nationality of the accused and victim, or of the country where the offence

---

13 Article 130 of the Third Geneva Convention of 1949 relative to the Treatment of Prisoners of War.

14 Article 5 of the UDHR states "No one shall be subjected to torture or to cruel, inhuman or degrading treatment or punishment."

15 Article 7 of the ICCPR states: No one shall be subjected to torture or to cruel, inhuman or degrading treatment or punishment. In particular, no one shall be subjected without his free consent to medical or scientific experimentation.

16 Article 4 of the ICCPR states that in a time of public emergency which threatens the life of the nation and the existence of which is officially proclaimed, the States Parties to the Covenant may take measures derogating from their obligations under the Covenant to the extent strictly required by the exigencies of the situation, provided that such measures are not inconsistent with their other obligations under international law and do not involve discrimination solely on the ground of race, colour, sex, language, religion or social origin. However, no derogation from articles 6, 7, 8 (paragraphs I and 2), 11, 15, 16 and 18 may be made under this provision.

17 The UN Convention Against Torture, and other Cruel, Inhuman or Degrading Treatment or Punishment, 1987 (CAT).

18 Article 5, CAT.

took place.[19] The prohibition of torture occupies an important place in international law and the extensive use of such practices has been codified as a "crime against humanity" under the Rome Statute of International Criminal Court.[20]

India has neither signed nor ratified the Rome Statute.[21] Although the Government of India signed the CAT almost 20 years ago, it has failed to ratify it till date. The Prevention of Torture Bill, 2010, introduced by the government in the Lok Sabha in the 2010 budget session, was criticized for lowering the standards set by the CAT, and in many ways was in direct opposition to the basic norm of adherence to the minimum standards set down with respect to the right to freedom from torture.[22] The Indian Penal Code, 1860, contains provisions such as Sections 330 and 331 for prosecuting public officials who resort to the use of torture. However, India is yet to enact a separate legislation to make the safeguards against torture more stringent.

Article 15 of the CAT provides that any statement which is established to have been made as a result of torture shall not be invoked as evidence in any proceedings, except against a person accused of torture.[23] As a State Party to the ICCPR, the Government of India must ensure that the

19 On 3 January 2013, Colonel Kumar Lama of the Nepal Army, deputed to UN peacekeeping in Sudan was arrested by the local police in London during his visit to the UK. He was accused of intentionally "inflicting severe pain or suffering" as a public official on two separate individuals between April and May 2005 at the Gorusinghe Army Barracks in Nepal. *The Himalayan Times*, 27 February 2014. Col Lama was charged under section 134 of the British Criminal Justice Act. He was, however, acquitted by the British court in August 2016.

20 Article 7, Rome Statute of the International Criminal Court, 1998.

21 Ramanathan Usha, India and the ICC, *Journal of International Criminal Justice*, Volume 3, 2005, pp. 627-634.

22 Though the eradication of torture is a matter of national importance, given its institutionalized practice and brutal effects, the progression of the Bill through the legislative process has been conducted in relative anonymity. Aside from select civil society groups facilitating discussions on the Bill, the Ministry of Home Affairs has not facilitated any public debate on this vital Bill, or called for public submissions on its provisions. Prevention of Torture Bill, 2010: A Critique, Commonwealth Human Rights Initiative, pp. 8.

23 International law provides a comprehensive set of rules to combat torture and that the inadmissibility of evidence found to have been obtained by coercion is an important tool designed to eradicate torture once and for all. For more details see: Thienel Tobias, The Admissibility of Evidence Obtained by Torture under International Law, Vol. 17, No. 2, *The European Journal of International Law*, 2006, p.349-367.

proposed domestic legislation relating to the prevention and prohibition of torture complies not only with the CAT but also with the provisions of the ICCPR, specifically: Article 7, prohibiting torture, Article 10(1) requiring all persons deprived of their liberty to be treated with humanity as well as Article 2, paragraph 3, requiring an effective legal remedy and redress for violations. Under both the CAT and the ICCPR, States parties have a duty to investigate allegations of torture or cruel, inhuman or degrading treatment.

Despite the international rules outlawing torture, there is a large gap between legal principles and actual practice in of many States.[24] During the 1970s, the British treated the IRA suspects harshly.[25] After the US invaded Afghanistan on 7 October 2001, the Taliban and al Qaeda suspects were transferred to the Guantanamo Bay US Naval Base and were subjected to enhanced interrogation methods.[26]

It has been said that torture, which was institutionalized in India during the British rule to silence people, continues to be used by "the present ruling classes for similar purposes, i.e., to counter people's movements.[27] The use of harsh methods for extraction of intelligence by armed forces personnel cannot be completely ruled out. Thus, it is necessary that the Indian Armed Forces impart the necessary training to their personnel to

24 Brunnee J. and and Stephen J. Toope. 2010. *Legitimacy and Legality in International Law: An Interactional Account*, Cambridge, UK: Cambridge University Press, p. 269.

25 The IRA suspects were interned *incommunicado* and (i) made to wear hoods over their faces except during interrogation; (ii) forced to stand-eagled in an uncomfortable position for hours; (iii) bombarded continuously with noise; (iv) prevented from sleeping; and (v) put on a diet of bread and water. McDonnell Thomas Michael. 2010. *The United States, International Law, and the Struggle Against Terrorism*, London and New York: Routledge, p. 47.

26 Prisoners were short-shackled, i.e., their wrists and ankles were shackled to a bolt in the floor, so that they remained in a foetal position for hours, and were compelled to urinate and defecate upon themselves. Some were subject to alternating cold and hot temperatures; some were subjected to loud music so that they could not sleep; some were beaten; some were sexually humiliated by female interrogators; some were daubed with fake menstrual blood; and some were intimidated by unmuzzled dogs. The CIA was authorized to use 'enhanced interrogation techniques' (EIT), including water boarding, dousing with cold water to bring the detainee two-thirds of the way toward hypothermia, putting them in crates, etc. McDonnell Thomas Michael. 2010. *The United States, International Law, and the Struggle Against Terrorism*, London and New York: Routledge, p. 49, 71.

27 Ferreira Arun, A Critical Appraisal of the Prevention of Torture Bill, 2010, *Economic & Political Weekly*, Vol. XLV, No. 21, 22 May 2010, p. 10-13.

ensure that interrogation/questioning techniques followed by them do not amount to an act of torture. The armed forces must also have one of their medical officers examine the detained person to find out whether he is fit to be interrogated. However, in such circumstances, the medical officer may face a conflict between his obligation to obey his military superiors and his ethical duties as medical practitioner. Rowe (2002; 190) is of the view that a military medical officer in such situations may act in breach of his medical ethics.[28] However, this may not be always true. An upright medical officer would assert that a suspect must not be subjected to torture, degrading or inhuman treatment at the hands of interrogators, and should this happen; he would bring it to light in his medical report strictly in accordance with medical ethics.[29]

In the absence of any law for protection against torture, the judiciary and the NHRC have played an important role in cases of reported custodial torture by public authorities. In a number of such cases, the NHRC has directed the Ministry of Defence and the Ministry of Home Affairs to pay compensation to the victim or his dependents. In 1993, the inhabitants of Barwah, in the Baramulla district of J&K had complained to the NHRC that Muhammad Akbar Sheikh of their village had died in military custody. In a proceeding under Section 19 of the Human Rights Act, the Ministry of Defence had replied that the said victim had voluntarily assisted the military unit in finding five hideouts from which weapons and ammunition were recovered. The time being the last week of December, the weather was harsh and the terrain difficult. The report attributed the death of Muhammad Akbar Sheikh to exhaustion when his body was handed over to the police in Baramulla on 29 December 1993. The Commission observed that the cause of the death was exhaustion as a result of the strain put upon him by the search party. Though the case was not one of custodial death, the situation was more or less akin to it. The NHRC directed the Ministry of Defence to pay Rs. 50,000 as compensation to the legal heirs of the deceased.

---

28 Rowe Peter. 2006. *The Impact of Human Right Laws on Armed Forces*, UK: Cambridge University Press, p. 190.

29 Principles of Medical Ethics relevant to the Role of Heath Personnel, Particularly Physicians, in Protection of Prisoners and Detainees against Torture and Other Cruel, Inhuman or Degrading Treatment or Punishment, UN General Assembly Resolution 37/194, dated 18 December 1982.

In another case, an individual named Moran was arrested by the personnel of the Jat Regiment on suspicion of having links with ULFA militants. The next day he was produced at the Doodooma police station by the military personnel. An FIR was registered and Moran was sent to jail on 8 February. At that time he had multiple injuries allegedly caused by the army personnel and he died on 19 February 2003. Following a complaint from the Deputy Superintendent of Police Dibrugarh, the NHRC investigated the matter and concluded that Moran had prima facie died due to torture while in military custody. The NHRC recommended the payment of Rs 5 lakh as relief.

On 9 October 2006, one Nipul Saikia of Kalahkowa village under Khowang police station in the Dibrugarh district of Assam was picked up by the troops of the Guard Regiment on suspicion of having links with the ULFA. He remained untraceable for the next four days. On the fifth day, the army personnel took him to a nursing home for treatment. Later, he was admitted to the Assam Medical College and Hospital, where the doctors found that the youth had suffered abdominal trauma which had led to the rectal bleeding and pain. The family members of the youth had also alleged that he had been subjected to electric shocks. The incident led to protesters blocking the national highway. The matter was investigated by a court of inquiry and the youth was shifted to the military hospital for further treatment. The army later punished two officers and four other ranks with disciplinary action including loss of seniority for promotion and pension.[30]

Torture is a gross violation of human rights and the perpetrators generally act with impunity. In order to prevent this, the government must ratify the UN Convention against Torture. The absolute prohibition of torture and ill-treatment under international law should be reflected in national law. An attempt to commit torture and complicity or participation must be criminalized. The chiefs of the military and paramilitary forces must condemn acts of torture and impress upon their staff that such acts will not be tolerated. Every individual in the armed forces must be educated about his right and duty to refuse to obey an order to torture. An individual while in the custody must not be taken to any secret place of detention and necessary medical examination by a medical officer

---

30 Talukdar Sushanta, Major among six punished for violating human rights of detenu: Victim tortured on suspicion of having ULFA links, *The Hindu*, 15 February 2008.

must be undertaken. Though the term 'least possible delay' is not defined in the AFSPA, the armed forces must ensure that the arrested person is handed over to a police station/judicial authority without any delay after being taken into custody. They must also ensure that complaints of torture brought to their notice are investigated by an independent and impartial court of inquiry and the text and findings of the inquiry are made public. The violator should be tried by a disciplinary court, and provided with the necessary legal assistance to defend his case. The victims of torture and their dependants should be entitled to obtain prompt reparation from the government including restitution, fair and adequate financial compensation and appropriate medical care and rehabilitation.[31]

Enforce Disappearance

An NGO has recently alleged that from 1989 to 2009, military and paramilitary forces deployed in Jammu and Kashmir were responsible for more than 8000 enforced and involuntary disappearances and nearly 70,000 deaths.[32] Another report relating to Manipur states that enforced disappearances were common in the early days of the armed conflict. However, sustained efforts of Manipuri civilians, human rights groups, relatives of victims, and civil society organizations forced the state government to take suitable steps to prevent such disappearances.[33]

Enforced disappearance is one of the most serious human rights violations. Once largely practiced by military dictatorships, it has become an almost global phenomenon. The term enforced disappearance has been defined in Article 2 of the UN Convention for the Protection of All Persons from Enforced Disappearance (CED).[34] Enforced disappearance is "the arrest, detention, abduction or any other form of deprivation of liberty by agents of the State or by persons or groups of persons acting with the

---

31 *Combating Torture: A Manual of Action*, Amnesty International, 2003, p. 169.

32 The report states that in the discourse of the Indian Armed Forces and the Jammu and Kashmir Police, the dead who were buried in unknown and unmarked graves are stated to be "foreign militants or terrorists". 'Unknown, Unmasked, and Mass Grave in Indian-Administered Kashmir, a preliminary report', International People's tribunal on Human Rights and Justice in Indian-Administered Kashmir, November 2009.

33 *These Fellows Must be Eliminated: Relentless Violence and Impunity in Manipur*, Human Rights Watch, September 2008, p. 56.

34 The International Convention for the Protection of All Persons from Enforced Disappearance, 2010 (CED) was signed by India in 2010, but has not been ratified.

authorization, support or acquiescence of the State, followed by a refusal to acknowledge the deprivation of liberty or by concealment of the fate or whereabouts of the disappeared person, which place such a person outside the protection of the law." Every enforced disappearance violates a range of human rights including: the right to security and dignity of person; the right not to be subjected to torture or other cruel, inhuman or degrading treatment or punishment; the right to humane conditions of detention; the right to a legal personality; the right to a fair trial; the right to a family life; and when the disappeared person is killed, the right to life. The CED requires a State to take appropriate measures to investigate acts defined in Article 2 committed by persons or groups of persons acting without the authorization, support or acquiescence of the State and to bring those responsible to justice. Further, the State should ensure that enforced disappearance constitutes an offence under its criminal law.

In order to ensure that the armed forces are not involved in enforced disappearances, the leadership must ensure that places of secret detention do not exist. Further, the minimum legal standards must be followed and records of detention must be maintained at the authorized places of custody and these records must be periodically examined by the commanding officers/commandants. The persons deprived of liberty are authorized to communicate with their family, counsel or any other person of their choice. The following guidelines issued by the Supreme Court in the case of *DK Basu* must be meticulously followed by the in-charge of the detention centre.[35]

(i)   The police personnel carrying out the arrest and handling the interrogation of the arrestee should bear accurate, visible and clear identification and name tags with their designations. The particulars of all such police personnel who handle interrogation of the arrestee should bear accurate, visible and clear identification and name tags with their designation. The particular of all such personnel who handle interrogation of the arrestee must be recorded in a register.

That the police officer carrying out the arrest shall prepare a memo of arrest at the time of arrest and such memo shall be attested by at least one witness, who may be either a member of

---

35   *D K Basu v State of West Bengal* AIR 1997 SC 610.

the family of the arrestee or a respectable person of the locality from where the arrest is made. It shall also be counter signed by the arrestee and shall contain the time and date of arrest.

(ii)   A person who has been arrested or detained and is being held in custody in a police station or interrogation centre or other lock up, shall be entitled to have one friend or relative or other person known to him or having interest in his welfare being informed, as soon as practicable, that he has been arrested and is being detained at the particular place, unless the attesting witness of the memo of arrest is himself such a friend or a relative of the arrestee.

(iii)   The time, place of arrest and venue of custody of an arrestee must be notified by the police where the next friend or relative of the arrestee lives outside the district or town through the legal aids organization in the district and the police station of the area concerned telegraphically within a period of 8 to 12 hours after the arrest.

(iv)   The person arrested must be made aware of his right to have someone informed of his arrest or detention as soon as he is put under arrest or is detained.

(v)   An entry must be made in the diary at the place of detention regarding the arrest of the person which shall also disclosed the name of the next friend of the person who has been informed of the arrest and the names land particulars of the police officials in whose custody the arrestee is.

(vi)   The arrestee should, where he so request, be also examines at the time of his arrest and major and minor injuries, if any present on his /her body, must be recorded at that time. The Inspector Memo' must be signed both by the arrestee and the police officer effecting the arrest and its copy provided to the arrestee.

(vii)   The arrestee should be subjected to medical examination by the trained doctor every 48 hours during his detention in custody by a doctor on the panel of approved doctor appointed by Director, Health Services.

(viii) Copies of all the documents including the memo of arrest, referred to above, should be sent to the magistrate for his record.

(ix) The arrestee may be permitted to meet his lawyer during interrogation, though not throughout the interrogation.

(x) A police control room should be provided at all district and State headquarters where information regarding the arrest and the place of custody of the arrestee shall be communicated by the officer causing the arrest, within 12 hours of effecting the arrest and at the police control room it should be displayed on a conspicuous notice board.

As in the case of torture, every incident of 'enforced disappearance' must be investigated and the perpetrators must be brought to justice. In the case of 'enforced disappearance', the 'victim' is not only the disappeared person but also any other individual who has suffered harm as the direct result of the disappearance, such as family members. These indirect victims have the right to the truth regarding the circumstances of the enforced disappearance, the progress and results of the investigation and the fate of the disappeared person. Reparations provided to victims should cover material and moral damages including appropriate restitution and rehabilitation, and guarantees of non-repetition. The government needs to take the necessary steps to provide adequate protection to witnesses of enforced or involuntary disappearances, human rights defenders acting against enforced disappearances and the lawyers and families of disappeared persons against any intimidation, persecution, reprisal or ill-treatment.

Offences against Women

Armed forces personnel have also been accused of committing offences against women ranging from harassment and molestation to rape. The armed forces have shown zero tolerance in such matters and have taken strict action against violators. Four BSF personnel were dismissed from service by the Union Home Ministry after a general security force court had convicted them for raping a woman during their deployment at

Chhaturgul village in Srinagar district on 23 December 1996. The court had also sentenced them to 10 years imprisonment. The J&K High Court has recently refused to interfere in the punishment awarded by the Force Court.[36]

In 2005, the Army dismissed an officer of the rank of Major for an offence of molestation. The officer, while on deputation with the Rashtriya Rifles, was found guilty of molesting a 12-year-old girl and her mother during a search operation in the night intervening 6 and 7 November 2004 at Bhadra Payeen in Kupwara district. The court martial found him guilty of charges of molestation, use of criminal force and not adhering to the procedure laid out for carrying out cordon and search operation. The allegation of rape could not stand the scrutiny of the court as the DNA report showed that the semen stains on the clothes of the complainant were of her husband and not of the Major. The officer had failed to take a woman police/officer along while searching the women and girl child, and had thus violated the 'don'ts' of the Armed Forces Special Powers Act 1990. In November 2006, two army soldiers were dismissed from service and sentenced to two years of imprisonment in civil jail after a court martial found them guilty of molesting a girl during an anti-insurgency operation in Arunachal Pradesh.

In a few other cases in which members of the armed forces had committed offences against women while being deployed in disturbed areas, authorities took prompt and stern action against the violators after due investigation. Trials in such cases usually proceed with exemplary speed and sentences can be harsh, up to 10 years imprisonment and dismissal/ cashiering from service. The Ministry of Defence has generally followed the directions issued by the National Human Rights Commission in such cases.[37] However, the details of such cases, the punishment awarded by the court martial and its promulgation are not generally available for public

---

36 J&K: HC Upholds Dismissal of 4 BSF Men For Rape, *Outlook*, 9 August 2011.

37 The NHRC took *suo motu* cognizance of a news item published on 20 April 1999 entitled "Jawan rapes mentally disturbed girl in public" and asked for a report from the Ministry of Defence (MoD). The MoD confirmed the allegation and an FIR was lodged in the matter. The victim was examined medically and the medical officer confirmed the offence. A summary general court martial tried the accused and awarded him 8 years rigorous imprisonment and dismissal from service. The district magistrate was directed to pay a sum of Rs. 25,000/- to the parents of the victim by way of immediate interim relief. National Human Rights Commission Annual Report 1999-2000, Assam Case No. 27/3/1999-2000.

scrutiny and research. This has given rise to the belief that the armed forces try to protect such offences.

To make matter worse, militants and their supporters have often falsely accused the armed forces of molestation and rape. Some writers/ studies have also made such allegations without authentic/reliable data to back their claims.[38] There seems to be a concerted effort by some to convey a message across the world that 'human rights violations in Kashmir Valley' are being legitimized by the armed forces in the name of 'national interest' and 'counter-insurgency'.[39] One of the most infamous cases related to unfounded allegations of rape against members of the armed forces at Shopian has been discussed in the next chapter.

Extrajudicial Killings and Fake Encounters

An extrajudicial killing (or extrajudicial execution) is the killing of a person by governmental authorities without the sanction of any judicial proceedings or legal process. This punishment is mostly seen by humanity to be unethical, since they bypass the due process of law. Extrajudicial killings often target leading political, dissident, religious, and social figures and are only those carried out by the state government or other state authorities like the armed forces or police, as extra-legal fulfillment of their prescribed role. This does not include cases where aforementioned authorities act under motives that serve their own interests and not the state's, such as to eliminate their complicity in crime or commissioning by an outside party. The US Torture Victim Protection Act contains a definition of extrajudicial killing: "a deliberate killing not authorized by a previous judgement pronounced by a regular constituted court affording all

---

38 In its efforts to crush the militant movement, India's central government has pursued a policy of repression in Kashmir which has resulted in massive human rights violations by Indian army and paramilitary forces. Rape is used as a means of targeting women whom the security forces accuse of being militant sympathizers. Rape has also occurred frequently during reprisal attacks on civilians following militant ambushes. See: Rape in Kashmir: A Crime of War, Asia Watch & Physicians for Human Rights, Volume 5, Issue 9.

39 Kazi Seema, Law, Governance and Gender in Indian-Administered Kashmir, Working Paper Series, Centre for the Study of Law and Governance, Jawaharlal Nehru University, New Delhi, CSLG/WP/20, November 2012, p. 26-29; Jamwal Anuradha Bhasin, Rapists in Uniform, *Economic and Political Weekly*, Vol. XLVIII, No. 8, 23 February 2013, p. 13-16; Pervez Ayesha, Sexual Violence and Culture of Impunity in Kashmir: Need for a paradigm shift, *Economic and Political Weekly*, Vol. XLIX, No. 10, 8 March 2014, p. 10-13; Hazarika Sanjoy, An abomination called AFSPA, *The Hindu*, 12 February 2013.

the judicial guarantees which are recognized as indispensable by civilized peoples. Such term, however, does not include any such killing that, under international law, is lawfully carried out under the authority of a foreign nation."

The NHRC, in its discussion with the UN Special Rapporteur on Extra-judicial Summary or Arbitrary Execution stated that it had received a few reports/complaints of 'injury or death caused due to police action', but that the number of such complaints was not high. The NHRC stated: ".... often it happens that while pursuing criminals or attempting to arrest them, criminals resort to the use of lethal weapons to fend off the police. In several such cases, while exercising their right to self-defence, the police end up injuring, and in some instances even causing the death of such criminals....the right to self-defence also applies to police personnel and is provided for under the Code of Criminal Procedure....extra-judicial killings have no sanction whatsoever, under Indian law." [40]

The NHRC has issued necessary instructions on this regard to the chief secretaries of the states and on the receipt of any such report, the NHRC investigates the case. Where it believes there was no apprehension of any possible injury or death to the police personnel at the hands of the criminal, and that the concerned police personnel made use of unjustified force, thus, causing grievous injury or death of an individual, the Commission is empowered to award compensation to the next of kin of the victim and recommend the prosecution of the errant official. In 2011, two labourers were killed in firing by the Border Security Force (BSF) in separate incidents in Tripura. The families of the victims immediately lodged complaints in the local police stations claiming that the persons killed were innocent, which the BSF registered complaints with police the alleging that the men were smugglers and that firing was resorted to in self-defence. In November 2013, the two families received a sum of Rs 7 lakh and Rs 5 lakh as compensation from the BFS in compliance with the NHRC directive.[41]

---

40 Discussion held on 22 March 2012 at 1130 hrs under the Chairmanship of Justice Shri GP Mathur, Member, NHRC. Record of discussion available at: http://nhrc.nic.in/ Documents/Reports/Record%20Note-%20UN%20Spl.Rapporteur%20on%20Extra-Judicial%20Powers.pdf, accessed 21 November 2014.

41 BSF compensates firing victims' families in Tripura, *The Hindu*, 20 November 2013.

The judiciary too has been proactive and taken cognizance of extra-judicial killings and fake encounters. The Guwahati High Court ordered the Army to pay Rs 4 lakh each to the next of kin of two deceased in one such case.[42] The two victims, who were residents of Naoherua Village in the Darrang district of Assam, were summoned separately by the Field Regiment of the Harisinga Army Station for interrogation during February-March 2004. It was alleged that they were killed subsequently in a fake encounter and that their bodies were handed over to the police on the night of 7 March 2004. Following the deaths, the family members of the deceased moved the Guwahati High Court. On 8 April 2008, the High Court directed the District and Sessions Judge of Darrang to inquire into the death of the two persons. Finding the army responsible for both the deaths, the High Court ordered for compensation. On 25 May 2010, in compliance with the order of the Guwahati High Court the Army paid Rs 4 lakh each to the next of kin of the two persons.

Notwithstanding the directions of the NHRC and the verdict of the court, the armed forces personnel face a serious difficulty while working in disturbed areas. The use of force against an individual in an encounter is often projected as extrajudicial execution or fake encounter by human rights activists and relatives of the victim. Quite often this is done to discredit the armed forces or to claim compensation. Even when the arms and ammunition have been recovered from the deceased, the forces have been accused of planting these to dress up the incident as a genuine encounter. The case of Pathribal encounter, discussed in the next chapter, is a case in point. Militants often use human-shields, predominantly women, to escape when confronted by the armed forces. This ruse enables them to allege misconduct on the part of the armed forces, and the authorities, who conduct subsequent investigations often fail to understand the difficulty faced by the armed forces while operating in a hostile environment. It is easier to comment on the 'effectiveness and competence' of the armed forces, and the use of 'disproportionate force' when one is removed from the scene of action. The following highlights the frustrations of an anonymous military person in this context.

> Armed forces personnel too are human beings and they too have human rights. To understand the problems faced by them one must go into the details of functioning in a disturbed area. The

---

42 Army pays compensation for custodial deaths, *The Shillong Times*, 28 May 2010.

AFSPA allows for the search of a house without warrant. Now tell me, if you get information that five militants are hiding in a place x, would you wait for a search warrant from a magistrate the next day, and take the police along to search the house? Is it practicable to do so, particularly in a disturbed area? By the time you reach, the militants would have finished their task and moved on. Also, in such areas the police, judiciary and the local media live in fear of the militants. No one wants to antagonise them, so there is a high possibility of information being leaked to them. Frivolous litigation against the armed forces is an age-old practice followed by militants. They have a good number of lawyers on their pay roll, who can file cases on behalf of so-called human rights defenders and they often receive funds from across the border. Further, how you ensure the safety of an armed forces person who has to appear in court after getting posted out?

The armed forces have effective procedures to deal with violations of law and few members have been found guilty of extra-judicial executions and fake encounters. In the Poonch district of Jammu and Kashmir, a special police officer (SPO) and a Territorial Army jawan conspired and stage-managed an encounter for personal benefits. They claimed to have killed a top ranking Lashkar-e-Taiba militant after a 12-hour encounter. It later came to light that they had picked up a mentally challenged man from Rajouri, taken him to a forested area and shot him dead the next day. On the basis of this input, the army later claimed to have eliminated a high-ranking terrorist, and recovered a pistol, a wireless set and a diary recovered from the encounter site. The two men who had attempted the fake encounter were later arrested and charged with murder. A similar incident took place in 2010 in Machil in the Kashmir Valley, where three unsuspecting youths were picked up from their houses on the pretext of being given jobs by a former SPO and his associates. Then an 'encounter' based on 'pinpoint information' was arranged at a remote place and the 'foreign terrorists' were killed.[43] The case was subsequently taken over by the Army. On 13 November 2014, a general court martial convicted

---

43 The Army had claimed that they had killed three infiltrators in the Machil sector along the Line of Control. The three victims were reportedly lured by a former SPO and later handed over to the Army. The trio was later allegedly shot dead in a staged gun-battle near the Line of Control. The case came to light when the police found discrepancies in the FIR lodged by the Army unit and launched an inquiry into the incident. Eleven persons including nine army officials and two civilians were charged under Sections 302

seven personnel, including two officers, for their involvement in the fake encounter and sentenced them to life imprisonment.[44]

Human Shield

In April 2017, a military unit under the command an officer of the rank of Major, was tasked in Budgam, Jammu & Kashmir (J&K) to rescue a party of 12 persons, consisting of four election duty persons, seven ITBP armed escorts and one J&K Police constable. The polling party and their escorts were surrounded by murderous mob intending to use lethal force, including petrol bombs and stones. The armed escorts to the polling party were from the central armed police force and could have used their weapons in self defence. However, in order to avoid any criticism of having killed/injured civilians; they preferred help from the army. The army contingent of 17 men encountered a mob of about 1,000 people. Appeals made to the crowd to disperse remained ineffective. The army could have used their weapons after due warning to the mob, which might have resulted in numerous civilian casualties. However, the officer commanding the contingent asked his men to arrest one of the stone-palter, who was tied to the bonnet of a military vehicle and was used as a "human-shield" to rescue election officials and security personnel. The said man was later released. Human rights organizations, a few politicians, and activists termed the incident outrageous, and raised a hue and cry, forcing the government to conduct an inquiry and punish the wrongdoer.

Human shields are noncombatants whose presence protects certain objects or areas from attack.[45] The use of civilians as human shields has been employed worldwide in both international and non-international armed conflicts. The use of civilians (including women and children) as human shields has been an essential tactics of insurgents in Jammu &

(murder), 364 (abduction), 120-B (criminal conspiracy) and 34 (common intent) of the Ranbir Penal Code (RPC).

44 Machil fake encounter: Seven soldiers sentenced to life for killing three Kashmiri civilians, *The Hindu*, 14 November 2014, available at: http://www.thehindu.com/news/ national/other-states/machil-fake-encounter-seven-soldiers-sentenced-to-life-for-killing-three-kashmiri-civilians/article6594347.ece.

45 The term "human shields" describes: The intentional use of a party to a conflict of one or more human beings, usually civilians, or captured members of the adversary's forces … placed between the adversary and themselves in a way meant to deter an attack against the forces using the human shields, for fear of killing or harming the unarmed shields. The use of human shields is illegal in international armed conflict.

Kashmir. The provisions of AFSPA are applicable in Jammu & Kashmir and there is no specific prohibition on human shields under the Act. The law of non-international armed conflicts contained in the Common Article 3 to the Geneva Conventions, and the 1977 Additional protocol II (AP II) are applicable in non-international armed conflict. The Common Article 3 states that anyone in the hands of/under control of a party to the conflict must "in all circumstances be treated humanely, without any adverse distinction founded on race, colour, religion or faith, sex, birth or wealth, or any other similar criteria. For this purpose a number of acts against protected persons "are and shall remain prohibited at any time and in any place," including "violence to life and person, in particular cruel treatment and torture, outrage upon personal dignity, in particular humiliating and degrading treatment." Hence Common Article 3 prohibits inhuman treatment. Article 4 of AP II reiterates the essence of Common Article 3 in relation to the ban on inhuman and degrading treatment. Perhaps, this was the reason that prompted the State Human Rights Commission to direct the government to pay compensation to Rs 10 lakhs to the victim.

The use of a human-shield by the military in Budgam to avoid casualty was, perhaps, one method to deal with the extraordinary situation. The tactics are not new; Israeli military has used such measures in the past to protect civilians and others from Palestinian stone-pelting. More innovative tactics could be used by the police and military personnel in the future. In short, military needs to be innovative in exercising options during non-international armed conflict, even imperfect under the laws of war, if situation so demands and it saves lives of innocents.[46] The emerging security environment is radically different from what it was even two decades ago. Geneva Conventions, drafted in 1949, could never envisage such situations. Who could have imagined that few terrorists would hijack a passenger-laden airliner and use it to destroy the World Trade Centre in the US?

Besides the serious offences that have been discussed the armed forces have also been accused of intimidation, harassment, looting, dacoity, etc.

---

46 The Chief of Army Staff General Bipin Rawat defended the use of human shield, stating that the army is facing a dirty war in J&K which has to be fought through innovative ways. According to army chief, the rules of engagement are there when the adversary comes face to face and fights with you. It is a dirty war…that is where innovation comes in. You fight dirty war with innovations. It would have been easier for the army to fight insurgents, if they used weapons instead of stones and petrol bombs.

These allegations have been promptly investigated by the armed forces and action has been taken against the culprits. Remedial measures have also been put in place to avoid reoccurrence of such offences. In 2011, the house of a civilian in Jorhat was raided by a few military personnel under the command of an officer of the rank of captain on the ground of the suspected presence of ULFA cadre. The woman who was present in the house, in a statement to the police, alleged that the Army personnel had covered their faces to conceal their identity and blindfolded the inmates. They had looted valuables, including Rs 1.5 lakh in cash, Rs 6.5 lakh worth of gold jewellery, a pistol, a laptop and four mobile phones. The raiding team had not followed the procedural requirement of informing the local police about the raid. After an FIR was registered under Sections 395/397, IPC at the local police station and the suspects were identified, the case was taken over by the Army under Section 125 of the Army Act, 1950 read with Section 475 of the Criminal Procedure Code, 1973. [47] The Army is yet to inform about the action taken against the culprits, a mandatory requirement under Rule 7 (1) of the Criminal Courts and Court-Martial (Adjustment of Jurisdiction) Rules, 1978.[48]

Problems Faced by the Armed Forces

The greatest problem in a disturbed area is that the local media is under the influence of the militants. Hence, the reports carried in the media are biased against the armed forces and have created the impression that they are the greatest violators of human rights. Unless members of the armed forces are also killed in an encounter, the civil society refuses to believe that

---

47 The 2011 Jorhat dacoity incident, which led to the then Army Chief Gen V K Singh ordering a promotion ban on then Lt Gen Dalbir Singh Suhag, previous Army Chief, is in the news again with the Supreme Court, on 19 August 2014, seeking responses of the Centre and Assam on a PIL seeking CBI inquiry into the crime. It has been alleged that the entire investigation was stalled/hijacked by the Army in order to save the Army officials.

48 Rule 7 of the Criminal Courts and Court-Martial (Adjustment of Jurisdiction) Rules, 1978, provides that when an accused has been delivered by the magistrate, the commanding officer of the accused or the competent military authority, shall inform the magistrate whether the accused has been tried by a court martial or other effectual proceedings have been taken or ordered to be taken against him. When the magistrate has been informed that the accused has not been tried or other effectual proceedings have not been taken or ordered to be taken against him, the magistrate shall report the circumstances to the State Government which may, in consultation with the Central Government, take appropriate steps to ensure that the accused person is dealt with in accordance with law.

it is genuine. When an innocent civilian is gunned down by the militants, no voice is raised;[49] however, in every case of collateral harm to a civilian, the media and the civil society try to portray the armed forces as an enemy of the local population. While every offence against civilians, be it an enforced disappearance or fake encounter, needs to be condemned and the violator punished severely, there is also a need to examine, why such incidents take place.

The Indian armed forces are looked upon as a nationalist institution, yet no one, not even the greatest political leaders, are quite clear about their role or significance in society. Independent India's two most important leaders, Mahatma Gandhi and Jawaharlal Nehru, had reservations about the use of armed forces. Nehru had strong distaste for the military.[50] Over the years, they have been used to clean up political messes in different parts of the country. They are controlled by civilian officials in the Ministry of Defence, which approves all promotions above the rank of Colonel. Bureaucratic control over the defence establishment has diminished the stature of the superior officers in the eyes of the men they command, and has weakened the command and control system within the services. Nothing changes this precedence given to the bureaucracy over the armed forces.[51] Not even wars, in which the forces are called upon to make supreme sacrifice in the service of the nation.

The pressure of working under this set-up has prompted a number of senior officers to lobby for political support to seek appointments, promotions, awards and transfers. Besides, the rot that has affected the society in general has pervaded the armed forces as well. Senior officers have tinkered with the selection boards to accommodate their own staff officers and relatives. Promotions and posting policies have been altered or reversed arbitrarily without serious thought.[52] All of this has led to a cynicism that prompts acts like those we are condemning today.

---

49 Militants have killed more than 10 panch members in J&K, who were elected in Panchayat elections of 2011.See: *The Times of India*, 18 April 2014 and 21 December 2014.

50 Cohen Stephen P. 2002. *India: Emerging Power*, New Delhi: Oxford University Press, p. 128.

51 While a significant body of literature exists on the nature of the Indian civil-military relations and the institutional structure of civilian control of the military, very little work has been done on addressing the changing balance between civil-military functions over time. Ray Ayesha. 2013. *The Soldier and the State in India*, New Delhi: Sage, p. 3.

52 Bedi Rahul, Desperate to reorder and modernize, *The Hindu*, 28 October 2010.

The Indian soldier has a hard life. He has to struggle with inadequate salary, poor accommodation, leave restriction, ineffective seniors and paltry pension. A retired officer writes:

> The loneliness of being away for long periods of duty in counter-insurgency areas, coupled with a growing sense of dismay at the callousness of the civilian administration and political authority, produces a frustration that is virtually complete. While trying to clean up the mess created by bureaucratic and political ineptitude, the soldier is also putting his neck on the line. The sense of honour that has been instilled in soldiering prevents him from walking away and leaving the mess as it was. [53]

Young officers too face similar situations when posted in a hostile environment. The tough call of duty takes a toll on the officers and the soldiers whom they command.[54] It may drive them to take extreme steps. Working under pressure from a result-oriented commander, an officer may be compelled to do things he ought not to have done.[55]

Law as Weapon in Internal Conflict

In India, law has been successfully used as a weapon of warfare (lawfare)[56] against the armed forces engaged in non-international armed conflict. Consider the following:

---

53 Jha U. C., Fake encounters, *The Hindu*, 14 May 2006, available at: http://www.thehindu. com/todays-paper/tp-features/tp-openpage/fake-encounters/article3225219.ece.

54 Kumar Vinay, Anxiety in Uniform, *The Hindu*, 21 March 2013.

55 In a petition filed in the Armed Forces Tribunal, the petitioner alleged that on the directions of his commander a 'false report' about killing of five militants on the night intervening 17 and 18 August 2003 was submitted by him to the higher authorities. Further, based on an anonymous complaint, the matter was investigated and the petitioner was made a scapegoat. He was tried by a court martial for making a false statement, committing a civil offence i.e. criminal conspiracy, and was dismissed from service. The Tribunal did not interfere in the punishment awarded by the court martial holding that the petitioner being the commanding officer was required to be more honest towards his duties and the personnel attached with him. *Col H S Kohli v Union of India*, TA No. 254/2009, in WPC No. 7827/2009, decide by the Armed Forces Tribunal, Principal Bench, New Delhi on 11 January 2010.

56 US Air Force General Dunlap was the first to use the term "lawfare" to denote a strategy of using or misusing law as a substitute for traditional military means to achieve a war-fighting objective. Lawfare is becoming a powerful 'force multiplier', reminding one of Sun Tzu, who once said, "To subdue the enemy without fighting is the supreme excellence." Russia, the People's Republic of China and Palestine Authority (PA) have

- Reacting to a petition filed by an NGO, the Supreme Court in its order of July this year has issued directions for the lodging of an FIR in every case of encounter death against members of the forces involved in counter-insurgency operations in Manipur.

- The J&K police was recently forced by the local leaders to register a case against an army unit reportedly involved in tying an alleged stone-palter to an army vehicle and using him as a human shield.

- In June 2016, the army had to move the Supreme Court against the orders of the J&K High Court on the alleged mass rape committed in Kunan-Poshora in 1991. Despite the conclusion of an independent investigation team that the allegation was a hoax orchestrated by militant groups, the issue has been kept alive by cases filed by activists.

- Between 2012 and 2016, nearly 200 complaints of human rights violations by defence personnel were filed in the states where the AFSPA is in force.

- In almost every encounter death in the areas infested with Maoists, activists move the human rights commissions and the courts, claiming the encounter to be fake.

- Pellet guns have been portrayed as inhuman weapons, compelling the government to limit their use.

Lawfare can substitute for armed conflict where it provides a means to compel specified behaviour with fewer costs than the use of weapons. In India, the reasons behind the rise of lawfare are the increasing reach of human rights organizations, revolution in information technology, unaccounted sources of finance and ease with which the Indian legal system can be exploited. The use of lawfare by the activists has resulted in engaging the armed forces in investigations ordered by the Supreme Court and special investigations and commissions of inquiry appointed by state governments. Lawfare poses a serious threat to the effective functioning of the armed forces and paramilitary in India. There is a need for a realistic assessment of this threat and the responses to it.

---

used "legal warfare" as a major component of their strategic doctrine. The PA is waging lawfare against Israel on the battleground and international organizations and treaties, and Palestinian NGOs are doing so on the battleground of national courts.

The Legal System

India has passed the Geneva Conventions Act 1960 to give effect to the Geneva Conventions of 1949. The punishment for grave breaches of the Conventions is contained in Section 3 of the Act, which provides that if a person subject to the Army Act commits a civil offence, he shall be tried only by a court martial. However, there is a need to update the legal system relating to the armed forces. The system must incorporate the crimes as well standards of 'command or superior responsibility'[57] specified in the Rome Statute. Articles 6, 7 and 8 of the Rome Statute define the crimes over which the ICC has jurisdiction, that is, genocide, crimes against humanity and war crimes. The definition of war crimes is of relevance to India, as its armed forces are deployed in humanitarian missions of the United Nations and also internally, in aid to civil power.[58] The advantage will be that international standards would be clearly defined in domestic laws and would allow the armed forces to continue their policy of trying service members alleged to have violated the law by a court martial.[59]

Certain members of the civil society have been demanding that the armed forces in India, while operating in disturbed areas, must observe

57 The Rome Statute applies rules of command responsibility not only to military commanders, but also to civilian superiors. Article 28 of the Rome Statute provides: "A military commander or person effectively acting as a military commander shall be criminally responsible for crimes within the jurisdiction of the Court committed by forces under his or her effective command and control, or effective authority and control as the case may be, as a result of his or her failure to exercise control properly over such forces, where: (i) That military commander or person either knew or, owing to the circumstances at the time, should have known that the forces were committing or about to commit such crimes; and (ii) That military commander or person failed to take all necessary and reasonable measures within his or her power to prevent or repress their commission or to submit the matter to the competent authorities for investigation and prosecution."

58 War crimes constitute acts contrary to the laws of international armed conflict, and entail penal accountability of the individuals who perpetrate the proscribed acts. Article 8, lists four different categories of crimes as "war crimes", i.e., (i) grave breaches of the Geneva Conventions of 12 August 1949; (ii) other serious violations of the laws and customs applicable in international armed conflict; (iii) in the case of an armed conflict not of an international character, serious violations of Article 3 common to the four Geneva Conventions of 12 August 1949; and (iv) other serious violations of the laws and customs applicable in armed conflicts not of an international character. Under each of these headings, the Statute goes on to list a series of specific crimes.

59 Jha U.C., 'ICC and the Indian Military Justice System', in Nainar Vahida and Saumya Uma (ed.). 2013. *Pursuing Elusive Justice: Mass crimes in India and Relevance of International Standards*, New Delhi: Oxford University Press, p. 327.

international standards of humanitarian law and human rights. They have repeatedly reminded the armed forces about the obligations and duties imposed under the Common Article 3 of the Geneva Conventions of 1949 and the Additional Protocol II to the Geneva Conventions. However, they fail to question the non-State actors about their human rights obligations. International law imposes obligations on parties to an internal armed conflict irrespective of any recognition granted by the State they are fighting against or by any third State. International humanitarian law, which applies during internal armed conflict, imposes certain duties on non-State actors.[60] The minimum protection offered by Common Article 3 to the four Geneva Conventions of 1949 contains obligations for "each Party to the conflict". These obligations are to "persons taking no active part in the hostilities" as well as to the "wounded and sick". The prohibitions include murder, violence to the person, cruel treatment, the taking of hostages, humiliating and degrading treatment, and sentences or executions without judicial safeguards. The non-State actors in India have indulged in all these prohibited acts against the civilian population in the last two to three decades. If Common Article 3 is indeed applicable, then its terms impose obligations not only on the armed forces but also on non-State actors operating in Jammu and Kashmir and the northeast.

The protection offered by AP II goes beyond the minimum standards contained in Common Article 3 although the minimum standards contained in Common Article 3 remain in effect even when AP II is applicable. The Protocol supplements these standards with extra protection for civilians, children, and medical and religious personnel. It also details the procedural guarantees that must be afforded to people interned or detained.[61] The important point in the present context is that it is applicable to both the sides in an armed conflict and the intensity of fighting has to be greater than that traditionally required for the application of Common Article 3. Besides, India is not a signatory to AP II.

---

60 For more details see: Clapham Andrew, Human rights obligations of non-state actors in conflict situations, *International Review of the Red Cross*, Vol. 88, No. 863, September 2006, p. 492-523.

61 According to Article 1(2) of AP II, the Protocol does not apply to situations of internal disturbances, riots and sporadic acts of violence. In addition Article 1(1) of the Protocol requires that the dissident armed groups be under responsible command and exercise such control over part of the territory that they are in a position to carry out military operations and implement the guarantees in the Protocol. This is generally considered to constitute a higher threshold than that for the applicability of Common Article 3.

Court Martial or Criminal Court

The AFSPA gives Indian military and paramilitary forces wide-ranging powers in the disturbed areas. There have been many instances where military persons engaged in the aid to civil power in the disturbed areas have been accused of killings, disappearances, torture, arbitrary detention, sexual violence and other serious crimes.[62] Such allegations are investigated by the military and if found true, the offenders are tried by a court martial under the Army Act. The human rights groups have alleged that investigations and prosecutions of human rights violations remain slow and a court martial consisting of military officers often shields the accused leading to impunity.[63] The military courts are primarily used to "discipline" the military and not to deliver justice. Further, the military overshadows and dominates not only the civilian population, but also civil administration, the judiciary and elected state governments.[64] They have been demanding that a military person accused of committing civil offence must be tried in a civil (criminal) court.[65]

A court martial is a criminal court as per the definition in the Criminal Procedure Code, 1973 (Cr PC).[66] The proceedings of a court martial are judicial in nature. A court martial is an important institution for disciplining the armed forces. It is constituted under the respective Acts

---

62 The AFSPA gives the armed forces wide powers to shoot to kill, arrest on flimsy pretext, conduct warrantless searches, and demolish structures in the name of "aiding civil power." Equipped with these special powers, soldiers have raped, tortured, "disappeared," and killed Indian citizens for five decades without fear of being held accountable. *Getting Away With Murder: 50 Years of the Armed Forces (Special Powers) Act*, Human Rights Watch, August 2008.

63 In July 2017, the Principal Bench of the Armed Forces Tribunal suspended the sentence of the officers convicted in Machil fake encounter case and released them on bail. Section 15 (6) (e) of the Armed Forces Tribunal Act, empowers the Tribunal to suspend a sentence of imprisonment awarded by a court martial. However, media as well as few activists portrayed entirely different account of the legal proceeding. See: Chakravarty Ipsita, They will never get justice, 29 July 2017, available at: https://kashmirobserver.net/2017/features/they-will-never-get-justice-21202, accessed 10 August 2017.

64 Mathur Shubh, Life and death in the borderlands: Indian sovereignty and military impunity, *Race & Class*, Vol. 54, No. 1, pp. 33-99.

65 Under Section 3 (viii) of the Army Act, the term "Criminal Court" means a court of ordinary criminal justice in any part of India. The expression 'criminal court' as applied in the Army Act does not mean only the courts created under Criminal Procedure Code, but it includes all courts of 'ordinary criminal justice'.

66 Sections 480 to 482, Criminal Procedure Code, 1973.

of the armed forces (i.e., the Army Act 1950, the Assam Rifles Act 2006, the Border Security Force Act, 1963, etc: henceforth the common term 'Army Act' will be used for these laws) and is an ad hoc tribunal empowered to award punishments, depending upon the nature of offence, up to the death.[67] It has no jurisdiction over civilians and cannot award damages in favour of an individual. A military court is subject to the superintendence of the Armed Forces Tribunal and the Supreme Court.

Offences Triable by Court Martial

In January 2013, a government instituted commission headed by a former Chief Justice of India, Justice Verma recommended that security forces be brought under the purview of ordinary criminal law instead of military law in cases involving sexual crimes against women. This recommended created confusion in the minds of many that military person are not amenable to civilian criminal justice system in India. The offences committed by persons subject to the military law can be classified into three categories:

(a) Offences triable exclusively by court martial, e.g., offences in relation to enemy, mutiny, desertion, illegal absence, unbecoming conduct, disobedience, etc.

(b) Offences triable by criminal court only, e.g., murder of a civilian, culpable homicide of a civilian, rape of a civilian, while not on active duty, at any place outside India or on a notified frontier post.

(c) Offences triable by court martial as well as a criminal court, e.g., counterfeiting coin, public nuisance, hurt, wrongful restraints, defamation, kidnapping, abduction etc.[68]

The Army Act section 69 provides that any person subject to this Act who at any place in or beyond India commits any civil offence shall

---

67 Under the Army Act 1950 a general court martial is empowered to award punishments of the death, imprisonment for life, imprisonment rigorous or simple up to 14 years, cashiering (only to officer), dismissal, and other punishments lower in scale like reduction in ranks, forfeiture, severe reprimand, stoppage of pay and allowances etc. Certain of these punishments could be awarded in combination. An officer shall be sentenced to be cashiered, before he is awarded the punishment of the death, imprisonment for life or imprisonment. See the Army Act 1950 section 71-74.

68 Sections 69 and 70, the Army Act, 1950.

be deemed to be guilty of an offence against the Army Act and shall be liable to be tried by a court martial. The offences covered by section 69 and described as civil offences fall in concurrent jurisdiction of court martial and criminal court and pertain to the third category. In case a military person is accused of murder, culpable homicide not amounting to murder, and rape against a person not subject the service Acts; he will be tried by a criminal court unless the offence has been committed while on active duty, outside India, or on a notified frontier post.

Concurrent Jurisdiction

Besides offences of a military nature, a court martial can try civil offences committed at any place in or beyond India, so long as they are deemed to be offences under the Army Act. It can try offences of murder, culpable homicide not amounting to murder and rape committed by a person subject to the Army Act against any person, if they are committed while on active service, or at any place outside India or at a frontier post specified by the Central Government. The commanding officer of an accused also has powers through which the majority of minor criminal and disciplinary offences against members of the armed forces are handled.[69]

The Army Act does not bar the jurisdiction of criminal courts in respect of acts or omissions which are punishable under the Army Act as well as under any other law in force. Section 125 of the Army Act provides that if the designated officer decides that the proceedings should be before a court martial he may direct the accused to be detained in military custody. Otherwise, he may handover a military accused to the magistrate for trial in a criminal court. Section 125 of the Army Act provides:

> When a criminal court and a court-martial have each jurisdiction in respect of an offence, it shall be in the discretion of the officer commanding the army, army corps, division or independent brigade in which to accused person is serving or such other officer as may be prescribed to decide before which court the proceedings

---

69 The Commanding Officer (CO) under the Army Act has the authority to hear a charge and impose up to 30 days of imprisonment and additional 14 days detention. The accused has no appellate rights against this award. In case of more serious offences, a CO has the authority to try an accused up to the rank of havildar by a summary court martial (SCM) and award punishment of one year imprisonment and dismissal from service. Unlike the Army, an accused in the paramilitary forces has no right to appeal against punishments awarded by a summary force court.

shall be instituted, and, if that officer decides that they should be instituted before a court-martial, to direct that the accused person shall be detained in military custody.

Section 126 of the Army Act dealing with the power of a criminal court to require delivery of military offender states: "When a criminal court having jurisdiction is of opinion that proceedings shall be instituted before itself in respect of any alleged offence, it may, by written notice, require the officer referred to in section 125 at his option, either to deliver over the offender to the nearest magistrate to be proceeded against according to law, or to postpone proceedings pending a reference to the Central Government."[70] Further, "In every such case the said officer shall either deliver over the offender in compliance with the requisition, or shall forthwith refer the question as to the court before which the proceedings are to be instituted for the determination of the Central Government, whose order upon such reference shall be final."[71]

The impact of section 126 of the Army Act is that if a criminal court is still of the opinion that proceedings should be instituted before it itself it may, by written notice, require the officer referred to in section 125 at his option either to deliver over the offender to the nearest Magistrate to be proceeded against according to law or to postpone proceedings pending a reference to the Central Government. Under sub-section (2) of section 126 if such a conflict arises the said officer must either deliver over to offender in compliance with the requisition which means a requisition by a written notice, or must forthwith refer the question as to the court before which the proceedings should be instituted for the determination of the Central Government, whose order upon such reference shall be final. It follows that the effect of sections 125 and 126 of the Army Act, when read together, is that the first option lies with the Army authorities and in case of conflict the Magistrate gets jurisdiction only if the Central Government decides that the accused person shall be tried by a criminal court. The Magistrate cannot by reason of section 126, assume jurisdiction to try an accused person unless he has given a written notice to the officer referred to in section 125 and then the Central Government decides that the case should be tried by the Magistrate.

70　Section 126 (1), the Army Act, 1950.

71　Section 126 (2), the Army Act, 1950.

The Central Government has made the Criminal Courts and Court-martial (Adjustment of Jurisdiction) Rules, 1978 under the powers conferred by section 475 (1) of the Cr PC. Under rule 5 of the said Rules, the first option has been given to the army authorities and they may give notice to the magistrate that the accused should be tried by a court martial. From the above discussion what emerges is this that under the Army Act, 1950, as well as the Rules the first option lies with the army authorities to decide the forum of trial. The magistrate gets jurisdiction only after a decision in his favour by the Central Government in case of a conflict between the army authorities and the magistrate. The Supreme Court in the case of *Union of India v. State of Punjab* [72] has summed up the issue relating the jurisdiction of court martial and criminal court:

(i) When both ordinary criminal court and court martial have concurrent jurisdiction to try the offence, the conflict of opinion whether the accused by tried by ordinary criminal court or court martial is to be resolved by Central Government.

(ii) Inherent jurisdiction under which criminal courts have to take cognizance of civil offences is not taken away by any of the provisions of Air Force Act or 475 Cr PC and rules framed thereunder.

(iii) If both criminal courts and court martial have concurrent jurisdiction, the first option lies with military authorities to try the accused. If military authorities had surrendered the accused in the ordinary criminal courts, it will be deemed that military authorities and exercised its option not to try the accused.

(iv) If accused has been tried by criminal court without objection by the military authorities such trial is not vitiated.

(v) First right is of the military authorities to try the offender – Once express their intention to do so – If they abdicate

---

72 Criminal Misc No. 10831 of 1999 decided on 3 June 1999: Criminal Courts and Court Martial (Adjustment of Jurisdiction) Rules, 1978, Rules 3 to 9 – Cr PC, Section 475 – Offence committed by a Military personnel – Accused whether be tried by Court Martial or Ordinary Criminal Court.

their right in favour of ordinary criminal courts, it is not open to them to try the offender.

In June 2016, the Armed Forces Tribunal's Mumbai bench observed that a general court martial did have the right to try offences under the Protection of Children from Sexual Offences (POCSO) Act, 2012. The tribunal made the observation while dismissing an appeal filed by a colonel, who had challenged the jurisdiction of the general court martial in dismissing him from service in a sexual assault case and sentencing him under POCSO Act. The Tribunal held that the Army Act confer discretion on the commanding officer to decide before which court the proceedings shall be instituted, when a criminal court and court martial each have jurisdiction in respect of an offence.

Another concern has been raised that under section 69 of the Army Act, 1950, a court martial can take cognizance of civil offences; however, it does not have jurisdiction over some of the serious crimes defined under the Rome Statute of the International Criminal Court (ICC). The war crimes defined in the Rome Statute are of relevance to India, as its armed forces are deployed in aid to civil power and also in UN peacekeeping missions.

The Army Act defines some war crimes as crimes under national law, and provides for universal jurisdiction over such crimes. Military personnel accused of committing torture, inhuman and degrading treatment, destruction of property, etc. can be tried under different provisions of the Army Act. For serious offences, a military accused could be tried under the Indian Penal Code. The punishments authorized under the Army Act are more severe than those prevailing under the Rome Statute.[73] The conviction rate in trials by court martial is over 90 per cent. Trials are speedy, and there are hardly any unnecessary adjournments. Courts martial are open courts and members of the public have the right to access, subject to certain limitations.[74] In fact, a military accused is always at a greater disadvantage during trial by a court martial, as compared to trial by a civil court. During the stages of arrest and investigations, he cannot avail himself of any legal

---

73 The maximum punishment, which the International Criminal Court (ICC) can award, is 30 years of imprisonment; however, in exceptional cases the Court may impose a term of life imprisonment. A general court martial or summary general court martial can award death sentence.

74 The Army Rules, 1954, Rule 80A.

assistance. The quality of legal aid during his trial may not be effective and his right to appeal against the verdict is limited.[75] The military commander is also empowered to adopt a shorter version of trial by ordering a summary general court martial,[76] besides suspending certain rules on the grounds of expediency or necessity of discipline.[77] Another summary form of trial is by constituting a summary court martial, which can try persons up to the rank of havildar and award a punishment of one year of imprisonment and dismissal. The appellate rights against the findings and sentence of a court martial can be exercised only by persons subject to the Army Act, Air Force Act and the Navy Act in the Armed Forces Tribunal. Personnel of the BSF, the Assam Rifles and other paramilitary forces have no such right. An added advantage of trial by a court martial is that, the Army Act section 139 (6) enables a court martial, when trying a person for a civil offence to find him not guilty of that offence but guilty of any other offence of which he might have been found guilty under the Cr PC.

The fact is that the armed forces have inherited their legal system from the British who made it for the governance of a mercenary force and if anything certain provisions of the Army Act could be termed 'draconian' and 'primitive'. Not being aware of the intricacies of the military legal system, members of the civil society in Jammu and Kashmir and the Northeast have always demanded that military accused be tried in a civilian court. The irony is that while the military accused always feels that had he faced a trial under the civilian system he could have succeeded in defending himself better; a civilian always gets the impression that the military legal

75 The 'rights' to a fair trial listed under Article 14 of the International Covenant on Civil and Political Rights, 1966, though available to an accused in a civil court are not available to an accused in a trial by a court martial.

76 The Army Act 1950, Section 112. A summary general court martial (SGCM) is constituted by three officers with minimum of one year of commissioned service, the senior-most member must not be junior to the accused, there may not be any judge advocate and the accused may seek help from a military officer to defend his case. A formal charge-sheet is not necessary, the statement of offence may be made briefly in any language sufficient to describe or disclose an offence under the Army Act. A SGCM can award punishment upto death, and it may not have any member qualified in law on its board. Though an SGCM is to be constituted only in extreme situations, the Indian Army held 156 SGCM during 1999-2003. Besides Bangladesh and Pakistan, no other democracy in the world has such a draconian and antiquated system of justice for its military members.

77 The Army Rules, 1954, Rule 36.

system protects the military accused. An acquittal of a military person by the higher judiciary is invariably viewed by the civil society as 'judicial collusion with the interest of the military'[78], or 'actively aiding impunity for the armed forces'.[79]

---

78 Pervez Ayesha, Sexual Violence and Culture of Impunity in Kashmir: Need for a paradigm shift, *Economic and Political Weekly*, Vol. XLIX, No. 10, 8 March 2014, p. 12. It has been incorrectly mentioned by the author that a court martial can either send an accused to jail or dismiss him from service. In connection with a case of acquittal of military person by the Jammu and Kashmir High Court the author has commented: "In an attempt to fortify its 'subservient position', the judiciary in Kashmir has also colluded with the interests of the military".

79 While referring to the decision of the Supreme Court in *Masooda Parveen v Union of India* (2007) 4 SCC 548, it has been alleged that 'the Court has appeared to have actively aided, through its rulings, the impunity for armed forces in Jammu and Kashmir'. See: 'Alleged Perpetrators - Stories of Impunity in Jammu and Kashmir', International Peoples' Tribunal on Human Rights and Justice in Indian Administered Kashmir, p.14.

4

Human Rights Violations: Five Cases

Kunan-Poshora Mass Rape

The alleged mass rape at Kunan-Poshora in the Kashmir Valley in February 1991 received wide publicity both locally and internationally and refuses to die down almost 25 years later.[1] Kunan-Poshora in the Kushwara district is a twin-helmet with about 120 households. On the night intervening 23 and 24 February 1991, the 4th Rajputana Rifles (Raj Rif) of the 68 Mountain Brigade conducted a cordon-and-search operation in the village. It was alleged later that up to 100 women of all ages and conditions (pregnant, deaf and mute, and elderly) were raped by one to seven men in an orgy of sexual violence from 11:00 pm to 04:00 am in the presence of their children and families.

According to the Army, Kunan-Poshora was a staging camp for infiltrators and weapon-carriers. It had been searched on two occasions by the paramilitary forces, before the operation by the Army. According to the military version, after intercepting a conversation about the presence of armed militants at Kunan-Poshora, 9 army officers accompanied by 9 junior commissioned officers (JCOs) and 107 other ranks (ORs) were detailed to conduct a cordon-and-search operation. According to usual procedure, villages and localities may be cordoned off at night but are searched by day. However, in exceptional circumstances, when an elusive or important

---

1 Prashant Jha, Unravelling a 'mass rape', *The Hindu*, 8 July 2013, available at: http://www.thehindu.com/opinion/op-ed/unravelling-a-mass-rape/article4892195.ece, accessed 12 August 2014.

catch is anticipated, places may be searched in night. Around 11:00 pm, an outer cordon around Kunan-Poshora was formed by about 60 army men. A second column, under the commanding officer (CO) of the 4th Raj Rif, picked up two J&K police constables from the Trehgam police station and reached the village after 01:00 am, moving through heavy snow.[2] After the 'informer' with the search party identified 11 suspected houses, the able-bodied men were asked to collect outside the village school. The first floor of the school served as an interrogation centre and command post. Six search parties comprising an officer/JCO and four to six men were formed. These search parties, accompanied by the two J&K policemen, searched the houses. No militant was found but the inmates identified certain other households, which too were searched. The men from all the suspected houses were interrogated and on the basis of the information provided by them, two AK-47s, one of them plastered into a wall, and a pistol were recovered with ammunition. The night search concluded at 04:00 am, however, no militant was found.

After the morning *azaan* (call to prayer), the two policemen used the same speaker and asked the men from all the houses to gather outside the mosque at 06:30 am. The CO distributed sweets among some children and a medical officer set up a clinic, which was attended by 23 persons, including eight women. Meanwhile, 10 search parties, accompanied by representatives of the village, conducted a general search of all the houses. The search was over by 08:30 am, with no complaints from any of the houses. Thereafter, some village notables and two J&K policemen signed a no-objection certificate, a standard procedural requirement, which was explained to the villagers. A few of the men were offered fruits and eggs and they later led the army to a catch of arms outside the cordon area. The Commander of the 68 Brigade also arrived for an inspection and spoke to the headman, the teacher and some others. No one complained or lodged any protest. The column left the village at about 09:00 am in a friendly atmosphere.

On 27 February 1991, a few villagers visited the Brigade Headquarters and informed the Commander that 'people in Handwara' were complaining that women had been molested at Kunan-Poshora during the search operation. When the Brigade Commander asked them for the names of

---

2 Maheshwari Anil. 1993. *Crescent Over Kashmir: Politics of Mullaism*, New Delhi: Rupa & Co, p. 152.

the women or their relative, they could not name anyone. Nonetheless, the Brigade Commander said that he would inquire into the matter and take severe action against anyone found guilty.

On 3 March 1991, the Deputy Commissioner Kupwara, informed his superior, the Special Commissioner, Baramulla that he had heard of some untoward incident in Kunan-Poshora. He was advised to visit the village, which he did after a few days. By this time, the village chowkidar also came with a report. The Deputy Commissioner of Kupwara visited Kunan-Poshora, accompanied by the Tehsildar, the SHO of Trehgam and two J&K police constables who had been with the Raj Rif cordon-and-search party on 23/24 February. He was informed that a number of women were raped during the cordon-and-search operation and was handed three empty bottles of whisky as evidence of the liquor the army personnel had consumed. He spoke to 23 women who made allegations of rape, and showed him blood-stained garments. He was informed that the other victims of rape had fled the village.

The Deputy Commissioner sent a confidential report to the Divisional Commissioner, Kashmir on 7 March with copies to several other persons. The report leaked out and newspaper accounts quoted the Deputy Commissioner as having stated that the members of the armed forces 'behaved like violent beasts.....a large number having entered into the houses of villagers and gang-raped 23 women at gunpoint without any consideration for their age, pregnancy, etc.' The report further stated, 'There was a hue and cry in the whole village.' An FIR was lodged at the Tregham Police Station under sections 375, 452 and 342 of the Ranbir Penal Code on 8 March 1991.

On learning of this, Brigadier H K Sharma, Deputy Brigade Commander of another Brigade conducted an inquiry on 10 March. A Defence Ministry release later dismissed the allegations as 'malicious and untrue'. *The Telegraph*, Calcutta in its issue of 14 March 1991 also brought out a story on the incident, which was contradicted by the Ministry of Defence.

Divisional Commissioner Wajahat Habibullah conducted an inquiry into the matter on 18 March. He was accompanied by the DG Police, a senior CRPF officer, the DC and SP Kupwara, and a PRO of the Ministry of Defence. Habibullah found that the number of rape victims had risen from 34 to 40 and then 53. Subsequent press reports put the figure at around 100. He noted several discrepancies: there was no consistency in the reported number of rape victims; it would have required more men (than those in the search party) to gang rape so many women; and the complaint was made several days later. Besides no one heard screams or cries for help, the villagers, who were addressed by the commanding officer the next morning, did not lodge a complaint and a no-objection certificate was signed by the village elders. The Divisional Commissioner also noted that some of the names of the rape victims tallied with those of the women who had voluntarily sought treatment by the army medical officer in the camp on 24 February. He concluded that the charges levelled against the army were grossly exaggerated, though he did find that some of the women in the village were genuinely angry.

A medical examination of 32 alleged rape victims was conducted at the primary medical centre, Kralpora on 15 and 21 March 1991 by the Block Medical Officer (BMO). His report stated that all the women barring four were married and that almost all of them had abrasions on the chest and abdomen. Further, while three women stated that they were raped, 19 said that they were molested, while the rest made no specific comment. It has been reported that 'abrasions on the chest and abdomen' are common among the village folk in Kashmir as they use kangris (earthen pots with burning coal) to ward off the winter chill.[3]

Several news papers, including the *New York Times* carried a chilling report about a women called Zarifa or Hanifa, aged about 25 years and nine months' pregnant who was raped by seven army men.[4] The report also said that she was kicked in the womb by a soldier and delivered a baby boy with a fractured arm in the Kupwara district hospital three days later. An independent committee[5] which investigated the incident, however, reported that Zarifa and her mother had separately stated that Zarifa had delivered a baby 6 days before the fateful night. Zarifa had said, "They hurt my baby of six days," while her mother said that around the time of *azaan*, three men took her daughter to another room. The Committee was given

---

3   Maheshwari Anil. 1993. *Crescent Over Kashmir: Politics of Mullaism*, New Delhi: Rupa & Co, p. 151.

4   Barbara Crossette, 'India Moves Against Kashmir Rebels', *New York Times*, 7 April 1991.

5   Comprising senior journalists B G Verghese and K Vikram Rao.

to understand from medical experts that babies can be born with fractured limbs if doctors change the position of the foetus to make the delivery safe.

The Verghese Committee formed at the behest of the Press Council of India in June 1991 to investigate accusations against the army, also reported on the incident. The Committee met almost all concerned.[6] It visited Kunan-Poshora and talked to several of the alleged rape victims in their homes, the male members of their family, and other men who said that they had been interrogated by the military or kept out in the cold all night while their houses were being searched. The Committee also met the village headman, a teacher, and two J&K policemen who were present in during the cordon-and-search operation. It reported that some women did offer resistance when the men from the suspected houses were being taken away for questioning during the night search. The report stated: "Even in remote villages, Kashmiri women, particularly in the militant-infested areas, are far from shy and docile and indeed quite aggressive in defending their men, shouting, screaming, beating their breasts and tearing their clothes, as experienced on other occasions."

Asia Watch, a division of the Human Rights Watch and the Physicians for Human Rights also came out with a report on the incident.[7] Its opening page stated: "In its efforts to crush the militant movement, India's central government has pursued a policy of repression in Kashmir which has resulted in massive human rights violations by Indian army and paramilitary forces. Throughout the conflict, the security forces have deliberately targeted civilians......, have assaulted civilians during search operations, tortured and summarily executed detainees in custody and murdered civilians in reprisal attacks." It alleged: "Indian government

---

6   The list included the Corps Commander, Divisional Commander, Brigade Commander, Battalion Commander, medical officers of the army, the Governor, the DGP, the Divisional Commissioner Kashmir, the Special Commissioner Baramulla, the DC and SP of Kupwara, the Tehsildar Kupwara, the Chief Medical Officer and Chief Physician Kupwara District Hospital.

7   In October 1992, representatives from Asia Watch and Physicians for Human Rights (PHR) traveled to Jammu & Kashmir to document rape and other human rights abuses and violations of the laws of war by Indian security forces. They also investigated incidents of abuse by armed militant groups who have also committed rape and other attacks on civilians. *Rape in Kashmir: A Crime of War*, Vol. 5, Issue 9, [The year of publication is not available].

authorities have rarely investigated charges of rape by security forces in Kashmir."[8] On the Kunan-Poshora incident, the report stated:

> The rapes allegedly occurred during a search operation in the village conducted by the army unit. The village headman and other village leaders claimed that they reported the rapes to army officials on 27 February and that the officials denied the charges and took no further action. Officials countered that no clear complaint was made. A local magistrate who visited the village requested that the commissioner order a more comprehensive investigation, only to be told that officials in Delhi had denied the charges without checking with officials in the state. A police investigation that was eventually ordered never commenced because the police officer assigned to conduct it was on leave at the time and was then transferred by his superiors.[9]

A video made around mid-April 1991 (carrying no credits) was distributed by human rights activists. In it 25 women and some men of Kunan-Poshora recounted what had happened to them on the night of 23/24 February. In the beginning, the narrator told the viewers that Kunan-Poshora was inhabited by poor and illiterate farmers. However, all the women in the video appeared well groomed and dressed for an occasion. Many of them used the same phrase, e.g., 'a night of andhi and toofan (storm)'. Several made special reference to heavy drinking by the army men and a few said that they had lost unconsciousness due to brutal rape. Almost all the women alleged that neither they nor their children could cry or scream because guns were pointed at them or they were gagged. A male narrator estimated that 50-60 women were found unconscious the next morning. At the end, a private teacher denounced the Divisional Commissioner, who being a Muslim, did nothing; and stated that Indians did not care for the honour of Kashmiri women and there was no democracy, minority rights, dignity and human rights in India.

The Verghese Committee dismissed the allegations of mass rape as bogus and concluded that it was a lie being spread at the behest of the militants. The members of the Committee also visited the medical examination room at 68 Brigade Headquarters on 12 June 1991. They found that 15-20 patients were waiting to be registered for treatment. Several of

8 *Ibid*, p. 3.

9 *Ibid*, p. 7.

them were local women and children who said that health facilities at the district hospital were very poor compared to those provided by the army.[10] Among the patients were two women and a man from Kunan-Poshora. They talked freely and expressed confidence in the army doctors. The committee also found that many patients had visited the army medical examination room regularly on the days immediately following the alleged rape which should have struck terror and caused disgust and hatred against the army. The Committee reported: "The mass rape theory was an afterthought, retailed and orchestrated by militants and their sympathisers and mentors to denigrate the Indian Army. It was the militant's revenge." The report concludes: "Unless far better evidence is forthcoming, the Kunan rape story stands totally unproven and completely untrue, a dirty trick to frame the army...."[11]

There are three petitions still pending before the Jammu & Kashmir High Court in the case: one by the survivors seeking investigation and prosecution, and two by the army — against the implementation of the State Human Rights Commission recommendations in this case and against the police probe ordered by the Judicial Magistrate, Kupwara, on 18 June 2013. In May 2016, the army has moved the Supreme Court against the orders of the Jammu and Kashmir High Court on investigation and compensation in the Kunan Poshpora case. The army has contended before the apex court that the allegations of rape and torture are "a hoax orchestrated by militant groups and part of a cleverly contrived strategy of psychological warfare to discredit the security forces and to jeopardise counter-insurgency operations".[12]

Kunan-Poshora lies in a militant-infested area along the main infiltration routes from Pakistan Occupied Kashmir through which arms supplies, trained personnel, ideological material and strategic doctrines flow. It is difficult to imagine that on a cold winter night, an entire column of military men, spent hours in ruthless abandon, gang-raping twenty-three, or thirty-two, or sixty-five or even one hundred women, when they would have been in fear of being attacked at any moment by militants. It

---

10 Maheshwari Anil. 1993. *Crescent Over Kashmir: Politics of Mullaism*, New Delhi: Rupa & Co, p. 161.

11 See: Maheshwari Anil. 1993. *Crescent Over Kashmir: Politics of Mullaism*, New Delhi: Rupa & Co, p. 148-166.

12 Army moves Supreme Court in Kunan Poshpora 'mass rape' case, *The Hindu*, 28 June 2016.

also defies logic that no one reported the matter to the commanding officer or the brigade commander who addressed the villagers in the morning, or that the villagers did not complain to the police authorities for 10 days or that some of these women and their neighbours sought treatment from the medical officer of the same formation in Kunan and subsequently at Trehgam. It would appear that the Verghese Committee was right in concluding that the mass rape story was stage-managed by the militants and their sympathisers. The local media fuelled it and the international media and NGOs were fooled. They published what was fed to them without any investigation. And once trapped, it has become difficult for the media to accept their failing gracefully. So, demands for fresh investigations are still being made.[13]

Pathribal Killings

On 20 March 2000, 36 Sikhs were killed by terrorists in Chittisingpora Village of the district Anantnag, J&K. It was reported that the terrorists were dressed in uniform with badges of rank similar to that of the military and were led by a man they addressed as 'commanding officer'. They addressed each other in Hindi and Punjabi, using Hindu names and attempted to portray that it was a cordon-and-search operation conducted by the security forces. They collected the locals and segregated male members in two groups, as is normally done during such operations. After the massacre, in an attempt to malign the army, they shouted *'Bharat Mata Ki Jai'*, divided themselves into 3-4 parties and retreated into in the neighbouring villages.[14] The sole survivor of the massacre, Nanak Singh Aulakh, recounted the events to reporters. A few claimed that the killings

---

13 A Festering Wound: The Kunan Poshpora mass rape case must be independently investigated (editorial), *Economic & Political Weekly*, 20 July 2013, Vol. XLVIII, No. 29, p. 9. Also see The Wire, 23 February 2017.

14 The massacre coincided with the visit of the US president Bill Clinton to India. In *The Mighty and the Almighty: Reflections on America, God, and World Affairs* (2006), Madeleine Albright accused Hindu Militants of perpetrating the crime. The publishers, Harper Collins later acknowledged in a public statement: "Page xi of the *Mighty and the Almighty* contains a reference to Hindu militants that will be deleted in subsequent imprints. This error was due to a failure in the fact-checking process". In 2010, the Lashkar-e-Taiba (LeT) associate David Headly, who reportedly confessed to the National Investigation Agency that the LeT carried out the Chittisinghpora massacre to create communal tension just before Clinton's visit.

were in fact carried out by Indian troops.[15] After the massacre, various ministers, government officials and military officers visited the place. The US condemned the killings but refused to accept the Indian government's accusation that it was the work of Islamist groups based in Pakistan.

Immediately thereafter, a search for the terrorists was launched in the entire area. On 25 March 2000, in a joint operation undertaken by 7 Rashtriya Rifles (RR) and the J&K police's Special Operation Group (SOG), five persons, purported to be terrorists, were killed at village Pathribal Punchalthan, situated inside a dense forest in Anantnag.[16] A seizure-memo was prepared and the arms and ammunition found with the bodies of the terrorists were handed over to the Field Ordnance Depot (FOD) by the military authorities.[17] The bodies were handed over to the police representative on the spot and were buried separately without any post-mortem examination. None of the local residents who saw the bodies could identify them. The medical officer who examined the bodies was of the opinion that cause of death was both burns as well as bullet injuries. Bullet injuries were present on all the bodies. The cause of the burns was explosive material from the firearms.

---

15 Celia W Dugger, 'Pall Cast by Sikh Slaying Settles Over Clinton Visit', *The New York Times*, 22 March 2000; [as quoted in *Everyone Lives in Fear: Patterns of Impunity in Jammy & Kashmir*, Human Rights Watch, Vol. 18, No. 11 (C), September 2006, p. 51]. The All Parties Hurriyat Conference accused the Indian government of carrying out the massacre to discredit the Kashmiri independence movement, while Syed Salahuddin, head of Hizbul Mujahideen said: "Mujahideen have nothing against the Sikh community which sympathizes with our struggle. We assure them that there never was and there will never be any danger to Sikhs from Kashmiri freedom fighters".

16 A complaint dated 25 March 2000 was sent to Police Station Achchabal, District Anantnag, J&K by the Adjutant, 7 RR, for lodging FIR stating that during a special cordon and search operation in the forests of Panchalthan on 25 March 2000, an encounter took place between terrorists and troops of that unit and in that operation, 5 unidentified terrorists were killed. On the receipt of the complaint, FIR No 15/2000 under section 307 of the Ranbir Penal Code (RPC) and sections 7/25 Arms Act, 1959 was registered against unknown persons.

17 A seizure memo was prepared by Major Amit Saxena on 25 March 2000 and was signed by two civilian witnesses. The 7 RR deposited the recovered weapons and ammunition with 2 Field Ordnance Depot. However, the local police insisted that the Army failed to hand over the arms and ammunition, which was tantamount to causing disappearance of evidence, constituting an offence under section 201 of RPC.

The operation was undertaken based on the intelligence provided by the police after the interrogation of a suspect. The then SSP Anantnag claimed in the media that the success of the operation was owing to the intelligence given by him. The IG Kashmir Range, in a statement made to the *Indian Express* on 25 March 2000 stated: "The operation was launched in Panchalthan, Pathribal, a village situated deep inside dense forest. The hideout was at least 20km away from the massacre site and was found after a lead given by the local militant who was arrested a few days ago. All the five were wearing army uniforms and were part of the group that conducted the massacre." The daily update for 25 March 2000, on an army website claimed: "5 foreign terrorists (Harkat-ul-Mujahideen and Lashkar-e-Toiba group) killed. These terrorists were involved in the massacre of 36 innocent Sikhs on the night of 20 March."[18] The Pathribal valley was an active area and in two separate encounters in August 1999, four terrorists were killed, while the army suffered three casualties in these operations.

At around the same time, two villagers complained that their family members had been abducted in the night of 24 March 2000 by a few masked gunmen. The first information report (FIR) was filed by the chowkidar two days after the alleged abduction, stating that two villagers (Jumma Khan Faqirullah and Jumma Khan Amirullah) had been kidnapped by unknown masked gunmen with the intention of killing them. It is not clear why the chowkidar waited for two days before filing the FIR. The relatives of two other missing persons, Bashir Ahmed Bhat and Mohammad Yusuf Malik, did not file FIRs. A missing persons report (MPR) were registered on 27 March, three days after their disappearance. The MPR stated that the family did not suspect foul play, and no FIR was filed. Relatives of Zahoor Dalal, another missing person, also filed a MPR on 27 March.[19] After hearing about the killing of militants at Panchalthan, Pathribal, some villagers went to the site of the killings, where they found some clothes belonging to two of the five missing men. The local residents then insisted that those killed were not militants but the abducted men who had been murdered in a fake encounter by the Army.

---

18 Army in Kashmir, Events in Jammu & Kashmir as on 25 March 2000, available at: http://www.armyinkashmir.org/updates/25032000.html, accessed 10 May 2012.

19 Families of terrorists shot dead in encounters have often filed MPRs shortly after the death of their relatives, hoping to secure compensation. Even if this was not the case in Panchalthan, the certitude with which it has been claimed that the victims were innocent people appears misplaced. Swami Praveen, Massacres and Mysteries, *Frontline*, Volume 17, Issue 24, 25 November - 08 December 2000.

Protests

On 30 March, the local authorities in Anantnag relented to growing public pressure and agreed to exhume the bodies and conduct and investigations into the deaths. With no action being taken with regard to the promised investigations into the Pathribal deaths, the local population grew increasingly restless. On 3 April, about 3000-4000 protesters marched to the city of Anantnag, where they intended to present a memorandum to the Deputy Commissioner demanding the exhumation of the bodies. When they reached the town of Barakpora, about 3km from Anantnag, a few protesters started throwing stones at a paramilitary camp. Members of the Central Reserve Police Force (CRPF) and SOG responded by opening fire on the protesters, killing seven and injuring at least 15 persons, of whom one later died of his injuries. On 5 April, the Chief Minister of J&K ordered the exhumation of the bodies. He also ordered for the constitution of a commission of inquiry headed by Justice S Pandian, a retired Supreme Court judge, to investigate the Barakpora firing in which seven people had been killed and several injured.[20]

Exhumation of bodies

Acting on the petitions filed by the relatives of the five civilians missing in the area, the CJM Anantnag ordered the DSP Anantnag to conduct an enquiry into the matter. The bodies of the five people killed in the Pathribal encounter were to be exhumed under the orders of the District Magistrate, Anantnag issued on 6 April 2000. On 7 April, the villagers forcibly took out the bodies from the graves that had been dug on the previous day, in order to ascertain the identity of the dead. While three of the bodies identified by their relatives, two others were identified on the basis of the clothes found in the graves. The villagers then took out the bodies from the graves and shouted slogans against the Army and called for strict action against the culprits. They initially took possession of all the bodies, but later agreed to restore two of them to the graves. They refused to hand over the other three bodies to the authorities saying that the dead belonged to their community and would be buried according to their religious rites. Several attempts by the authorities to persuade the villagers turned futile. The authorities

---

20 The report indicted seven men of the Central Reserve Police Force (CRPF) and the J&K police's Special Operation Group (OPG) for opening unprovoked firing on a group of marching protesters. The report has also pointed out the inaccuracies in police versions about the accountability and the control of SOG in the Barakpora firing.

maintained that the identity of the bodies would be confirmed only after the DNA tests reports and refused to endorse or deny the claim of the villagers.[21]

The head of the department of forensic medicine, Government Medical College Srinagar along with a team of doctors took samples from the 5 bodies. Blood samples of the relatives of the missing persons were also taken on 7 and 8 April 2000 and sent to the CDFD Hyderabad and CFSL Kolkata for establishing the identity of the five killed in the encounter.[22] A post-mortem was also conducted on the bodies and the report mentioned that the deaths were caused by burn and arms injuries. All the injuries were ante-mortem and the bodies had 95-98 per cent burns. All the bodies, though badly burnt and mutilated, were identified by the relatives and handed over to them for burial; pending the result of the DNA tests by the forensic laboratories.

The forensic analysis, suggested that the identification process may have been less than reliable. For example, body believed to be that of Jumma Khan Amirullah, was identified by his son and wife. Amirullah's face had been blown apart by a bullet, and his body had suffered 95 per cent burns during the encounter, however, a black plastic shoe on his foot, remained intact. So did a brass ring, with an embedded red stone on one finger. The ring ought to have left a distinctive burn mark, but the forensic examiners found none. The son also said he recognised his father by a gap in the dentition caused by the extraction of a tooth years earlier. This gap was indeed visible in Amirullah's jaw, but the son did not appear to know of several other such gaps, which the forensic experts found. The alleged body of Zahoor Dalal was identified on the basis of a shirt and sweater in a plastic bag lying next to the corpse. Had soldiers forced Dalal to change his shirt before his death, it is unlikely that they would have left his clothes behind so neatly packed. The bag also contained pieces of a jaw and a nose which were identified by Amirullah's wife and son. But the corpse they eventually identified had its nose intact. The alleged corpse of Jammu Khan Faqirullah, which had suffered 97 per cent burns and was covered in

---

21 'Angry villagers take on authorities in Anantnag', *Hindustan Times*, 7 April 2000.

22 A forensic team from the Government Medical College, Srinagar, led by Dr Balbir Kaur exhumed the bodies and sent the samples to the Centre for DNA Fingerprinting and Diagnostics in Hyderabad and Central Forensic Science Laboratory, Kolkata.

a white fungal growth, was identified on the basis of a 'partial grey beard present over the left side of (the) lower jaw'.[23]

The CJM Anantnag directed the local police to register FIRs on the basis of the complaints of the relatives of dead and accordingly two FIRs were registered at PS Anantnag on 11 April 2000. According to the DSP Anantnag, 7 RR conducted the fake encounter and killed five civilians to save face in view of the public criticism of their operational inefficiency and lack of control in the area in the wake of the Chittisingpora massacre. While the army maintained that it was a genuine encounter conducted by the commanding officer of 7 RR and his personnel alongwith the SOG of the local police. How the police reached the conclusion that local people could not be involved in militant activities is unclear, as the identification of the dead did not mean that they were not involved in militant activities.

Forensic Investigations

The CDFD Hyderabad and CFSL Kolkata conducted the necessary tests on the samples received by them and opined that they were fudged. In March 2002, the CDFD Hyderabad informed the J&K police that in one case, the samples supposed to be from a female relative of one of the deceased were actually from a male, and in another case, samples from an alleged female were in fact composed of the blood of two different men.[24] Subsequently, forensic experts from CDFD Hyderabad and CFSL Kolakata visited Anantnag and got the bodies exhumed once again. Fresh samples from the dead bodies and blood samples from the relatives were collected in April 2002. After conducting the tests, both the laboratories opined that the dead bodies were of the five persons reported missing. Based on the forensic report, the DSP Anantnag submitted a report to the CJM, concluding that the five persons killed in the encounter by 7 RR were local civilians and not foreign militants, as claimed earlier.

The information about the fudged DNA samples was leaked to the media. The National Human Rights Commission on 14 March 2002, issued a notice to the Government of J&K about reports of tampering with the DNA testing. It said, "In view of these media reports, which have not come

---

23 Swami Praveen, Massacres and Mysteries, *Frontline*, Volume 17, Issue 24, 25 November - 08 December 2000.

24 Varadarajan Siddharth, State of Discontent, *Newsline*, June 2002; Also see Swami Praveen, In Search of the Truth, *Frontline*, Vol. 19, Issue 07, 30 March-12 April 2002.

as a surprise to the Commission because of the reservations it has had on the performance of the concerned public servants reported earlier to the Commission not being found very satisfactory, the Commission requires the Government of J & K to submit a comprehensive up to date report of the action taken in this matter together with that in contemplation to correctly identify the five deceased as well as the follow-up action."[25] On 8 March 2002, the Chief Minister ordered a commission of inquiry headed by retired high court judge G A Kuchai to investigate the alleged fudging of DNA samples.[26] The Kuchai Commission submitted its report on 12 December 2002, however, the report was not made public.

According to press reports, the inquiry found that SSP Farooq Khan may have organized the manipulation of DNA samples. The Commission also questioned the conduct of DSP Abdul Rahman, who had been responsible for organizing the collection of the DNA samples from the relatives of the deceased. The donors were not properly identified by the paramedical staff escorted by Rahman. The conduct of the police, the paramedical staff and the doctors, the Commission found, "gave enough opportunity to fudge the material." The Committee concluded that "only those persons related to the killings (of the five civilians) would be interested in the destruction or falsification of evidence." Based on the committee's recommendations, disciplinary action was ordered against DSP Rahman for subverting proper evidence gathering. Strong displeasure was conveyed to Dr. Balbir Kaur, who had headed the team of forensic experts that collected the samples, blaming them for "lack of proficiency and diligence."[27]

---

25 NHRC issues notice to the government of Jammu & Kashmir," National Human Rights Commission, available at: http://www.nhrc.nic.in/disparchive.asp?fno=149, accessed 07 June 2017.

26 J&K Government set up a 'one man commission' to conduct a probe into the DNA fudging in the case. The government appointed retired High Court Judge, Justice GA Kuchaai to enquire whether the samples of those killed in Village Panchalthan of the District Anantnag in April 2000, which were sent for DNA test to Kolkata were fake/spurious? The commission was also to enquire the circumstances under which the samples were collected and to fix the responsibility of persons, directly or indirectly involved in the DNA fudging.

27 *Everyone Lives in Fear: Patterns of Impunity in Jammu & Kashmir*, Human Rights Watch, Vol. 18, No. 11 (C), September 2006, p. 55.

Investigation by the Central Bureau of Investigation

On the request of the Government of J&K, a notification was issued by the Central Government on 22 January 2003 and an investigation into the encounter at Pathribal was taken up by the Central Bureau of Investigation (CBI). The CBI conducted simultaneous investigations into the: (i) killing of 36 Sikhs at Chittisinghpora on 20 March 2000; (ii) killing of five civilians at Pathribal on 25 March 2000; and (iii) killing of eight persons on 3 April 2000 at Barakpora on 25 March 2000.

The CBI filed a charge-sheet in connection with the Pathribal encounter before the chief judicial magistrate cum special magistrate (CJM) in May 2006, according to the charge-sheet, three officers and one junior commissioned officer committed an offence punishable under s 120B (criminal conspiracy) read with s 342 (wrongful confinement), 364 (kidnapping for murder), and 302 (murder) read with 342, 364 and 302 of the Ranbir Panel Code (RPC); while one officer was charged under s 120B (punishment of criminal conspiracy) read with 201 (causing disappearance of evidence or giving false information to screen offenders) of the RPC.

The CBI alleged that it was a fake encounter, and held Colonel Ajay Saxena, Major Brajendra Pratap Singh, Major Sourabh Sharma, Subedar Idrees Khan and some members of the troops of 7 RR responsible for the killing of innocent persons. Major Amit Saxena (Adjutant) prepared a false seizure memo showing recovery of arms and ammunition in the said incident, and also gave a false complaint to the police station for registration of the case against the said five civilians showing some of them as foreign militants and false information to the senior officers to create an impression that the encounter was genuine and, therefore, caused disappearance of the evidence of commission of the aforesaid offence.

There was apparently a difference of opinion between the CBI's investigation team and the legal panel as to whether to file a charge-sheet the army officers. The *Indian Express* reported that the decision to charge-sheet the army officers was delayed because former Director US Mishra could not take final decision given the division in the agency. The CBI was convinced that the encounter was fake because it presumed that the army unit (7 RR) was under tremendous psychological pressure to show some results in the wake of the massacre of 36 innocent Sikhs on 20 March 2000. It also felt that in any genuine encounter there would be some military casualties as well. Going by the same logic, it would not be improper to presume that the CBI was also under tremendous pressure to implicate the Army personnel in the Pathribal killings. [28]

The CJM Srinagar could not proceed in the matter since the Armed Forces J & K (Special Powers) Act 1990 (AFSPA), offered protection to persons acting under the said Act. The CJM, therefore, an granted opportunity to the Army to exercise the option of trial by court martial under the provisions of Section 125 of the Army Act 1950.[29] The CBI was of the opinion that since this was not a genuine encounter, "The acts of the accused do not come under the purview of discharge of official duties as provided by the AFSPA."

On 24 May 2006, the army officers filed an application before the court pointing out that no prosecution could be instituted except with the previous sanction of the Central Government in view of the provisions of Section 7 of the AFSPA[30] and, therefore, the proceedings be closed by returning the charge-sheet to the CBI. The CJM, by an order dated 24 August 2006, dismissed the application holding that the said court had no jurisdiction to go into the documents filed by the investigating agency and it was for the trial court to find out whether the action complained of fell within the ambit of the discharge of official duty or not. Aggrieved by the order of the CJM, the army officers filed a revision petition before the Sessions Court, Srinagar and the same was dismissed by an order dated 30 November 2006. However, the Sessions Court directed the CJM to give one more opportunity to the army officials for the exercise of the option under Section 125 of the Army Act.

The army officers, thereafter, approached the High Court. The Court, by an order dated 10 July 2007, affirmed the orders of the lower courts and held that the very objective of the sanctions under the AFSPA was to enable

---

28 Sarin Ritu, Officers face charge-sheet for killing innocent, *Indian Express*, 27 April 2006.

29 According to the Army Act 1950, when a criminal court and a court martial each have jurisdiction in respect of an offence, it shall be the discretion of the officer commanding the army, army corps, division or independent brigade in which the accused person is serving to decide before which court the proceedings shall be instituted.

30 The Armed Forces (Jammu and Kashmir) Special Powers Act 1990 (AFSPA) section 7 dealing with the protection of persons acting in good faith under the AFSPA provides: No prosecution, suit or other legal proceeding shall be instituted, except with the previous sanction of the Central Government, against any person in respect of anything done or purported to be done in exercise of the powers conferred by the AFSPA.

army officers to perform their duties fearlessly by protecting them from vexatious, malafide and false prosecution for acts done in performance of their duties. However, it had to be examined whether their action fell under the AFSPA and the CJM did not have the power to examine such an issue at the time of the committal of proceedings. It could only examine whether any case has been made out and, if so, who the offence is triable by. Not satisfied with the decision of the High Court, the army authorities files an appeal in the Supreme Court.

The Supreme Court Decision

The Supreme Court passed its judgment in *General Officer Commanding v. Central Bureau of Investigation* on 1 May 2012.[31] It decided two appeals by a common judgment, taking the Criminal Appeal No. 257 of 2011 as a leading case, since the subject matter of both the appeals was similar.[32] The cases addressed the issue of the need for sanction to prosecute Army personnel under the Armed Forces Special Powers Act (AFSPA). In both cases, it has been alleged that the Army officers had staged fake encounters and the CBI had been directed to investigate the matter. The CBI had claimed that the people who were killed were indeed victims of fake encounters and moved the court to initiate prosecution against the accused Army officers. The officers claimed that they could only be prosecuted with the prior sanction (permission) of the Central Government. The officers relied on provisions of the AFSPA, 1958 and the Armed Forces J & K (Special Powers) Act, 1990 to support their claim. These provide that legal proceedings cannot be instituted against an officer unless sanction is granted by the Central Government.

The Supreme Court held that the AFSPA, or the Armed Forces (J&K) Special Powers Act, empowers the central government to ascertain if an action is 'reasonably connected with the discharge of official duty' and is not a misuse of authority. The courts have no jurisdiction in the matter. In making a decision, the government must make an objective assessment of the exigencies leading to the officer's actions. The Court ruled that under the AFSPA, or the Armed Forces (J&K) Special Powers Act, sanction is

---

31 *General Officer Commanding v Central Bureau of Investigation*, (2012) 5 SCR 599.

32 The second Criminal Appeal No. 55 of 2006 was preferred against the impugned judgment and order dated 28 March 2005 passed by the High Court of Guwahati. In this case five people were killed by the Army in Assam in a counterinsurgency operation in 1994.

mandatory, but that the need to seek sanction would only arise at the time of cognizance of the offence. Cognizance is the stage when the prosecution begins. Sanction is therefore not required during investigation. The Supreme Court directed:

1. The competent authority in the Army shall take a decision within a period of eight weeks as to whether the trial would be by the criminal court or by a court-martial and communicate the same to the Chief Judicial Magistrate concerned immediately thereafter.

2. In case the option is made to try the case by a court-martial, the said proceedings would commence immediately and would be concluded strictly in accordance with law expeditiously.

3. In case the option is made that the accused would be tried by the criminal court, the CBI shall make an application to the Central Government for grant of sanction within four weeks from the receipt of such option and in case such an application is filed, the Central Government shall take a final decision on the said application within a period of three months from the date of receipt of such an application.

4. In case sanction is granted by the Central Government, the criminal court shall proceed with the trial and conclude the same expeditiously.

The Army opted for a court martial. The five military accused were served a tentative charge-sheet under the Army Act 1950 on the charges levelled by the CBI and the case was adjourned for the purpose of reducing the evidence to writing.[33] The families of the victims and other witnesses were summoned to Nagrota, the 16 Corps HQs in Jammu, on 20 September 2012 for recording of 'summary of evidence'[34]. In order to

---

33 The Army Rules 1954, Rule 22.

34 Contrary to its nomenclature, 'summary' of evidence is a detailed recoding of statement and evidence against the accused, and also in his favour, if he so desires (Rule 23, Army Rules 1954). In the armed forces, the 'summary of evidence' is a basic document for initiation of disciplinary proceedings against an accused. It is used to assist the officer having the power to convene a court martial in determining whether the case shall go for trial by court martial and if so, on what charges. The summary of evidence also helps the officers of the judicial branch (judge advocate general) of the three services to examine the case and advise the convening authority accordingly.

facilitate the appearance of witnesses before it, the venue of the summary of evidence was subsequently shifted to Awantipora. After the recording of evidence was concluded, the officer with the power to convene the court martial (convening officer) did not find enough evidence to initiate the prosecution of the military officer and JCO.[35] The charges were therefore dismissed under the provisions of the Army Rules.[36]

In many instances of serious crimes being committed by militants, including rape and murder, the local population has blamed the security forces. Militants have used military uniforms and availed themselves of local hospitality to carry out operations, and disappeared with the help of sympathisers or sleeper cells. Villagers have been unable to distinguish between uniforms, ranks and different nomenclatures.[37] After the Chittisingpora massacre, it was rumoured that central security forces were under tremendous pressure to arrest the culprits as the area was under the operational command of 7 RR of the Army, which was being blamed for being inefficient and ineffective. In reality, the State police and the not the army was responsible for the law and order problems of the district.[38] The district police officials were, in fact, under tremendous pressure to arrest or eliminate the culprits responsible for the massacre. After the encounter, an FIR was lodged by 7 RR and the bodies of those killed were handed over to the local police. Military personnel were not involved in the events that followed. The weapons recovered by the military after the operation were duly recoded, sealed and kept in safe custody.

---

35 The summary of evidence, after recording, is considered by the commanding officer who has three options; (i) remand the accused for trial by a court martial; (ii) refer the case to the proper superior authority; or (iii) if he thinks it desirable, re-hear the case and either dismiss the charges or dispose of it summarily (Rule 24, Army Rules 1954). The commanding officer/convening officer is bound to seek advice of the judge advocate general in all cases of civil offences before arriving at a conclusion.

36 The Army Rules 1954, Rule 24.

37 Maheshwari Anil. 1993. *Crescent Over Kashmir: Politics of Mullaism*, New Delhi: Rupa and Co., p. 171.

38 The CBI in its report presumed that the military authorities were under pressure to arrest the culprits responsible for the said massacre, mainly because the area was under the operational command of 7 RR, which had to bear the blame of operational inefficiency and ineffectiveness. However, even when the armed forces are deployed under the AFSPA, the overall administration of the area as well as the responsibility for law and order remains with the district authorities.

The killing of innocent civilians is a serious crime in municipal as well as international law; and need to be condemned by one and all. There is an urgent need to prove conclusively as to who was behind the Pathribal killings. Was there a sinister plan by a militant organization to abduct the five civilians, assemble them in an isolated place and lure the police/military to use force against them. Was the police fed with fake intelligence on which the operation was planned? For instance, during inquiries by Justice Pandian (Commission to investigate the Barakpora firing of 3 April 2000), Assistant Sub-Inspector Bashir Ahmad had stated that he had received a telephone call from a shopkeeper informing him of the presence of foreign militants in the neighborhood.[39] Why was no post-mortem conducted by the police before the burial of the five persons killed in the operation? Who was behind the fudging of the DNA samples?

Killing of Manorama Devi

Thangjam Manorama Devi, a 32-year-old women, was a resident of Bamon Kampu village, in the Imphal East district of Manipur. The Assam Rifles[40] suspected her of links with an underground separatist group and raided her house a little after midnight on 11 July 2004, asking the family to wait outside while they questioned her. The soldiers signed an 'arrest memo', an official acknowledgement of detention and took her away. No female police or paramilitary official was available at the time of the arrest. The next morning, villagers found Manorama Devi's bullet-ridden body near her house. She had been shot through the lower half of her body, leading to suspicion that the bullet wounds had been used to hide evidence of rape.[41]

---

39 Assistant Sub Inspector Ahmad further stated to the Commission that he was part of an operation led by the 7 RR and had fired 20-22 rounds of ammunition. Eventually, the firing stopped and he found charred bodies on the ground. *Everyone Lives in Fear: Patterns of Impunity in Jammy & Kashmir*, Human Rights Watch, Vol. 18, No. 11 (C), September 2006, p. 57.

40 The Assam Rifles is a paramilitary force officered by the Army, but administratively under the Ministry of Home Affairs. The Assam Rifles Act 2006 declares that it is an Armed Force of the Union for ensuring the security of the borders of India, to carry out counter insurgency operations in specified areas and to act in aid of civil authorities for the maintenance of the law and order.

41 Sushanta Talukdar, 'Manipur's Protest', *Frontline*, Vol. 21, Issue 17, 14-27 August 2004.

The Assam Rifles claimed that Manorama Devi was an active member of the People's Liberation Army and had taken part in many of its operations. According to the army, she was responsible for a number of bomb blasts, including one that killed some soldiers. Most human rights activists and journalists agreed in private that she was a member of an underground group, but differed on the details, including the role she played. However, her family insisted that she was a peaceful activist and not involved in any criminal activities.

Protest

The killing of Manaroma Devi received widespread media attention. Protests erupted in Manipur, while domestic and international human rights groups demanded an immediate investigation and the prosecution of those responsible. Students, lawyers, traders, mothers, journalists, and human rights activists marched every day, demanding justice. After Manorama's killing, 32 organizations formed a network called Apunba Lup to demand the repeal of the AFSPA. On 15 July 2004, a group of Manipuri women, members of the Meira Paibi (torch bearers) stripped in front of the Assam Rifles camp Imphal, and wrapped a banner around themselves. The banner said, "Indian Army Rape Us." It was claimed by a certain group that the protest was stage-managed and that the women were hired for the purpose. Anti-social elements took advantage of the situation and the demonstrations turned violent. Protesters set ablaze government offices, five youths attempted immolation, and a young man cut off one of his fingers. Emotions ran high all over the state, as people thronged curfew-bound streets, defying rubber bullets and tear gas shells, in protest against the atrocities committed by security forces and demanding the immediate withdrawal of the AFSPA.[42]

Investigation by the Assam Rifles

The Assam Rifles later stated that it had ordered an internal inquiry, however, the findings of the inquiry were never revealed. The court of inquiry could not be concluded until forensic tests had been completed. Once the laboratory sent a report that semen had been found on Manorama's clothes indicating sexual assault, the army ordered DNA testing to identify the perpetrators. Over 30 personnel of 17th Assam Rifles including two officers of the rank of majors provided blood samples for DNA testing.

---

42 Sushanta Talukdar, Manipur's Protest, *Frontline*, Vol. 21, Issue 17, 14-27 August 2004.

There were unconfirmed reports that a major and four others were accused in the killing at the court of inquiry. There was no information from the army about prosecution of any of its member for procedural lapses, the killing or alleged rape of Manorama Devi in the night of 11 July 2004.[43] The Ministry of Defence released a statement on 28 July 2004 stating that the court of inquiry had found some "lapses" by Assam Rifles personnel.[44] The Vice Chief of the Army Staff, while speaking to the media, said that the Army had documents to prove that Manorama Devi had links with a terrorist outfit in Manipur, but termed the incidents leading to her death as 'unfortunate'.[45]

Commission of Inquiry

On 12 July 2004, after the discovery of Manorama's body, her brother Thangjam Dolendro Singh filed a written complaint at the Irilbung police station. Based on the complaint, the police registered a FIR to investigate the alleged murder. It ordered forensic tests to determine if rape had been committed and DNA testing to identify the perpetrators. In responses to the protests, the Manipur government ordered the institution of a commission of inquiry headed by retired district judge C. Upendra Singh. The terms of reference of the commission were (i) to enquire into the facts and circumstances leading to the death of Monorama Devi on 11 July 2004; (ii) to identify responsibilities on the person/persons responsible for the death; (iii) to find out any matters incidental thereto; and (iv) to recommend measures for preventing the recurrence of such incidents in future. The commission was to submit its report to the state government within one month from the date of issue of the notification.[46]

---

43 *These Fellows Must be Eliminated: Relentless Violence and Impunity in Manipur*, Human Rights Watch, September 2008, p. 37.

44 Major SD Goswami, defence spokesman in Imphal said: "There were some lapses by the Assam Rifles personnel in the implementation of the instructions issued by the army for such operations. We are holding further enquiries and anyone found guilty will be dealt with severely."

45 Manorama devi had links with terrorists: Army, *Times of India*, 11 December 2004.

46 Government of Manipur Secretariat, Home Department, Notification No 8/1(1)/2004-H (Pt-2), dated 12 July 2004. It was issued in exercise of powers conferred by Section 3 of the Commissions of Inquiry Act, 1952.

Arrests

Manipur had been declared a disturbed area by the Governor of the State by a notification dated 31 May 2004 in exercise of the powers conferred upon him by Section 3 of the AFSPA for a period of one year with effect from June 2004. The personnel of 17th Assam Rifles were deployed in the state to act in aid of civil power for the purpose of containing the unlawful activities of certain terrorist organizations. They had the power to arrest, search, and use force for a variety of reasons under the AFSPA.

According to the Assam Rifles, they received information from confirmed sources on 10 July 2004, that a member of the banned People's Liberation Army (PLA), identified as PLA No. 1262, Corporal Manorama Devi alias Henthoi, a militant since 1995, was in the area of Bamon Kampu Mayai Leikai. She was identified as an expert in improvised explosive devices (IEDs) and as an informer of the PLA. Based on this information, the officials posted at Sinjamei were alerted to her presence in the area. A little after midnight, on 11 July, a preliminary check post was set up in the area, which confirmed that Manorama was at her residence in the village. The Assam Rifles immediately launched an operation and troops were dispatched to cordon off the area. At around 3:00am, the troops entered her house. Manorama Devi was arrested and the in-charge of the arrest party provided an arrest memo and took her into custody.[47] Manorama's mother and brothers were asked to sign a 'no claims certificate' which stated that they had no claims against members of the Assam Rifles who had searched the house and made the arrest and that the troops "have not misbehaved with women and not damaged any property". Though Manorama's brother Dolendro Singh said that he had not seen anything being recovered from the house, an affidavit submitted by the Assam Rifles stated that, "one Singapore-made Kenwood Radio Set and one Chinese-made fragmentation type hand grenade" were found in Manorama's house.[48]

---

47 Havildar Suresh Kumar of the 17th Assam Rifles (service number 123355) signed an arrest memo. Rifleman T. Lotha (service number 123916) and Rifleman Ajit Singh (service number 173491) signed as witnesses. The memo stated that she was being arrested on the suspicion of being a militant and that no incriminating evidence was found during a search of the house. Sushanta Talukdar, 'Manipur's Protest', *Frontline*, Vol. 21, Issue 17, 14-27 August 2004.

48 Writ Petition No 5187/2004, in the case of *Col. Jagmohan Singh v The State of Manipur*, Guwahati High Court, dated 19 August 2004.

Custodial interrogation and death

Manorama's bullet-ridden body was found at around 05:30 am on 11 July 2004 by villagers about four kilometres from her house. After that a statement was issued by the Assam Rifles that during interrogation Manorama had disclosed that one of her militant colleagues, a woman called Lt. Ruby, had an AK-47 assault rifle and that this information "led to a hot chase". However, when the group reached the area based on Manorama's directions, she said that she had made an error and then proceeded to lead the soldiers to a number of different locations, each time saying that she had made a mistake.

According to the affidavit submitted by the Assam Rifles, after almost two hours of driving around like this, at daybreak, Manorama requested that she may be allowed to relieve herself. Thereupon, the vehicle was stopped and the party accompanying her took position about 30-35 metres away to allow her privacy. Then all of a sudden she started to flee. The guard commander shouted for her to stop and fired a short burst in the air to warn her. The other members of the guard party instinctively fired towards her legs. As a result she suffered bullet injuries, which caused her death.[49]

Human Rights Violations

Human Rights organizations and the members of the civil society raised a number of issues relating to procedural failure and illegality in the arrest and killing of Manoram Devi.

- The raid at the house of Manorama Devi and her arrest was conducted without the presence of a woman constable.

- The civil police was not informed, though the house was cordoned off, and there was no FIR pending against Manorama Devi at the time of her arrest.

- Why did the members of Assam Rifles not run to catch unarmed woman and stop her. Since her hands were tied while she was in custody, it would have not been difficult for a soldier to run and arrest her.

---

49 Ibid.

- Why did the Assam Rifles not inform the local police after the firing and the death of Manorama.

- No blood was found near the body, though Manorama had six bullet wounds, raising suspicions that she was killed elsewhere and her body was dumped later. According to the police surgeon and forensics specialist who deposed before the inquiry commission, the nature of the bullet wounds suggested that the shots were fired at close range and that Manorama was lying down when she was shot.

The Assam Rifles claimed that there was an attempt to procure a female constable before taking Manorama into custody but their request was refused by the Imphal West police station. However, the police later said that the person who had come to the police station was asked to make a formal application to the superintendent of police. According to the police, the person left and did not return.

Allegation of Rape

Manorama's body bore scratch marks and a gashing wound on the right thigh. According to her relatives, there were bruise marks on her body. Her body also bore bullet marks on the genitals, which led to the public perception that she was raped before being shot dead.[50] However, the post-mortem report did not mention sexual abuse or torture. Manorama Devi's mother demanded that another autopsy be carried out as she had doubts about the post-mortem report.

A second post-mortem was, therefore, ordered by the state government. Dr. Manglem, who along with two other forensic experts conducted the second post-mortem examination, reported that because of the injuries in the lower part of the body no conclusive opinion could be passed on whether Manorama was raped. Manorama's family refused to accept her body, until the "guilty" Assam Rifles personnel were punished and the AFSPA was withdrawn from the state. The state government ordered the cremation of the body after the completion of the second autopsy and the cremation was carried out under tight security arrangements.[51]

---

50 Sushanta Talukdar, Manipur's Protest, *Frontline*, Vol. 21, Issue 17, 14-27 August 2004.

51 For more details see: *These Fellows Must be Eliminated: Relentless Violence and Impunity in Manipur*, Human Rights Watch, September 2008, p.10-11.

The Use of Force

Manorama Devi was unarmed and was shot while trying to escape. The use of firearms against an unarmed, handcuffed woman, supposedly wearing a sarong, which hinders free movement, appears excessive by any standards. Paramilitary forces are expected to abide by certain basic principles relating to the use of force while acting in the aid of civil power. The 1990 UN Basic Principles on the Use of Force and Firearms by Law Enforcement Officials[52] declares that law enforcement officials have a vital role in the protection of the right to life, liberty and security of a person, as guaranteed in the Universal Declaration of Human Rights, 1948 and reaffirmed in the International Covenant on Civil and Political Rights.

According to the UN Basic Principles, whenever the lawful use of force and firearms is unavoidable, law enforcement officials shall exercise restraint in such use and act in proportion to the seriousness of the offence and the legitimate objective to be achieved. They will minimize damage and injury, and respect and preserve human life and ensure that assistance and medical aid are rendered to any injured or affected persons at the earliest possible moment. Further, they shall ensure that the relatives or close friends of the injured or affected person are notified at the earliest possible moment. Where injury or death is caused by the use of force and firearms by law enforcement officials, they shall report the incident promptly to their superiors.[53]

The Rule states that law enforcement officials shall not use firearms against anyone except in self-defence or defence of others against the imminent threat of death or serious injury, to prevent the perpetration of a particularly serious crime involving grave threat to life, to arrest a person presenting such a danger and resisting their authority, or to prevent his or her escape, and only when less extreme means are insufficient to achieve these objectives. In any event, intentional lethal use of firearms may only be made when strictly unavoidable in order to protect life. In case of unavoidable circumstances, where the use of firearms becomes necessary, the law enforcement officials shall identify themselves as such and give a clear warning of their intent to use firearms, with sufficient time

---

52 Adopted by the Eighth United Nations Congress on the Prevention of Crime and the Treatment of Offenders, Havana, Cuba, 27 August-7 September 1990.

53 Rule 22 of the 1990 UN Basic Principles on the Use of Force and Firearms by Law Enforcement Officials.

for the warning to be observed, unless to do so would unduly place the law enforcement officials at risk or would create a risk of death or serious harm to other persons, or would be clearly inappropriate or pointless in the circumstances of the incident.[54] Going by these basic norms, the use of force against an armed woman in legal custody appears excessive and avoidable.

Court Proceedings

The Assam Rifles personnel did not appear before the Justice Upendra Singh Commission. The counsel for the Assam Rifles claimed that the men were not available because of an ongoing internal court of inquiry in the matter. He also cited safety concerns, saying that armed groups had planned to attack personnel who attended the hearing, and filed an application requesting that the hearings be held inside the army camp. It was finally agreed that some witnesses would be examined privately in the judge's chambers (in camera). However, the Assam Rifles was slow to provide the list of personnel who participated in the operations that led to Manorama's death. It did not provide a list of witnesses either. According to Justice Upendra Singh, the Assam Rifles clearly did not want to cooperate with the inquiry. Justice Upendra Singh issued arrest warrants against the four Assam Rifles personnel who failed to appear before the commission and instructed the Director General of Police to execute the warrant.

In August 2004, Assam Rifles personnel filed two writ petitions before the Guwahati High Court stating that the state government had no authority to appoint a commission of inquiry to examine the conduct of federal armed forces and thus the personnel could not be compelled to appear before such a commission. It also claimed that an army court of inquiry was in progress and thus there was no need for another inquiry covering the same aspects. In response to Writ Petition 5817, filed by Col Jagmohan Singh, the high court passed an order observing the Commission could examine the petitioners in camera. In Writ Petition 6187, the high court (single judge) provided that the commission may proceed with the enquiry, but shall not publish the report or any other material without prior leave of the court and the findings of the commission shall be subject to the final decision in the said writ petition.

---

54 Rule 11, the 1990 UN Basic Principles on the Use of Force and Firearms by Law Enforcement Officials (Rule 11).

The Writ Petitions had submitted that the commission of inquiry had been virtually asked to look into the working, conduct and jurisdiction of the Assam Rifles and the state government had no jurisdiction to appoint the commission as it was not the 'appropriate government', defined in Section 2(a) of the Commission of Inquiry Act, 1952. Also, the act of the commission to summon the Assam Rifles personnel to appear before it and to produce documents was irregular. The coercive measures taken by the commission in publishing summons in the newspapers was an infringement on the working and conduct of the armed forces of the Union deployed in the state. It was claimed that the subject matter of the enquiry related to Entry-2A of List-I of the Seventh Schedule and, therefore, only the Central Government was competent to appoint a commission to look into the matter.

In the high court's opinion, the report submitted by the commission of inquiry to the state government could not be treated as a report within the meaning of Section 3 of the Commissions of Inquiry Act, 1952. It could, however, be treated as a report by a fact-finding committee/body appointed by the state. The court disposed of both the writ petitions with a direction to the state of Manipur to hand over the report of the commission of inquiry report to the Ministry of Home Affairs, Government of India without delay. The Union Home Ministry, represented by the Secretary, will examine the report and pass orders/take appropriate action against the 17th Assam Rifles personnel, if any, indicted in the report without loss of time. The Union Home Ministry shall also take an immediate decision about publication of the report in tune with the citizens' right to information...to restore the confidence of people of Manipur in the Constitution and the laws.[55]

Manorama Devi's family filed an appeal against the high court judgment with the help of the Human Rights Law Network (Manipur). On 31 August 2010, a division bench of the Guwahati High Court allowed the government of Manipur to act upon Justice Upendra Singh's inquiry

---

55 Writ Petition (C) No. 5817 of 2004 was filed by Col Jagmohan Singh, Commandant of 17th Assam Rifles challenging the competence of the State of Manipur to appoint a Commission of Inquiry by the Notification No. 8/1(1)/2004/H(Pt-2), dated 12 July 2004 with prayer for other consequential reliefs; and Writ Petition (C) No. 6187 of 2004 was filed by JC-172262F Nb Sub Digambar Dutta of 17th Battalion Assam Rifles and three others also challenging the aforesaid notification. The High Court disposed of both the petitions by a common judgment and order. *Col Jagmohan Singh and others v The State of Manipur*, decided by the Gauhati High Court on 23 June 2005; AIR 2006 Gau 33.

report on the facts and circumstances leading to Manorama's killing.[56] Since the government failed to comply with the order, Manorama's family filed a writ petition in the High Court in January 2011 for opening the inquiry report and initiating a fresh probe by the CBI for punishing the guilty Assam Rifles personnel. Though the matter was listed for hearing, it had to be deferred as the Central Government (Secretaries of Union Defence and Home Affairs) and commandant of 17 Assam Rifles filed a SLP in the Supreme Court challenging the ruling of the division bench of the Guwahati High Court. On 18 December, the Supreme Court directed the Central Government to give interim compensation of Rs 10 Lakh to the kin of Manorama Devi.[57]

In view of the large-scale protest against the killing of Manorama Devi and the revocation of AFSPA from Manipur, the Central Government constituted the Jeevan Reddy Committee in November 2004, to 'review the working' of the AFSPA. The committee's 147-page report was submitted to the government in June 2005 but is yet to be made public. The issues brought out by the Justice Reddy Committee are discussed in Chapter II.

Problems in Manipur

State officials as well as residents of Manipur say that armed groups have a tremendous hold over the people, forcing them to build alliances with one group to ensure protection from the rest. Many impose a variety of diktats and implement such orders with force. Some groups have been responsible for attacks on ethnic minorities. For example, in March 2008,

---

56 Division Bench of the High Court comprising Justices Amitava Roy and BD Agarwal, which heard the case, stated in its order: "The impugned judgment and order is thus interfered with. The impugned Notification dated 12 July 2004 is hereby adjudged legal and valid. The State of Manipur is left at liberty, if so advised, to deal with the report submitted by the Commission strictly in adherence with the provisions of the Commission of Inquiry Act, 1952, and other relevant provisions of law pertaining thereto." The High Court delivered its judgment to various petitions [WP(C) No 5817/2004; WP (C) No 6187/2004, Writ Appeal No 560/2005 and Writ Appeal No 561/2005] challenging the legality or otherwise of the constitution of the commission of inquiry into the rape and murder of Manorama Devi following her arrest in 2004 by the Assam Rifles.

57 On 18 December 2014, the Supreme Court Bench headed by Justice T S Thakur agreed to hear the Government's appeal challenging Gauhati High Court order of 2010 in which the Court had directed the state government to open and act upon the report submitted by Justice Upendra Singh on the facts and circumstances leading to death of Manorama Devi.

militants killed 14 migrant labourers from othern states and left behind a note warning others to leave Manipur. In January 2006, armed cadres belonging to United National Liberation Front (UNLF) and Kangleipak Community Party (KCP) allegedly raped 21 Hmar tribal girls in Manipur's Churachandpur district. Militants have also been responsible for the indiscriminate use of landmines, bombs, political killings, and attacks upon those they consider being informers or traitors. The people complain the most about the militant groups' culture of extortion against which the state is unable to provide protection. Even manipuri activists do not dispute the need for strong law enforcement to end the violence perpetrated by the militants. Some want the army to remain to combat the militants, while others want the army to be withdrawn.[58] However, whichever side one may belong to, the fact remains that Manorama's family is still waiting for justice, eleven years after her death, and that her killers need to be identified and punished.

Manipur: Extra-judicial Executions

In 2012 a Writ Petition (WP)[59] under Article 32 of the Constitution was filed in the Supreme Court by the Extra Judicial Execution Victim Families Association (EEVFAM)[60] and Human Rights Alert. The petitioners had compiled a list of 1528 alleged extra-judicial executions carried out by the police and security forces (the Assam Rifles and the Army) in Manipur during the period May, 1979 to May, 2012.[61] It was alleged that a majority of these executions have been carried out in cold blood while the victims were in custody and the victims were also subjected to torture. Of these 1528 cases documented by the petitioners, they made

---

58 *These Fellows Must be Eliminated: Relentless Violence and Impunity in Manipur*, Human Rights Watch, September 2008, p.10-11.

59 Writ Petition (Criminal) No. 129 of 2012. Another WP No. 445 of 2012 was filed by Dr Th. Suresh Singh in individual capacity which urged the Supreme Court for directions that the areas in Manipur declared as "disturbed area" in terms of Section 3 of the Armed Forces (Special Powers) Act, 1958 (AFSPA) be withdrawn and the notification issued in this regard be quashed. The Supreme Court declined to consider prayer made in WP 445.

60 A registered trust having as its members the wives and mothers of persons whom they say have been extra-judicially executed by the Manipur Police and the security forces (mainly the Assam Rifles and the Army).

61 See: *Extra Judicial Execution Victim Families Association (EEVFAM) v Union of India* (2013) 2 SCC 493.

an elaborate documentation of 62 cases of extra judicial executions. The petitioners referred to 10 specific cases (out of 62) where eye-witness were available to support extra-judicial executions but the police and the security forces justified them as encounters with militants. Out of the ten cases, eight encounter killings were allegedly committed by the state police commandos; one by members of the armed forces, while in one case the perpetrator was not mentioned.

According to the petitioners, no First Information Report (FIR) has been registered by the Manipur police against the police or the security forces even though several complaints have been made in respect of the alleged extra-judicial executions. As a result of the failure of the Manipur police to register an FIR, no investigation or prosecution has commenced and the cries of anguish of the families of the victims have fallen on deaf ears. Further, the victims of the extra-judicial executions included innocent persons with no criminal record whatsoever but they are later on conveniently labeled as militants. The complaint to Manipur State Human Rights Commission could not be made as the organization remains defunct due to the non-appointment of members and non-allocation of resources. The petitioners also alleged that the National Human Rights Commission (NHRC) which is mandated to investigate human rights abuses and recommend punishment of the guilty has turned out to be a toothless tiger. The petitioners urged the Supreme Court to appoint a special investigation team comprising police officers of integrity from outside the state to investigate all the killings.

Justice Hegde Commission

The Supreme Court, by an order dated 4 January 2013 constituted a commission of inquiry headed by Justice Hegde. [62] The Commission was established to make a thorough investigation in the six cases detailed in the petition, with a further direction to the Commission to record a finding regarding the past antecedents of the victims and the circumstances in

---

62 The Commission was headed by Justice N. Santhosh Hegde (retired Judge to Supreme Court and former Solicitor General of India), having Mr. J. M. Lyngdoh (former Chief Election Commissioner of India) and Dr. Ajai Kumar Singh (former Director General of Police, Karnataka state) as members. The State Government and all other agencies were directed to hand over to the three-member Commission all relevant records. The Commission was free to devise its own procedure, address the larger question of the role of the State Police and the security forces in Manipur and to make recommendations. The Commission was to give its report within twelve weeks.

which they were killed. It was also mandated to evaluate the role of the security forces in Manipur. The Commission submitted its report to the Court on 30 March 2013.[63]

The Commission found that the state police did not have any credible, verified, and specific information concerning the identity of the seven victims in the six cases it investigated. It was of the view that the security forces have violated the procedure and used disproportionate force against the victims. It also felt that the security forces had been transgressing the legal bounds in their counter-insurgency operations in the state. The Commission was of the view that the state police was grossly inadequate to face the challenges (of militancy) before it and recommended that the state government should draw up and implement a five-year plan for strengthening, equipping and training the State police so as to do away with the deployment of Union forces in the aid of civil power. It also suggested that the guidelines laid down in the *Naga People's Movement case* must be scrupulously adhered to in letter and spirit by the security forces.[64]

Some of the concerns raised by the Commission were: the security forces had gone prepared for an encounter, the number of security forces personnel was very large as compared to the number of suspects, they were better armed, they did not attempt to overpower or apprehend the victims, they did not disable the victims by aiming at non-vital parts, they used disproportionate force in self defence and a large quantity of ammunition was used to eliminate an individual, and in all the cases of encounter they had no casualties. The Commission also commented on the misuse of power under the AFSPA in Manipur: "Normally, the greater the power, the greater the restraints and stricter the mechanism to prevent its misuse or abuse. But here in the case of AFSPA in Manipur this principle appears to have been reversed. We should not forget that power corrupts and absolute power corrupts absolutely."[65]Some of the recommendations of the Commission were as follows:[66]

---

63 The Commission had several sittings including public sittings at Imphal, Manipur, and having received many written submissions, documents, affidavits including personal appearances by witnesses for the petitioners and the respondents (Government of India, Ministry of Home Affairs, Assam Rifles, Home Department of Manipur, Manipur Police).

64 See chapter 2 of the book.

65 Para 4.13 of the Hegde Commission Report dated March 30, 2013.

66 See Justice Hegde Commission report dated March 30, 2013, page 97-105.

- The continuous use of the AFSPA in Manipur State for decades has evidently had little effect on the situation. The six cases, which have shown to be not real encounters, are egregious examples of the AFSPA's gross abuse.

- The Commission has gone through the Jeevan Reddy Committee report and is in respectful agreement with the same.

- It is time to progressively de-notify more areas of the State under Section 3 of the AFSPA.

- The Do's and Don'ts laid down in *Naga Peoples Movement case* may be given statutory status.

- A sensitive, proactive and responsive administration in the State including people-friendly policing would go a long way in normalizing the situation and winning the confidence of the peoples.

- A District Police Complaints Authority with at least one representative from the civil society be constituted in all the districts of the State.

- All the cases of police encounter resulting in death to be investigated by police officers not below the rank of Dy SP (SDPO in the State of Manipur).

- The cases of encounters resulting in death to be tried by a special court constituted for this purpose.

While these recommendations may appear serious to a person conducting an inquiry, those who undertake such operations and face death at every moment may have an entirely different viewpoint. Such observations do not take into consideration the fact that military personnel are trained to kill and destroy. To expect them to catch a violator and use only non-lethal force in an unfavourable environment would amount to putting an unrealistic demand on them.

The Central Government informed the Supreme Court that it has adopted a zero tolerance approach towards fake encounters and assured that anyone guilty of such extra-judicial killings would be dealt with sternly. It also said that several militant organizations active in the state were employing every possible method to separate the state from the country with the help of massive ill-gotten money gathered through extortion, killings and with help from outside the country.[67] The Government alleged that the Commission had followed a faulty procedure that was prejudiced against the personnel of the security forces and that during the inquiry process; these personnel were denied the minimum rights under the Criminal Procedure Code, 1973 and were compelled to be witnesses in cases where they were likely to be incriminated. The Government also claimed that the findings of the Hegde Commission which doubted the genuineness of the operations/encounters in the said cases were absolutely incorrect and legally untenable.

Submissions by the Government

The Government of India in its affidavit submitted to Supreme Court in September 2013 gave a broad overview of insurgency in the north-eastern states of India. With specific reference to Manipur, it was stated that a large number of terrorist groups are active in the state with varying demands including outright secession from India. These terrorist groups have safe havens across the border and they have been indulging in the cold blooded murder of dignitaries, security force personnel and innocent citizens including political leaders, bureaucratic functionaries etc. These groups have resorted to burning copies of the Constitution of India and the national flag and have, to a certain extent, subverted the local administration and muzzled the voice of the people by violence and threats of violence. It was further stated that the armed forces conduct operations within the framework of the military ethos wherein local customs and traditions are deeply valued and respected and restraint is exercised. This is reflected, significantly, in the number of casualties suffered since 1990 - approximately for every two terrorists killed, one security force personnel has been killed and for every two security force personnel killed, three of them have been wounded in operations.

---

67 The Home Ministry said, "The Union government shall not tolerate even one false encounter and shall not spare anyone guilty of false encounter, but at the same time, it is necessary to ensure that no innocent security personnel is harassed for an official act performed in good faith and without any mala fide intention." Mahapatra Dhananjay, Zero tolerance for fake encounters: Modi govt tells SC, *The Times of India*, New Delhi dated 16 August 2014.

The Government of India made another submissions to the Supreme Court on 4 May 2016 and pointed out that "a militant or terrorist or insurgent, is an 'Enemy' within the definition of the Army Act, 1950,[68] and it is the bounden duty of all army personnel to act against a militant or a terrorist or an insurgent, while he is deployed in a 'disturbed area' under AFSPA. In case army personnel do not act against an enemy or show cowardice, it is a court martial offence under the Army Act section 34, punishable with death."

Supreme Court Order dated 8 July 2016

The Supreme Court in its order of July 2016, disregarded the submission made by the Attorney General that: "It is only due to the efforts of the Manipur Police and the armed forces of the Union that the security environment in Manipur has not deteriorated but has vastly improved over the years. The efforts made in the past and the successes gained, the efforts being presently made and the efforts that will be made in the future should not get hamstrung through wanton and sometimes irresponsible allegations of violations of human rights and use of excessive force. These have a deleterious and demoralizing impact on the security forces to no one's advantage except the militants, terrorists and insurgents. This is apart from the submission that the deaths caused were justified, being deaths of militants, terrorists and insurgents in counter insurgency or anti terrorist operations."[69]

The Supreme Court was of the opinion that, "....the situation in Manipur has never been one of a war or an external aggression or an armed rebellion that threatens the security of the country or a part thereof. No such declaration has been made by the Union of India – explicitly or even implicitly - and nothing has been shown that would warrant a conclusion that there is a war or an external aggression or an armed rebellion in Manipur." Further, "All that we can and do say is that in such a situation, our Constitution recognizes only an internal disturbance, which is what the situation in Manipur is and that ought to be dealt with by the civil

---

68 Section 3(x) of the Army Act, 1950 states: "enemy" includes all armed mutineers, armed rebels, armed rioters, pirates and any person in arms against whom it is the duty of any person subject to military law to act.

69 *Extra Judicial Execution Victim Families Association (EEVFAM) v. Union of India*, WP (Criminal) No. 129 of 2012, judgement dated 8 July 2016.

administration with the services of the armed forces that are available in aid of the civil power."

The Court was of the opinion that though an internal disturbance is cause for concern, it does not threaten the security of the country or a part thereof unlike an armed rebellion which could pose a threat to the security of the country or a part thereof. Since the impact of a proclamation of emergency under Article 352 of the Constitution is rather serious, its invocation is limited to situations of a threat to the security of the country or a part thereof either through a war or an external aggression or an armed rebellion, but not an internal disturbance. To put it negatively, an internal disturbance is not a ground for a proclamation of emergency under Article 352 of the Constitution.

Prior to the amendment of Article 352 by the Forty-fourth Amendment of the Constitution it was open to the President to issue a proclamation of emergency if he was satisfied that a grave emergency exists whereby the security of India or of any part of the territory thereof is threatened whether by war or external aggression or "internal disturbance". By the Forty-fourth Amendment the words "internal disturbance" in Article 352 have been substituted by the words "armed rebellion". The expression "internal disturbance" has a wider connotation than "armed rebellion" in the sense that "armed rebellion" is likely to pose a threat to the security of the country or a part thereof, while "internal disturbance", though serious in nature, would not pose a threat to the security of the country or a part thereof. The intention underlying the substitution of the word "internal disturbance" by the word "armed rebellion" in Article 352 is to limit the invocation of the emergency powers under Article 352 only to more serious situations where there is a threat to the security of the country or a part thereof on account of war or external aggression or armed rebellion and to exclude the invocation of emergency powers in situations of internal disturbance which are of lesser gravity. This has been done because a proclamation of emergency under Article 352 has serious implications having effect on the executive as well as the legislative powers of the States as well as the Union."

However, a proclamation of emergency could be made in the event of an internal disturbance (not covered by Article 352 of the Constitution) by resort to Article 356 of the Constitution. The Court stated the issue has been so held in *Naga People's Movement of Human Rights* in the following words: "There can be a situation arising out of internal disturbance which may justify the issuance of a proclamation under Article 356 of the Constitution enabling the President to assume to himself all or any of the functions of the Government of the State. That would depend on the gravity of the situation arising on account of such internal disturbance and on the President being satisfied that a situation has arisen where the Government of the State cannot be carried on in accordance with provisions of the Constitution."

According to Supreme Court, there is a clear distinction between an armed rebellion that threatens the security of the country or a part thereof and an internal disturbance. The former comes within the purview of Article 352 and Article 356 of the Constitution while the latter comes within the purview only of Article 356 of the Constitution and not Article 352 of the Constitution.

The Supreme Court also analyzed the provisions of the Army Act, 1950, containing the offences in relation to the enemy which are punishable with death, offences not punishable with death and offences that are more severely punishable while on active service. According to Court, while functioning under the AFSPA, the armed forces are entitled while maintaining public order in a disturbed area to cause the death of an enemy, that is a militant, terrorist, insurgent, underground element or secessionist who belongs to or is associated with a terrorist organization or terrorist gang or unlawful association and is threatening or is likely to threaten the unity, integrity, security or sovereignty of India.

The Supreme Court clarified distinction between the right of self-defence or private defence and use of excessive force or retaliation. Very simply put, the right of self-defence is a right that can be exercised to defend oneself but not to retaliate. Referring to its decision in *Rohtash Kumar v. State of Haryana* (2013) 14 SCC 290 the Court cautioned against the use of retaliatory force even against a dreaded criminal. Merely because a person is a dreaded criminal or a proclaimed offender, he cannot be killed in cold blood. The police must make an effort to arrest such accused. In a given case if a dreaded criminal launches a murderous attack on the police to prevent them from doing their duty, the police may have to retaliate and, in that retaliation, such a criminal may get killed. That could be a case of genuine encounter. Therefore, while a victim of aggression has a right of self-defence (recognized by Sections 96 to 106 of the IPC) if that victim exceeds the right of self-defence by using excessive force or retaliatory measures, he then becomes an aggressor and commits a punishable offence.

When the State uses such excessive or retaliatory force leading to death, it is referred to as an extra-judicial killing or an extra-judicial execution or administrative liquidation.[70]

The Supreme Court also referred to the report of the National Human Rights Commission: "... one cannot be oblivious of the fact that there are cases where the police, who are performing their duty, are attacked and killed. There is a rise in such incidents and judicial notice must be taken of this fact. In such circumstances, while the police have to do their legal duty of arresting the criminals, they have also to protect themselves. The requirement of sanction to prosecute affords protection to the policemen, who are sometimes required to take drastic action against criminals to protect life and property of the people and to protect themselves against attack. Unless unimpeachable evidence is on record to establish that their action is indefensible, mala fide and vindictive, they cannot be subjected to prosecution."[71]

The Supreme Court considered two questions in this case:

- Has there been use of excessive force by the Manipur Police and the armed forces in the 1528 cases compiled by the petitioners through fake encounters or extra-judicial executions during the period of internal disturbance in Manipur as alleged by the petitioners?

- Has the use of force by the armed forces been retaliatory to the point of causing death and was the retaliatory force permissible in law on the ground that the victims were 'enemy' as defined in Section 3(x) of the Army Act?

On the question of the use of excessive force and retaliation the Court referred to its decision in the case of *Darshan Singh v. State of Punjab* (2010) 2 SCC 333, wherein it has held: "When there is real apprehension that the aggressor might cause death or grievous hurt, in that event the right of private defence of the defender could even extend to causing of death. A mere reasonable apprehension is enough to put the right of self-defence into operation, but it is also a settled position of law that a right of

---

70 *Extra Judicial Execution Victim Families Association (EEVFAM) v. Union of India*, WP (Criminal) No. 129 of 2012, judgement dated 8 July 2016, para 118-122; *People's Union for Civil Liberties v. Union of India* (1997) 3 SCC 433.

71 *Extra Judicial Execution Victim Families Association (EEVFAM) v. Union of India*, WP (Criminal) No. 129 of 2012, judgement dated 8 July 2016,   para 127.

self-defence is only a right to defend oneself and not to retaliate. It is not a right to take revenge." The Court came to conclusion that in all the six cases investigated bb Hedge Commission, the individuals were killed in a fake encounter or that the force used against them was excessive.

On the second question of retaliation against an enemy, the Court concluded, "even while dealing with the 'enemy' the rule of law would apply and if there have been excesses beyond the call of duty, those members of the Manipur Police or the armed forces who have committed the excesses which do not have a reasonable connection with the performance of their official duty would be liable to be proceeded against.[72] The Court also referred to the "Ten Commandments (supplementary)" issued by the Chief of Army Staff, and stated that minimum force is to be used even against terrorists, militants and insurgents. The Court observed that the commandments were in tune with the Geneva Conventions and the principles of international humanitarian law.

COAS TEN COMMANDMENTS (Supplementary)

- Remember that people you are dealing with, are your own countrymen. All your conduct must be dictated by this one significant consideration.

- Operations must be people friendly, using minimum force and avoiding collateral damage – restrain must be the key.

- Good intelligence is the key to success – the thrust of your operations must be intelligence based and must include the militant leadership.

- Be compassionate, help the people and win their hearts and minds. Employ all resources under your command to improve their living conditions.

- No operations without police representative. No operations against women cadres under any circumstances without *mahila* police. Operations against women insurgents to be preferably carried out by police.

---

72 *Extra Judicial Execution Victim Families Association (EEVFAM) v. Union of India*, WP (Criminal) No. 129 of 2012, judgement dated 8 July 2016, para 149.

- Be truthful, honest and maintain highest standards of integrity, honour, discipline, courage and sacrifice.

- Sustain physical and moral strength, mental robustness and motivation.

- Train hard, be vigilant and maintain highest standards of military professionalism.

- Synergise your actions with the civil administration and other security forces.

- Uphold Dharma and take pride in your country and the army.

The Supreme Court in para 152 of the judgment made clear that Section 6 of the AFSPA and Section 49 of the UAPA[73] presently have no application to this case. It has yet to be determined whether the deaths were in fake encounters as alleged or whether the deaths were in genuine encounters in counter insurgency operations and it has also to be determined whether the use of force was disproportionate or retaliatory or not. If any death was unjustified, there is no blanket immunity available to the perpetrator(s) of the offence. No one can act with impunity particularly when there is a loss of an innocent life.

The Supreme Court also referred its decision in *General Officer Commanding, Rashtriya Rifles v. Central Bureau of Investigation* (1012) 6 SCC 228 where the provisions of the Armed Forces (Jammu and Kashmir) Special Powers Act, 1990 and the AFSPA were considered. Relying upon *Matajog Dobey* it was held in this case that the criminal court lacks jurisdiction to take cognizance of the offence unless sanction is granted by the Central Government. The Court concluded: "... the law is very clear and if an offence is committed even by Army personnel, there is no concept of absolute immunity from trial by the criminal court constituted under the

---

73 Section 49: Protection of action taken in good faith - No suit, prosecution or other legal proceeding shall lie against - (*a*) the Central Government or a State Government or any officer or authority of the Central Government or State Government or District Magistrate or any officer authorised in this behalf by the Government or the District Magistrate or any other authority on whom powers have been conferred under this Act, for anything which is in good faith done or purported to be done in pursuance of this Act or any rule or order made thereunder; and (*b*) any serving or retired member of the armed forces or paramilitary forces in respect of any action taken or purported to be taken by him in good faith, in the course of any operation directed towards combating terrorism.

Cr PC. The result of the interplay between Section 4 and Section 5 of the Cr PC and Sections 125 and 126 of the Army Act makes it quite clear that the decision to try a person who has committed an offence punishable under the Army Act and who is subject to the provisions of the Army Act does not always or necessarily lie only with the Army – the criminal court under the Cr PC could also try the alleged offender in certain circumstances in accordance with the procedure laid down by the Cr PC.[74]

The Supreme Court reiterate that in the event of an offence having been committed by any person in the Manipur Police or the armed forces through the use of excessive force or retaliatory force, resulting in the death of any person, the proceedings in respect thereof can be instituted in a criminal court subject to the appropriate procedure being followed. The Court directed:

(a) Of the 62 cases that the petitioners have documented, their representative and the *Amicus* will prepare a simple tabular statement indicating whether in each case a judicial enquiry or an inquiry by the NHRC or an inquiry under the Commissions of Inquiry Act, 1952 has been held and the result of the inquiry and whether any First Information Report or complaint or petition has been filed by the next of kin of the deceased.

(b) The representative of the petitioners and the *Amicus* will revisit the remaining cases (1528 minus 62) and carry out an identical exercise as above. This exercise is required to be conducted for eliminating those cases in which there is no information about the identity of the victim or the place of occurrence or any other relevant detail and then present an accurate and faithful chart of cases in a simple tabular form.[75]

Curative Petition

On 18 April 2017, the Supreme Court rejected a curative petition submitted by the Central Government against its order of July 8, 2016.

---

74 *Extra Judicial Execution Victim Families Association (EEVFAM) v. Union of India*, WP (Criminal) No. 129 of 2012, judgement dated 8 July 2016, para 163-164.

75 *Extra Judicial Execution Victim Families Association (EEVFAM) v. Union of India*, WP (Criminal) No. 129 of 2012, judgement dated 8 July 2016, para 175.

[76] The Government had pleaded that the cases of alleged extra-judicial killings by security forces personnel who had been given clean chits by courts of enquiry should not be re-investigated by a court-appointed special investigations team; as a fresh judicial probe would hamper the functioning of security forces in Manipur. The Attorney General had made a submission that it was an extremely important petition not only for armed forces' personnel which face extreme danger to their lives during every counter-insurgency operation, but also equally important for the security and sovereignty of the country. He said the Army was sensitive to human rights and was not seeking immunity from inquiry by military authorities into complaints of excesses. Further, empirical data as compiled from Manipur proves the point — 18,670 (90%) insurgents have been apprehended by security forces from 1990 to 2015 as compared to 1,881 (10%) insurgents/terrorists who have died in encounters. During the same period, Army and Assam Rifles lost 928 personnel to insurgents and 1,463 more were injured during counter-insurgency operations in Manipur alone. The members of the armed forces need to be given the requisite measure of protection.

The Supreme Court, however, upheld its direction for mandatory registration of FIR against armed forces personnel, even in disturbed areas under AFSPA, for every encounter death despite the Central Government pleading that this order could jeopardize efforts to maintain peace and security.[77]

---

76 In a chamber hearing without the presence of law officers for the Central Government, a bench of Chief Justice J S Khehar, Justices Dipak Misra, J Chelameswar, Madan B Lokur and U U Lalit had dismissed the Union government's curative petition against the judgment delivered in July 2016. The Supreme Court in *Rupa Ashok Hurra v Ashok Hura* (2002) 4 SCC 388 had devised the curative jurisdiction whereby a litigant could, as the last recourse, seek reconsideration of a judgment even after a review petition had been dismissed, on grounds of alleged violation principle of natural justice and bias. A curative petition is considered in chamber by a bench that includes the three senior-most judges of the Supreme Court and the judges who had delivered the judgment in question, if the latter were still available.

77 The Attorney General was of the opinion that the process for curative petitions was "unfair and flawed" on three accounts: (1) If the judges who had delivered the judgment and dismissed the review petition were to be part of the bench to hear the curative petition, then it is obvious that the result would go the same way as the fate of the review petition. If the intention is to have a relook at the judgment, then the curative petition must be placed before a bench which does not include the judges who had delivered the judgment. (2) In camera proceedings in deciding curative petitions are contrary to the notion of dispensation of justice under public gaze. The court proceedings in

Probe by Special Investigation Team (SIT)

Based on a statement filed by the petitioner in the case, the Supreme Court directed constitution of a Special Investigating Team (SIT) to investigate 60 specified cases of alleged fake encounter. The Court made observation that in none of the cases any FIR has been registered against the Manipur Police or any uniformed personnel of the armed forces of the Union. On the contrary, FIRs have been registered against the deceased for alleged violations of the law.

Commenting upon the submission made by the Attorney General that in a number of cases compensation has been paid to the next of kin for the unfortunate deaths and therefore it may be not necessary to proceed further in the matter; the Court observed, "Compensation has been awarded to the next of kin for the agony they have suffered and to enable them to immediately tide over their loss and for their rehabilitation. This cannot override the law of the land; otherwise all heinous crimes would get settled through payment of monetary compensation. Our constitutional jurisprudence does not permit this and we certainly cannot encourage or countenance such a view."

The Supreme Court directed the Director CBI to nominate SIT consisting of five officers, which will go through the records of the 60 specified cases, lodge necessary FIRs and to complete the investigations by 31 December 2017. Where necessary the SIT will also prepare charge sheets against offenders. The CBI has been directed to complete the investigation and submit the report by second week of January 2018.[78]

India are open to public, except in exceptional circumstances. (3) The absence of petitioner's counsel to argue before the bench dealing with the curative petition was not in accordance with the principles of natural justice. In fact, there is no provision in the Constitution regarding curative petition. After the dismissal of an appeal, the only opportunity a litigant can avail of is Article 137, which empowers the top court to review any judgment or order pronounced by it.

78 *Extra Judicial Execution Victim Families Association (EEVFAM) v Union of India*, WP (Criminal) 129 of 2012, judgement dated 14 July 2017.

Shopian Rape and Murder Case

The town of Shopian in Jammu and Kashmir is located on the bank of the river Rambi Ara Nallah, which has a number of tributaries that are 10 to 15 feet wide and 2 to 3 feet deep. An incident that occurred on the night of 29/30 May 2009, shattered the calm and tranquility of the place and brought the harmonious and easy life of the inhabitants to a grinding halt. Two young girls, Neelofar (22) and Asiya (15), who had left their home on foot around 04:00 pm on 29 May 2009 for their orchard located across the river, did not return. Shakeel Ahmad, the husband of Neelofar and brother of Asiya returned from his shop at 0700 pm, and upon not finding the girls, went looking for them with his friend Showkat Ahmad Dalal. They searched all around the orchard, but could not trace the girls. Shakeel them approached the police station and a search party was constituted by the police. Several relatives of Shakeel Ahmad accompanied the search party, which conducted an intense search on both sides of the river. The search was called off at 02:30 am on 30 May 2009 and resumed again in the morning by the relatives of the missing girls and the police party.

Recovery of the dead bodies

Neelofar's body was found at about 06:00 am further upstream from the orchard. The SHO permitted the dead body to be dragged out of the shallow part of the river, where it was resting on boulders and taken to the bank. A *feran* was draped over the body by one of Neelofar's relative, though her clothes were not torn. Gold ornaments were present on the dead body of Neelofar when her dead body was recovered.

Another search party, looking for Asiya, found her dead body in one of the streams flowing into the Rambi Ara river nearly one-and-a-half km downstream from the bridge. The body had a wound on the forehead and a bleeding nose. Although the body was fully clothed, it was covered by a blanket by her relatives. The SHO failed to inform the relatives and the members of the search party not to touch the body, to ensure that evidence was not disturbed or tampered with. The bodies were sent to the hospital for post-mortem, and since Neelofar's husband had not complained of rape and murder of his wife, no offence under Section 302 or 376 RPC was registered.

Post-mortem

The medical examination of the bodies was conducted by a team of three doctors.[79] After examining the body of Miss Asiya on 30 May 2009, Dr Bilal reported an injury of 2 to 3 cm on the forehead, a cut on the nasal bridge and minor cuts on both sides of the forehead. The injury on the forehead was 1 cm deep and had been caused by a sharp-edged weapon, according to the doctors. There was no froth from the mouth. There was no discoloration of the tongue and the nails were pale. There were no blood stains on the inner garments and no marks of violence around genitals. Upon dissection of the body, no external bleeding of the heart or stomach was seen. In his opinion, death could not have been due to strangulation and the cut on the forehead could have caused concussion of the brain. The injury was ante-mortem. According to Dr Bilal, there were no external injuries on the body of Neelofar, and no indication to suggest that the death was by strangulation. The lungs were removed and a floating test was performed. The test result ruled out the possibility of death by drowning. The uterus was sent to the Forensic Science Laboratory. According to Dr Nazia, the medical examination of the body of Asiya could not be conducted because of rigor mortis; however, there was a wound on her head. Dr Bilques could not perform any test on the bodies as she was scared of the crowd which had entered the hospital premises. After the post-mortem, the bodies were handed over to the relatives. The locals were agitated because they suspected foul play.

As soon as the news about the incident spread, the entire area was rocked by spontaneous protests. Hundreds of people, including a large number of women, took to the streets, shouting anti-India and pro-freedom slogans. They alleged that the duo were first raped and then murdered by members of military/paramilitary forces. They demanded a fresh post-mortem by a team of 'neutral' doctors from outside the district. The deputy commissioner, M R Thakur, later consulted the director, health services, after which a team of doctors from Pulwama conducted a second post-mortem.

---

79 The first team which conducted post-mortem consisted of Dr Bilal, Dr Nazia and Dr Bilques.

Second Post-mortem

The second team of doctors [80] arrived at the Shopian hospital around 01:45 pm and conducted the second post-mortem in 20 to 25 minutes. Dr Nighat, heading the team reported a wound of 2 to 3 inches in the frontal region of the skull of Asiya. The injury was one cm deep and sufficient to cause compression of the brain, resulting in cardiac arrest and death. The team also reported three sharp cuts on the forehead between the eyes and one each on the right and left side of the body. The nasal bridge bore a cut from a sharp-edged weapon and the left nostril was bleeding profusely at the time of the examination of the body. According to Dr Nighat, the injury on the head could not have been caused by a fall in the river because it was a sharp cut and not very deep and death occurred between 03:00 and 04:00 am. There were no apparent marks of injury or violence in the genital area, though deeper injury could not be ruled out because per speculum examination was not possible. Hymen was freshly torn and was no fresh bleeding. Vaginal swab were taken and after an examination, it was reported that a sexual assault had been committed, though the morphology of the private parts did not suggest that a gang rape had been committed. In the view of the doctors, death could have been due to haemorrhage shock because of bleeding from the multiple cuts. According to Dr Nighat, on physical examination of the body of Neelofar, no marks of violence or injury were seen except mild echymotic patches (bruises) on the buttocks. There were no marks of violence in the genital area and no hymen was present. The skulls of dead bodies were not opened and samples of brain and heart were not taken from both either body for forensic analysis.

After completing the post mortem, the team of doctors told the district magistrate that they were of the opinion that Asiya had been molested before her death, but could not give any opinion regarding Neelofar. It has been reported that in the presence of the DC and SP, the relatives of the victims urged the doctors to say on oath whether rape had been committed. The doctors had replied in the affirmative, and even the SP had confirmed this and promised full support to the relatives. When the mob waiting outside the hospital heard that both the girls had been raped and murdered, it pelted stones at the hospital and had to be dispersed with tear gas and cane-charge. The bodies were taken by the relatives for burial and were buried in the evening.

---

80 The team of doctors which conducted the second post-mortem was consisted of Dr Nighat, Dr Ghulam Qadir and Dr Mohammad Maqbool.

Protest

The initial cause of public anger and resentment was the indifferent and casual attitude of the police and their refusal to register an FIR on 30 May 2009 on the recovery of the bodies. The protesters accused the state government and the police of hiding facts. The non-performance of the investigating agency added fuel to the fire and provided an easy opportunity to antisocial and disgruntled elements to hijack the situation, instigate the people, and call for an indefinite strike. There were violent protests against the incident, with protesters accusing the Indian armed forces of raping and murdering Neelofar and Asiya. From 30 May to 13 July there were around 900 civilian injuries and one death due to police action. Around 60 armed personnel were also injured. Many pro-freedom leaders were put under house arrest or jailed. Offices, schools, colleges, business establishments, civic amenities and even hospitals remained closed. The anger and hatred generated by dissenting political parties completely alienated the people from the administration.[81]

PIL by Bar Association of Kashmir

A public interest litigation (PIL) was filed by the Bar Association of Kashmir, which sought the registration of a FIR under RPC 376 (gang rape) and 302 (murder).[82] It also pleaded that the High Court monitor the investigations in the case on a daily basis. While admitting the PIL, the division bench comprising Chief Justice Barin Ghosh and Justice Hakim Imtiyaz Hussain issued a notice (on 5 June 2009) to the state government directing it to file its reply within a short period of time. It also directed the chief secretary, DGP, SSP Shopian and SHO Shopian to present a detailed report before the division bench on 29 June.

On 9 June 2009, the High Court Bar Association probing the matter independently released its fact-finding report which concluded that the duo were abducted, gang-raped and murdered. It demanded that the police file a case under Sections 363, 366, 376, 120B of RPC for kidnap of

---

81 The deaths triggered one of the longest-running street protests in the valley in two decades. Moderate Hurriyat leader Bilal Lone said the separatists received funds from "both sides" but later backtracked and stated: "I never named Pakistan". 'Shopian Women not murdered or raped: CBI', *The Times of India*, 15 December 2009.

82 Advocate G N Shaheen, Advocate M Abdullah Pandit, Advocate R A Joo and Advocate B A Sidiq argued on behalf of the Bar Association.

a minor, abduction of a major, rape, murder and conspiracy respectively.[83] The report said that the SP had forced the doctors to change statements and that the SP, SHO and doctors of the hospital were all guilty of failure of duty and destruction of proof.

On 30 May 2009, the Director General of Police ordered the constitution of a 3-member special investigation team (SIT) for the expeditious investigation of the case. An FIR under Section 302 RPC was registered on 8 June. The team was to investigate the case under the supervision of the DIG South Kashmir Range. The team failed to find any clue, even though it announced an award of Rs 20 lakh to anyone who provided any information about the culprits involved in the case.

Commission of Inquiry

The Government of Jammu & Kashmir appointed a commission of enquiry[84] to enquire into the matter. The terms of reference of commission of inquiry were:

(a)   To enquire into the causes and circumstances which led to the deaths.

(b)   To ascertain whether there has been any foul play and if so, to identify the person/persons responsible.

(c)   To recommend action as deemed necessary against the person/persons found involved/responsible.

---

83 The Bar Association's investigation recorded witnesses as stating, "The body of one of them was lying half naked on dry sand. Her clothes were torn and hair, clothes and body were dry. Blood was dripping from her nose and it appeared "sindoor" had been smeared on forehead." "During our investigations," association leader GN Shaheen said, "we found that the perpetrators belonged to a particular community and they had even vandalised the bodies of the victims." In case anyone had missed the point, Mr. Shaheen added the rapists were "fanatic Hindus." Swami Praveen, Exhuming the truth on Shopian, *The Hindu*, 28 December 2009, available at: http://www.thehindu.com/opinion/lead/exhuming-the-truth-on-shopian/article71564.ece, accessed 15 August 2014.

84 Amidst public outcry, the Government of Jammu & Kashmir appointed a Commission of Inquiry headed by Justice Muzaffar Ahmad Jan to investigate the case. The Commission was appointed by the government in exercise of the powers conferred by the Jammu and Kashmir Commission of Inquiry Act 1962, section 3, under Notification No. SRO 160 dated 1 June 2009. The Superintendent of Police, Dr Haseeb Mughal and the Chief Prosecuting Officer, Abdul Majid Dar were to assist in the probe.

(d)   To suggest remedial measures, as may be necessary, to ensure that such incidents do not occur in the future.

(e)   To ascertain whether there was any failure on the part of any department in the government in the conduct of an investigation or handling of the post incident situation.

Justice Muzaffar Jan (Retd) was appointed to the one man commission of inquiry, which was required to submit its report within one month from the date of issuance of the notification.[85] It commenced its proceedings on 2 June 2009 and issued a public notification on the next day, whereby all individuals, group of persons, associations, institutions and organizations with direct or indirect knowledge of the facts and circumstances relating to the matters referred to the Commission, and having interest in the proceedings, before the Commission, or who wished to assist the Commission in making suggestions, were invited to furnish their statement of facts/allegations, in the form of affidavits duly verified by the deponents and sworn before any court or magistrate or notary, along with three photostat copies before the secretary of the commission, either in person or by a duly appointed attorney. During the course of the proceedings, nine affidavits were submitted by members of the family of the deceased girls and other independent witnesses and the statements of 28 witnesses were recorded.

Since the beginning of the proceedings the people of the town went on continuous strike, resulting in the closure of government institutions,

---

85 The J&K High Court Bar Association rejected the probe ordered by the government demanding that a sitting judge of High Court or Chief Justice should carry out the probe instead of a retired Justice, Muzaffar Jan. The Shopian Bar Association also formed a six-member 'fact finding committee' which included Advocates S M Iqbal, Ajaz Hussain, Ghulam Hassan Dar, Sheikh Mubarak and A M Mir and headed by Advocate MY Bhat. While, Syed Ali Shah Geelani demanded Amnesty International to probe the incident and also urged the High Court Bar Association to probe the matter at their own level so that the people could know the truth. However, the Advocate General of J&K, Muhammad Ishaq Qadri commented that the Commission of Inquiry headed by a sitting or a retired judge does not make any difference regarding the legality of its findings, which are recommendatory in nature in both the cases. The leader of the opposition in the assembly and the PDP president, Mahbooba Mufti, also rejected the government's inquiry commission into the case, and called upon the Prime Minister, Dr Manmohan Singh, to review the performance of the state's ruling coalition personally as according to her, it had failed to extent of not registering an FIR of rape and murder in the case.

schools, colleges, hospitals, private business establishments and even the highway from Shopian to Srinagar. The closure of roads disturbed the working of the commission and hampered the collection of facts for the compilation of the final report. It appears that the commission came to a conclusion without finalizing its proceedings. Its interim report stated:

> The Commission is aware of the sensitivity of the incident and also the anger and wrath of the public towards the persons who committed the gruesome crime. The murder of two innocent young girls has touched the soul of all citizens and inflicted pain on the entire society. Unmindful and undaunted by the loss of business, medical facilities, education of children and the total shut down of civic facilities provided by the state, the entire populations of the town of Shopian are continuing their protest for the long duration of 22 days without a break. The breakdown of basic amenities has multiplied the miseries of the common man and adversely affected….. There does not seem to be any relenting by the public till some confidence building measures are taken to restore the faith and trust of the people, and make a breakthrough by softening this psychological barrier. [86]

Protest Continued

The chairman of the Hurriyat Conference (G), Syed Ali Geelani called for a state-wide strike and peaceful protest against the incident. A complete shutdown was observed throughout Jammu and Kashmir with all government offices, shops, schools, banks remaining closed. In Srinagar, people took to the streets, shouting pro-freedom slogans. The police cane-charged and used tear gas canisters to disperse the mob. In the process one of the person was critically injured. In Ganderbal, a complete shutdown was observed. In Sopur, people held demonstrations against the incident. In Kulgam, protesters blocked roads by erecting barricades and burning tyres. Several people were injured in the ensuing police action. In Bandipora, the police used force against protesters who pelted stones. Several people were injured. The widespread disturbances caused a complete breakdown of law and order.

---

86   Justice Muzaffar Jan, Commission of Inquiry report, page 2-3 (Part 4).

Report of the Commission

The one-man commission submitted a 400-page report to the government. The Commission recommended action against the doctors who conducted post-mortem and four police officers for failing to preserve the evidence. Later, four police officers were suspended and arrested, but were released after the SIT failed to produce any evidence against them in the court of single bench. A few observations made by the commission are as follows.

a. Professional capability of police

All the police officers dealing with the incident appear to be ignorant of their professional responsibility and their duty to uphold the honour of their uniform. By their negligence, incompetence and flagrant violation of laws and rules, they have eroded the image of the entire department, embarrassed the administration, and hurt the sentiments of the citizens of the state. They deserve no leniency in punishment. This would be appropriate to straighten the system and correct the indolent and incompetent officers of the police force.[87] The Commission recommended that the SI Gazi Ab. Kareem, SHO Shafeeq Ahmad, DSP Rohit Baskotra and SP Javid Iqbal Matoo be placed under suspension and a departmental enquiry be initiated for their failure to comply with the mandatory provisions of the Criminal Procedure Code (Cr PC), police manual and relevant rules governing the course of investigation in criminal cases. The commission was of the view that all these officers, in one way or the other contributed to the destruction, dissipation and suppression of evidence. The commission recommended that prosecution under the appropriate provisions of the RPC may be considered against them.

b. Conduct of medical examination

On the professional conduct of Dr Bilal and Dr Nighat, who conducted the post-mortem examination of the bodies of Neelofar and Asiya, the commission observed: "[these doctors] have not opened the skull of both the dead bodies and have not taken the samples of brain and also of heart. This omission does not appear to be accidental in a sensitive case of present nature......

---

87 Justice Muzaffar Jan, Commission of Inquiry report, page 31-32 (Part 4).

The relatives of the deceased trusted both the medical teams and cooperated with the post-mortem proceedings inside the hospital. It is this breach of trust by Dr Bilal and Dr Nighat that triggered the unrest and added fuel to the fire, which engulfed the entire town. Whatever was the motive of Dr Bilal and Dr Nighat, it does not seem to be holy." The observations of the Commission were based on the statement made by Dr Fareeda Noor, head of the forensic medicine department of the Government Medical College, Srinagar, that it was professional requirement to open the skull, remove the brain and send it for analysis. The Commission recommended that a departmental enquiry be initiated against both doctors to assess as to whether they were capable of handling professional requirements of a similar nature, pending which they may not be entrusted with any serious duty in the hospital.

c.   Forensic Science Laboratory, Srinagar

On the functioning of the Forensic Science Laboratory Srinagar, the Commission reported that it received the samples of vaginal smear from the bodies of Neelofar and Asiya on 01 June 2009 around 10:30 am. Javed Iqbal, who was in-charge stated before the commission on 14 June 2009, that two of his officials had formed their opinion regarding the samples on 01 June 2009. The opinion certificate was regarding the presence of human spermatozoa on the bodies. Javed Iqbal received the opinion certificate complete in all respects on 2 June, but retained the certificate in his office for five days without any justification. The certificate was delivered to the police on 6 June 2009.

d.   The role of the media

The Commission criticized journalists for publicizing unconfirmed and incorrect information and for fermenting public unrest. A few of these observations are as follows.

1.   The print and electronic media gave wide publicity to the last mobile call of Neelofar to her husband, alleging that she was being chased by CRPF persons around 0700 PM on 29 May 2009 near Rambi Ara River. However, Shakeel Ahmad (husband of Neelofar), Syed Zeerak Shah (brother of Neelofar) and Posha (cousin Neelofar) had stated in

their statement before the Commission, on oath, that Neelofar did not have a mobile phone and never called. The investigating team of the Commission scrutinized 32686 calls and found that Neelofar did not have a mobile phone on 29 May 2009.

2. It was reported that Neelofar was pregnant, but Dr Bilal, who conducted post-mortem examination on the bodies reported that she was not pregnant.

3. The press had described orchard as extending over hundreds of kanals, with thousands of fruit trees, but the Commission found that the orchard was a migrant property measuring 1 kanal and 16 marlas and was in a neglected condition, full of weeds, wild grass and with around 35 fruit trees in a bad shape.

4. It was reported that the garments of the two women were torn. During enquiry, the Commission found that this was not true.

5. It was reported that Asiya had a 'sindoor mark' on her forehead. The Commission found that there was a grave injury on the forehead of Asiya, which was bleeding even at the time of post-mortem. The blood on her forehead was projected as 'sindoor'.

6. The press has reported that Constable Mohammad Yaseen had made several calls while conducting a search of the bodies. On analyzing the calls made from the mobile, the Commission found that only four calls had been made during the day and no calls had been made from 10:00 pm on 29 May to 06:00 am on 30 May 2009.

7. It was reported that there were multiple injuries on Neelofar's body, however, both the teams of doctors had stated that there were no visible external injuries on the body.

8. Though it had been widely reported that the girls had been gang-raped; during the enquiry made by the Commission, it was revealed that the teams of medical experts were of the view that there was no evidence of gang-rape.

Failure to identify Shopian culprits

Though the Commission failed to identify the culprits involved in the unnatural deaths of the two women, it said that the involvement of Jammu and Kashmir police could not be ruled out completely. In its final report, submitted to the government on 7 July 2009, it called for further investigation and suggested that the killings were most likely the result of a family feud. The J&K government accepted the commission's report, and decided to hand over the case to the Central Bureau of Investigation (CBI) on 12 August 2009.

A number of human rights activists[88] and organizations also expressed their view on the unnatural deaths; albeit quoting unconfirmed sources and without due verification. The Delhi-based Independent Women's Initiative for Justice (IWIJ), which had sent its team to the valley on a fact-finding mission, in its report alleged that the Jammu and Kashmir government was involved in a major hush-up of the case.[89] The report argued that as for "accidental drowning of the two women in the nallah (stream), where no one in recent or living memory has ever drowned, we would need to be more than merely credulous to believe that." The IWIJ claimed that during its team's visit to Shopian, the members found that the water in the stream was only ankle-deep—not enough for anybody to drown in it.[90]

---

88 "The tragedy of Shopian is a wake-up call for the state and the central government." Mattoo Amitabh, Kashmir After Shopian, *Economic and Political Weekly*, Vol. XLIV, No. 28, 11 July 2009, p. 39-43. "From the infamous gang rapes in Kunan-Poshora in 1990 to Shopian's spine-chilling double rapes and murders, and the equally shocking cover-up by official investigating agencies....exemplify the victimization and vulnerability of women in militarised conflict." Jamwal Anuradha Bhasin, Rapists in Uniform, *Economic and Political Weekly*, Vol. XLVIII, No. 8, 23 February 2013, p. 13-16.

89 The team comprising Uma Chakravarti, Usha Ramanathan, Vrinda Grover, Anuradha Bhasin Jamwal, Seema Misra and Dr Ajita reported: "The Shopian rapes and murders epitomise the wrongs and injustices perpetrated on the people living in a militarised society. The incident not only manifests the extent of fear psychosis, denial of security and democratic rights to the people, it also demonstrates the abject refusal of those at the helm of affairs to bring the culprits of gross violation of human rights to book". The report ended with, "Two women sacrificed at the altar of national security".

90 In its report submitted to the J&K High Court, the CBI concluded that the women had accidentally drowned in the Rambiara nullah. The report showed that the stream, according to the state flood and irrigation department, had sharp increase in water discharge around 26 May 2009. Further, the discharge would have been peaking on the day the women died. Available at: http://indiatoday.intoday.in/story/Exclusive:+Shopia n+truth+nailed/1/83795.html, accessed 1 July 2014.

The CBI Investigation

On 28 September 2009, the CBI exhumed the bodies of the two women. The bodies were examined by a team of doctors from the All India Institute of Medical Sciences (AIIMS) in presence of three executive magistrates and family members of Neelofar and Asiya. The team took 23 samples from the lungs, uterus, bone, hair, etc from the exhumed bodies. The AIIMS post-mortem report contradicted the previous report by the Shopian and Pulwama teams in crucial areas. The AIIMS team did not find any injury on Neelofar's body whereas the Pulwama team had claimed to have found injury marks on her body. The Pulwama team had claimed that Asiya was sexually assaulted and the hymen torn in rags. The AIIMS team found that Asiya's hymen was intact. The Pulwama team had claimed that Asiya's nasal bridge was fractured, but the CBI showed the post-mortem witnesses that no bone was fractured. The CBI report ruled out rape and murder in the case.[91] The forensic report from the AIIMS stated that soil and water were found in the two women's lungs and other organs. The doctors reportedly concluded had the women been murdered and then thrown into the river, their bodies would have got air-locked, preventing soil and other river material from entering their organs.

On 14 December 2009, the CBI submitted its 66-page report on Shopian case to the Jammu and Kashmir High Court. The CBI officials gave a power point presentation prepared by the agency to the court where the media persons were not allowed. The CBI report concluded that both the women had died due to drowning in the river. The CBI probe uncovered a two-pronged attempt to defame the security forces.[92] First, the two teams of doctors, with the exception of one doctor, prepared false post-mortem reports which suggested that Neelofar and Asiya had been raped

---

91 On 14 December 2009, the CBI submitted its 66-page report on Shopian case to the Jammu and Kashmir High Court. The CBI officials gave a power point presentation prepared by the agency to the court where the media persons were not allowed. The CBI report concluded that both the women had died due to drowning in the river.

92 The CBI has ripped apart the claims of the secessionist-linked J&K Bar Association, politicians like People's Democratic Party leader Mehbooba Mufti and much of the media. Backed by forensic detective work by the AIIMS Department of Forensic Medicine and Toxicology, the Central Forensic Sciences Laboratory in New Delhi, the Forensic Sciences Laboratory in Madhuban and the Indian Agricultural Research Institute, the CBI has concluded that the women were neither raped nor murdered. Swami Praveen, Exhuming the truth on Shopian, The Hindu, 28 December 2009, available at: http://www.thehindu.com/opinion/lead/exhuming-the-truth-on-shopian/article71564.ece, accessed 15 August 2014.

and murdered. Second, certain advocates of the Shopian Bar Association coerced witnesses to corroborate the claims of the doctors. Some of the findings of the CBI were as follows.

- A deliberate conspiracy was hatched against the police and the security forces and concerted efforts were made to create false evidence. The doctors at the Shopian and Pulwama hospitals created false post-mortem reports, fudged slides of samples taken from the alleged victims' bodies and resorted to inducing and threatening the witnesses to give false testimony.[93]

- The first team of doctors prepared four reports making "additions/extrapolations to suit the changing circumstances" even though per vaginal (PV) examination could not be conducted because rigor mortis had set in. A piece of tissue preserved by Dr Bilal as a sample of the lungs of Neelofar turned out to be a pience of tissue from the heart. One member of the post-mortem team, Dr Bilkees, did not sign the report and fled from the hospital after the assembled crowd at Shopian started pelting stones. The first team also misled the Justice Jan commission through false affidavits and post-mortem reports.

- Dr Bilal and Dr Nazia wrongly mentioned a lacerated wound on Asiya's temple as an incision wound. They falsely attributed the cause of death to haemorrhagic shock and bleeding from Asiya's multiple injuries.

- Dr Nighat, who was on the second team, concluded that they had been raped without even examining their vaginas. Dr Nighat and her associates falsely mentioned in their postmortem report that Asiya's hymen was ruptured.

- The per vaginal (PV) examination slides were not prepared in the postmortem theatre. The slides were not prepared from the vaginal smear of the deceased. The fudged slides were prepared subsequently by Dr Nighat from some other source. The slides were not sealed and sent as claimed by the second team of doctors.

---

93 Baweja Harinder, Exclusive: Shopian truth nailed, *India Today*, 13 February 2010.

Dr Nihgat reportedly confessed to the CBI that she submitted her own vaginal swab samples instead of the victims.[94]

- Dr Nighat falsely claimed to have conducted the lung flotation test to rule out drowning as the lungs were found to be intact at the time of exhumation of the two bodies. Dr Nighat and her associates said Nilofar died due to neurogenic shock; while, the AIIMS team found that she died due to asphyxia as a result of ante-mortem drowning.

- The evidence suggested that the post-mortem reports of the victims were fudged at the behest of the Majlis Mashawarat, an organization that was at the forefront of the agitation against the security forces. This was confirmed after conversations between a Majlis representative and two doctors were taped by the J&K Police.[95]

The AIIMS forensic experts found several pieces of evidence inside the bodies of the victims, suggesting drowning. Pin-sized petechial haemorrhages were found on the membranes of their lungs and bronchi. Larger patches of Paltauf's haemorrhages (bluish-red areas found in the lungs of about half of all drowning victims), were also visible. Doctors also discovered accumulations of fluid within the alveoli, suggesting pulmonary oedema, another sign of drowning. Based on the expert's report, the CBI concluded that both Neelofar and Asiya had died of drowning. It also filed a charge-sheet against 13 people, including six doctors, two witnesses and some advocates for destroying evidence and creating disturbances in the state by claiming that the women were raped and murdered by security personnel. The CBI's report sparked anger in the Kashmir valley; copies of the report were burnt on the streets. The Majlis-e-Mushawarat called for a strike, with support from the Hurriyat Conference's moderate faction.[96]

---

94 See:http://www.ndtv.com/article/india/shopian-case-doctor-submits-own-vaginal-swab-11589, accessed 13 August 2014.

95 The Abdullah government gave the clearance for tapping the phones of Majlis representatives, the doctors and lawyers of the Shopian bar council. Baweja Harinder, Exclusive: Shopian truth nailed, *India Today*, 13 February 2010.

96 See http://www.ndtv.com/article/india/shopian-bandh-after-cbi-rules-out-rape-murder-13097, accessed 12 August 2014.

High Court Monitoring

A Division Bench of the High Court, headed by Chief Justice M M Kumar and Justice D S Thakur was of the view that the very basis of the findings and conclusions of Justice Muzaffar Jan had been found to be absolutely false. Delivering the order, the Bench ruled out re-investigation into the case of Asiya Jan and Neelofar. However, it clarified that if any additional evidence or factors other than those already on record became available and has an important bearing on the case, nothing would prevent the trial court from examining the same. Since the CBI had completed its investigation and presented the charge-sheet, the bench was of the opinion that no further monitoring was required by the High Court.

In three of the five cases discussed in this chapter deliberate attempts were made to malign the security forces and arouse public sentiments. In Manoram Devi's case, members of the paramilitary forces apparently used excessive force. The Assam Rifles and the government have not informed the people about the action taken against the wrongdoers. Such acts too undermine the people's confidence in the security forces and are used by secessionists and other antisocial elements to foment trouble. In the case of extra-judicial executions alleged in Manipur, the CBI is yet to complete the investigation and file charge-sheet.

5

Human Rights and Fundamental Freedoms: Armed Forces

The members of the armed forces and paramilitary forces (referred to as 'armed forces') are citizens of India and are entitled to the fundamental rights contained in the Indian Constitution. However, some of their rights have been restricted by the Constitution itself to ensure discipline and the proper discharge of duties by them.[1] These rights relate to membership of any trade union, addressing political meetings and taking part in demonstrations for political purposes and communication with the press or publication of any document.[2]

Unlike other citizens, members of the armed forces could be called upon to perform duties which may necessitate killing other people or sacrificing their own lives. They may have to serve under harsh or extreme conditions. They may have to live and serve in hostile areas, away from their

---

1   Article 33 of the Constitution provides: Parliament may, by law, determine to what extent any of the rights conferred by Part III shall, in their application to (a) the members of the armed forces; (b) the members of the forces charged with the maintenance of public order; (c) persons employed in any bureau or other organization established by the State for purposes of intelligence or counter intelligence; or (d) person employed in, or in connection with the telecommunication systems set up for the purposes of any force, bureau or organization referred to in clauses (a) to (c); be restricted or abrogated so as to ensure the proper discharge of their duties and maintenance of discipline among them.

2   Section 21 of the Army Act, 1950 provides that the Central Government may make rules restricting the right of persons subject to the Army Act: (a) to be a member or associated with any trade union or labour union, or any society, institution or association; (b) to attend or address any meeting or to take part in any demonstration organised for any political purposes; and (c) to communicate with the press or to publish any book, letter or other document. These provisions have been further elaborated in the Army Rules 1954, rules 19 to 21. Similar provisions are contained in the other service Acts as well as the law relating to the paramilitary forces.

family and in conditions where there may be very little separation between private life and official duties, e.g., in barracks. They must always be ready and capable of ensuring the internal security and guarding the frontiers of the country. It is true that these special factors call for placing limitations on the human rights of armed forces personnel. However, should armed forces personnel not be entitled to certain basic human rights?

The Importance of Human Rights in the Armed Forces

Article 21 of the Constitution of India guarantees the right to life with dignity.[3] If we respect the human rights of members of the armed forces and make them feel that they are a valued part of the society, if we protect them against misuse and oppression by the government or the by their commanders, only then we can expect them to be sensitive to the human rights of others. When the members of the armed forces function in 'aid to civil power' they are required to integrate human rights into their day-to-day operations. They would be better prepared for this if they themselves operate in an environment in which these rights are protected.[4]

Whilst taking into account the special characteristics of service life, members of the armed forces should enjoy certain rights guaranteed by the Constitution of India. No derogations should be permitted in relation to: the right to life (except in respect of deaths resulting from lawful acts of armed conflict, whether internal or international), the right to a fair trial, the prohibition of torture and inhuman or degrading treatment or punishment, the prohibition of slavery and servitude, the principle that no punishment can be inflicted without a law and the right not to be tried or punished twice.

Right to Life: Every individual joining the armed forces takes a pledge that he/she would bear true faith and allegiance to the Constitution of India, obey all commands of superiors and would not hesitate to sacrifice his life for the country.[5] Members of the armed forces are trained to fight

---

3   Enjoyment of a quality life by people is the essence of the guarantees right under Article21 of the Constitution. *H L Tiwari v Kamla Devi* (2001) 6 SCC 496 : AIR 2001 SC 3215.

4   For more details see: *Handbook on Human Rights and Fundamental Freedoms of Armed Forces Personnel.* 2008. Poland: OSCE/Office for democratic Institutions and Human Rights (ODIHR).

5   The true text of the oath/affirmation administered to every person joining the Army is contained in the Army Rules, 1954, Rule 9: "I,......do swear in the name of God/

a war, kill enemies and destroy property. That being so, to talk about the human rights and in particular the 'right to life' of armed forces personnel may appear absurd to some. International humanitarian law (IHL),[6] has however, laid down certain norms regarding the use of weapons and methods of warfare and protects those who are *horse de combat*. Though IHL does not give any 'right' to a soldier, it imposes obligations on a State to take certain actions, for instance to protect a prisoner of war or non-combatants.[7] IHL is applicable during international armed conflict or war as well as in internal armed conflict.

A soldier knows that he may have to sacrifice his life while fighting for his country. He undergoes rigorous training, for instance, climbing cliff faces at night, rigorous swimming, jungle training, or even low flying. He is aware of these hazards to his life, but he may be not aware that he may get killed because of the recklessness of his fellow soldiers or the lack of proper equipment. A pilot may get injured/killed while flying an obsolete aircraft. A soldier may get killed by another disgruntled or mentally disturbed soldier. He might get killed in an IED explosion, if the vehicle provided by the State does not have protection against such devices. A soldier who he has been provided with a faulty GPS set, may get killed for intruding into enemy territory accidently. A soldier may get killed in an accident in mountainous terrain, if the vehicle provided to him is unfit for use on such terrain. He may die because of snake bite, if the State fails to provide him with suitable boots for jungle terrain infested with leeches, poisonous insects and snakes. The question which arises in such cases of negligence by the government is whether the death of a soldier in these circumstances

---

solemnly affirm that I will bear true faith and allegiance to the Constitution of India as by the law established and that I will, as in duty bound, honestly and faithfully serve in the regular Army of the Union of India and go wherever ordered by land, sea or air, and that I will observe and obey all commands of the President of the Union of India and the commands of any officer set over me even to the peril of my life." Other legislations dealing with the military and paramilitary establishment provide similar provisions.

6   International humanitarian law (IHL) has been defined as "international rules, established by treaties and customs, which are specifically intended to solve humanitarian problems directly arising from international or non-international armed conflicts and which, for humanitarian reasons, limit the rights of the parties to a conflict to use the methods and means of warfare of their choice or protect persons and property that are, or may be, affected by conflict." Y Sandoz, *Commentary on the Additional Protocols of 8 June 1977 to the Geneva Conventions of 12 August 1949*, Geneva: ICRC, p. xxvii.

7   Rowe, Peter. 2006. *The Impact of Human Right Laws on Armed Forces*. UK: Cambridge University Press, p. 2-4.

would amount to human rights violations. Could the next-of-kin of the deceased soldier prefer a claim against the government for human rights violations? Or, could the government can claim 'combat immunity' in such cases and refuse to pay compensation for its neglect? While there may not be any jurisprudence on such issues in the Indian legal system, the British Supreme Court has recently decided a few such cases where the Ministry of Defence had claimed combat immunity.

In the first case, a British soldier lost his life and two other servicemen sustained serious injuries while serving in Iraq. On 25 March 2003, Corporal S Allbutt, Lance Corporal D Twiddy and Trooper A Julien, serving with the British Army, took part in an offensive by British troops to take Basra. They were in one of the Challenger II tanks which had been placed near a dam in hull down positions to minimise chances of their being spotted by the enemy. Just after midnight, another Challenger II tank, commanded by Lt Pinkstone, crossed over to the enemy side of a canal to take up a guarding position some distance from the dam. At about 0050 hrs Lt Pinkstone identified two hot spots through his thermal imaging device. He thought those might be personnel moving in and out of a bunker. He described the location to Sgt Donlon, who was unable to identify the hot spots because the description he was given was incorrect. After Lt Pinkstone had identified another four hot spots in the same area, he was given permission to fire by Sgt Donlon.

Lt Pinkstone's tank fired two high-explosive shells. The hot spots that he had observed were in fact men on top of Cpl Albutt's Challenger II tank at the dam. The first shell landed short of the tank, but the explosion blew off the men who were on top of it. The second shell entered the tank and killed Cpl Allbutt, and caused serious injuries to Trooper Julien and Lance Corporal Twiddy. It also killed Trooper David Clarke. Lt Pinkstone did not know of the presence of another Challenger II tank at the dam. He did not realize that he was firing back across the canal, as he was disorientated and believed that he was firing in a different direction.

Ms Deborah Allbutt, wife of Corporal Allbutt, Corporal Daniel Twiddy and Trooper A Julien preferred a claim in the British Court for negligence. They alleged failures by the Ministry of Defence (MoD) to equip the tanks properly and to give soldiers adequate recognition training during pre-deployment and also in theatre. The MoD argued that the claims should not be admissible: (a) on the principle of combat immunity (which operates to exclude liability for negligence in respect of the acts or omissions of those engaged in active operations against the enemy), and (b) because it would not be fair, just or reasonable to impose a duty of care on the MoD in the circumstances of the case. The Supreme Court, in June 2010, ruled that the British troops were not protected by human rights laws on the battlefield. The judgment overturned a controversial earlier ruling that soldiers' human rights must be guaranteed, even in the heat of battle. The British Defence Secretary hailed the Supreme Court judgment and was of the view that 'instructions given in the heat of battle should not be questioned by lawyers at a later date'. It was feared that officers would then be prevented from giving orders because of the risk of being sued. However, the ruling was a blow for the families of troops killed or injured because of being sent into conflict without the right equipment.[8]

In June 2013, the Supreme Court reconsidered the issue whether Article 2 of the European Convention on Human Rights (ECHR)[9] places positive obligations of the UK to secure the right to life of its soldiers in the field. This case arose out of the deaths of soldiers using vulnerable Snatch Land Rovers in Iraq. The families accused the MoD of negligence as they claimed that the MoD was already aware that the Snatch Land Rovers, originally designed for Northern Ireland, were unsuitable. More robust armoured vehicles were available but were only belatedly deployed. The families accused the MoD of failing to take all reasonable steps to avoid risks to the lives of soldiers. [10]

---

8   Allen Vanessa. Human rights do not apply on the battlefield: Supreme Court quashes landmark ruling, available at: http://www.dailymail.co.uk/news/article-1290813/ Soldiers-human-rights-protection ruling-quashed-Supreme-Court.html, accessed 21 August 2014.

9   Article 2 of the European Convention on Human Rights, to which the UK is a party, provides: (1) Everyone's right to life shall be protected by law. No one shall be deprived of his life intentionally save in the execution of a sentence of a court following his conviction of a crime for which this penalty is provided by law. (2) Deprivation of life shall not be regarded as inflicted in contravention of this article when it results from the use of force which is no more than absolutely necessary: (a) in defence of any person from unlawful violence; (b) in order to effect a lawful arrest or to prevent escape of a person lawfully detained; (c) in action lawfully taken for the purpose of quelling a riot or insurrection.

10 In 2005 Private Phillip Hewett was deployed near the town of Al Amarah in Iraq. His mobile unit, consisting of three Snatch Land Rovers (a light armoured), was sent to patrol around Al Amarah. The vehicle was designed to provide limited protection against ballistic threats, such as those from small arms fire. It provided no significant protection, against improvised explosive devices (IEDs) and had no electronic counter

In the light of the European Court's *Al-Skeini* judgment,[11] the Supreme Court unanimously reversed its earlier ruling of 2010. The Court held that the British troops remain within the UK's jurisdiction when deployed on active service abroad, and so attract the protections of the Human Rights Act, 1998. Further, the principle of combat immunity did not negate the MoD's duty of care during the military activities in question. The Court also ruled that families of soldiers killed by 'friendly fire' from Challenger tanks could sue for negligence on the grounds that the doctrine of combat immunity did not cover decisions "far removed from active operations against the enemy".[12]

---

measures (ECMs) to protect it against the threat of IEDs. It was escorted into, but not around, the town by warrior fighting vehicles, which were heavily armoured and tracked, and were capable of carrying seven or eight personnel as well as the crew. Pte Hewett was in the lead Snatch Land Rover as its driver with 2/ Lt Richard Shearer. At about 0115 hrs on 16 July 2005 an explosion was heard in the vicinity of the stadium in Al Amarah. 2/ Lt Shearer decided to investigate the explosion. As the Snatch Land Rovers were driving down the single road to the stadium, an IED detonated, explosion killing Hewett and 2/ Lt Shearer while two other occupants of the vehicle were seriously injured. See: Thomas Tugendhat and Laura Crof, The Fog of Law: An introduction to the legal erosion of British fighting power, available at: http://www.policyexchange.org. uk/images/publications/the%20fog%20of%20law.pdf, accessed 12 January 2015.

11 In this case, the relatives of six Iraqis brought a suit against the UK, each claiming that the British had failed to conduct an adequate investigation into the deaths of their family members – all of whom were civilians. The first five individuals had died in separate incidents involving British troops, the sixth, Baha Mousa, died in a military prison whilst in British custody. The European Court of Human Rights held that the UK, through its soldiers engaged in security operations in Basra, exercised authority and control over individuals killed in the course of such security operations – therefore creating a jurisdictional link between the deceased and the UK for the purposes of Article 1 of the Convention, making the UK liable. *Al-Skeini and Others v The United Kingdom* – 55721/07 [2011] ECHR 1093.

12 *Smith v The Ministry of Defence, Ellis v The Ministry of Defence* and *Allbutt v The Ministry of Defence*, [2013] UKSC 41, decided on 19 June 2013. The European Convention on Human Rights is not applicable to India; however, decision of the British Supreme Court relating to negligence claims is of considerable interest. In the British system, the Crown and its agents enjoy what has been called 'combat immunity', which is a shield from liability for negligence in the heat of battle that is predicated on the assumption that it would be unfair, unjust and unreasonable to impose liability for decisions taken or omissions made in the context of active combat. But the claims in these appeals were different: it was alleged that the Ministry of Defence had been negligent in failing to provide equipment that would have prevented the injuries and deaths in question, some of which resulted from 'friendly fire'; the argument was that combat immunity ought not to apply to negligence in procuring defective equipments and pre-battle planning.

Since the last decade or so, the British military has been facing a foe of a different kind. Arising from the conflicts in Iraq and Afghanistan, an unprecedented number of cases have been brought against the MoD in British courts under human rights laws. So far there have been two public inquiries, more than 200 judicial reviews and more than 1,000 damages claims made against the MoD on human rights grounds. The cost of these legal challenges is around £85m, over half of which has gone on inquiries into the killings of Baha Mousa and Al-Sweady by British troops in Iraq in 2003 and 2004. In May 2015, the International Criminal Court, responding to a complaint by Phil Shiner of Public Interest Lawyers, announced that it was launching a preliminary examination of 60 alleged cases of unlawful killing and 170 of mistreatment of Iraqis by British troops.[13] However, the ICC will only exercise its jurisdiction over these matters when a state is unable or unwilling to investigate and prosecute the perpetrators itself.

The Delhi High Court has recently made reference to the case of *Smith v The Ministry of Defence* [2013] in awarding compensation to an Indian Air Force (IAF) pilot. On 2 May 2017, the High Court awarded Rs 55 lakh to a IAF pilot injured in 2005 MiG-21 crash. The petitioner had sustained injuries on 04 April 2005 while bailing out of MiG 21 aircraft. The manner in which the ejection took place, the petitioner suffered physical injuries. Due to the injuries, he was placed into a medical category lower than the one that was required of him to continue as a fighter pilot. This affected his career prospects. The petitioner claimed that the aircraft which he was flying lacked airworthiness, induced by purely human factors, resulted in, violation of his right to life under Article 21 of the Constitution, more specifically, his right to work in a safe environment. The IAF relies on the Hindustan Aeronautics Limited (HAL) for manufacture, assemblage and maintenance of its aircrafts.

The petitioner sued for compensation and an apology from the government. The core basis for the petitioner's claim for compensation was that his right to work in a safe environment, an un-enumerated but integral component of the fundamental right to life and liberty under Article 21 of the Constitution was violated by the respondents (the Union of India and the HAL).

---

13 Soldiers and Human Rights: Lawyers to right of them, lawyers to left of them, *The Economist*, 9 August 2015.

The Delhi High Court exercising its jurisdiction under Article 226 (2) of the Constitution held that the fundamental right to life and liberty under Article 21 of the Constitution of India occupies a transcendental position. It commended, "Over the years, the right to life has been expanded to include within its fold, various facets of what is considered to be the essential facets of a life of dignity; a life that represents the minimum that the State must ensure and seek to protect. Amongst these facets of "life" is the right to work in a safe environment. It denotes that an individual engaged in public employment, shall at the very least, work in an environment that is secure and does not expose him to unnecessary harm."

Referring to the case of *Smith*, the High Court held the Union of India was liable to compensate the petitioner by Rs 5 lakhs for the trauma and agony which he underwent all the while and is also liable for non-disclosure of relevant information relating to an unsafe workplace. The HC held the HAL liable to compensate the petitioner Rs 50 lakhs for exposing him to more than the reasonable and ordinary risk due to the inadequate and less than standard workmanship. The HC further commented, "A soldier or officer's honour and dignity is as much a part of his right to life; it is to be respected just as much, if not more, for the reason that it is offered unhesitatingly and fully in defending the borders of the nation. Unlike "hired guns" they stand guard so that the rest exercise our liberties. Denying them the right to a safe workplace with standard equipment constitutes violation of their right to life and dignity."[14] It is a welcome change in the approach of higher judiciary in India and first decision of its kind. It will open a Pandora Box for similar petitions in the future. We have to wait as the Supreme Court on 24 May 2917 has granted a stay on the order of the Delhi High Court.

Democratic Rights: Members of the armed forces are being deprived of certain basic human rights. The democratic rights and freedoms, which should have been extended to all ranks in the armed forces, are being curtailed in particular in the case of the lower ranks in the name of 'service ethos'. The Minister of Defence responding to a question in Rajya Sabha

---

14 The Court was of the view that because of the nature of their profession, there was an inherent assumption of risk by fighter pilots, however, it does not extend to the acceptance of risk due to negligence in manufacturing aircraft. The Court made it clear that that it was not passing judgement on the airworthiness of the MiG-21, the workhorse of the IAF fighter fleet and an aircraft that has gained a reputation for being dangerously unreliable. *Sanjeet Singh Kalia v Union of India* WP (C) 3414/2013, Delhi High Court, decision pronounced on 02 May 2017.

regarding extending democratic rights and freedom to defence personnel stated: "All democratic rights and freedom are extended to all ranks..... There is no master-servant relationship of colonial days prevalent in the Army (i.e. *sahayak* or batman). The relationship is based on soldierly ethos embedded in 'leader' and 'led' values as comrades in arms."[15] The Defence Minister was perhaps not correct in making the statement as the system of *sahayak* or batsman still prevails in the Indian Army and some of the paramilitary forces.

The *Sahayak* is not a listed trade in the armed forces, but usually young combatants do this task for a few years. Their duties may include acting as a 'runner' to convey orders from the officer to subordinates; maintaining the weapons, uniform and personal equipment of the officer/ JCO; carrying and operating radio sets, maps etc during exercises; and other miscellaneous tasks the officer does not have the time or inclination to do. In fact the list of 'miscellaneous' tasks may include looking after domestic chores, taking care of children, walking dogs and cleaning vehicles. A letter addressed to the editor (*The Hindu*), describes: "I was once admitted to the military hospital for an eye injury. A jawan was in the same ward, though he appeared fit and healthy. I asked him, after a couple of days, why the hospital did not discharge him. He said innocently that although he was fit to be discharged, he had been given the duty of fetching milk for the family of the colonel (eye surgeon) every morning. He would be discharged after the colonel saheb got a *sahayak*."[16]

The Defence Minister in a reply to another question in the Rajya Sabha later stated, "*Sahayaks* are authorized to officers and junior commissioned officers in the Army as per their entitlement, while serving with formations functioning on war establishments.[17] These *syahahks* are combatant soldiers who are entitled to regular pay, allowances and other benefits befitting their rank in the hierarchy. Further, as per the recommendations

---

15 The Minister of Defence Sri A K Antony, responding to a question in Rajya Sabha regarding extending democratic rights and freedom to defence personnel (Question No. 255, answered on 29 August 2012).

16 Available at: http://www.thehindu.com/opinion/letters/sahayak-woes/article4567611. ece, accessed 20 August 2014.

17 The scale of authorization of *sahayak* is as follows: One for every field officer and above, one for every two officers of the rank of captain and below, one for every subedar major, and one for every two junior commissioned officer of the rank of subedar and below. For more details see: Standing Committee on Defence (2008-2009) Report on Stress Management in Armed Forces, October 2008, p. 21.

of the Standing Committee of Defence, the system of *sahayaks* has been taken up for review."[18] The Parliamentary Standing Committee on Defence in a 2010 report had asked the government to abolish the system of employing jawans as *sahayak*, a legacy of the British era.[19] However, the Defence Ministry had tried to justify before the Committee that *sahayaks* help officers in communications and other tasks during operations.[20]

The employment of a combatant in such duties may contribute to increasing stress levels and lowering self-esteem, resulting in incidents of suicide and fratricide. It has been reported that every three days a jawan of the paramilitary forces is lost - not to enemy bullets, but to suicide. Stress, overwork and poor working conditions are some factors leading to a high rate of suicide. Ministry of Home Affairs' data reveals that 536 paramilitary personnel committed suicide in the last five years. The CRPF accounts for nearly 40 per cent of the suicides that occur in all paramilitary forces.[21] The situation is equally frightful in the three defence services, which are losing more soldiers due to suicide than in action.[22] The case of an Army man

---

18 The Minister of Defence Sri A K Antony, responding to a question in the Rajya Sabha regarding the employment of soldiers as '*sahayaks*' in the Army (Question No. 3604, answered on 3 September 2012).

19 Contrary to popular perception, the recommendations of Parliamentary Standing Committees are not binding on the government or the cabinet.

20 On 20 March 2017, the Government while debating issue in Parliament, strongly defended the *sahayak* system in the Army, holding that it provides "essential support" to the officers and junior commissioned officers fulfilling their assigned duties both in tomes of peace and war. The Union Minister of State for Defence further added that "exhaustive instructions" are repeatedly issued to all Army units to stress that *sahayak* should not be employed on menial tasks which are not in conformity with the dignity and self-respect of combatant soldiers. In Parliament, Centre defends 'sahayak' system of the Army, *The Times of India*, March 22, 2017.

21 It has been brought out in a recent report that 80-89 per cent of CRPF personnel remain on deployment at any given time, about 80-85 per cent of them are continuously deployed in 10 militancy/insurgency affected states. Owing to extremely difficult and sub-human working conditions, the CRPF personnel are usually not able to fulfil their social obligations. Long separation from the family deprives the individual of normal married life which results in a biological, emotional and psychological torture. Very few parents prefer their sons and daughters to marry the ward of CRPF personnel. They also undergo trauma in family matters and are unable to ensure good education for their children. 'Posting in conflict zones traumatizing CRPF men', *The Times of India*, 12 January 2015.

22 Replying to a question in the Rajya Sabha (Question No. 1422) on 22 July 2014, the Defence Minister said, "The armed forces lost 597 personnel to suicide in the last five years (498 from the Army, 83 from the Air Force and 16 from the Navy), while 1,349

who spent five days atop a mobile phone tower in the heart of Delhi in August 2012 to highlight his grievances epitomized the crisis. Incidents of 'fragging', or fratricidal killing of fellow soldiers or superiors are also on the rise.[23]

Working Hours: The armed forces do not follow any specific rules on work hours, based on the premise of the permanent availability of military personnel. A research carried out by Georg Nolte and Heike Krieger (2003) shows that in Europe, the average period of work for armed forces personnel is between 36 and 50 hours per week. In Belgium, armed forces personnel generally work 38 hours per week.[24] In Denmark, working hours follow those of other civil servants with modifications for the effectiveness of the armed forces. For instance, it is normally required in Denmark to grant employees 11 hours of free time within each 24-hour period. Since military exercises sometimes last for several days, and it is not possible to comply with this provision, compensation is granted. In Italy, the regular working time is 36 hours per week. Overtime compensation can be provided in money or in time. In some European countries, the organization of working time is still based on the principle of the permanent availability of soldiers. This is true of France, for example, where a soldier can be requested to be on duty at all times in accordance with Article 12 of the General Statute on Military Personnel. Recently, however, the French Ministry of Defence adopted a system of compensation for overtime for armed forces personnel. On the basis of this regulation, armed forces personnel were granted 15 extra days of annual leave, in addition to the existing 60 days.[25] The UK follows the approach that it is necessary for a professional armed forces to

officers quit the Army during the same period. The highest number of suicides took place in the Army in 2010 when 116 troops committed suicide."

23 The Government in response to a question in Rajya Sabha intimated that the armed forces continue to lose over 100 personnel in stress-related deaths in form of suicides and fratricide every year. There have been 11 cases of fratricide since 2014. In February 2014, a soldier of Rashtriya Rifles in J&K shot dead five of his colleagues while they were asleep and then killed himself. The Stress in Killing: Suicides, fragging claim over 100 a year, *The Times of India*, New Delhi, August 9, 2017.

24 In Belgium, members of the armed forces have a right to annual holidays and holiday allowances. Unlike India, the regulations for the soldiers in this regard do not differ much from the other civil servants. Argent Pierre d', 'Military Law in Belgium', in Nolte George (ed.). 2003. *European Military Law Systems*, Berlin: De Gruyter Recht, p. 183-232.

25 For more details see: Nolte George (ed.). 2003. *European Military Law Systems*, Berlin: De Gruyter Recht, p. 101-103.

make service conditions attractive, since the very existence of the military depends on the recruitment.

Restrictions on the exercise and enjoyment of social and economic rights by armed forces personnel need to be specific. General restrictions should be avoided. The Ministries of Defence and Home Affairs should take all possible measures to ensure that provisions related to working conditions are implemented in accordance with national law and international obligations. If armed forces personnel are required to work for longer than the legally defined hours, they must be monetarily compensated.

Poor Working and Living Conditions: After 68 years of Independence, military establishments still do not provide housing for all ranks. It may take two years or more before a person below the rank of officer is allotted family accommodation in a military station. By that time he has to be ready for the next posting. Security experts say that jawans posted far away from their native places are under tremendous stress due to the lack of contact with their families. Denial of leave adds to the stress.

Several researches have revealed that stress, overwork and poor working conditions are some of the major factors responsible for the high attrition rate and suicides among armed forces personnel. Counter insurgency operations often lead to stress-related anxiety and depression and in extreme cases, it may lead to suicide. The other reasons for the high suicide rate are domestic, and financial problems.

The high attrition rate in the paramilitary forces has become a cause for worry. This impelled the government to commission a study by IIM-Ahmedabad in 2012. The study cited continuous posting in difficult areas, long working hours, sleep deprivation, denial of leave, lack of healthcare facilities, delay in promotions and pay parity as causes of stress.[26] However, the trend is continuing. In 2016-17 the number of personnel opting for voluntary retirement from service (VRS) in central paramilitary forces has gone to around 450 per cent as compared to previous year.[27] While personal and domestic reasons are stated in applications for VRS; career stagnation, lack of pay parity and tough working conditions play important part in voluntary retirement. A CRPF man recounts experiences of serving in

---

26 For more details see: Dixit K C, *Addressing Stress-Related Issues in Army*, IDSA Occasional Paper No 17, Institute for Defence Studies and Analyses, New Delhi, 2011.

27 The total numbers of voluntary retirement from the service (VRS) in 2016-17 were 9,065; whereas in 2015-16 figure was only 2,105.

Chhattisgarh: "We face two enemies, the 'double M' of Maoists and malaria. You are either going to die of a bullet or of a mosquito bite. The healthcare facilities are poor and at times we have to spend out of our own pocket for treatment that too after travelling great distances in treacherous terrains."[28] Besides, there are vast difference between the promotion, entitlement of leave, ration and financial incentives of members of the defence forces and those of the paramilitary forces. This causes disgruntlement, as in a given situation both the forces, defence and paramilitary, might be employed in a similar task.

Archaic Legal System: The legal system which governs the armed forces contains archaic provisions which were drafted by the colonial masters to serve their purpose. These provisions are harsh and have not been updated keeping in view the progressive development in the Indian penal system and the norms of international human rights. For instance, it was only in 1996, the Supreme Court of India held[29] that a provision similar to the Criminal Procedure Code 1973 Section 428 should be incorporated in the Border Security Force Act 1968 so as to safeguard the interests of under-trials and entitled them to the benefit of set-off of the period of detention already undergone during the process of trial. The Border Security Force Act 1968 was amended by the Amendment Act 2000. Incidentally, this provision was incorporated in the Army Act 1950 only in 1993 (section 169-A), while the Air Force Act 1950 is yet to see this change. Some other provisions which need modernization are summary court martial, legal aid and appellate rights.

Summary Court Martial: In the Army, the Assam Rifles and the Border Security Force (BSF) the commanding officers or commandants are empowered to try an accused up to the rank of havildar by a summary court martial (SCM). The commanding officer alone constitutes the court, and acts as judge and prosecutor. The proceedings of a summary court-martial are attended by two other persons, who may be officers or junior commissioned officers. They are not supposed to take any part in the

---

28 Heavy attrition, suicides bleed paramilitary forces, *Times of India*, 22 October 2012. Also see: Home Ministry promises action as figures show a jawan commits suicide every three days over 'stress and poor working conditions', *Mail Online India*, 20 June 2013, available at: http://www.dailymail.co.uk/indiahome/indianews/article-2345351/Jawan-suicides-Home-Ministry-promises-action-figures-death-days-stress-poor-working-conditions.html, accessed 20 August 2014.

29 *Union of India v. Anand Singh Bisht* (1996) 10 SCC 153.

proceedings and have no right to vote in determining either the findings or the sentence. The trial procedure is summary in nature and the accused has no right to defend himself through any military or civilian counsel. There is no need for a detailed judgment or even a reasoned decision in these trials. An accused cannot claim that he should be governed by the principles of natural justice which apply to a civil servant under Article 311 of the Constitution. An SCM may award a sentence of up to one year's imprisonment and dismissal from service. There is no right to appeal against the decision of the court in the Assam Rifles and the BSF. In the case of the Army, the convicted person has the right to approach the Armed Forces Tribunal, constituted under the Act of 2007 if his punishment is of dismissal or exceeds imprisonment for more than three months.

Trials held under the SCM have been criticized by the high courts and the Supreme Court for awarding excessive and harsh punishments, denying procedural rights guaranteed under Article 14 of the Constitution, lack of evidence, arbitrariness, lack of justice, and non-compliance with the rules. The Supreme Court has recently criticized the rampant abuse of recourse to SCM by the military authorities.[30] The Court referred to the recommendations of the Committee of Experts appointed by the Defence Minister,[31] and held: "that the provision of SCM should be used sparingly and exceptionally and preferably only in operational areas where resort to a regular trial is not practicable or when summary/ administrative action would not meet the requirements of discipline. Further, SCM is an exception and not the rule and was not even originally meant to be a peace-time provision or regular recourse. In the times to come, the desirability of even having such a provision on the statute book may be examined with the suitability of a replacement by a more robust system meeting the aspirations of judiciousness and Constitutional norms. SCM ....may not be treated as a routine recourse when other effective tools of enforcing discipline are available."

Such an arbitrary system of justice is violative of Article 14 of the International Covenant on Civil and Political Rights (ICCPR) and is not followed in any other democratic country. There is an urgent need to abolish this arbitrary system of trial.

---

30 *Union of India v. Vishav Priya Singh*, Civil Appeal No. 8360 of 2010, decided on 05 July 2016.

31 The Committee of Expert was appointed by the Minister of Defence. The Committee headed by Lt Gen Mukesh Sabharwal (Retd) submitted its 255 page report in 2015.

Legal aid: Legal aid is the professional legal assistance given either free or for a nominal sum to indigent persons in need of such help. It is a modern concept derived from the 'rule of law'. The rule of law and equality before law are fundamental principles of a democracy. Developed countries, like the USA, UK, Australia and Canada have adopted schemes for legal aid to armed forces personnel, seeing it as an essential part of the democratic system. In the US, a military member suspected of an offence must be informed of his or her right of legal aid before being questioned.[32] Uniform Code of Military Justice 1950, Article 31(b) provides: "No person subject to this chapter may interrogate, or request any statement from an accused or a person suspected of an offence without first informing him of the nature of the accusation and advising him that he does not have to make any statement regarding the offence of which he is accused or suspected and that any statement made by him may be used as evidence against him in a trial by court-martial." Thus, the military member has the right to ask for an attorney and can choose not to make a statement to investigators. These rights are binding on both commanders and military police.

In India, legal aid has been prescribed as an instrument for achieving equality before the law as provided under Article 14 of the Constitution. Legal aid is a form of State assistance to ensure equality before the law, the most fundamental of the Fundamental Rights guaranteed under the Indian Constitution.[33] However, in the armed forces, the rights of an accused to effective legal aid are restricted. A suspect does not have the right to remain silent, or to consult a lawyer at the time of arrest and pre-trial confinement. He can be interrogated by the department police or any other authority. Even when evidence is recorded against him, he is not entitled to any legal help. An accused has the right to engage a civilian counsel at his own

---

32 Uniform Code of Military Justice 1950, Article 31(b) provides: "No person subject to this chapter may interrogate, or request any statement from an accused or a person suspected of an offence without first informing him of the nature of the accusation and advising him that he does not have to make any statement regarding the offence of which he is accused or suspected and that any statement made by him may be used as evidence against him in a trial by court-martial. Thus, the military member has the right to ask for an attorney and can choose not to make a statement to investigators.

33 Article 39A of the Constitution provides: "The State shall....., in particular, provide free legal aid, by suitable legislation or schemes or in any other way, to ensure that opportunities for securing justice are not denied to any citizen by reasons of economic or other disabilities."

expense in a general or district court-martial.[34] However, the convening authority may deny the services of a civilian counsel if he feels that it is not expedient to allow the appearance of such a counsel. If an accused is charged with an offence punishable with death, he is entitled to a defence counsel at State expense. The maximum amount payable to the counsel is Rs 500 for each day of appearance.[35] This amount is, however, grossly inadequate for hiring the services of a counsel where an accused is charged with a serious offence.

The purpose of the right to defence has four important aspects:

(i) Technical—the counsel for the defence provides the accused with the technical skills necessary to enable him to make full use of rights afforded by criminal procedure law, including the fundamental rights guaranteed by the constitution. The principle of 'equality' enshrined in the constitution plays an important role here.

(ii) Psychological—once an individual is accused of a criminal act, he becomes emotionally involved in the dispute. He needs the assistance of a reasonable and well controlled person for rational analysis and insight into the case. It is necessary that the person be qualified and experienced to give psychological support to the client.

(iii) Humanitarian—involvement in criminal proceedings is a source of enormous stress. The feeling of forlornness and desperation are particularly strong when the accused is arrested and detained. The assistance of a counsel serves the humanitarian aim of providing the defendant with a human companion to lessen the feeling that he has been abandoned by everyone and is to be dealt with by a hostile system.

---

34 If an accused does not have financial resources, he may have to depend upon the services of a defending officer (a serving officer qualified in the law) provided by the convening authority. An accused may not have any confidence in the quality of legal aid being provided by a serving officer, who remains under command influence. Re *Estrella v Uruguay* (1983) (74/180), the Human Rights Committee held that the military court had violated the defendant's right to choose counsel by limiting him to a choice between two appointed attorneys.

35 Regulations for the Army 1987, Vol. I, Para 479(c).

(iv)   Structural—the right to defend ensures that the accused has an active role in the proceedings, the role of a subject rather than an object. The right of an accused to defend himself with the assistance of counsel enables the accused to influence the course of the proceedings. It also ensures the personal dignity of the accused.[36]

Appellate Rights: The first landmark judicial intervention in the military legal system in India occurred in 1982, when the Supreme Court, in *Lt Col PPS Bedi's* case, criticized the military justice system, calling it archaic and antiquated. The Court also pointed out a glaring deficiency in the Army Act, *viz* the absence of the remedy of appeal against the orders of courts-martial. In addition, the court called attention to the changes effected in the military justice systems in the UK and the US, and observed that Parliament should pass similar legislation, consistent with the changed value system. The judgement stirred a debate on the need for an appellate court for the armed forces. The three services were, however, not in agreement on the matter. Buckling under pressure, the Ministry of Defence proposed the setting up of an armed forces tribunal and on 20 December 2005, the government introduced the Armed Forces Tribunal Bill in Parliament. The Bill was referred to the Parliamentary Standing Committee on Defence for comments and report. Finally, after a prolonged gap of 25 years since the Supreme Court's decision in *PPS Bedi's* case, Parliament passed the Armed Forces Tribunal Act, 2007. The Tribunal has original jurisdiction over service matters and appellate jurisdiction against the order, finding or sentence of a court-martial.

Appeal proceedings tend to become more technical than the proceedings at the first instance. The provisions governing appeal under the Armed Forces Tribunal Act are strict, particularly with regard to the requirement of time limit to be respected. Thus, in such proceedings there is an even greater need, in the interest of justice, for the accused to be assisted by a qualified counsel. As the Armed Forces Tribunal has the power to increase the severity of a sentence awarded by the court-martial,

---

36 Swart Bert (ed.). 2011. The Legacy of International Criminal Tribunal for the Former Yugoslavia, Oxford: Oxford University Press, p. 184. Also see: Trechsel Stefan. 2005. *Human Rights in Criminal Proceedings*, Oxford: Oxford University Press, p. 244-248; Zapalla Salvatore. 2003. *Human Rights in International Criminal Proceedings*, Oxford: Oxford University Press.

the accused must be provided with the help of a counsel for approaching the Tribunal.

The personnel of the paramilitary forces have no such forum of appeal. Dissatisfied with the system, a large number of paramilitary force personnel have approached the higher courts for the redressal of their grievances, which demonstrates a gradual erosion of faith in the system of governance. The large number of cases that have come up before the superior civil courts in recent years show that the appellate system falls short of the aspirations of the men in the paramilitary forces. Instead of creating an independent tribunal for the central police and paramilitary forces (CPFs), the government is trying to amend the Central Administrative Tribunal Act, 1985 so as to bring matters relating the CPFs under the purview of the Central Administrative Tribunal.[37] As and when such a forum of appeal is created for the paramilitary forces, the government must ensure that it has the power of 'civil contempt', a shortcoming being faced by the Armed Forces Tribunal.

Grievance Redressal System: The military and paramilitary personnel have the right to make complaints seeking the redress of their grievances.[38] The Regulations of various forces provide different procedures for the processing of complaints.[39] The senior commanders and even the Defence Ministers have claimed that the armed forces have a time-tested, well established and transparent mechanism to address complaints.[40] If the grievance redressal system in the armed forces was so effective and

---

37 The Rajya Sabha Question No. 513, answered on 13 August 2014.

38 Section 26 of the Army Act 1950, provides that any person below the officer rank (PBOR) who deems himself wronged by any superior or other officer may complain to the commanding officer (CO) for the redress of his grievance. When the officer complained against is the officer to whom the complaint should be preferred, the aggrieved person may complain to the officer who is next in superiority to such officer. Section 27 of the Act provides that any officer who deems himself wronged by his CO or any superior officer, and who on due application made to his CO does not receive the redress to which he considers himself entitled, may complain to the Central Government. Redress applications by the officers are to be addressed to the Central Government and by the PBORs to the Chief of the Army Staff (COAS). Similar provisions are contained in laws relating to the air force, the navy and the central paramilitary/armed police forces.

39 The Regulations for the Army, Volume I, 1987, para 364 (as amended).

40 'Time tested mechanisms are in place for redressal of grievances of service personnel'; Minister of Defence, Shri Arun Jaitley in a written reply to Question No. 672 in Rajya Sabha, answered on 15 July 2014. For more details on the subject see: The Parliamentary Standing Committee on Defence (2005-2006) Tenth Report dated 25 May 2006.

time tested, as claimed, the Government would not have established the benches of the Armed Forces Tribunal in 2009. The Minister of State for Home Affairs has recently claimed that every paramilitary force has a proper grievance redressal mechanism. In addition, Standing Committees against any sexual harassment and other grievances of women personnel have also been established under the chairpersonship of a lady officer.[41]

The problem with grievance redressal in the armed forces is the unfair processing of a complaint, which damages the effectiveness of a statutory right.[42] During the processing of a complaint, the complainant is not informed about the comments of the section commander and intermediate authorities on his grievance.[43] Undue delays in the processing

---

41 To address the personal as well as official problem/service complaints of the members of the paramilitary forces personnel, each Force has a proper grievance redressal mechanism in place at Battalion, Range, Sector, Frontier, Zone & Directorate level. Nodal officers have been earmarked at each level for this purpose and the applicants are apprised about the factual position/facts with reference to their grievances/complaints within stipulated time. For each Force, the Director General of the Force concerned is the highest authority for redressal of the grievances. If an individual is not satisfied with the reply of the Nodal Officer or does not get any reply, he/she is free to appear before the Director General in person for redressal of his/her grievance(s) with the approval of his/her Head of office. Standing Committees against any sexual harassment and other grievances of women personnel have also been established in the Forces. The Minister of State Home Affairs informed the Rajya Sabha in reply to Question No. 513 (answered on 13 August 2014) regarding "Establishing tribunals for redressal of grievances in paramilitary forces".

42 For instance, some of the common errors in investigations in the cases of sexual harassment could be: (i) Not identifying discrimination because of a lack of awareness of the relevant human rights principles before starting the investigation. For example, an investigation may wrongly conclude that discrimination did not occur because there was no intention. (ii) Not being impartial or having pre-conceived ideas about what the outcome of the investigation will be. (iii) Discounting the perspective of the person who has raised the allegations because of an assumption that they must be lying, despite the absence of a reasonable basis for such an assumption. (iv) Relying on irrelevant factors to undermine the credibility of the person who has raised the allegations. For example: taking into account the past sexual history of a woman who has alleged sexual harassment. (v) Being overly sympathetic to the feelings of "victimization" and "impact on reputation" raised by the person accused of discriminatory conduct. This may lead to a failure to appropriately address discriminatory conduct. (vi) Excluding the person who has raised the allegations. (vii) Concluding that there was no sexual harassment because a person was a willing participant or had consented to sexual activity in the past.

43 In the case of Union of India v. Maj Gen Arun Roye (2008), the Calcutta High Court opined: "...non-furnishing of comments of the intermediate authorities to the complainant who lodged the statutory complaint is tantamount to violation of the principles of natural justice." The Court further stated; "This is because the comments that are furnished by the intermediate authorities to the Central Government are essential to the complainant,

and disposal of complaints are another source of problem. Often, the delay is justified under the pretext that the chain of command is engaged in making investigations. There is also no fixed time-frame for the Central Government to give its final decision in the matter. There have been cases where the final decision on a grievance has been delayed until the complainant retires. The delay in the finalization of a complaint frustrates the very purpose of the system.[44]

All levels of the hierarchy in the armed forces are entitled to seek legal advice on a complaint. However, the aggrieved person is not provided any legal help for preferring his complaint. The persons objected to may participate in disposing of the objection.[45] If the grievance is against the commander or higher authorities, the affected individual or his family may also face social seclusion and harassment. There have been allegations that those lodging complaints against their superiors have been transferred to far-flung places, causing harassment to them and their family members. Further, the decision on an application is not required to be a "reasoned" order and it could be conveyed in a brief sentence, such as: "Your application has been rejected by the competent authority as being devoid of merit." Such rejection orders reinforce the doubt that complaints are treated arbitrarily and against the principles of natural justice.

The Way Ahead

The armed forces cannot stay cocooned since the personnel they recruit belong to and interact with the wider society, which has undergone significant change. An individual joining the armed forces, particularly in the ranks has a hard life. As the armed forces constitute the most powerful weapon of the executive, their internal management and other functional systems are required to be efficient, modern and in tune with the times. The following issues must be considered by the government to ensure

---

so as to enable that person to know what has been commented against him/her by the said military authority while forwarding the complaint to the Government."

44 The Delhi High Court in the case of *AVM MS Brar v. Union of India* CWP 2600/2002 decided in July 2002 has observed that while disposing of representation by the Air Force authorities, the petitioner has been deprived of his valuable rights, as he was not given a reasonable opportunity of hearing. The decision on the application for extension of service was given after the retirement of the petitioner. The Court imposed a penalty of Rs 50,000 on the Union of India.

45 The Supreme Court in the case of *Lt Col PPS Bedi v. Union of India* AIR 1982 SC 1413 has observed that such practice leads to bias.

that the members of the armed forces enjoy the basic human rights and fundamental freedoms in the context of their service. A soldier whose human rights are protected by the State is likely to be more disciplined and operationally effective,[46] and also less likely to violate the human rights of others.

The Right to Life: Article 21 of the Constitution of India guarantees "right to live with human dignity".[47] Members of the armed forces also have the right to life and should not be exposed to situations where their lives would be put at risk without a clear and legitimate purpose or in circumstances where the threat to life has been disregarded. Every suspicious death or alleged violation of the right to life of a member of the armed forces should be investigated by an independent and effective inquiry.

Freedom from Torture, Inhuman or Degrading Treatment or Punishment: The government must take effective measures to ensure that the members of the armed forces are not subjected to torture, inhuman or degrading treatment or punishment. In case any member makes a complaint of such a treatment or punishment, the highest authority in the respective organization must ensure investigation of the matter by an independent and effective official. The respective military/paramilitary organization must take measures to encourage the reporting of acts of torture or ill-treatment within the forces and to protect from retaliation those reporting such acts. Persons under detention should be treated humanely ensuring respect for the inherent dignity of all human beings. Members of the armed forces should not be used to perform tasks incompatible with their assignment to national defence and security duties, with the exception of emergency and civil assistance carried out in accordance with the law.

Procedural Guarantees and Fairness: Conduct which constitutes a threat to discipline, good order, safety or security has been defined as offence in the codes of the armed forces.[48] Discipline should be balanced by fairness

---

46 See: Bal Suryakant, The Human Element in Military Effectiveness: A Systems Approach, *Journal of Defence Studies*, Vol. 5, No. 1, January 2011, p. 134-146.

47 The guarantee by Article 21 is available to every person and even the State has no authority to violate that right. *PUCL v. State of Maharashtra*, Criminal Appeal No. 1255 of 1999, decided by the Supreme Court on 23 September 2014.

48 The three armed forces of India, i.e., the army, the navy and the air force are governed by the Army Act 1950, the Navy Act 1957 and the Air Force Act 1950 respectively. They are based on the British Indian Army Act of 1911. The paramilitary forces like the Assam Rifles, the Central Reserve Police Force and the Border Security Force are governed by

and procedural guarantees. Allegations of infringement of disciplinary rules by a member of the armed forces should be reported promptly to the competent authority, which should investigate it without undue delay. On the other hand, anyone who is arrested or detained should be informed promptly of the reasons for his arrest or detention, the charges against him, and his procedural rights. The severity of the punishment imposed by the authorities or disciplinary tribunal should be proportionate to the offence.

The Right to a Fair Trial: Every individual must have the right to a fair hearing which should include adequate time to prepare his defence, communication with the counsel of his choosing, defending himself in person or through the counsel and free legal assistance, if he is unable to procure legal assistance due to the pecuniary reasons. An accused must have the chance to examine the witnesses against him and obtain the attendance of witnesses on his behalf and must not be compelled to testify against himself or to confess his guilt. The affected person should also be given the opportunity to appeal to a higher and independent body.[49]

Grievance Redressal Mechanism: The armed forces must have an effective grievance redressal mechanism and must ensure a reasoned decision on every petition. The Supreme Court has held that failure to give reasons amounts to denial of justice.[50] A decision is arbitrary if it is not based on reasons and as such amounts to an interference with the principles of justice. There must also be a uniform policy framework and timeframe for the redress of grievances. The final order must be made within three months of submission of a grievance. Coercive provision contained in the regulations needs deletion.[51]

---

the Assam Rifles Act 2006, the Central Reserve Police Force Act 1949 and the Border Security Force Act 1968 as amended in 2000, and the rules made under these Acts. The laws governing the Assam Rifles, the Central Reserve Police Force and the Border Security Force are also obsolete and based on the Indian Army Act 1950.

49 The procedural guarantees are contained in Article 14 of the International Covenant on Civil and Political Rights, 1966. The Government of India has signed and ratified this Covenant.

50 The Supreme Court held, "reasons are live links between the minds of the decision taker to the controversy in question and the decision or conclusion arrived at. Reasons substitute subjectivity with objectivity." *Arunima Baruah v. Union of India* (2007) 6 SCC 1201.

51 The Regulations for the Army (Paragraph 364. 8) states that if a complainant has made an accusation in the grievance application, he/she is required to render a certificate, "I undertake that any false statement or false accusation made by me in this complaint

Compensation: Those who sustain injuries in service must be provided with adequate healthcare facilities; while the families of those who are killed must be liberally compensated. An appropriate compensation scheme should be available to persons leaving the armed forces due to injuries or disability as a result of service. The compensation schemes must be similar for members of the military and paramilitary forces serving in similar situations. Those leaving the armed forces should be provided with appropriate benefit packages and training for rehabilitation in civilian life. The existing compensation provided to the families of the armed forces personnel by the central and state governments is woefully inadequate.[52]

---

will render me liable for disciplinary action." In cases of the use of abusive language, misbehaviour and sexual harassment, which may take place in private, it may not be possible for a victim to support his/her accusation with any documentary proof or witness. Then the victim would be liable to disciplinary action based on the certificate rendered with his/her petition. The punishment for false accusation under Section 56 of the Army Act is imprisonment up to five years. This often deters the victim from seeking redress and makes the statutory right meaningless.

52 The Central Government pays an ex-gratia to the next of kin of the personnel of armed forces killed in action, as shown in the following table:

S. No.	Circumstances	Ex-gratia amount in Rs
1	Death occurring due to accidents in the course of the performance of duties	25 lakh
2	Death in the course of performance of duties attribute to acts of violence by terrorists, anti-social elements etc.	25 lakh
3	Death occurring in border skirmishes and action against militants, terrorists, extremists and sea pirates	35 lakh
4	Death occurring while on duty in the specified high altitude, inaccessible border posts, on account of natural disasters, extreme weather conditions	35 lakh
5	Death occurring during enemy action in war or war-like engagements, which are specifically notified by the Ministry of Defence, and death occurring during evacuation of Indian nationals from a war-torn zone in a foreign country	45 lakh

Besides, the State Governments have their own policies for the payment of ex-gratia which varies from Rs 2.5 to 20.0 lakhs. It is strongly felt that the recommended amount of ex-gratia compensation is too meagre in the present circumstances; besides there is very little difference between categories 2 to 5. Incidentally, in its decision of 24 February 2016, the Delhi government clarified that the next of kin of deceased Delhi police personnel would continue to be eligible to receive Rs 1 crore as ex-gratia. The Central Government must enhance the amount of ex-gratia compensation to 1.2 crore.

In addition, potential recruits for the armed forces should be provided with full and detailed information about all aspects of recruitment, the induction process and the specific nature of the commitments involved. In the case of recruits who are under the age of 18, this information should also be provided to their parents or legal guardians. Accommodation provided for members of the armed forces and their families should meet the basic requirements of health and hygiene. The members of the armed forces should receive training to heighten their awareness of human rights, including their own human rights. They should be informed that they have a duty to object to a manifestly unlawful order given by their superiors amounting to a war crime or torture.

6

Domestic Deployment in Other Countries

There is an ongoing debate on using the armed forces in the fight against militancy and terrorism. The core issue is whether a State can deploy its armed forces against militants in internal conflicts, and if so, whether and to what extent they should be given the power to shoot to kill.[1] The most important right that any government owes its citizens is the right to personal safety, i.e., the right to live, work and move about peaceably, secure in one's person and property. Militants have threatened this right and caused serious damage to the welfare of the people as well as the security of nations. The military cannot sit idle while government property is being destroyed and innocent citizens are being killed. International law not only permits but requires States to protect their citizens, without discrimination, by responding effectively to security threats. The use of lethal force to prevent a terrorist attack similar to that which occurred on September 11 poses significant challenges for the military and the police, particularly in relation to balancing necessity against the right to life. The practice of employment of the armed forces for internal security duties in Australia, Canada, Germany, Japan, the UK, and the USA are discussed in this Chapter.

---

1   All armed forces have both domestic and international responsibilities. As a general rule, the less democratically and economically developed a State, the more these responsibilities and capabilities focus on domestic control and the greater the political role and share of defense budgets that go to armies rather than navies and air forces. As countries mature both economically and politically, maintaining domestic order through the use or threat of force usually declines, while concern over the preservation of one's territory, borders, and trade routes increases. Sheldon W. Simon, Asian Armed Forces: Internal and External Tasks and Capabilities, *The NBR Analysis Series*, Vol. 11, No. 1, May 2000, p. 1-28.

Australia

Under the Australian federal system, the maintenance of law and order is primarily the responsibility of the States. The Constitution makes provision for Commonwealth assistance to the States in the maintenance of law and order in limited circumstances. The term 'aid to the civil power, has been defined as the use of members of the Defence Force (i) to execute and maintain the Constitution and the laws of the Commonwealth; (ii) to protect a Commonwealth interest; and (iii) on the application of the Executive Government of the State, to protect the State against domestic violence.[2] On a number of occasions and for a variety of reasons, the Australian Defence Forces (ADF) have rendered assistance to the civil authorities. These includes extending technical help to police force in connection with minor matters beyond the expertise of the police, providing aircraft and crew for ceremonial flying on festive occasions and assisting the police in maintaining law and order.

Section 119 of the Australian Constitution provides: "The Commonwealth shall protect every State against invasion and, on the application of the Executive Government of the State, against domestic violence." For the application of the provisions of Section 119, it is necessary for a state of 'domestic violence' to exist and for the Common Wealth to receive a request for assistance from the state government. Section 119 does not authorize unilateral action by the Commonwealth. The need for this provision is linked with the fact that the states are unable to raise a military force themselves.[3]

On several occasions, the Commonwealth has refused assistance sought by the states under Section 119 on the basis of its own assessment of the presence of situations of domestic violence. Although it has been argued that the Commonwealth is bound to give assistance sought under Section 119(8), practice suggests that the Commonwealth has the right to

---

2   Ewing Brigadier M. J., Military Aid to the Civil Power, *Defence Force Journal*, No. 57, March/April 1986, p 21-30.

3   At Federation in 1901, the military power was handed over to the Commonwealth under Section 51 (xxxi) of the Constitution, the colonial defence forces were transferred to the Commonwealth by Section 69, and the states were forbidden to raise military or naval forces without the consent of the Commonwealth Parliament under Section 114. Residual authority over domestic law and order remained in the hands of the states and their police force. Head Michael and Scott Mann. 2009. *Domestic Deployment of the Armed Forces: Military Powers, Law and Human Rights*, USA: Ashgate, p. 126.

make its own assessment in relation to the degree of unrest and that the mere allegation of unrest by a state will not invoke the section.

Bowral Call-out of 1978

In general, the invoking of 'military aid to the civil power' has been a relatively rare event in Australia, confined in the most part of peaceful use in national emergencies, such as floods, cyclones and earthquakes. Only major mobilization of the defence forces in urban areas occurred in February 1978, when a bomb exploded outside the Hilton Hotel in Sydney, killing three people, two garbage collectors and a police officer. Several others were seriously injured in the incident.[4] The hotel was host to the Commonwealth Heads of Government Regional Meeting (CHOGRM). The blast set off a security scare which ultimately saw an official call-out of the army by the Governor-General.[5] It involved the deployment of nearly 2000 heavily armed troops of the ADF, some with bayonets fixed, accompanied by armoured personnel carriers and helicopters. Units took position along a major highway on Sydney's outskirts. For three days, the ADF troops patrolled the Southern Highlands towns near the site of a scheduled CHOGRM summit. They also safeguarded rail and road links between Bowral and Sydney. Helicopter support was provided by the Royal Australian Air Force (RAAF). The call-out was clearly not an exercise of Section 119 of the Constitution because there was no application by the state.

Following the precedent established by the post-Hilton call-out, the Cabinet Intelligence and Security Committee formally decided in September 1978 to adopt a policy of deploying the ADF whenever 'appropriate' in response to alleged terrorist attacks. However, the decision

---

4   During rescue and recovery, the NSW Police requested assistance from the Army Bomb Disposal Unit. Concurrently, Prime Minister Fraser and the Cabinet agreed that armed troops were to be deployed in NSW; without a formal request but with the concurrence of Premier Wran. The Governor-General, in his capacity as Commander-in-Chief, issued an order calling out the ADF for the purposes of 'safeguarding the national and international interests of the Commonwealth of Australia' as well as 'giving effect to the obligations of the Commonwealth of Australia in relation to the protection of internationally protected persons'. Commonwealth, Defence Legislation Amendment (Aid to Civil Authorities) Bill 2000 (Cth), Bills Digest No 13 2000-01 (2000).

5   The order for call out was made on 13 February 1978 (Commonwealth of Australia Gazette No S 30, 14 February 1978) and revoked on 20 February 1978 (Commonwealth of Australia Gazette No S 33, 20 February 1978).

that the ADF would be authorized to use force in domestic deployment was never made public, nor was there any public debate.[6]

In the years following the Hilton attck, the Commonwealth has deployed the ADF several times to protect national or Commonwealth interests. For instance, in 1983, the RAAF were requested by the federal government to undertake photographic sorties over southwest Tasmania with the intention of establishing and obtaining evidence relating to work being undertaken by the Tasmanian Government. In 1989, Prime Minister Hawke employed the services of the RAAF again during the airline pilot strike of that year. In addition, the Prime Minister used Australian military personnel to guard the Nurrungar military base.[7]

After the terrorist attack of September 2001, the perspective of Australian society on the involvement of the military in internal disturbances has changed. A large number of military personnel were deployed for the 2000 Sydney Olympics, the 2003 Rugby World Cup and the 2006 Malbourne Commonwealth Games. The Australian Royal Navy was dispatched to repel asylum seekers, with power to use lethal force on boats and transport their passengers to remote islands. The ADF has participated in anti-terrorist exercises in urban areas along with police and intelligence officials. The ADF was used during the US President's visit to Australia in 2003.[8] Apart from minor differences, the deployment of the ADF in these operations was supported by major political parties in Australia.

Domestic Deployment Law

Australia has made an attempt to establish a statutory code governing the domestic deployment of the armed forces. The first set of legislation was introduced in 2000.[9] This was extended in 2006, giving the Federal

---

6   It was later revealed in a partial release of documents by the National Archives of Australia in 2009. For more details see: Head Michael and Scott Mann. 2009. *Domestic Deployment of the Armed Forces: Military Powers, Law and Human Rights*, USA: Ashgate, p. 141-142.

7   Laing Norman Charles, Call-out the Guards – Why Australia Should no Longer fear the deployment of Australian Troops on Home Soil, *UNSW Law Journal,* Volume 28 (2), 2005, p. 507-522.

8   Head Michael and Scott Mann. 2009. *Domestic Deployment of the Armed Forces: Military Powers, Law and Human Rights*, USA: Ashgate, p. 126.

9   The Defence Legislation Amendment (Aid to the Civil Authorities) Bill 2000 (Cth) was introduced to provide the statutory mechanism that would enable the ADF to

government and the chief of the ADF explicit peacetime powers to call out troops if 'domestic violence is occurring or is likely to occur' that 'would be likely to affect Commonwealth interests' or if the protection of a state or territory is necessary. Both sets of legislations were justified as urgent response to potential threats of terrorism during the 2000 Sydney Olympics and the 2006 Melbourne Commonwealth Games. Though no acts of violence occurred at those events, the laws have remained and their language goes beyond countering terrorism.

The original call-out legislation of 2000 limited the deployment of the ADF to where the government felt that a danger of 'domestic violence' existed which required the protection of 'Commonwealth interests' or the protection of a state or territory where the sate or territory could not, or was unlikely to be able to, protect itself.[10] However, the term 'domestic violence' was not defined anywhere in the legislations. The term was derived from American usages and meant to relate to intense political, industrial or social crises that endangered the very existence of the State. Section 4, Article IV of the US Constitution specifies that the United States shall protect each state, on the application of its legislature, against 'domestic violence'. The amendment to the Defence Act in 2006 enhanced the scope of deployment of the army, the air force and the navy routinely to deal with incidents that fall short of insurrections, including any alleged act or danger of terrorism, and threats to physical property, judged by the ministers to be 'critical infrastructure.[11] The counter-terrorism laws passed in Australia since 2001 define terrorism broadly.[12]

---

be called out. The insertion of Part IIIAAA was specifically aimed at dealing with the utilization of the defence force to protect the interests of the Commonwealth, the states and self-governing territories, against domestic violence. Part IIIAAA provides that ADF personnel acquire a number of powers such as the power to search and recapture buildings and people, free hostages and seize dangerous articles such as weapons and ordnance.

10 The Defence Act 1903 (Cth), sections 51A, 51B and 51C.

11 According to the Explanatory Memorandum of the Defence Act 1903 (Cth) sections 51CB, the amended Act would apply to 'mobile terrorist incident', allowing for military mobilization under the broad banner of combating terrorist acts.

12 According to Criminal Code 1995 (Cth) 100.1: A 'terrorist act' includes anything done 'with the intention of advancing a political, religious or ideological cause' and with the intention of 'coercing, or influencing by intimidation' any government (including a foreign government) or 'intimidating the public or a section of the public', if the act causes death, serious harm to a person, serious damage to property, serious risk

The Defence Act, Section 51

The operation of Section 119 of the Constitution is reflected in Section 51 of the Defence Act 1903 (Cth) which reads:

> Where the Governor of a State has proclaimed that domestic violence exists therein, the Governor-General, upon the application of the Executive Government of the State, may, by proclamation, declare that domestic violence exists in that State, and may call out the Permanent Forces and in the event of their numbers being insufficient may also call out such of the Emergency Forces and the Reserve Forces as may be necessary for the protection of that State, and the services of the Forces so called out may be utilized accordingly for the protection of that State against domestic violence.

> Provided always that the Emergency Forces or the Reserve Forces shall not be called out or utilized in connection with an industrial dispute.

The Prime Minister or two other 'authorizing ministers' can, in the event of a 'sudden and extraordinary emergency' call out the ADF by a simple telephone call, without a written order. Alternatively, standing orders can be issued for the activation of the ADF whenever the chief of the defence staff considers it necessary. Once deployed, the members of the defence forces have unprecedented peacetime powers. They are authorized, among other things, to shoot down aircraft, sink ships, use deadly force, interrogate civilians, issue orders, enter and search premises and seize documents.[13] Potentially lethal force can be used where an ADF member considers it necessary 'on reasonable grounds' to protect himself or another person or any infrastructure that the government designates as 'critical'.

On the use of reasonable and necessary force, the Defence Act provides: (1) A member of the Defence Force may, in exercising any power, use such force against persons and things as is reasonable and necessary in the circumstances. (2) However, a member of the Defence Force must not, in

---

to health or safety of a section of the public or seriously interferes with an electronic, information, financial or transport system.

13 Head Michael and Scott Mann. 2009. *Domestic Deployment of the Armed Forces: Military Powers, Law and Human Rights*, USA: Ashgate, p. 128.

using force against a person: (a) do anything that is likely to cause the death of, or grievous bodily harm to, the person unless the member believes on reasonable grounds that doing that thing is necessary to protect the life of, or to prevent serious injury to, another person (including the member); or (b) subject the person to greater indignity than is reasonable and necessary in the circumstances. (3) In addition, if a person is attempting to escape being detained by fleeing, a member of the Defence Force must not do anything that is likely to cause the death of, or grievous bodily harm to, the person unless the person has, if practicable, been called on to surrender and the member believes on reasonable grounds that the person cannot be apprehended in any other manner.[14]

Citizens have no right to refuse to answer questions or hand over material on the grounds of self-incrimination. Instead they could be jailed for non-compliance.[15] Further, under the 2006 amendments, all ADF members are protected by a defence of 'superior order', which protects them from criminal liability, unless the order they obeyed was 'manifestly unlawful'. The members of the ADF are also exempted from wearing their name tabs during operations.[16] Any criminal prosecution of the ADF members associated with call-out duty is to be handled by federal authorities under federal laws, overriding state laws.[17]

Other legal provisions on the use of troops for non-defence purposes occur in two sets of regulations: (i) Australian Military Regulations (AMRs), Part V-Duties in Aid of the Civil Power During Domestic Violence,[18] and (ii) Air Force Regulations (AFRs), Part IX-Duties in Aid of Civil Power[19]. The two sets of regulations are similar and derive from common law as it evolved in eighteenth-century Britain. The regulations incorporate the notion that the civil power is paramount and apply the doctrine of minimum force. The major requirement is that a magistrate accompanies the forces. The role of the magistrate is to 'read the riot act' (AMR 407). If the magistrate concludes that the police are unable to cope with the riot,

---

14 The Defence Act, section 51T.

15 The Defence Act, section 51 SO.

16 The Defence Act, section 51 S(1)(b).

17 The Defence Act, section 51 WA.

18 The Regulations 398-415.

19 The Regulations 491-511.

then he is called upon to request the commander of the military forces to take action (AMR 408).

Regulation 400 states that officers called out for the protection of a state against domestic violence should ensure that the forces under their command are not utilized unnecessarily or to an unnecessary extent. Regulation 404 provides that except in cases of great and sudden emergency, the troops must not take any action, until a requisition in writing has been received from a civil authority. The civil authority must arrange for a magistrate to meet the forces and the magistrate must remain as near as possible to the commander of the military forces (Regulations 405 and 406). Regulation 410 requires the commander of the forces to warn 'the people' that if the troops are ordered to fire, the fire will be effective.

Although the provisions of the AMR and AFR are directed at a call-out to control domestic violence in a state, there is a provision for the application of these rules, as far as possible, when troops are employed by the Commonwealth on its own initiative to protect its servants or property, or safeguard its interest (AMR 415, AFR 511).

Procedure for call-out

Under the Australian system, an order for calling out the ADF need not be in writing. The Prime Minister or two other 'authorizing ministers', i.e., the Defence Minister and the Attorney General, can order the calling out of the ADF. Alternatively, one authorizing minister, together with the Deputy Prime Minister, Foreign Affairs Minister or Treasurer, can give the order. In addition, standing orders can be issued for the activation of the ADF whenever the chief of the armed forces deems it necessary. Alternatively, authorizing ministers can request the Governor-General to make a written call-out order.[20] The 2006 amendments also permit the authorizing ministers to dispense with a previous requirement to notify both Houses of Parliament (as well as the general public) within 24 hours of the declaration of a 'general security area.'[21]

---

20 The Defence Act sections 51 CA, 51CA (2), 51AB and 51A.

21 The Defence Act section 51K requires a recall of both the Houses of Parliament within six days of a declaration of a 'general security area', but provides that failure to do so 'does not make a declaration ineffective to any extent'. Under the 2006 amendments, section 51K (2AA) permits the authorizing minister to avoid notifying Parliament and the public of such a declaration, if they are satisfied that it 'would prejudice the exercise of power'.

The principal provisions of the rules of engagement are: (i) never use more force than the minimum necessary to carry out the duty; (ii) always try to handle situations by means other than opening fire; (iii) if forced to fire, fire only aimed single shots and do not fire more rounds than are absolutely necessary; (iv) whenever possible, give a clear and loud warning before firing; and (v) when operating collectively, open fire only when ordered to do so. Depending upon the circumstances, the minimum force necessary to restore law and order can vary from the mere appearance of troops to the use of all the force at a commanders' disposal. A soldier can meet force with force. If his life is endangered he does not have to wait until the terrorist is almost successful.[22]

In 2007, the Australian High Court in *Thomas v Mowbray*[23] sanctioned the substantial use of the federal defence power in peacetime and for domestic purpose. The judges also expanded the doctrine of 'judicial notice' to accept the many untested assertions about the 'war on terror' made by federal and state governments and their security agencies. They were of the view that groups of zealots forming part of or associated with Al Qaida were making common cause of hatred against communities posing no threat to them and planning to undertake violent and suicidal attacks upon institutions and persons of these communities.

In 2008, the Australian Prime Minister appointed a former military general to the new post of National Security Advisor. This was for the first time that a former military general headed the nation's domestic security set up. It gave further impetus to the militarization of domestic security. The terrorist attacks over the last 15 years have demonstrated that terrorism and extremist activities around the world do not distinguish between individuals. This environment of terror has created an overriding shift in the attitude towards the ADF being called out. It is now expected by Australians that they will be accorded adequate protection against any threat or attack on their lives. Thus, there is a possibility that the deployment of the ADF in domestic matters will not only continue, but will increase.

---

22 Ewing Brigadier M. J., Military Aid to the Civil Power, *Defence Force Journal*, No. 57, March/April 1986, p 21-30.

23 [2007] HCA 33.

Canada

A few instances of military operations against civilians, including French colonists and the Aboriginal people, find mention in Canadian history. Canada maintained small armed forces, trained and equipped for a range of contingencies from humanitarian assistance to war and deployment on operational missions abroad.[24] However, the domestic use of the forces was not given high priority till September 11.[25] The military assumed a supporting, rather than a lead role in most domestic operations. After September 11, the Canadian federal government tightened financial restrictions on potential fund-raising by identified terrorist groups. It also introduced new legislation and bureaucratic structures focused on security issues, and better coordinated intelligence gathering and information sharing across government agencies and with principal allies.

Since September 11, the Canadian forces have made considerable investment in developing specialized counter-terrorism capabilities, particularly in regard to tactical assault and detecting and handling of weapons of mass destruction. The Joint Task Force 2 and the Canadian Joint Incident Response Unit are highly trained and mobile military units, capable of rapid deployment. Military first responders also include forces involved in the patrol of Canada's air and sea approaches as well as military elements called out in times of emergency and crisis. The command, control, and coordination of those military forces is the responsibility of the Canada Command, a single strategic military headquarters with purview over Canadian and continental operations, in close touch with the government, provincial and territorial authorities, and the military commands of Canada's principal ally and neighbour. In the event of any terrorist attack, Canada would likely receive assistance from the United States based on affiliation, integration, and existing military arrangements.

---

24 Robert W. Murray and John McCoy, From Middle Power to Peace-builder: The Use of the Canadian Forces in Modern Canadian Foreign Policy, *American Review of Canadian Studies*, Vol. 40 (Summer 2010), p. 178.

25 To some extent the underlying sentiment finds expression in Canadian legal system. The Constitution Act of 1867 established a military-civilian demarcation. While the militia (armed forces) were paced under the exclusive jurisdiction of the federal government by sub-section 91 (7), law enforcement and public safety was placed in the hands of the provinces. Head Michael and Scott Mann. 2009. *Domestic Deployment of the Armed Forces: Military Powers, Law and Human Rights*, USA: Ashgate, p. 63.

In support of the 2002 G8 Summit in Kananaskis, the Canadian forces deployed more than 5,000 personnel, as well as air defence weapons, CF-18 fighters, Hercules transport aircraft and helicopters. As part of their commitment to the North American Aerospace Defence Command (NORAD), Canadian fighter aircraft have increased their patrols to ensure the safety of skies following the attacks of September 11. The Vancouver 2010 Olympic Games witnessed the deployment of about 1,800 military personnel in a supportive security role.[26]

The Canadian forces possess inherent capacity to deal with terrorist threats as part of broader government efforts to improve preparedness in the event of an emergency or crisis. These material and personnel resources augment the existing arrangements in the civilian sphere of emergency preparedness at the national, provincial, territorial, and municipal levels. Where the federal government decides to use the force for domestic deployment, the Canadian military is approached through the established chain of command. In the interim, the military offers advice, expertise, and recommendations if asked.

The deployment of the forces on domestic operations related to terrorism or terrorist acts perpetuated on Canadian soil must respect certain restrictions and limits under Canadian laws and statute. Canada's inherited British tradition of parliamentary democracy contains a strong suspicion of standing armed forces as well as the costs and liability associated with them. The use of the military on home territory is considered exceptional, usually for a defined period of time and particular purpose. The fundamental nature of the Canadian society and the consciousness of the citizens compel the military to takes into account issues of privacy, use of force, as well as safeguarding persons and property in the course of planning and operations.

The defence intelligence agencies and the military are prohibited from collecting information and intelligence on Canadian citizens and permanent residents inside Canada. The National Defence Act of Canada stipulates that the activities of the Communications Security Establishment 'not be directed at Canadians or any person in Canada' and 'protect the

---

26 Kevin Johnson, Olympic Security doesn't stop at Canadian border. *USA Today*, 8 February 2010. Available at: http://www.usatoday.com/sports/olympics/vancouver/2010-02-07-olympic-security_N.htm, accessed 27 June 2014.

privacy of Canadians in the use and retention of intercepted information.[27] Exemptions, however, may be made should the minister of national defence deem such action in the national interest, for a defined period of time. The military may not gather and retain information and intelligence on Canadians during domestic operations as a normal course of business. The military response to terrorist threats and acts inside Canada, therefore, lies within definite legal bounds in respect to information and privacy.

The use of force during domestic operations related to terrorism is also bound by numerous legal norms. Military members have neither the status of peace officers nor powers of arrest and detention beyond those of any Canadian citizen.[28] Should another Canadian be killed or seriously injured through military action, officers and soldiers could become liable to prosecution or civil remedies before the courts. To avoid such possibilities, troops deployed on domestic operations almost always work in formed units and groups under the command and orders of superior officers. Armed violence, when necessary, becomes a collective responsibility. Issued rules of engagement govern when force may be used and under what conditions.[29] These rules of engagement are approved by the chief of defence staff and passed down through the Canada Command to subordinate formations and units. In general, military planners and soldiers are expected to deploy the minimum force so authorized depending upon the situation, though specific rules of engagement may allow both deadly and non-deadly means. Thus, armed violence with weapons could be reasonable and appropriate to stop identified terrorists from acting, while crowd control and protection of private property with no threat to life would likely call for measures of a lower scale.[30] However, a terrorist threat or act does not alter the basic requirement to comply with Canadian law and the policy that derives from it.

The Canadian force members, like all Canadian citizens, possess the inherent right to self-defence under the Criminal Code of Canada when faced with imminent threat perceived to be dangerous to one's own person and life.[31] The use of force in self-defence is justified as long as it is

---

27 National Defence Act, R.S.C. 1985, c. N-5, s. 273.64(2).

28 B-LG-007-000/AF-001, *Domestic Operations - Collection of Documents* (2007).

29 CFJP-5.1(B-GJ-005-501/FP-001), *Use of Force for CF Operations*, (2008).

30 B-GJ-005-307/FP-090, *Crowd Confrontation* (31 May 2003).

31 Criminal Code of Canada, R.S.C. 1985, c. C-46, s. 34(1).

reasonable and no more than necessary in the given situation. Invoking self-defence, however, becomes problematic in respect of protecting other non-military persons and property. In either case, military members are prevented from using deadly or lethal force as a matter of legal requirement and forces policy, especially in the domestic context.[32] This leads to a paradoxical situation in which the military has a duty to protect civilians from terrorist action, though, the extent of force it can reasonably use is strictly circumscribed other than in the case of special units like the Joint Task Force 2. Canada primarily treats terrorists as armed criminals subject to arrest rather than urban guerrillas or freedom fighters engaged in an armed struggle against a political state or way of life. Military response must be tailored to the degree of risk posed to the apparatus of government and its officials rather than be geared to protecting civilians at large from harm.

In 2005, in response to global terrorism and possibility of its having an impact on domestic security, the Canadian Minister of National Defence made a new international policy statement aimed at increasing the strength of the Canadian forces and their future role in domestic deployment. The document stated:[33]

> The heavy demands on our military, both domestically and internationally, will not diminish—they may well increase. Canada must possess a military that is well adapted to the evolving security environment and ready to respond to the country's future needs...The first challenge is to strike the right balance between the Canadian Forces' domestic and international roles. In the current security environment, where the lines between these roles are less distinct than ever, the military must continue to carry out operations at home and overseas. Current threats demand that we pay increased attention to the safety and security of our citizens at home, the most fundamental responsibility of any government.... To improve their ability to carry out the domestic, continental and international roles described above, the Canadian Forces will be increased by 5,000 Regular and 3,000 Reserve personnel....These new Regular and Reserve personnel will also help the Canadian

---

32 B-GJ-005-314/FP-000, *CF Joint Force Protection* (2006), s. 103.

33 The Honourable Bill Graham, Minister of National Defence, Canada's International Policy Statement: A Role of Pride and Influence in the World; Defence, 2005, p. 32.

Forces better respond to domestic crises, such as natural disasters and terrorist attacks.

Domestic Deployment: Command and Control

In 2006, Canada established a separate military command with the specific task of preparing and conducting internal operations—the first such in history. A defence policy statement in 2006 announced: "To better protect Canada and Canadians, the Canadian Armed Forces will be reorganized to more effectively and quickly respond to domestic crises, as well as support other government departments as required."[34] The Prime Minister of Canada also promised rebuilding the Canadian forces into a first-class modern military, keeping citizens safe and secure.[35]

The national command authority of Canada for responding to terrorist threat is located in its capital, Ottawa. Under the Canadian parliamentary system, the prime minister exercises overwhelming power to commit military forces to operations, with or without the concurrence of ministers in cabinet and elected members of parliament from the ruling and opposition parties. The minister of national defence and minister of public safety are the next important political figures on issues relating to national security and terrorism by virtue of their departmental portfolios, though other ministers and bureaucrats are also involved.[36] The prime minister may or may not consult with them while directing the employment of military forces and national police in response to identified terrorist threats or actions in the country. The National Command Centre (NCC), a war room operating on a 24X7 basis, collates available information from military and civilian feeds as a central location and provides meeting space for senior decision-makers. Liaison with other government departments and agencies is also actively maintained during times of crisis. The NCC is at the disposal of the prime minister and the minister of national defence for real-time situational awareness and consultation with senior military leadership. Requests for assistance from other government departments and provincial and territorial authorities are channelled through the minister of national defence. Though a permanent fixture, the NCC could

---

34 Backgrounder BG 10.001, *Canada Command* (January 2010).

35 Department of National Defence, Canada 2008, p. 1.

36 B-GJ-005-308/FP-010, *Inter-Agency Handbook for Domestic Operations* (15 May 2005).

also be used as a crisis management location within the national defence headquarters.

Routine, contingency, and emergency matters affecting Canada are handled by the standing military strategic headquarters, Canada Command, also located in Ottawa. Canada Command provides the main command, control, and coordination functions to operationalize a military response to any terrorist threat against Canada and North America.[37]

Canada Command first receives requests from civilian authorities for assistance, stays connected with other government departments, provincial and territorial authorities, and police forces, and provides an established point of interaction with similar American commands in regard to any operations performed by militaries in the two countries and across borders. Six regional joint task forces throughout Canada fall under Canada Command: North, Pacific, West, Central, East, and Atlantic.[38] This framework provides extensive and continuous coverage of the country and is aimed at anticipating developing threats and marshaling suitable military forces in response.

Below the levels of Canada Command and the regional joint task forces, command and control essentially rests on the basic structure of the Canadian forces and dispersion of regular force and reserve units in Canada. A military presence exists in most urban centres and selected rural settings by way of military bases, installations, armouries, and naval reserve divisions. Consequently, some military forces would be reasonably nearby in the event of an emergency. Military-owned facilities may also serve the potential as command and control centres or hubs in times of terrorist threat or crisis.

Legal Mechanism

The terms 'national security' or 'security of Canada' now appear in more than 30 Canadian statutes, and have created new government powers or limited government obligations. Canada has two statements of basic rights, although neither expressly prohibits or curtails the domestic mobilization of the Canadian Forces to suppress political or social unrest. *The Canadian*

---

37 *Canada Command Direction for Domestic Operations* (Ottawa: Canada Command, 2006).

38 Woiden, K.L. 2007. *Domestic Operations in Canada: The Relevance and Applicability of Mission Command*, research paper, Toronto: Canadian Forces College, p. 10-11.

Charter of Rights and Freedoms and the *Canadian Bill of Rights* protect the rights of citizens during an emergency, but permit parliament to curtail some of the rights. Canadian courts have generally treated military and national security considerations as overriding procedural fairness.[39] In addition, phrases like 'reasonable limits', 'unreasonable' and 'arbitrary' in the *Charter* provide enough scope for military intervention during domestic deployment.

Domestic operations are conducted in response to requests from outside the control of the Canadian forces and can take almost infinite form. The response of the CF is, however, strictly bound by the legal responsibilities that enjoin defence activities, and the accountability of commanders at all levels for personnel and material resources under their command.[40] The National Defence Act allows for considerable use of the armed forces to suppress political unrest and dissent. Part VI of the Act deals with aid to civil power. It permits the Attorney General of a province to request 'military aid to civil power' to suppress a riot or disturbance. The request must be made in writing, addressed directly to the Chief of the Defence Staff (CDS) or any other designated officer. The CDS or the designated officer is authorized to call out the forces as considered necessary for suppressing or preventing any actual riot or disturbance. Officers and non-commissioned officers (NCOs) of the defence forces, while employed in aid of the civil power shall have additional power, have additional powers and duties of police officers. These include power of arrest, search and seizure and the use of lethal force as well as the powers they hold as soldiers.[41] Members of Canadian forces act only as a military body and are liable to obey only the orders of their superior officers.[42] Canadian force

---

39 *Chiarelli v Canada* (Minister of Justice) [1992] 1 SCR 711.

40 NDHQ Instruction DCDS 2 of 1998, Guidance for the Conduct of Domestic Operations 10 July 1998, para 2.

41 Deployment of the Canadian Forces (CF) in aid to civil power is the ultimate law enforcement action of a provincial/territorial government. Such use of the CF as a force of last resort should not occur until all other options have been exhausted, or have been judged insufficient. The CF may use all necessary legal force to restore the situation to normalcy. The very prospect of such a CF deployment should be seen as a powerful deterrent, and any commitment of personnel or resources must be deliberate and decisive. NDHQ Instruction DCDS 2/98, Guidance for the Conduct of Domestic Operations 10 July 1998, para 62.

42 The National Defence Act, sections 275-283.

units deployed for domestic operations are to use their integral vehicles, equipment and weapons within the restrictions placed on their use by the circumstances of a particular operation. Instructions concerning the deployment and potential use of specific types of equipment or weaponry will be specified in each case by the CDS.[43]

The Canadian Emergencies Act permits the government to rule by executive orders and regulations during any 'national emergency', broadly defined as an "urgent and critical situation of a temporary nature that seriously endangers the lives, health or safety of Canadians or seriously threatens the ability of the Government to preserve the sovereignty, security and territorial integrity of the country". The Act provides for four kinds of emergencies: natural disasters, internal security, international threats to security and war. In addition, martial law may also be declared.[44]

Liaison with the US

Canada enjoys a close relationship with the United States as a neighbour, economic trading partner, and military ally. Any terrorist threat or attack against continental North America invites a shared military response from the two countries.[45] The Canadian forces have a good working relationship with the US military to the point of inter-operability and cross-exchange postings. The US is central to Canada's security from external threat, whether direct military or terrorist. Canada Command deals directly with Northern Command, the American military headquarters that exercises responsibility for continental defence and homeland security. The North American Aerospace Defense Command (NORAD), is a historical bilateral defence organization that focuses on air defence and surveillance.[46] Both commands are located near each other in Colorado for the purposes of coordination. Canada maintains responsibility for Canadian airspace and keeps military members at US locations to participate in the day-to-day

---

43 NDHQ Instruction DCDS 2/98, Guidance for the Conduct of Domestic Operations 10 July 1998, para 92.

44 Head Michael and Scott Mann. 2009. *Domestic Deployment of the Armed Forces: Military Powers, Law and Human Rights*, USA: Ashgate, p. 67.

45 Mason Dwight N., The Future of Canadian-US Defense Relations, *American Review of Canadian Studies*, Volume 33, Spring 2003, p. 80-81.

46 Victor E. Renuart, Jr., The Enduring Value of NORAD, *JFQ: Joint Force Quarterly* , Volume 54,(3rd Quarter), 2009, p. 95.

running of the commands. A suspected terrorist threat from air or sea would go through NORAD, Northern Command, and Canada Command for political and military decision in Washington and Ottawa.[47]

Germany

The Germans look upon their armed forces (*Bundeswehr*) as an institution designed to guarantee homeland defence and security. The Constitution [*Grundgesetz* or Basic Law] provides that a member of the government (in peacetime the Minister of Defence; and the Chancellor once the federal parliament has determined that a situation requiring defence has arisen) shall have the supreme command over the armed forces.[48] In 1968, Article 97a was inserted in the Constitution to incorporate a domestic emergency rule. The main purpose of the article was to ensure that the armed forces would not be ordered to act domestically in any manner other than that which was explicitly permitted by the Constitution.[49]

During the forty-five years of Cold War, Germany limited its defensive actions to its own territory. There were never any official plan to cross borders and take steps for the defence of the homeland outside its borders.[50] After the end of the Cold War and unification, attitudes toward the deployment of the armed forces have been adapted to new international challenges. Germany has shifted to a security posture which in principle accepts the need for German participation in military interventions outside the traditional NATO (North Atlantic Treaty Organization) context of collective defence.[51] The main task of the armed forces is no longer territorial defence. Instead, its focus is on an asymmetric security threat from international terrorism, non-State actors and failing States.

Germany's constitution, called Basic Law (*Grundgesetz*), does not solely bind the processes of legislation and jurisdiction, but is applicable to

---

47 Madsen Chris, Military Responses and Capabilities in Canada's Domestic Context Post 9/11, *Journal of Military and Strategic Studies*, Volume 13 (3), Spring 2011, p. 1-18.

48 Articles 115 and 65 of the German Constitution.

49 Nolte George and Heike Krieger, 'Military Law in Germany', in Nolte George (ed.). 2003. *European Military Law Systems*, Berlin: De Gruyter Recht, p. 337-426.

50 Klose Col. Gerhard J., The Weight of History: Germany's Military and Domestic Security, *The Quarterly Journal*, Fall 2007, p. 37-57.

51 Hanns W. Maull, Germany and the Use of Force: Still a "Civilian Power"? *Survival*, Volume 42/2 (2000), p. 56–80.

every citizen. Laws that are found to be in conflict with the Basic Law are automatically overruled a special Court of Constitution which interprets affairs with a constitutional dimension. The judgments of the Court of Constitution bind the government and the parliament. There are many cases where laws that had passed both chambers of parliament had to be repealed and reworked under clear restrictions established by the Court of Constitution

In response to a series of incidents (including the hijacking of a Lufthansa plane) leading to a death of 34 people in 1973, the government imposed a 'contact ban', on suspected terrorists and their lawyers. The period referred to as "German Autumn", saw the passing of legislation in 1977 to regularize such bans. The law provided that in circumstances in which there was imminent threat to the life, physical integrity or liberty of a person, and there was a reasonable suspicion that this threat came from a terrorist organization, a contact ban could be ordered.[52] The administrative order could be issued by the federal government, a designated high federal state authority or, if more than one federal state was affected by the offence, the federal minister of justice. The Act contained a provision for the judicial review of such orders. The order could restrict all contacts of a detained person with other detained persons, the 'outside world' (friends and family) and lawyers.[53]

The German Constitutional Court considered the constitutional validity of the law in 1978 and concluded that the right to life of potential victims overrode the right to a fair trial and that within the framework of Basic Law, human rights had the highest value of all. The Court said that a conjoint reading of Article II (1) and Article II (2) clarified that in respect of the high value attached to life, the most serious duty of the State was to protect citizens from the unlawful deprivation of life by others.

Laws were also updated to allow police officers to use lethal force as a last resort against a criminal in circumstances where their own life or the life of a hostage was under threat.[54] These laws significantly eroded the accused's right to choose his lawyer; provided for his trial in absentia;

---

52 Contact Law 1977.

53 Hufnagel S., German Perspective on the Right to Life and Human Dignity in the "War on Terror", *Criminal Law Journal*, Volume 32, 2008, p. 102-103.

54 Some of the laws passed or updated were: Anti-Terror Act 1974, Anti-Terror Act 1976, Contact Law 1977, Raid Act 1978, Act Amending the Criminal Code and the Act on

and permitted the temporary incommunicado detention of prisoners. Membership of a terrorist organization was made a crime and powers were granted to search entire apartment blocks.[55] The German Court held that a terrorist remains a 'general, continuous threat' to society and could therefore be legitimately eliminated even if he is not an immediate threat to the life of a person. Further, the authorities were empowered to eliminate any such terrorist at any time.

The Constitution also provides for the use of the armed forces for the purposes of collective security and domestic operations in the event of an internal emergency, natural disaster or humanitarian catastrophes.[56] Under Article 87a (4) of the Constitution, in order to avert any imminent danger to the existence or free democratic order of the Federation or a *Lander* (State) the federal government may use the armed forces to support the police and the Federal Border Guard in the protection of civilian property and in combating organized and militarily armed insurgents, if the conditions as envisaged in Article 91 (2) are met and the use of police forces and the Federal Border Guard is insufficient.[57] The Law of Military Discipline, 2001 regulates the disciplinary powers and disciplinary measures of the members of the armed forces.

Post-September 11, following the lead of the US and UK, leading German politicians called for increasing the involvement of troops in the war on terror, both internally and externally. A political consensus also supported a limited peacekeeping role beyond the NATO borders. In 2001, the Chairperson of the Christian Democrats (CDU) called for constitutional amendments to allow the German military to deploy inside the country in the case of a serious terrorist threat.[58] A range of anti-terrorism laws were introduced, with a serious impact on civil and

---

Assemblies against Terrorism 1985, Passport Act Amending the Code of Criminal Procedure 1986, and Act for the Fight Against Terrorism 1986.

55 Campbell Colm, 'Beyond Radicalization: Towards an Integrated Anti-Violence Rule of Law' in Ana Maria Salinas De Frias, Katja Lh Samuel and Nigel D White (ed). 2012. *Counter-Terrorism: International Law and Practice*, Oxford: Oxford University Press, p. 261-262.

56 Articles 87a (2) and 24 (2) of the German Constitution.

57 Nolte George and Heike Krieger, 'Military Law in Germany', in Nolte George (ed.). 2003. *European Military Law Systems*, Berlin: De Gruyter Recht, p. 353.

58 Head Michael and Scott Mann. 2009. *Domestic Deployment of the Armed Forces: Military Powers, Law and Human Rights*, USA: Ashgate, p. 95.

democratic rights. In addition, 17 existing laws and five regulations were amended, bringing about consequential changes in nearly 100 laws.[59] Ban on the detainee's contact with lawyers was extended to where there might be a risk of the lawyer concealing evidence from the investigators.[60]

The 2003 Defence Policy Guidelines promulgated by the minister of defence declared:

> Defence as it is understood today means more, however, than traditional defensive operations at the national borders against a conventional attack. It includes the prevention of crises and conflicts, the common management of crises, and post-crises rehabilitation. Accordingly, defence can no longer be narrowed down to geographical boundaries, but contributes to the safeguarding of our security wherever it is in jeopardy.[61]

In 2003, a mentally ill person hijacked a small aircraft and threatened to crash it into the European Central Bank building. A new law, the Air-transport Security Act, was enacted by the parliament in June 2004. It entered into effect on 15 January 2005, after Federal President Horst Kohler put aside his concerns about constitutionality and signed the law. The law rearranged provisions of existing statutes under the rubric of the new Air-transport Security Act. It also introduced new competencies for the security agencies. The most prominent provision of the statute empowered the minister of defence to order that a passenger airplane be shot down, if it could be assumed that the aircraft would be used against the life of others and if downing it was the only means of preventing the danger. The statute empowered the minister of defence, as the commander of the German Air Force, to undertake appropriate countermeasures if a hijacked plane was believed to have been converted for use as a terrorist weapon. Section 14

---

59 After 11 September 2001, Germany saw an incredible increase in security legislation. The lawmakers of both *Bund* (federation) and *Lander* (federal states) enacted several new statutes intended to ameliorate the general level of security in the country. Almost all of these statutes curtailed civil rights by limiting individuals' freedom. Lepsius Oliver, Human Dignity and the Downing of Aircraft: The German Federal Constitutional Court Strikes Down a Prominent Anti-terrorism Provision in the New Air-transport Security Act, *German Law Journal*, Volume 7, No. 9, p. 761-776.

60 Hufnagel S., German Perspective on the Right to Life and Human Dignity in the "War on Terror", *Criminal Law Journal*, Volume 32, 2008, p. 102-108.

61 Defence Policy Guidelines promulgated by Minister of Defence Peter Struck, 21 May 2003, Berlin.

(3) provided for the shooting down of an airplane if there was no other way of dealing with the situation. It was this provision, in particular, that triggered widespread debates among the general public and legal fraternity.

In 2006, the Constitutional Court declared the law to be unconstitutional on the grounds that it violated the right to dignity (Article 1) and the right to life (Article 2). In particular the Court emphasized that the provision treated the innocent passengers in such a plane as objects without providing them legal protection.[62] The Court held:

> Under the Aviation Security Act they [the claimants' rights] become the mere objects of governmental actions. By their killing being used as a means to save others, they are treated as objects and at the same time deprived of their rights; with their lives being disposed of unilaterally by the state, the persons on board the aircraft, who, as victims, are themselves in need of protection, are denied the value which is due to a human being for his or her own sake. The value of their lives is judged on a quantity basis and according to how long they can still be expected to live with regard to the circumstances of the particular case....The State may not protect a majority of its citizens by intentionally killing a minority, in this case the flight crew and the passengers on the airplane. Balancing life against life on the basis of how many people might possibly die on the one side and how many on the other, is inadmissible. The State may not kill human beings based on the assumption that it will save more lives than it will destroy by killing these people.

However, the Court said that aircraft occupied by only terrorists could be shot down without infringing the Basic Law. It also ruled that the law invalidly expanded the latitude for using the military within Germany. The judges conceded to domestic deployment of the military with the condition that it would not be allowed to deploy any specific military means which the police was not permitted to use.

Some are, however, of the view that when the threat is grave, and the when consequences might be catastrophic, lives may have to be sacrificed

---

62 Lespius Oliver, Human Dignity and the Downing of Aircraft: The German Federal Constitutional Court Strikes Down a Prominent Anti-terrorism Provision in the New Air-Transport Security Act 7, *German Law Journal*, Vol. 7, No. 9, 1 September 2006, p. 761-776.

and rights may have to be infringed upon. People subscribing to this view justify their stand by involving extreme scenarios such as dirty bombs in urban areas or even the case of the rogue plane brought before the German court. On the one hand, the killing of innocent civilians by the State seems morally and constitutionally unacceptable, while on the other, allowing a plane to crash into a densely populated area seems equally unthinkable. In 2006, during the FIFA World Cup finals, the interior minister and other prominent politicians urged the deployment of the German Army for internal security and in spite of the ruling of the Constitutional Court, the German Defence Minister publicly stated in 2007 that hijacked planes would be shot down, justifying such action by a 'supra-statutory state of emergency'.[63]

The deployment of armed forces for domestic security got an impetus in August 2012, when the Constitutional Court ruled 15 to 1 that armed soldiers can be deployed on streets, but only in exceptional cases. The ruling said that the German Army could be employed inside Germany if there was a threat of "damage of catastrophic dimensions", but not to control demonstrations. The decision has lowered the threshold for the use of the Army domestically and permits it not only to reinforce the police, but also to use weapons such as fighter jets and tanks. The decision overturns severe restrictions put in place following the Nazi era and has made Germany broadly in line with European allies including Italy, France and Britain. The Court ruled that combat weapons can only be used 'as a last resort', and must be approved by the federal government. In a dissenting opinion, judge Reinhard Gaier said that the court had gone too far and that the

---

63 Most contemporary deontologists were of the view that deontological injunctions can be overridden under certain circumstances. Even if one concedes that shooting down a plane carrying 50 passengers in order to save 50 victims is not justified, what about shooting down 50 passengers to save 1000? What about a 10,000? And what about shooting down 2 to save 50? The issue surely must not hinge on playing with the numbers. As a matter of principle, there must be some ratio of victims to potential victims that would indeed justify the downing of the plane. This is not merely an abstract observation of moral philosophers. The duties to protect are an established component of many constitutions, including the German Federal Constitution. The duty to protect includes a duty to protect the potential victims of a terrorist attack and such a duty may require, under certain circumstances, infringing some people's rights. See: Harel Alon and Assaf Sharon, "Necessity Knows No Law" On Extreme Cases and Uncodifiable Necessities, available at: http://law.huji.ac.il/upload/necessity-updated(1).pdf, accessed 1 October 2014.

government should seek an amendment to the Constitution if it aims to deploy the military on German soil.[64]

The judgment marks a turning point in the history of the Federal Republic similar to the passage of Emergency Laws in May 1968. At that time, the German parliament amended 28 articles of the constitution to permit the government to suspend or restrict basic democratic rights in the event of war, a domestic state of emergency or a natural disaster.[65] The Emergency Laws allowed the deployment of the German Army domestically, but only in order to avert an imminent danger to the existence or free democratic order of the Federation or a state, or to combat organized armed insurgents.

Japan

The State-building process in Japan was summarized in the slogan of *fukoku kyohei* (rich nation, strong army), which emphasized the development of a strong domestic economy and technologies and complementary military capabilities.[66] In the eyes of many Japanese the country's defeat in World War II discredited the role of the military as the primary means to achieve security. Japan's demilitarization under the Allied occupation, and the growth of anti-militaristic and antinuclear views in Japanese society ensured that the role of the military would be heavily circumscribed. Japanese policy-makers, however, did not ignore the role of military power in security affairs. Japanese Prime Minister Yoshida Shigeru signed a security treaty with the US in 1951, later revised in 1960.

---

64 The critics believe that the criterion--damage of catastrophic dimensions--is so vague that it can be stretched at random and applied to every form of social or political protest. German court sanction for domestic deployment of the military, 23 August 2012, available at: http://www.wsws.org/en/articles/2012/08/pers-a23.html, accessed 12 June 2017.

65 When the Emergency Laws were passed in 1968, Europe and the US were in social turmoil. On 30 May 1968, the day of the vote in the German parliament, neighboring France was on the edge of revolution. Ten million workers had been on general strike for two weeks. The day before, President de Gaulle had fled to Baden-Baden to consult with his military leadership. The student revolt raged and unrest in the factories was widespread. Three weeks previously, student leader Rudi Dutschke had been seriously injured by a right-wing would-be assassin. The Emergency Laws were directed against insurgent youth and workers.

66 Samuels, Richard J., Reinventing security: Japan since Meiji, *Daedalus*, Volume 120 (4), 1991, p. 47-68.

This led to light rearmament and the subsequent formation of Japan's military forces, the Self Defence Force (SDF), in 1954.[67] It also highlighted a pragmatic perception that alignment with and security guarantees from the US were essential to Japan's survival in the midst of intensifying Cold War pressures in East Asia.

Article 9 of the post-war Japanese Constitution stated that "land, sea, or air forces or other war potential, will never be maintained."[68] Deprived of any military capability after 1945, the nation had only occupation forces and a minor domestic police force on which it relied for security. However, later cabinets interpreted the constitutional provision as not denying the nation the inherent right to self-defence and, with the encouragement of the US, the Self Defence Forces (SDF) was developed in a phased manner.[69] Under the terms of the Mutual Security Assistance Pact, ratified in 1952 along with the peace treaty Japan had signed with the US and other countries, the US forces stationed in Japan were to deal with external aggression against Japan while Japanese forces, both ground and maritime, would deal with internal threats and natural disasters. Since 1972, the Japanese government has maintained that being a member of the UN, Japan possesses the right of collective self-defence and the right to provide military support to any country to repel aggression.

---

67 To avoid the appearance of a revival of militarism, Japan's leaders emphasized constitutional guarantees of civilian control of the government and armed forces and used nonmilitary terms for the organization and functions of the forces. The overall organization was called the Defence Agency rather than the Ministry of Defence. The armed forces were designated the Ground Self-Defence Force (GSDF), the Maritime Self-Defence Force (MSDF), and the Air Self-Defence Force (ASDF), instead of the army, navy, and air force.

68 Japanese Constitution Article 9 states: "Aspiring sincerely to an international peace based on justice and order, the Japanese people forever renounce war as a sovereign right of the nation and the threat or use of force as means of settling international disputes. To accomplish the aim of the preceding paragraph, land, sea, and air forces, as well as other war potential, will never be maintained. The right of belligerency of the state will not be recognized." There has been widespread and continuing public support for Article 9.

69 The Parliament (or Diet), established the Self Defence Forces (SDF) in 1954. Although they were equipped as a conventional military force, they were, by law, an extension of the police, created solely to ensure national security. Due to the constitutional debate concerning the Forces' status, any attempt at increasing the Forces' capabilities and budget tends to be controversial. The Rules of Engagement were strictly defined in the Self-Defence Forces Act 1954.

By the early 1980s, as US-Japan security cooperation increased. Japan, encouraged by the US, upgraded its national military capabilities and range of missions in support of US power projection functions in the region. Post-September 11, Japan has shared US concerns about the spread of terrorism. At the regional level, these concerns have been reflected in the problems of potential links between *Al-Qaeda* and insurgency in the Philippines and Indonesia. Japan has feared even more the proliferation of weapons of mass destruction (WMD) in East Asia and beyond. In January 2007, the Japan Defence Agency was upgraded to Ministry of Defence, a Cabinet-level ministry.[70] Today, Japan has one of the largest armed forces in the world. The Japanese SDF consists of over 250,000 personnel including a 160,000-person ground forces, a sophisticated air force and a formidable navy. Its military establishment designs and builds weaponry and other war equipment equal to those of any of the developed nations.

During the July 2008 G8 Summit, in addition to more than 20,000 police personnel providing ground security, 12 warships, Patriot surface-to-air-missiles, and AWACS reconnaissance aircraft were deployed.[71] The SDF has not been used in police actions so far,[72] however, its deployment in internal security tasks in the future cannot be ruled out.

---

70 The Defence Agency and the SDF comprise the same defence organization. However, the term Defence Agency is used to denote an administrative organization responsible for the management, operation, etc., of the GSDF, MSDF and ASDF, while the term SDF is used to mean armed organizations that conduct unit activities for the defence of the nation and for other purposes. The SDF are under control of the civilian Defence Agency, subordinate to the prime minister. Thus, of the 10 bureaucratic appointments to JDA, at least four are assigned from other ministries. This is the result of a deliberate effort to ensure continued civilian control.

71 Head Michael and Scott Mann. 2009. *Domestic Deployment of the Armed Forces: Military Powers, Law and Human Rights*, USA: Ashgate, p. 110.

72 The National Police Agency (NPA) is responsible for policing the entire nation and protecting against foreign espionage and terrorism. It is similar to US FBI. It is also the most influential intelligence apparatus in Japan. The NPA's information gathering depends on not only 300,000 police force (the number is greater than Japanese military services), but also occupation of chief intelligence positions of other agencies. Through the Cold War period, the main duty of Japanese intelligence was to monitor communist activities in Japan and the NPA was suitable for the duty. The role of the Japanese military forces was very limited in the period. For example, in 1976, when a lieutenant of the Soviet air force, flew to Japan with MIG-25 fighter jet seeking for political asylum, the Japanese military services were not allowed to check the jet. They were excluded from the investigation by the NPA, and the Army Chief of Staff resigned expressing his strong protest against the humiliating incident.

Italy

Italy's national defence comprises all political, military, economic, industrial, and financial activities that are carried out by the State to ensure its own security and national integrity in all circumstances. National security is managed by military defence and civil defence, which are strictly interconnected through a permanent structure called the Agency for Civil-Military Cooperation (COCIM), which is the responsible for dealing with extraordinary circumstances. This structure is controlled by the Military-Political Nucleus (*Nucleo Politico Militare*), which is part of the prime minister's cabinet and is headed by the prime minister (or his delegate).[73]

The use of the military in domestic deployment has been a regular phenomenon in Italy. Successive governments have turned to the military to carry out safety and security tasks and have endowed soldiers with special police functions and powers. The armed forces have participated in a broad range of operations in support of the civil authorities since the end of World War II. These range from protecting key facilities and critical infrastructure to providing relief in response to natural disasters. During the 1960s Italy faced an insurgency in the northern region of Alto Adige. The insurgents belonged to the German-speaking minority, who were demanding a higher level of autonomy from Rome. The army was called to assist the police forces, and a number of military units were deployed along the border with Austria to prevent the illegal movement of armed groups across the Alps. Units were deployed in the rest of the region to secure essential services like railways and electric power stations, and to guard national institutions. The military provided direct support to the police in cordon-and-search operations and other related activities. The deployment required an average of 10,000 men under the command of the Fourth Army Corps of Bolzano. After about 7 years, the problem was resolved politically and the army units returned for their normal duties.

In the 1970s, the soldiers performed similar functions throughout Italy to secure public facilities against possible attacks by the Red Brigade terrorist group. Italian Army units were active in disaster relief operations, most notably in the Vajont Dam disaster in 1963, in which over 3000 people

---

73 Cabigiose Lt. Gen. Carlo, The Role of Italy's Military in Supporting the Civil Authorities, *The Quarterly Journal*, Fall 2005, p. 59-82.

died in the wake of a landslide, and the earthquake in Friuli in 1976, which killed a thousand and rendered 150,000 homeless.

The domestic deployment of the armed forces has increased since 1992 and the military has been involved in a greater range of internal security tasks than in any other country in Europe. In 1992, the Italian military undertook operation 'Forza Paris', in which 5,000 troops were deployed. This operation, which lasted about two months, was designed to demonstrate the government's will to maintain control over its territory. During the operation, mainly designed to curtail the freedom of activity of local criminal groups, Army units conducted military training operations in the central portion of the island. The troops deployed in the operation did not have special police powers.

In 1992, in the wake of the assassination of two Italian magistrates, the local authorities were unable to cope with the distrust of the population and were not effective in countering the organized Mafia in Sicily. The Italian government deployed nearly 10,000 soldiers in Sicily in an operation called 'Sicilian Vespers'. The soldiers conducted territorial control operations throughout Sicily, including surveillance, patrols, checkpoints, and infrastructure security operations which lasted for nine years. During this period, all 19 brigades of the Italian Army were deployed to Sicily in a 60 day rotational cycle. The average strength of the army in Sicily during this operation was about 6000. The soldiers were deployed as 'public security agents' under an act of parliament which entrusted them with law enforcement powers, including the authority to detain and arrest suspected persons. This enabled army units to act independently of the police. The army checked nearly a million persons and 665,000 vehicles, and arrested 1,225 persons. [74]

As the violence in the Balkan region increased in the later part of 1990s, Italian military units were pressed into service to secure Italy's external borders. The efforts included controlling illegal immigration along Italy's land border with Slovenia, and illegal maritime immigration along the southeast coast. These operations involved an average presence

---

74 Italian law sets forth three categories for law enforcement agents: full police authority, public security agency, and a "reduced" public security function. Soldiers employed in the operation enjoyed public security agency authority and were empowered to shoot to kill. Cabigiose Lt. Gen. Carlo, The Role of Italy's Military in Supporting the Civil Authorities, The Quarterly Journal, Fall 2005, p. 59-82.

of about 5,000 soldiers who were endowed with limited police powers, which enabled them to stop and arrest suspects.

After the September 11 attacks the range of tasks undertaken by the military increased. In October 2001, the Italian Army commenced Operation Domino. It involved about 4000 soldiers, and was designed to provide protection for 150 critical installations as well as enhanced security for the US military bases in Italy. In contrast with other operations, the military did not possess special police powers, and thus could not, on their own, stop and arrest suspects. The intensity of the operation was reduced after 2006, however, certain facilities are still under enhanced protection.

In 2002, over 2,000 troops were sent to Sicily to combat the Mafia. In 2008, the Italian armed forces were deployed to crack down on illegal immigrants and provide enhanced security in Italy's urban streets. Operation "Secure Streets" commenced in May 2008 by executive decree, later authorized by law number 125 of 24 July 2008. This operation was designed to support the police and Carabinieri[75] units by increasing the presence of security forces on Italian streets. Specific tasks included ensuring the external security of immigration centres in 16 provinces (involving about 1000 soldiers); securing 52 sensitive locations in Rome, Milan, and Naples, mostly embassies and consulates (involving 750 soldiers) and joint police-army patrols in nine cities (involving 1500 soldiers). The law enforcement powers of the soldiers were limited to stopping and searching suspicious individuals. Suspected individuals were to be turned over to law enforcement authorities immediately. The joint patrols were carried out in high-traffic areas, such as bus and train stations, as well as in major tourist

---

75 The Carabinieri is the national military police of Italy, policing both military and civilian populations. It was originally founded as the police force of the Kingdom of Sardinia. During the process of Italian unification, it was appointed the "First Force" of the new national military organization. They are fully recognized as an independent service and possess the full status of a police force as well as that of a military force. They report to the chief of staff for defence regarding their military duties and to the Ministry of the Interior in relation to their tasks in the areas of policing, public order, and public security. They also provide special units to the Ministry of Health, Ministry for the Environment, Ministry of Culture, Ministry for Social Policies, Ministry for Agriculture, and Ministry for Foreign Affairs to carry out compulsory regulatory activities related to the application of their ordinances. The total strength of the Carabinieri is about 120,000. Their organization partially reflects the structure of the army (similar ranks, disciplinary code, name of units and command structure). Since 2001, Carabinieri has been one of the four Italian armed forces.

areas. In the first year of operation, it resulted in the searches of nearly 300,000 people and 150,000 vehicles.

Following a six-month trial, in 2009, the government implemented the second phase of "Operation Safe Streets" and deployed about 30,000 soldiers. Of these, 1,000 troops were deployed to manage refugee internment camps, called 'identification and classification centres'; while another 1,000 were deployed in sensitive public places. Armed troops, some in body armours, were deployed to patrol streets in the capital and other major cities along with the police.[76] However, this deployment invited severe criticism from domestic and international communities. In the beginning of 2009, military units were also deployed to make arrests and break up illegally erected shacks in Rome.[77] There were allegations that gypsies and other migrants were targeted as economic and social conditions deteriorated in 2008 and 2009.

While deploying the armed forces, Italy uses a concept known as "presence and surveillance." This concept has three operational domains: territorial defence, disaster relief, and territorial control. Under Italian law, the military is considered a full partner of the police in a number of domestic contingencies. Under the law that established the Agency for Civilian Protection (225/92), the armed forces were designated the 'operational branch' of the national civil protection service, which though primarily concerned with coordinating Italy's response to disasters, has become increasingly involved in working with security organizations to enhance public security.

The Italian Constitution, Article 117 (d), provides that the state has exclusive legislative powers in matters concerning "state security; armaments, ammunition, and explosives". The weapons, munitions, and explosives of the "Armed Forces and the Armed Corps of the State," are regulated by law and authorization is required to use them.[78] While the phrase Armed Corps of the State includes the police, these provisions exempt the police from the need to receive authorization to use weapons, weapon parts, ammunition, and explosives in the exercise of their duties.

---

76 Cabigiose Lt. Gen. Carlo, The Role of Italy's Military in Supporting the Civil Authorities, *The Quarterly Journal,* Fall 2005, p. 59-82.

77 Head Michael and Scott Mann. 2009. *Domestic Deployment of the Armed Forces: Military Powers, Law and Human Rights,* USA: Ashgate, p. 106-107.

78 Royal Decree Nos. 773 and 635 and Law No. 110 of 1975.

Presidential decree sets forth rules governing what weapons are available to the National Police. It states that the use of weapons must be adequate and proportionate to the protection of the public order and safety, the prevention and punishment of crime, and other institutional duties.[79] Under the Italian Criminal Code, public officers cannot be punished for using or authorizing the use of a weapon or other means of physical coercion in the line of duty in order to overcome resistance to authority or prevent violent acts or crimes such as murder, manslaughter, armed robbery, kidnapping or drowning someone, or causing a shipwreck, aviation disaster, or train wreck.[80]

All military units deployed in aid to police for purposes of homeland security are given specific rules of engagement to be followed in case the use of force is required. Weapons can generally be used only for self-defence, and proportionality must be observed in relation to the severity and nature of the offence. The use of weapons is allowed: (i) by individual initiative, to face an attack that endangers a soldier's own life or the lives of others, (ii) on order, given by the commander of the unit, when it is necessary to counter threats against the unit or to safeguard the lives of others.

The Italian public's reaction to most of these operations involving the use of military has been uniformly positive. They have generally concurred with the decision to deploy soldiers to carry out these non-military tasks. On a few occasions, there have been demonstrations in favour of more military involvement, as the armed forces are now seen in Italy as an organization that "gets things done". The factors responsible for the positive public opinion are: (i) the operations enhanced the image of the military in Italy, where the armed forces have not generally been viewed as highly competent; and (ii) the operations brought stability in certain disturbed parts. The domestic operations were useful in procuring additional funds for the military. It is anticipated that the government will continue to look to the military to provide a growing range of support to law enforcement,

---

79 Presidential Decree Number 359 of 1991.

80 In addition, police must (i) diligently secure their weapons and responsibly maintain them; (ii) carry out in all circumstances the security measures established for the handling of the weapon; and (iii) receive training, actively practice the techniques learned, and participate in drills organized by the authorities. The Italian Military Code of Peace contains a similar provision concerning military personnel. Police Weapons in Selected Jurisdictions, Council of Europe, The Law Library of Congress, Global Legal Research Centre, September 2014, p. 53-56.

as well as engage in civil support operations. However, there have been increased tensions between the Carabinieri and the other branches of the Italian armed forces, particularly the army.

Nigeria

The 1999 Constitution of Nigeria which provides for the military in Article 217 states the duties of the military, that is the Army, Navy and the Air Force to defend Nigeria from external aggression, maintain its territorial integrity and securing its borders from isolation on land, sea or air, suppressing insurrection and acting in aid of civil authorities to restore order when called upon to do so by the President but subject to such conditions as may be prescribed by an Act of National Assembly. The military is also to perform such other functions as may be prescribed by an Act of the National Assembly. Article 217 (c) of the Constitution forms the basis of involvement of the military in internal security operations in Nigeria: "suppressing insurrection and acting in aid of civil authorities to restore order when called upon to do so by the President but subject to such conditions as may be prescribed by an Act of National Assembly". The Constitution empowers the President to use federal forces to combat domestic disturbances. The Armed Forces Act, Section 8(1) provides that the President shall determine the operational use of the Armed Forces; which includes the use of the armed forces for the purpose of maintaining and securing public safety and public order.

Article 305 of the Constitution empowers the president to issue a proclamation of state of emergency in the following situations: (i) When there is actual breakdown of public order and public safety in the federation to such an extent that requires extraordinary measures to restore peace and security; (ii) In case there is a clear danger of an actual breakdown of public order and public safety in the federation requiring extraordinary measure to avert any such dangers; and (iii) There is an occurrence or imminent danger or the occurrence of any disaster or national calamity affecting the community or a section of the community in the federation, or there is any other public danger which clearly constitutes a threat to the existence of the federation. In addition, Article 305 of the Constitution also empowers the President to issue a proclamation of state of emergency and deploy the military internal security operations. This state of emergency shall be declared in the following situations: (i) When there is actual breakdown of public order and public safety in the federation or any part thereof to such extent as to require extraordinary measures to restore peace and security; (ii) If there is clear and present danger of an actual breakdown of public order and public safety in the federation or any part thereof requiring extraordinary measures to avert such danger; or (iii) There is an occurrence or imminent danger or the occurrence of any disaster or natural calamity affecting the community or a section of the community in the federation, or there is any other public danger which clearly constitutes a threat to the existence of the federation.

Though the duty to restore law and order within the country is that of the civil authorities through the use of the Nigerian Police, but under the provisions of Article 217, the armed forces can be called upon to aid civil authorities to restore public order in any part of the country. Under these provisions, the Nigerian military has been requisitioned for internal security operations since the days of colonialism.[81]

The activities undertaken by the Nigerian military while performing internal security operations include the following: cordon and search operations (sealing off a village to search for offenders, weapons or equipment); urban and rural patrols, possibly joint patrols with police or paramilitary forces; manning observation posts; guard duties at key points or for VIPs; road blocks or vehicle check points (VCPs); identity checks; controlling peaceful demonstrations; controlling or dispersing unlawful assemblies or demonstrations (riot situations); enforcing curfews; making arrests; detaining persons; acting as a reserve or reinforcement, i.e. quick reaction duties on standby for incidents; keeping sides apart (manning a "peace line" or "green line"); escort duties for the police, civil defence units, the fire brigade; hostage rescue; ambush; securing or picketing routes, for example to ensure safe passage of supplies through sensitive areas; and bomb disposal, or dealing with improvised explosive devices (IEDs).[82]

---

81 Internal security operations relates to duties undertaken by the domestic security agents such as the Police, Customs, Immigration Services, and others for the purpose of containing domestic threats to the security of the country. These threats often relate to cases of riots, demonstrations, strikes, communal clashes, and terrorism which normally fall outside the constitutional duty of the military. Zainab Brown Peterside, The Military and Internal Security in Nigeria: Challenges and Prospects, *Mediterranean Journal of Social Sciences*, Vol. 5, No. 27, December 2014, pp.1-7.

82 Epiphany Azinge San, Military in Internal Security Operations: Challenges and Prospects, Paper Presented at the Annual General Conference, Nigerian Bar Association, 28 August 2013, pp. 29.

The Nigerian military has participated in a number of internal security operations.[83] However, involvement of the Nigerian military in the internal security operations over the years has been controversial. Owing to the perceived excesses of soldiers in that context, there have been popular outcries to the effect that these soldiers are "usurpers, oppressors, or intruders."[84] For instance, during the Onitsha crisis (2006), the Governor of Anambra State, Mr Peter Obi, called on President Goodluck Jonathan to direct the deployment of military troops to the State with the intent to restore peace, law, order and public security. Accordingly, the President directed the deployment of soldiers to work in collaboration with the police in order to ameliorate the raging crisis. As the operations lasted, some members of the Joint Army and Police Team resorted to untoward acts, in which there were massive extra-judicial killings, torture, extortion, rape, and the likes. A few soldiers exhibited extreme barbarism in the use of force. It was reported that a man escorting his two sisters to a place was killed while the two sisters of his were raped by soldiers. Such atrocities engendered widespread outcries and resentment against the military and the government. The military excesses were also reported during the Zaki Biam (2001) and Odi (1999) operations. In these operations indiscriminate use of force by the military was reported in addition to rape of women and the wanton killings of innocent villagers. In the cases of Odi and Zaki Biam, the entire villages were raided, leading to mass dislocation of families. In the recent incident at Farikin Ladi in Plateau State, the villagers were forced to evacuate their traditional abodes and squat in unfriendly and unhealthy destinations in their immediate and remote neighbourhood.[85] In December 2015, the army killed 347 members of the Shia Islamic

---

83 Some of these include: The Egba Revolt (1914); The Aba security operations (1929-1930); The Tiv Riots (1964-1965); Western Region Political Crises (1965); The Nigerian Civil War (1967-1970); Maitatsine Religious Disturbances (1980, 1984); Political crisis following the annulment (1993) elections; Operation Second 11; The Odi Crisis (1999); Tiv-Jukun and zaki Biam crisis (2001); Kaduna religious Crisis (2000, 2002); The Niger Delta Operation (Op RESTORE HOPE); The Jos/NE Operation (Operation restore Order); The Operation PULO SHIELD, and The Onitsha Crisis (2006).

84 Nwolise, O.B.C. (2007). "Military Assistance to Civil Authority as a Constitutional Duty of the Nigerian armed Forces: Sources of Public Agonies and Outcries, Bad Military Image, and Their challenges for Political Leadership, Military Command and Professionalism" in Ogomudia A. (ed), *Peace Support Operations, Command and Professionalism: Challenges for the Nigerian Armed Forces in the 21st Century*, Ibadan: Gold Press.

85 Okoli, Al Chukwuma and Orinya Sunday, Evaluating the Strategic Efficacy of Military Involvement in Internal Security Operations (ISOPs) in Nigeria, *IOSR Journal Of*

Movement of Nigeria (IMN) after a road blockade by the group in Zaria. Across the country, allegations of abuses including arbitrary arrests and detention, torture, forced disappearance, and extrajudicial killings continue to trail military operations in Nigeria.[86]

The atrocities perpetrated by certain Nigerian military personnel constituted gross violations of the tenets of Nigeria's constitution. For instance, Article 34(1) of the Constitution provides for "respect for the dignity" of every Nigerian. This provision is supported by Article 19(b) which states that "the sanctity of the human person shall be recognized and human dignity shall be maintained and enhanced". Similarly, Articles 33 to 37 guarantees fundamental human rights to citizens, among which are right to life, right to personal liberty, right to privacy, etc. The increasing role taken by the military in internal security operations have been criticized on the grounds that the members of the army are not that trained to manage internal operations like other civil authorities such as the police. In order to improve the situation, the recommendations are: (i) There is the need for domestic legislation to regulate the operations of the military during internal operation; (ii) The rules of military engagement should be well defined; and (iii) There should be re-orientation of the soldiers involved in internal security operations and the populace as well.[87]

Nigeria has initiated reform its security sector as part of the transition from military to civilian rule at the start of the new millennium. Key reform issues include the prevention of coups, the demilitarization of society, the subordination of the military to civilian control, the use of the military for policing functions, the need to build the capacity of the military to combat insurgency, and criminal justice system reform.[88] On 5 August 2017, the Acting President of Nigeria, Yemi Osinbajo has appointed a seven-man Judicial Commission to review compliance of the armed forces with human rights obligations and rules of engagement, especially in local conflict and

---

Humanities And Social Science (IOSR-JHSS), Volume 9, Issue 6 (March - April 2013), pp. 20-27.

86 World Report: 2017, Human Rights Watch, p. 451.

87 Peterside, Zainab Brown, The Military and Internal Security in Nigeria: Challenges and Prospects, *Mediterranean Journal of Social Sciences*, Vol. 5, No. 27, December 2014, pp. 1301-1307.

88 Aiyede, E R. "Democratic Security Sector Governance and Military Reform in Nigeria" in Bryden, A and Chappuis, F (eds.). 2015. *Learning from West African Experiences in Security Sector Governance*, London: Ubiquity Press, pp. 97–116.

insurgency situation with Boko Haram. The Commission is empowered to review the rules of engagement applicable to the Armed Forces of Nigeria and its compliance during internal armed conflict. It is also empowered to investigate alleged acts of violation of IHL and human rights law under the Constitution of the Federal Republic of Nigeria, Geneva Conventions Act, African Charter on Human and Peoples' Rights (Ratification and Enforcement) Act and other relevant laws relating to Nigerian security agencies. The Commission, headed by a Justice of the Court of Appeal, is to submit its report in 90 days.[89]

The United Kingdom

Throughout British history, troops have been mobilized against civilians during the periods of acute political and social conflicts. The military has played an essential role in securing the State against internal political disaffections. The Army was involved in the suppression of industrial action by trade unions in 1926, and the eviction of the Bonus Army in Washington in 1932. In colonial India, the British Indian Army was used to suppress the demand for independence and in Ireland, British military forces, along with locally recruited forces such as the Black and Tans, conducted a prolonged counterinsurgency campaign against Irish insurgents fighting for the liberation of Ireland. The British Army exercised primacy in Northern Ireland operations from 1970 to 1976, a period in which the police in that province were unable to assert full control.[90]

---

89 Osinbajo Inaugurates Judicial Committee to Review Military Compliance with Human Rights, 05 August 2017, available at: https://www.360nobs.com/2017/08/osinbajo-inaugurates-judicial-committee-review-military-compliance-human-rights/, accessed 7 August 2017.

90 The commitment of troops in 30-year counterinsurgency operations has negatively affected British law and British democracy. The British government has felt it necessary to cloud in secrecy different aspects of the security situation in Northern Ireland. The Northern Ireland Office has refused to make available basic data, such as the number of deaths attributable to the security forces and to the terrorists. The Director of Public Prosecutions has refused to make public a list of killings by the security forces that have resulted in criminal proceedings. The army's doctrine for internal security is unavailable for public scrutiny. Even the "Yellow Card," the one-page instruction which tells the soldier when to use lethal force, is classified and not available for public scrutiny. The government says it would not be in the public interest to make this information available, while in reality the very opposite is true. Rasmussen, Maria Jose Moyano, *The Military Role in Internal Defence and Security: Some Problems*, The Centre for Civil-Military Relations, The Naval Postgraduate School California, Occasional Paper 6, October 1999, p. 30-31

Common Law imposes a duty on every citizen, including armed forces personnel, to go to the aid of the police/civil power, when requested, to assist in the enforcement of law and order, where it is reasonable to do so and where they have the resources and ability to do so. This forms the main (but not the only) basis for military aid to civil authority.[91] Section 2 of the 1964 Emergency Powers Act (EPA) and the 2004 Civil Contingencies Act (CCA) provide a statutory basis for the Military Aid to the Civil Power (MACP).[92] Queen's Regulations place an additional duty on military commanders to act on their own responsibility without a request by the civil power where, in very exceptional circumstances, a grave and sudden emergency has arisen, which in the opinion of the Commander demands his immediate intervention to protect life or property.[93]

Power to Make Emergency Regulations

The Crown has the same power as a private individual of taking all measures which are absolutely and immediately necessary for the purpose of dealing with an invasion or other emergency. The Crown further has the prerogative power to take action to maintain peace. It has been held that the power to take action to maintain the peace includes the power to supply equipment to a chief constable where the equipment is necessary to deal with either an actual or an apprehended threat to the peace. [94] The Crown may, by Order in Council, make emergency regulations if satisfied that: (1) an emergency has occurred, is occurring or is about to occur; (2) it is necessary to make provisions for the purpose of preventing, controlling or mitigating an aspect or effect of the emergency; and (3) the need for provision is urgent. A senior Minister of the Crown may make

---

91 The Military Aid to Civil Authority (MACA) has three sub-categories: Military Aid to the Civil Power (MACP) for maintenance of law, order and public security; Military Aid to Other Government Departments (MAGD) for assistance on urgent work of national importance and services essential to life, health and safety; and Military Aid to the Civil Community (MACC) like assistance during natural disasters. Waring Marc, The Domestic Deployment of the British Army: A Case for Third Force, *RUSI Journal*, June/July 2013, Volume 158, No. 3, p. 62-69.

92 Operations in the UK: The Defence Contribution to Resilience, Joint Doctrine Publication 02 of September 2007, chapter 4.

93 The Queen's Regulations for the Royal Navy, J4801 to 4802 and J4805 to 4806, The Queen's Regulations for the Army, J11.001 to 11.010 and The Queens Regulations for the RAF, J852.

94 *R v Secretary of State for the Home Department, ex p Northumbria Police Authority* [1989] QB 26, (1987) a All ER 282 DC.

emergency regulations if satisfied that (a) the conditions in Provisions (1) to (3) are satisfied; and (b) it would not be possible without serious delay to arrange for an Order in Council. Further, emergency regulations must be prefaced by a statement by the person making the regulations specifying the nature of the emergency in respect of which the regulations are made. The statement must declare that the person making the regulations: (i) is satisfied that the conditions in heads (1) to (3) are met; (ii) is satisfied that the regulations contain only provision which is appropriate for the purposes of preventing, controlling or mitigating an aspect or effect of the emergency in respect of which regulations are made; (iii) is satisfied that the effect of the regulations is in due proportion to that aspect or effect of the emergency; (iv) is satisfied that the regulations are compatible with human rights; and (v) in the case of regulations made by a senior Minister of the Crown, is satisfied that it would not possible without serious delay to arrange for an Order in Council.[95]

Meaning of Emergency

For the purposes of emergency powers legislation, the term 'emergency' means:

    (a) An event or situation which threatens serious damage to human welfare in the United Kingdom or in a Part or region,

    (b) An event or situation which threatens serious damage to the environment of the United Kingdom or of a Part or region, or

    (c) War, or terrorism, which threatens serious damage to the security of the United Kingdom.

The 'event or situation' may occur or be inside or outside the United Kingdom. For the purposes of sub-para (a) above, an event or situation threatens damage to human welfare only if it involves, causes or may cause: (i) loss of human life, (ii) human illness or injury, (iii) homelessness, (iv) damage to property, (v) disruption of a supply of money, food, water, energy or fuel, (vi) disruption of a system of communication, (vii) disruption of facilities for transport, or (viii) disruption of services relating to health. For the purposes of sub-para (b) above, an event or situation threatens damage to the environment only if it causes or may cause (i) contamination of

---

95   Civil Contingencies Act 2004, section 20 (5)(b).

land, water or air with biological, chemical or radioactive matter, or (ii) disruption or destruction of plant life or animal life. The Secretary of State may by order provide that in so far as an event or situation involves or causes disruption of a specified supply, system or facility or service, it is to be treated as threatening damage to human welfare, or it is no longer to be treated as threatening damage to human welfare.[96]

Purpose and Scope of Emergency Regulations

Emergency regulations may make any provision which the person making the regulations is satisfied is appropriate for the purpose of preventing, controlling or mitigating an aspect or effect of the emergency in respect of which the regulations are made. In particular, for the purpose of: (i) protecting human life, health or safety, (ii) treating human illness or injury, (iii)   protecting or restoring property, (iv) protecting or restoring a supply of money, food, water, energy or fuel, (v) protecting or restoring a system of communication, (vi) protecting or restoring facilities for transport, (vii) protecting or restoring the provision of services relating to health, (viii) protecting or restoring the activities of banks or other financial institutions, (ix) preventing, containing or reducing the contamination of land, water or air, (x) preventing, reducing or mitigating the effects of disruption or destruction of plant life or animal life, (xi) protecting or restoring activities of Parliament, of the Scottish Parliament, of the Northern Ireland Assembly or of the National Assembly for Wales, or (xii) protecting or restoring the performance of public functions.[97]

Emergency regulations may make provisions of any kind that could be made by an Act of Parliament or by the exercise of the Royal Prerogative. In particular, regulations may:

(a)   confer on a Minister of the Crown, on the Scottish Ministers, on the Wales Ministers, on a Northern Ireland department, on a appointed coordinator or on any other specified person a function, in particular a power or duty to exercise a discretion, or a power to give directions or orders whether written or oral;

---

96   Civil Contingencies Act 2004, section 19.

97   Civil Contingencies Act 2004, section 22 (1) and (2).

(b)   provide for or enable the requisition or confiscation of property (with or without compensation);

(c)   provide for or enable the destruction of property, animal life or plant life (with or without compensation);

(d)   prohibit, or enable the prohibition of, movement to or from a specified place;

(e)   require, or enable the requirement of, movement to or from a specified place;

(f)   prohibit, or enable the prohibition of, assemblies of specified kinds, at specified places or at specified times;

(g)   prohibit, or enable the prohibition of, travel at specified times;

(h)   prohibit, or enable the prohibition of, other specified activities;

(i)   create an offence of (i) failing to comply with a provision of the regulations; (ii) failing to comply with a direction or order given or made under the regulations; (iii) obstructing a person in the performance of a function under or by virtue of the regulations;

(j)   disapply or modify an enactment or a provision made under or by virtue of an enactment;

(k)   require a person or body to act in performance of a function (whether the function is conferred by the regulations or otherwise and whether or not the regulations also make provision for remuneration or compensation);

(l)   enable the Defence Council to authorise the deployment of Her Majesty's armed forces;

(m) make provision (which may include conferring powers in relation to property) for facilitating any deployment of Her Majesty's armed forces;

(n) confer jurisdiction on a court or tribunal (which may include a tribunal established by the regulations);

(o) make provision which has effect in relation to, or to anything done in (i) an area of the territorial sea, (ii) an area within British fishery limits, or (iii) an area of the continental shelf;

(p) make provision which applies generally or only in specified circumstances or for a specified purpose;

(q) make different provision for different circumstances or purposes.

A person making emergency regulations must have regard to the importance of ensuring that Parliament, the High Court and the Court of Session are able to conduct proceedings in connection with the regulations, or action taken under the regulations. The emergency regulations must specify the parts of the UK or regions in relation to which the regulations have effect. Emergency regulations are limited in relation to the creation of offences and may not amend powers or provisions of the Civil Contingencies Act 2004 or the Human Rights Act 1998. They lapse at the end of the period of 30 days beginning with the date on which they are made or such earlier time as may be specified in the regulations themselves.[98] They must be laid before Parliament as soon as it is reasonably practicable. According to Walker (2006), once emergency has been declared, the authorities in UK can assume almost boundless powers. They can prohibit assemblies, ban movements, create offences, deploy the armed forces and confer emergency powers on any individual.[99]

Military personnel during domestic deployment in aid to civil power have no specific statutory powers but the Ministry of Defence (MOD) guidelines assert substantial common law powers, including the use of lethal force and making arrests. The MOD provides that soldiers must act within the law and have no special legal powers beyond those available to an ordinary citizen.

---

98 Civil Contingencies Act 2004, section 23 (5) and 26.

99 Walker, C. and Broderick, G. (2006). *The Civil Contingencies Act 2004: Risk, Resilience and the Law in the United Kingdom*, Oxford: OUP, p. 161.

Fundamental Principles of the Law of Armed Conflict

Under the British Army Field Manual, the four fundamental principles of the laws of armed conflict (LOAC) are military necessity, humanity, distinction and proportionality. Military necessity permits the use of only that degree and kind of force, not otherwise prohibited by LOAC, which is required in order to achieve the legitimate purpose of the conflict, namely the complete or partial submission of the insurgent at the earliest possible moment with the minimum expenditure of life and resources. Humanity forbids the infliction of suffering, injury or destruction not actually necessary for the accomplishment of legitimate military purposes. Distinction requires a marked difference between the treatment of combatants and non-combatants and between objects that might legitimately be attacked and those that are protected from attack. Proportionality requires that unavoidable losses (such as incidental civilian casualties and collateral damage to civilian property) resulting from legitimate military action should not be excessive in relation to the concrete and direct military advantage anticipated from the attack as a whole, rather than any isolated or particular part of it.[100]

Adherence to Law

Adherence to the law is crucial for the legitimacy and campaign authority of any operation. All military operations have a legal dimension; there must be a legal basis for the operation and it must be conducted in a lawful manner. The legal framework is as much an operational enabler as a constraint; it confers a freedom to act, as well as a constraint on military activity. Accordingly, legal advice is essential, not only in the strategic decision to commit UK Armed forces, but also in the interpretation of that decision and its application at the operational and tactical levels. The Legal Adviser (LEGAD) is one of the commander's principal staff officers and advisers, and has a pivotal role in campaign planning and execution. [101]

The use of the armed forces in an operation must be consistent with the UK's obligations in international law and the applicable domestic law.

---

100   British Army Field Manual, Volume 1, Part 10, Countering Insurgency, Army Code 71876, October 2009, paragraph 12-17.

101   Joint Doctrine Publication (JDP) 0-01 *British Defence Doctrine* (BDD) (3rd Edition), paragraphs 160 -163.

Operational law is broader than the LOAC. It encompasses all legal aspects of operations from routine service discipline, through local purchase contracts abroad, to the use of force and everything in between. The Director Central Legal Services is the primary source of operational law and LOAC adviser to the MOD. The Director Central Legal Services provides strategic legal advice to the Government as well as providing oversight of operational legal advice and LEGADs deployed with subordinate formations in joint operations. Additionally, all three services have uniformed lawyers who provide commanders and their staffs with legal advice at the operational and tactical levels, including legal aspects of operations. Each of the three heads of the legal services is responsible for the availability of appropriately trained service lawyers to support operations.

Military lawyers should be involved in all aspects of operational planning and review all draft orders and instructions to ensure that operations are in accordance with the law and extant policies. In counterinsurgency, the LEGAD should also be involved in military activities that lie partly or wholly outside the control of a military commander. In so doing, the LEGAD has a role in coordinating and influencing a range of non-military individuals and groups such as local legal entities and NGOs.

Each counterinsurgency campaign must be conducted in accordance within the applicable legal framework. Therefore the tactics, techniques and procedures that are permissible in one campaign may not be permitted elsewhere or, perhaps, even during the same campaign if the legal framework changes. For instance, it would be plainly illegal for troops, when responding to a domestic riot at the request of the local police, to establish ambush positions with a view to killing those attempting to leave the area. However, if the insurgency has developed to the point that it has become an international armed conflict then it would be legally sustainable to establish an ambush of this type so long as the engagement was authorised by the military chain of command and those targeted were positively identified as falling within the target set as approved by the government and set out in the applicable rules of engagement (ROE) and Targeting Directive.[102]

---

102 British Army Field Manual, Volume 1, Part 10, Countering Insurgency, Army Code 71876, October 2009, paragraph 12-4.

Use of Force

British domestic law (Section 3 Criminal Law Act 1967 and common law) recognize that all persons (including soldiers) have the right, wherever they are in the world, to use such force as is reasonable and necessary in the circumstances in their own defence or defence of another. The degree of force used in defence has to be proportionate to the threat. The courts have recognized that in acting in self-defence a person cannot weigh to a nicety the exact amount of force to be applied. A person can also use force to ward off an anticipated attack provided that it is anticipated as imminent. If an individual believes that there is an imminent threat to life and there is no other way to prevent the threat, he or she may use lethal force to prevent the threat. Therefore, any force used has to be limited to the degree, intensity and duration necessary for self-defence.[103] Military law provides that the troops must obey lawful commands. The ROE, a classified document, duly approved by the MOD are issued to soldiers. In the past, both common law and parliament have condoned the use of deadly force to deal with disturbances.

London Olympics

Before the Olympics of 2012, the British Government made a security assessment and identified the four highest risks areas: (i) international terrorism, including the use of chemical, biological, radiological or nuclear (CBRN) materials; and of terrorism related to Northern Ireland; (ii) cyber attack, including by organised crime and terrorists; (iii) international military crises; and major accidents or natural hazards. To maintain security at the London Olympic Games, the government deployed Reaper drones, helicopters with snipers and the biggest warship in the Royal Navy's fleet. Up to 13,500 ground troops were deployed to provide security, backed by more than 20,000 private guards.

The MOD took the unprecedented step of erecting surface-to-air missile batteries on top of multiple residential locations around East London. A group of local council tenants lost their battle in the High Court to prevent the military missile encampment from being stationed on the roof of their tower block before and during the Olympics. The action to use their residential block as a military base was signed by the British Prime

---

103 British Army Field Manual, Volume 1, Part 10, Countering Insurgency, Army Code 71876, October 2009, paragraph 12-14.

Minister, Deputy Prime Minister, Home Secretary and Defence Secretary in 'defence of the realm'. The Judge presiding over the case maintained that the MOD had no duty to consult with residents, nor would they be responsible for their relocation or any compensation as a result of the domestic military operation.[104]

Jeffery K (1985) in 'Military Aid to Civil Power in the UK' has categorically stated: "Domestic security is an inescapable responsibility for an army. The defence of the state must include the capability to assist in the maintenance of public order and the suppression of internal unrest, insurrection or even revolution." However, has been an increasing demand for the creation of a third force (similar to the French *gendarmerie* or the Japanese riot police) to deal with MACP.[105]

The United States

The US military has provided support to civil authorities in response to civil emergencies and natural disasters from the Truman era.[106] Various

---

104 The Defence Secretary was accused by the residents for breaching Article 8 and Article 1 of Protocol I of the European Convention on Human Rights. It protects an individual's right to a private life and peaceful enjoyment of their home. The decision by the MOD to opt for residents' homes as domestic military staging areas placed residents firmly into the category of 'human shield'. **Patrick Henningsen and Daisy Jones,** Olympic Verdict Places British Residents Under Military Rule Indefinitely, available at: http://www.infowars.com/olympic-verdict-places-british-residents-under-military-rule-indefinitely/, accessed 02 October 2014.

105 Unlike many of its European neighbours, the UK does not have a third force to assist the police in times of emergency. Consequently, the danger remains that the armed forces might find themselves undertaking an ever-greater range of national-resilience tasks, including public order, without appropriate resources. Waring Marc, The Domestic Deployment of the British Army: A Case for Third Force, *RUSI Journal*, June/July 2013, Volume 158, No. 3, p. 62-69.

106 On 1 December 1950, by authority of Executive Order 10186, President Harry S. Truman established the Federal Civil Defence Administration and requested legislation providing statutory authority for the agency. As enacted on 12 January 1951 and amended through 1981, the Federal Civil Defence Act of 1950 stated the intent and policy of Congress: "a system of civil defence for the protection of life and property in the United States from attack and from natural disaster". The Act provided that the responsibility for civil defence is "vested jointly in the Federal Government and the several states and their political subdivisions." The federal government is to provide "necessary direction, coordination, and guidance." The President or Congress, by concurrent resolution, may proclaim a state of civil emergency if a determination is made that an enemy attack has caused or may cause substantial injury to civilian property or persons. During this period of emergency, the president is authorized to

terms have been used for this function over the years: military assistance, or military support to civil authorities; military support of civil defence; and employment of military resources in natural disaster emergencies within the US. During the Nixon administration of 1969-74, regulations were introduced to authorize the use of troops against civil disturbances.

The Los Angeles Riots

The Los Angeles riots of 1992, or the Rodney King riots, were catalysed by the acquittal of four white Los Angeles Police Department officers, who were tried for savagely beating King, an African-American. A private citizen videotaped the incident, which took place on 3 March 1991 and an edited version of the videotape was constantly broadcast on national television during the 12 months that elapsed between the beating and the beginning of the officers' trial. The televised version omitted footage that showed King resisting arrest and attacking one of the police officers. The jury at the trial viewed the complete videotape and found it exculpatory. On the basis of the televised version, the citizens of Los Angeles, the American public and public officials including President George Bush, expected convictions. The verdict in the trial was announced on 29 April 1992, at 1515 hrs and one hour later, the rioting began. Even though the verdict precipitated the riots, there were two other factors that contributed to the violence: the killing of Latasha Harlins[107], and social conditions in South Central Los Angeles. During the period of rioting from 29 April to 4 May

---

"direct, after taking into consideration the military requirements of the Department of Defence, and Federal department or agency to provide" personnel, materials, and facilities to aid the states, as well as emergency shelter. A few months before passage of the Federal Civil Defence Act of 1950, Congress enacted Pub. L. No. 81–875, the intent of which was to provide "an orderly and continuing means of assistance by the Federal Government to the States and local governments in carrying out their responsibilities to alleviate suffering and damage resulting from major disasters." Major disasters were defined as floods, droughts, fires, hurricanes, earthquakes, storms, or other catastrophes.

107 Latasha Harlins was a 15-year-old African-American girl who was unlawfully shot and killed by Soon Ja Du, a 51-year-old Korean store owner. Her death came 13 days after the videotaped beating of Rodney. Du was fined and sentenced to probation and community service but no prison time for her crime, some sources cited the shooting as one of the causes of the Los Angeles Riots.

there were 54 deaths, 2,400 cases of injuries and nearly 11,000 incidents of fire in the riot-hit areas.[108]

Since the regular police as well as National Guards were unable to control the situation; on May 1, the third day of rioting, the President authorized the deployment of Regular Army troops and Marines, and federalized the California National Guard. By May 2, nearly 10,500 guardsmen, 2,023 soldiers and 1,508 marines were in Los Angeles, in addition to 1,717 other federal law enforcement officers. Every guardsman, soldier and marine deployed in Los Angeles had to sign a copy of very restrictive Rules of Engagement (ROE), in order to acknowledge his/her understanding and acceptance of these rules. The ROE stated that: The use of deadly force is authorized only where all three of the following circumstances are present: (a) all other means have been exhausted, (b) the risk of death or serious bodily harm to innocent persons is not significantly increased, and (c) the purpose of its use is one or more of the following: (i) self-defence, (ii) prevention of a crime, (iii) defence of others, and (iv) detention or prevention of the escape of persons. The ROE stipulation that deadly force could be used only after "all other means have been exhausted" implied that non-lethal weapons were available to the military troops. However, this was not the case and only a few troops were equipped with riot batons and face shields. The troops were also not trained in the use of these non-lethal weapons. Thus, military intervention could have resulted in a bloodbath;[109] however, the troops performed the missions with enormous restraint.[110]

---

108 James D. Delk. 1995. *Fires and Furies: The L.A. Riots*, Palm Springs, CA: ETC Publications, pp. 46, 95, 138, 180, and 222.

109 Rasmussen, Maria Jose Moyano, The Military Role in Internal Defence and Security: Some Problems, The Centre for Civil-Military Relations, The Naval Postgraduate School California, Occasional Paper 6, October 1999.

110 On occasion, marines accompanied police officers responding to a domestic dispute. On receiving a request to "cover me," the marines fired over 200 bullets into a house where there were children. The problem was one of vocabulary as well as training: in police parlance, "cover me" means "have your weapon ready and prepare to fire only if I am in danger;" whereas in marine parlance, "cover me" means "open fire at once." Police officers are trained to respond to crime and violence with the minimum force necessary to accomplish the task. This principle of minimum force was alien to a soldier. Rasmussen, Maria Jose Moyano, The Military Role in Internal Defence and Security: Some Problems, The Centre for Civil-Military Relations, The Naval Postgraduate School California, Occasional Paper 6, October 1999, p.11-12

The Constitution

The American Constitution restricts military appropriations to two years, designates the President as the civilian commander-in-chief and empowers Congress to regulate the armed forces.[111] The 'guaranty clause', contained in Article IV, Section 4, provides that the military may only be used to protect a state against 'domestic violence' if requested by a state legislature or executive, when the legislature cannot be convened.[112] The First, Second, Third, Fourth and Fifth Amendments to the Constitution also promise individual rights, a civilian militia, freedom from the quartering of soldiers in private homes without the owner's consent during the peacetime, freedom from unreasonable search and seizure and no deprivation of life , liberty or property without due process. The Supreme Court has been the protector of these rights. It struck down an attempt, via a presidential order, to use the armed forces to seize and operate the country's steel mills which were threatened by a nationwide strike. The Court held that the President's constitutional and statutory powers as were not sufficient to support such an executive order, when Congress had specifically refused to grant such an authority by statute. However, the Court refused to order the military to stop collecting information about civilians.[113]

The courts have been reluctant to recognize the authority of the military tribunals over civilians. In 2008, in the case of *Boumediene v Bush*, the Supreme Court ruled that Guantanamo detainees could immediately file habeas corpus petitions in the US district courts challenging the legality of their confinement. However, it did not question the executive branch's power to declare someone as 'enemy combatant'. The US government has asserted that the commander-in-chief has unchallengeable authority to imprison anyone without charges for the duration of a global war on terror. According to Doyle (2000), the courts in the US have failed to enunciate a wider constitutional principle against military intervention, even in the

---

111 The US Constitution, Article 1, section 8, clauses 12 and 14; Article 2, section 2.

112 Article IV, Section 4 of the US Constitution provides: The United States shall guarantee to every state in this union a republican form of government, and shall protect each of them against invasion; and on application of the legislature, or of the executive (when the legislature cannot be convened) against domestic violence.

113 *Youngstown Steel and Tube Company v Sawyer* 343 US 579 (1952) and *Laird v Tatum* 408 US 1 (1972).

context of the Posse Comitatus Act,[114] where the judges have generally avoided any examination of its possible constitutional underpinning.[115] The Supreme Court has been of the view that the President does not require express Congressional or statutory authorization to exercise the power of mobilizing the force as commander-in-chief. The US President is authorized by the Constitution and laws of the US to employ the armed forces to suppress insurrections, rebellions, and domestic violence under various conditions and circumstances.

NORTHCOM

The September 11 event and the subsequent creation of a homeland security infrastructure have accelerated processed leading towards a greater mobilization of the US armed forces, both at home and abroad. A separate military command, called Northern Command (NORTCOM) was established in 2002. It assumed responsibility within the Department of Defence (DoD) for homeland security and homeland defence missions. Homeland security is defined as: "The preparation for, prevention of, deterrence of, preemption of, defence against, and response to threats and aggression directed towards US territory, sovereignty, domestic population, and infrastructure; as well as crisis management, consequence management, and other domestic civil support." General William F. Kernan, then Commander of Joint Forces Command, outlined the role of the military in homeland security. He proposed an order of response to domestic emergencies to start with the first-responders, then the National Guard, and finally the reserves and active components. The First-responders are primarily local organizations, such as law enforcement, emergency medical personnel, fire departments, and emergency crews from the transportation and communications industries. Homeland defence is: "The protection of

---

114 Posse Comitatus Act (PCA) stands as a strict prohibition against using the military for civilian law enforcement, complete with criminal penalties for violation. It text states: "whoever, except in cases and under circumstances expressly authorized by the Constitution of Act of Congress, willfully uses any part of the army, or Air Force as a posse comitatus or otherwise to execute the laws shall be fined under this title or imprisoned for not more than two years, or both." (18 USC, Section 1385).

115 Doyle, C. 2000. *The Posse Comitatus Act and Related Matters: The Use of the Military to Execute Civilian Law*, CRS Report ofr Congress, 1 June 2000, Washington DC: Congressional Research Service.

US territory, sovereignty, domestic population, and critical infrastructure against external threats and aggression."

The NORTHCOM area of responsibility encompasses Mexico, Canada, the Caribbean nations, and European possessions in the Caribbean. NORTHCOM also has responsibility for the territories of Puerto Rico and the US Virgin Islands, and for the 49 US states on the North American continent. Friendly forces available to NORTHCOM to conduct its homeland security mission—principally the National Guard[116] elements— largely belong to the state governors, with the military components under the control of the state's Adjutant General (AG). In 28 states, the AGs are also the directors of the state's emergency management agency or directorate, with control over all emergency management components, both civilian and military. Within the military departments of 23 states and the Territory of Puerto Rico are the additional State Defence Forces (SDFs),[117] which, like the state or territorial National Guard, are under the command of the governor through the Adjutant General. Thus SDFs constitute a third tier of military forces (the first two are federal forces, both active and reserve, and the dual-status National Guard forces, which may be either under federal or state control).

Troops from NORTHCOM have been assigned domestic deployment tasks on a number of occasions. These include sports events, States of the Union addresses, G-8 summits, presidential inaugurations and funerals, and political conventions.[118] During the 1996 Atlanta Olympics, more than 10,000 soldiers were deployed on the pretext of deterring terrorism. It has also become customary to involve the military in the security for national

---

116 The National Guard is state-based military force (although primarily funded by the federal government and trained in accordance with federal standards) that is the only military force shared by the states and the federal government. The National Guard's unique ability to work in three legal statuses makes them the most versatile DoD force available to the federal government for homeland security (HLS), homeland defence (HD), and military assistance to civil authorities (MACA).

117 State Defence Forces, controlled and funded by the state or territory, are composed of volunteers who are paid only when called to active duty by the governor. Nearly half of the governors have standing SDFs, while all the remaining states have the authority to raise such forces. State Defence Forces include both land and naval elements and are state-controlled military forces that may not be called to federal service.

118 Ehling, M., US Military Will Have Role in RNC Security, *Twin Cities Daily Planet*, 29 June 2008.

conventions of both Republican and Democratic parties. In 2004 and 2008, about 4,000 troops and Coast Guards were deployed for the conventions of both the parties, declaring them 'National Special Security Events'.[119] The troops were placed under the command of the US Army North, the Army's component of the NORTHCOM.

Military Assistance for Civil Disturbances

The Department of Defence Directive of 1994 on 'Military Assistance for Civil Disturbances' (MACDIS) provides that the President is authorized by the Constitution and laws of the United States to employ the armed forces to suppress insurrections, rebellions, and domestic violence under various conditions and circumstances. The primary responsibility for protecting life and property and maintaining law and order in the civilian community is vested in the State and local governments. Supplementary responsibility is vested by statute in specific agencies of the federal government other than the DoD. The President has additional powers and responsibilities to ensure that law and order are maintained. According to the DoD directive, the employment of the military forces to control civil disturbances shall be authorized by the President through an executive order directing the Secretary of Defence to act in a specified civil jurisdiction under specific circumstances. Military forces shall not be used for MACDIS unless specifically authorized by the President. Military forces employed in MACDIS operations shall remain under military command and control at all times. The pre-positioning of military forces for MACDIS operations shall not exceed a battalion-sized unit unless a larger force is authorized by the President. [120]

The Directive further provides that the Secretary of the Army, as the DoD Executive Agent, shall provide for participation by all the components of the army in MACDIS planning, and ensure that readiness of the active and reserve components of the army to execute plans for MACDIS. He shall promulgate orders, rules and regulations to govern all MACDIS operations in which the use of force or deadly force is or can be authorized, and provide all essential guidance on the applicability of the Insurrection

---

119 Head Michael and Scott Mann. 2009. *Domestic Deployment of the Armed Forces: Military Powers, Law and Human Rights*, USA: Ashgate, p. 56.

120 The US Department of Defence Directive Number 3025.12, dated 4 February 1994.

Act and the Posse Comitatus Act. He will also ensure that all Joint Task Force or other commanders who are authorized to execute MACDIS missions promulgate supplemental rules of engagement and rules for the use of force, to cover each MACDIS operation.[121]

Rules of Engagement

Rules of Engagement (ROE) are "directives issued by competent military authority which delineate the circumstances and limitations under which United States forces will initiate and/or continue combat engagement with other forces encountered."[122] In general, ROE differ in wartime to reflect the increased justification for using force. Wartime ROE permit US forces to open fire upon all identified enemy targets, regardless of whether those targets represent actual or immediate threats. By contrast, the standing ROE merely permit engagement in individual, unit, or national self-defence. The legal grounds for the use of force during peacetime are traceable to self-defence.

The principles of necessity and proportionality are applicable for the justification of peacetime use of force in self-defence. The necessity principle permits forces to engage only those forces which are committing hostile acts or clearly demonstrating hostile intent. A 'hostile act' is an attack or other use of force, while 'hostile intent' is the threat of imminent use of force. The precise meanings of these definitions become important when the ROE describe specific behaviours as hostile acts or equate particular objective characteristics with hostile intent. Standing ROE do not limit a commander's inherent authority and obligation to use all necessary means available and to take all appropriate action in self-defence of his/her unit and other US forces in the vicinity. The SROE principle is contained in the mnemonic RAMP;

- **R - Return fire with aimed fire.** Return force with force. You always have the right to repel hostile acts with necessary force.

---

121 The US Department of Defence Directive Number 3025.12, dated 4 February 1994.

122 ROE are rules that govern the use of force to reflect the will of the civilian and military leadership. ROE constrain the actions of forces to ensure their actions are consistent with domestic and international law, national policy, and objectives. ROE are based upon domestic and international law, history, strategy, political concerns, and a vast wealth of operational wisdom, experience, and knowledge provided by military commanders and operators. JP 1-04 *Legal Support to Military Operations*; The US Air Force Doctrine Document 1-04 , Legal Support to Operations, 4 March 2012, page 23.

- **A - Anticipate attack.** Use force if, but only if, you see clear indicators of hostile intent.

- **M - Measure the amount of force** that you use, if time and circumstances permit. Use only the amount of force necessary to protect lives and accomplish the mission.

- **P - Protect with deadly force only human life,** and property designated by your commander. Stop short of deadly force when protecting other property.

Threat Perception

The 2010 Quadrennial Defence Review establishes defence of the US and support of civil authorities at home as key missions of the Department. It directs enhancements to improve the readiness and flexibility of DoD to respond to and manage chemical, biological, radiological, and nuclear (CBRN) threats/attacks in recognition of the proliferation of destructive technologies and the potent ideologies of violent extremism. The 2011 National Strategy for Counterterrorism gives primacy to efforts to counter terrorism, highlights the danger of terrorist pursuit of weapons of mass destruction (WMD), and directs the continuation of investments in aviation, maritime, and border-security capabilities and information sharing to make the US a hardened and increasingly difficult target for terrorists to penetrate.

According to an assessment, US military personnel and facilities are visible symbols of American power, and they will remain primary targets for homegrown violent extremists (HVEs), including 'insider threats' within the armed forces. The growing pattern of attempted and actual attacks on military personnel and facilities – such as recruiting centers, National Guard armouries, Armed Forces Reserve Centres, and the Pentagon – pose a significant, growing, and enduring challenge to military force protection and anti-terrorism requirements. The challenges include the detection, monitoring, and interdiction of threats in the air and maritime domains. Illicit trafficking and transnational criminal organizations also pose a continuous challenge to the security and integrity of all homeland domains, including US land borders with Canada and Mexico and maritime borders in the Caribbean Sea and Pacific Ocean. The US's national security strategy is built upon the following key assumptions:

- The likelihood of a conventional military attack on the US homeland by a nation-state is very low.

- Threats to the homeland will significantly increase when the US is engaged in contingency operations with an adversary abroad.

- Potential nation-State adversaries will continue to refine asymmetric attack plans against the homeland as part of their concepts of operation and broader military strategies of confrontation with the US.

- State, non-State, and criminal cyber attacks on DoD networks will grow in number, intensity, and complexity, as will attacks on public-private information systems and critical infrastructure networks on which DoD depends.

- Terrorists will continue to pursue attacks inside the homeland, including use of WMD to inflict mass casualties.

- Loosely-networked or individually motivated violent extremists will continue to exhort followers and encourage violent extremism in the homeland. Military members and facilities will remain prominent targets of terrorists, particularly HVEs.

- The DoD will be called upon to provide significant resources and capabilities during a catastrophic event in the homeland. The National Response Framework will remain the primary instrument for applying federal capabilities during disaster response.

Homeland security is the first priority for the US and its military. The Strategy for Homeland Defence and Defence Support of Civil Authorities, released in February 2013, emphasizes innovative approaches, greater integration, deepening of external partnerships, and increased effectiveness and efficiencies in DoD's homeland activities. It calls for the use of the vital capabilities of the Total Force – in the Active and Reserve Components – to make the nation more secure and resilient. This strategy identifies two priority missions for the Department's activities in the homeland from 2012 to 2020. These are: (i) Defend US territory from direct attack by State and non-State actors; and (ii) Provide assistance to domestic civil authorities in the event of natural or manmade disasters. These priority missions are reinforced, supported, or otherwise enabled through the pursuit of the following objectives: (a) Counter air and maritime threats at a safe distance; (b) Prevent terrorist attacks on the homeland through support to law enforcement; (c) Maintain preparedness for domestic CBRN incidents; and (d) Develop plans and procedures to ensure Defence Support of Civil Authorities during complex catastrophes.

Military forces, particularly the ground forces, have often provided key support to governments, and in almost all the cases discussed in this chapter, except Japan, have supplanted them. The US and Canada, have created separate military commands, specifically tasked with internal security. In many new democracies, due to the traditional involvement of the military in law enforcement missions, when violence breaks out the government and the civil society consider it appropriate that the military should be brought in. In all the cases discussed above, once the armed forces are deployed they have sweeping powers, which includes the authority to use lethal force, shoot down civilian aircraft, issue orders to civilians, raid premises and seize documents. The rules of engagement (ROE), issued by the military to authorize and specify the level of force to be used by its members during domestic deployment remains highly classified. There is an international trend towards establishing greater executive powers to deploy the armed forces for domestic and political purposes. In Japan, where the military fascist dictatorship dominated before the Second World War, serious attempts have been made to reinterpret the Constitution, enabling the deployment of the armed forces. The scope of military call-out powers have been enlarged in the democracies with a substantial increase in the size and sophistication of weaponry. France has recently deployed 10,000 troops for internal security duties after the killing of 17 people by Islamist militants in Paris in January 2015. The People's Liberation Army (PLA) in China, which has not seen combat since its brief 'punitive war' against Vietnam in 1979, is fully trained and equipped for war. However, China's soldiers have been deployed time and again not to fight external enemies, but to respond to internal security issues such as violent mass demonstrations, and episodes of ethnic unrest.

The 'war on terror' has provided a justification for the domestic deployment of military forces, however, the military interventions in domestic affairs have gone well beyond terrorism. It is understood internationally that the military must be ready and willing to protect the nation against its domestic enemies. However, if soldiers are deployed, they need to be given powers, which must include the authority to arrest, use lethal force, shoot down domestic enemies, interrogate, raid premises and seize documents. In order to do their duties, the armed forces need special protection to maintain operational efficiency.

7

Conclusion and Recommendations

The northeastern region of India comprises seven states: Arunachal Pradesh, Assam, Manipur, Meghalaya, Mizoram, Nagaland and Tripura. The region shares borders with Bangladesh, Bhutan, China, Myanmar and Nepal and is home to more than 50 ethnic groups; some of which are demanding complete secession, while others are fighting for ethnic identities and homelands. A large number have no political ideology and are running insurgency as an industry to make easy money.[1] In Jammu and Kashmir (J&K), insurgency began in the 1980s as an indigenous movement mainly as a result of the discontent among the local population with the political and economic failures of the state government. It was later fuelled by Pakistan with the aim of wresting Kashmir from India.[2]

In the Northeast and J&K the activities of non-State actors, supported by certain foreign militaries has been responsible for the killing of civilians, internal displacements, fear and a sense of insecurity amongst the local population, derailment of the criminal justice system, closure of educational institutions, abductions and demands for ransom. All this has led disillusionment with the state machinery for not providing adequate protection and a sense of alienation in the local population due to slow developmental activities. Militants took advantage of the alienation and created further instability in the affected areas. To counter the threat posed by non-State actors, the Union Government has declared certain parts of

1   Grewal D.S. and Kamal Kinger, 'Role of Armed Forces in Internal Security Management in North Eastern States of India', in Adhikari Shekhar and Sanjeev Nhaduria (ed.). 2014. *India's National Security in the 21ˢᵗ Century*, New Delhi: Pentagon Press, p. 395-408.

2   Patankar V.D., 'Insurgency, Proxy War, and terrorism in Kashmir', in Ganguly Sumit and David P. Fidler (ed.). 2009. *India and Counterinsurgency: Lessons Learned*, London: Routledge, p. 65-78.

the northeast and J&K as 'disturbed areas' and deployed the armed forces in the northeast and J&K as 'disturbed areas' and deployed the armed forces in aid of civil power. The role of armed forces in the disturbed areas has been: (i) segregation and elimination of non-State actors; (ii) identification and neutralization of organizations favourable to these actors; and (iii) confidence building and winning the support of the local population.[3] In order to achieve these tasks, the armed forces deployed in the disturbed areas need certain additional powers which have been provided to them under the Armed Forces Special Powers Act (AFSPA).

The State is empowered to adopt all lawful and constitutional means and create a vigilante force to counter violence. The underlying rationale of self-defence, resting on the concept of necessity, is often expressed in the maxim *salus populi, suprema lex esto* (the safety of the people is the highest law). The concept of 'reason of State' also advocates the exercise of unrestricted penology of measures by the State when faced with existential challenges.[4] According to Carl J Friedrich (1957), "reason of State" are considerations, which exist 'whenever' it is required to ensure that the survival of the State must be ensured by the individuals responsible for it, no matter how repugnant such an act may be to them in their private capacity as decent and moral men.[5] Every State has the right to defend itself; the right needed is inherent in the necessity of the State.[6] The State is entitled to protection against those who seek to destroy it.[7] Going by the opinion of the International Court of Justice, a State can even use nuclear weapons lawfully in an extreme circumstance of self-defence, in which its survival would be at stake.[8]

3   Grewal D.S. and Kamal Kinger, 'Role of Armed Forces in Internal Security Management in North Eastern States of India', in Adhikari Shekhar and Sanjeev Nhaduria (ed.). 2014. *India's National Security in the 21ˢᵗ Century*, New Delhi: Pentagon Press, p. 402.

4   Singh Ujjwal Kumar. 2007. *The State, Democracy and Anti-Terror Laws in India*, New Delhi: Sage Publications, p. 311.

5   Carl J Friedrich. 1957. *Constitutional Reasons of State—The Survival of the Constitutional Order*, Brown University Press.

6   Crozier Brian. 1974. *A Theory of Conflict*, London: Hamish Hamilton.

7   Maogoto Jackson Nyamuya, *Battling Terrorism: Legal Perspectives on the Use of Force and the Law on Terror*, England: Ashgate, p. 162.

8   *Legality of the Threat or Use of Nuclear Weapons*, Advisory Opinion, International Court of Justice (ICJ), 8 July 1996, ICJ Reports 1996, para 97. The Court held: "…in view of the present state of international law viewed as a whole, as examined above by the Court, and of the elements of fact at its disposal, the Court is led to observe that it cannot reach a definitive conclusion as to the legality or illegality of the use of nuclear weapons by a

International law not only permits but requires a States to protect all its citizens, without discrimination, by responding effectively to security threats. Calling out the armed forces to deal with civil unrest[9] is one of the most drastic and potentially life-threatening actions that a government can take against members of the society. Such instances are not uncommon. The governments of the United States, the UK, Canada, Germany, Italy, and Australia have deployed the armed forces under special legislations. There is an international trend towards establishing greater executive powers to deploy the armed forces for domestic and political purposes.

In Australia, legislation was introduced in 2000, and extended in 2006, giving federal governments and the chief of the Australian Defence Force explicit peacetime powers to call out troops if 'domestic violence is occurring or is likely to occur' that 'would be likely to affect Commonwealth interests'. Post-September 11, separate military commands were established in the United States and Canada to prepare for and conducting internal operations. The Canadian Defence Policy Statement in 2006 announced: "To better protect Canada and Canadians, the Canadian Armed Forces will be reorganized to more effectively and quickly respond to domestic crises, as well as support other government departments as required." In Italy, government troops were on the streets of major cities in 2008 and 2009 to combat crime and illegal immigration.

Jeffery K (1985) in 'Military Aid to Civil Power in the UK' has categorically stated: "Domestic security is an inescapable responsibility for an army. The defence of the state must include the capability to assist in the maintenance of public order and the suppression of internal unrest, insurrection or even revolution." The fundamental right that any government must ensure for its citizens is the right to life and personal safety. The activities of non-State actors have threatened this right, and caused serious damage to the welfare of the people as well as the security of

---

State in an extreme circumstance of self-defence, in which its very survival would be at stake."

9 The terminology varies in different states. Some refer to a 'state of siege' (France, Belgium, Argentina), others to a 'state of war' (Italy, Netherlands) and yet others to a 'state of emergency' (Ireland, South Africa). In some constitutions (Australia, Canada and the US) the power to take emergency measures is implied from more general powers in the constitution (i.e., the power to make laws for peace, order and good government). Emergency powers have three principal characteristics: they are extraordinary in scope; they confer wide discretionary and enhanced powers on the government; and the powers are temporary and arise only at the time of crisis.

the nations. In normal circumstances, conflicts should be settled through peaceful measures. When it cannot be resolved through peaceful measures, it is resolved through the use of force. In India, when the state police forces have been inadequate in dealing with threats from non-State actors, the Union Forces consisting of armed forces and paramilitary forces have been deployed in aid to the state authorities. The armed forces cannot sit idle while government property is being destroyed and innocent citizens are being killed.

Human rights organizations, NGOs and a few members of the civil society have alleged that while working under the AFSPA, the armed forces have been responsible for systematic and widespread human rights violations amounting to war crimes. They have claimed that the provisions of the AFSPA are against the international norms of human rights and questioned the effectiveness of the national laws in preventing the abuse of power by the armed forces. They have called the AFSPA is a draconian legislation and argued it be scrapped. No doubt there have been a few instances where the armed forces personnel have exceeded the powers given to them under the AFSPA and have indulged in serious violations of human rights. However, the military as well as the civil legal system have been prompt in taking cognizance of such behaviour.

On the other hand, not much has been done to explore the links between certain human rights NGOs, sections of the media and insurgents. The free flow of foreign funds through hawala channels and NGOs to sustain insurgency and the separatist movements in Kashmir and certain part of the northeast are the major issues of concern for the government.[10] The emergence of NGOs represents an organized response by the civil society in areas in which the State has either failed to act or done so inadequately. However, this may not be true in the case of India, as the existence and

---

10 Recently, the Central Bureau of Investigation (CBI) informed the Supreme Court that the country has a 'mind-boggling' number of NGOs and most do not file audit reports with authorities. For instance, in West Bengal alone there were 234,000 NGOs but only 16,000 (about 8 per cent), had filed their audited reports on receipt of grants and expenditure. The Supreme Court had entrusted the CBI with the gigantic task of compiling information about all registered NGOs in the country, their funding and audit reports. 'Mind-boggling number of NGOs in India', *The Times of India*, 9 July 2014. The hawala trade, as also the booming narcotics business, is controlled from across the border, by elements working in close coordination with the ISI. For more details see: Madhav Nalapat, Foreign NGOs used Rahul as protector, *The Sunday Guardian*, 22 June 2014.

functioning of a large number of NGOs is dubious. In January 2017, the Supreme Court directed the Centre and state governments to scrutinize the accounts of NGOs and voluntary organizations. These organizations were accused of misusing grants and donations as only 10 per cent of the 32.97 lakh registered NGOs had their accounts audited. Besides, a few activists portray themselves as human rights crusaders and make irresponsible statements about the functioning of the state forces in the process. The judiciary, unaware of the ground reality, often gets influenced by these activists and places unjustified restrictions on the forces' functioning.

The award of fellowships to Indian researchers by a few foreign institutions to denounce the AFSPA and accuse the Indian Army of human rights violations is another aspect that must be investigated. Such papers get undue attention as military officers are not encouraged to write about their experiences of counterinsurgency operations. Thus, what the civil society gets to know is one-sided, and often exaggerated stories of military functioning in counterinsurgency operations.

A few NGOs and section of the media have played a major role in distorting and sensationalizing incidents and spreading distrust amongst minority groups. The armed forces lack the means to counter such propaganda and the mechanism to deal with such people. The defence public relations officers (PRO) in the present hierarchical set-up is placed under the ministry of defence and not the military leadership, the military hierarchy is hardly trained in handling the media.

Several NGOs have demanded that a soldier who kills a civilian in disturbed areas in the course of duty be tried in a civil court.[11] If we allowed this, it would lead to an anomalous situation: if a soldier kills a man in obedience to his superior's orders, the question as to whether his action was more than reasonably necessary (i.e., excessive use of force) to encounter the threat would be decided by a judge. While if he disobeys his superior's orders because he regards them as unlawful (as excessive use of force), the question as to whether they were actually unlawful would be decided by a court-martial. For obvious reasons the judge and the court-martial are likely to take different views as to the reasonable necessity and therefore the lawfulness of such an order. Therefore, for the sake of fairness and to protect the interest of a soldier performing his duty, it is necessary that

---

11 Amnesty International India briefing, AI Index: ASA 20/042/2013, dated 8 November 2013.

he be tried by a court martial and not by a civil court. The justice systems of the armed forces, however, need certain reforms. The question of trial aside, the government must ensure that victims of human rights violations are provided effective reparation, including adequate compensation and rehabilitation.

The armed forces play an important role in nation-building and national security. Their primary task relates to the security of the borders of India, to carry out counterinsurgency operations in specified areas and to act in aid of civil authorities for the maintenance of the law and order. In emergent situations, the armed forces can be asked to provide support to the civil authorities and their military expertise and capabilities can be utilized to fill gaps in a very wide range of activities in support of the civilian systems. They are controlled by civil authorities and have little lobbying power. They remain available for any task which may come up. "Let the military do it" is a phrase often heard in India when a task—such as rescue and rehabilitation after an earthquake or flood—exceeds the abilities of the local and regional authorities. Shamefully enough, they have been requisitioned by the district authorities to recover children from bore-well pits, erect a foot-bridge or even fight mosquito menace during the Commonwealth Games. Military forces are often looked upon as people waiting for something to do. And since engaging the military in a civil security task is often free of cost and risk, the temptation on the part of civil authorities to "let the armed forces do it" is great.

The insulated existence of the armed forces has cut them off from the rest of the society and prevented society from appreciating their role and acknowledging their basic rights. There is a need for a more authentic projection of the armed forces, and of their traditions and style of working. There is a need to redefine the rights and duties of armed forces personnel. If the people expressed their faith in the forces by treating them with dignity, fairness and equality under the law, the morale and discipline of the troops would be enhanced.

It is information that most Indians do not know that the Indian armed forces have the best articulated and most consistent set of professional values in the world today. They face the unique challenge of combating violence while keeping in view an overall political objective of their mission. They have the additional responsibility of use of force only for socially approved purposes in a socially approved manner.[12] They have to control violence through discipline, continuous training and laying ethical standards. Socially acceptable violence (in a conflict) is regulated through accepted laws of war. For instance, civilians are not to be harmed, poison should not be used and the prisoners should be treated humanely. These norms have existed since ancient times and find a place in customary laws of war and even in Chanakya's *Arthashastra*.[13] The Hague Conventions of 1899/1907, the Geneva Conventions of 1949 and international human rights law have laid down a set of principles that are acceptable internationally, even if not always followed. These apply to both the parties to a conflict, regardless of the justness of the conflict. These are meticulously followed by the armed forces during non-international armed conflict.[14] However, aberrations may take place.

The main reason from deviation from the principles of armed conflict by members of the armed forces is combat stress. Stressors include exposure to extreme weather, uncertainty, sleep deprivation, extreme fatigue, fear, grief, guilt, frustration and injury. A soldier under prolonged stress may resort to misconduct; which may include killing, torturing a detainee,

---

12 According to Huntington military profession has three special characteristics: expertise, responsibility and corporateness or sense of duty. The expertise of the military profession is in combat, i.e., controlled application of violence to achieve political aim. A soldier is recruited, clothed, armed, and trained to ensure that he fights well when the political leadership demands. The expertise is shared universally through the ranks and files. Officers of every armed service, regardless of their specialist cadre or rank are directed to aim their efforts towards the accomplishment of political mission. Huntington Samuel P. 1957. *The Soldier and The State: Theory and Politics of Civil-Military Relations*, Dehradun: Natraj Publishers, p. 8-10.

13 Kangle, R P. 1988. *The Kautilya Arthasastra*, Part III, Delhi: Motilal Banarsidas, p. 259-260.

14 The Army's sub-conventional doctrine (2006), which was released in 2006 states that since the centre of gravity for such operations is the populace, operations have to be undertaken with full respect to human rights and in accordance with the laws of the land. The doctrine further provides that in order to obviate inconvenience to the populace; the military operations must be conducted on the basis of: (i) Deep respect for human rights and scrupulous upholding of laws of the land; (ii) Ensuring awareness amongst all ranks on human rights; (iii) Expeditious investigation and disposal of alleged human rights violations; and (iv) Promulgation of punishment meted out to defaulting personnel for deterrent effect. Doctrine for Sub-Conventional Operations, Integrated Headquarters of Ministry of Defence (Army), Headquarters Army Training Command, Shimla, December 2006.

raping, looting, desertion and even fragging.[15] Other factors that could increase misconduct are monotonous duties, atrocities on members of the forces by the adversaries, the perception that the civilian population is hostile or untrustworthy, the lack of support from the political leadership, and the loss of confidence in the military leadership. The shortage of personnel in the officer cadre is also a cause of stress among junior and middle-level officers who have to perform multiple functions, and hence, do not have adequate time and opportunity for the intimate administration of personnel under their command.[16]

Buckling under public pressure to repeal the AFSPA, the government, in 2005, appointed a five-member committee headed by Justice Reddy. The committee in its report, which has neither been accepted nor rejected by the government, recommended the repeal of the AFSPA. It stated that the AFSPA is "too sketchy, too bald and quite inadequate in several particulars". However, it revealed that the people in the northeast, while demanding that the AFSPA be repealed, wanted the Army to remain to fight the militants and guard the borders.

At a meeting of the Cabinet Committee on Security headed by the Prime Minister in April 2014, the changes as proposed by the Administrative Reforms Commission were discussed and it was decided that the AFSPA would continue in its present form. The armed forces had opposed the repealing or dilution of the law in any form because while the violence parameters in the states have improved, the threat from terror groups continues. A recent report states that the Union Home Ministry may give up its power to impose the 'disturbed areas' tag on Assam and Manipur[17]

Imagine a scenario in which a high alert has been declared in the capital. The central police forces deployed for the security of the Supreme Court complex have been briefed about the possibility of a suicide bomber

---

15 Navlakha Gautam, A Force Stretched and Stressed, *Economic and Political Weekly*, 18 November 2006, p. 4722-4723.

16 In today's modern society certain values or ethos are not universally shared by civilian society, which leads to misunderstanding between the military and the civilian community. Added factor to such misunderstanding is dissociation of a military member from civil society and media. Reinke Saundra J. and Randall Miller, 'The Profession of Arms and the Management of Violence', in Weber Jeffrey A. and Johan Eliasson (ed.). 2008. *Handbook of Military Administration*, New York: CRC Press, p. 305-307.

17 Singh Vijaita, Assam, Manipur can now decide on AFSPA, The Hindu, August 16, 2017.

attacking the complex. The time is 1100 hours and Guard X, who has taken position behind a temporary post surrounded by sandbags, observes a man slowly approaching the gate. The individual is wearing a big jacket and appears suspicious. Guard X alerts his colleagues, suspecting that the man might be wearing an explosive belt inside. He asks the individual, who is about 15 metres away, to halt. The individual continues walking and tries to put his hand inside the jacket. Fearing that he is trying to switch on an explosive belt, Guard X shouts that he should halt. However, the man continues moving. Without losing any time, Guard X fires a shot, killing the person instantaneously.

There are two possibilities in this hypothetical case. First, the local police arrives and cordons off the area. It is found that the individual was indeed wearing an explosive belt. Because of the guard's alertness and quick action, a serious terrorist attempt has been thwarted. The police, intelligence agencies and government officials take due credit for their active networking. Guard X is promoted out of turn, felicitated and awarded by NGOs and interviewed by the media. Even the chief justice appreciates his soldiery action.

The second possibility is that the individual had come to meet his lawyer in the Supreme Court. He was hard of hearing, has a large dependent family and had no criminal background. The advocates' association files a petition for the removal of armed police from the Supreme Court complex. A protest is held at 'Jantar Mantar' and the police, paramilitary and even armed forces are criticised. Human rights activists call for a candle march and raise funds for the deceased's family. The human rights commission asks the government to pay compensation of Rs 50 lakh for the violation of human rights. Guard X is arrested, suspended, charge-sheeted, tried by a disciplinary court and imprisoned. His appeal in the high court is rejected on the grounds that he exceeded the right of private defence. He too has a dependent family, but no one cares.

This hypothetical case raises two important questions: (a) how certain soldiers should be that a given individual is a terrorist/insurgent and not a civilian before using lethal force against him, and (b) how far soldiers should risk themselves and their comrades to reduce the risk of killing a civilian mistakenly. These questions are very relevant in India, where the security forces face a great challenge not only from insurgents/terrorists, but also from human rights activists and NGOs. Some activists portray themselves as human rights crusaders and make irresponsible statements about the functioning of the State forces in the process. The judiciary often gets influenced and places unjustified restrictions on the forces' functioning.

The dividing line between a terrorist and civilian is not readily visible, either on the ground or in the law. Since insurgents/terrorists do not follow any rules of engagement and adhere to extreme violence and cruelty, it is becoming increasingly difficult for a soldier to religiously follow the principle of distinction. Moreover, this principle does not specify a level of certainty that soldiers must achieve or a level of risk they must accept to achieve that level of certainty. While a soldier has a duty not to harm a civilian, he cannot take a chance when there is a likely threat to comrades or persons he is protecting. While judicial officers have ample time to decide a case, a soldier on the ground has to take life-and-death decisions in a split second. It is a crime to intentionally kill an innocent civilian, but our legal luminaries must understand that no set of legal rules can replace human judgement, eliminate human error, or prevent the loss of civilian lives in the fog of present-day conflict.

Recommendations

Once soldiers are deployed, to quell domestic violence, they need to be given special powers under the Armed Forces (Special Powers) Act (AFSPA), including the authority to use lethal force, shoot down domestic enemies, interrogate civilians, raid premises and seize documents. They also need special protection to ensure operational efficiency to protect the rights of soldiers. The civil society and media must understand that the armed forces are called upon to rein in the chaos created by political failure to fulfil promises made to the people, and administrative failures in dealing with insurgents. They must remember that members of the armed forces are answerable for their lapses and that the powers given to them under the AFSPA are not unlimited and cannot be resorted to at will. Whether the AFSPA should be invoked or revoked is a political decision and is beyond the scope of this work. The following recommendations relate better compliance with the laws of war and human rights and should the armed forces continue to be deployed under the AFSPA.

Deployment of the Armed Forces: The military may provide short-term relief during a public order crisis. However, such crises are normally the result of complex political and social problems, and inadequate and corrupt law-enforcement and judicial systems. Unless the political and social issues are addressed, the military might have to be redeployed, and may become less of a deterrent in due course of time. Overzealous use of power may prove counterproductive and exacerbate the problem they were designed to solve. Resort to the power to declare an area as 'disturbed' and the deployment of the armed forces should not be prolonged further than is absolutely necessary.

Manual of Laws of War: The government must establish an expert committee to draft a common manual of the laws of the war for the three services. Some of the issues which could be included in the manual are: the application of laws during international and non-international armed conflict; the role of combatants and civilians; the means and methods of warfare which can be applied; the protection of the civilian population; the protection of the wounded and sick and cultural property; the laws applicable during sea and air warfare. It must also explain the customary principles of the laws of war like necessity, proportionality, distinction and humanity. A chapter on the enforcement of the laws of war, the responsibility of commanders and the role of non-governmental organizations, media and the International Committee of the Red Cross (ICRC) would remove uncertainties regarding the functions these agencies during an armed conflict. In order for operations to be conducted in compliance with the law, the law must be an integral part of (i) manual, (ii) education, (iii) training, and (iv) sanctions.

Amendments to AFSPA: Section 4 of the AFPSA gives powers to certain members of the armed forces in disturbed areas. There have been allegations that wide powers have been given to the low-ranking non-commissioned officer. In order to avoid any ambiguity in the matter the following provision may be added to the section: *The responsibility for deciding as to the strength and composition of any force to be utilized for the suppression of violence in a disturbed area shall lie with the military authorities. Whenever possible a sufficient number of officers/junior commissioned officers (JCO) shall be included to ensure that an officer/ JCO will be available to command each body that may be required to operate separately.*

The Act [18] provides that no suit or other legal proceeding shall be instituted, except with the previous sanction of the Central Government against any person in respect of anything done or purported to be done in the exercise of the powers conferred by the AFSPA. There have been allegations that this provision gives complete immunity to a person operating in a disturbed area and that the government rarely accords sanctions for prosecution. In order to allay such misgivings, it is recommended that the following provision be added to section 6/7 of the Act: *The Central Government while rejecting any such sanction shall give brief reasons in support thereof.*

Right to Compensation: The emergence of compensatory jurisprudence for protecting the right to life and personal liberty is a great contribution made by the Indian judiciary to the cause of human rights. Compensation to victims is a recognized principle of law that is being enforced through the civil courts. Under the law of torts victims can claim compensation in case of wrongful confinement and restraint. But it takes decades for the victims to seek redress in a civil court. [19] The government must devise a system to ensure that persons whose human rights have been violated by members of the armed forces (due to undue arrest or detention in disturbed areas) are duly compensated.[20]

Military Justice System: The military legal system must be reformed. There is a need to ensure that all violations of the laws of armed conflict and war crimes and the standards of 'command responsibility' are incorporated in

---

18 Section 6 of the Armed Forces Special Powers) Act, 1958 and Section 7 of the Armed Forces (Jammu and Kashmir) Special Powers Act, 1990.

19 The provision of a remedy and reparations for victims of violations is a fundamental component of the process of restorative justice. It is the duty of the State to provide a remedy and reparations forms a cornerstone of establishing accountability for violations and achieving justice for victims. While monetary compensation may certainly be central to this process, it is necessary that the violator is identified and suitably punished. Such process is fundamental to both the peace and security of any State since it eliminates the potential of future revenge and any secondary victimization that may result from the initial violation.

20 In a case in which British soldiers, while being stationed in Afghanistan, detained a civilian in illegal military custody for 135 days, the British Supreme Court held that the Ministry of Defence was liable to pay compensation for unlawful detention. *Serdar Mohammed v Ministry of Defence* [2014] EWHC 1369 (QB).

military law.[21] The existing justice system of the military and paramilitary forces is command centered. A commander has absolute powers to decide to try or not to try an accused; prefer charges; detail officers to constitute the court; return the proceedings for revision; and to confirm or not confirm the proceedings. The court members, prosecutor, defending officer and even the judge advocate function under command influence.

Such a system is seen as arbitrary and unjust by the civil society. The powers of the commander need to be rationalized. The justice system of the military and paramilitary forces must be transparent to ensure that the public has confidence in the administration of justice.[22] The findings of military/ paramilitary courts must be reasoned and the proceedings, except any part which may affect the affairs of the State, be available for public scrutiny. An accused must be afforded the right to a fair trial and must have the right to appeal against the verdict in an independent civilian tribunal.[23] Unfortunately the Government still maintains that the existing military laws are up to date and in synchronization with human rights, humanitarian laws and the prevalent criminal and service jurisprudence.[24]

---

21 There is a need to incorporate the crimes spelt out in the Rome Statute into the manuals of laws relating to the military and paramilitary forces. The jurisdiction of the Rome Statute of the International Criminal Court (ICC) is based on the principle of complementarity. The ICC would not hear any case unless the State is 'unwilling or unable genuinely' to prosecute the offender. It will remove the shortcoming of the legal system and comply with international criminal standards. Jha U. C. 'ICC and the Indian Military System', in Nainar Vahida and Saumya Uma (ed.). 2013. *Pursuing Elusive Justice: Mass Crimes in India and Relevance of International Standards*, New Delhi: Oxford University Press, p. 315-333.

22 Fidell Eugene R., Accountability Transparency & Public Confidence in the Administration of Military Justice, *The Green Bag*, Second Series, Summer 2006, Volume 9, Number 4, p. 361-366.

23 Article 14 of the International Covenant on Civil and Political Rights states that everyone shall be entitled to a fair and public hearing by a competent, independent and impartial tribunal established by law. Human rights standards and principles relating to the administration of justice fully apply to military courts. Independence of judges and lawyers, United Nations General Assembly document A/68/285, 7 August 2013.

24 The Government in a written reply to question in informed that the Rajya Sabha informed, "While the three services, viz. Army, Navy and Air Force, have their own Acts and Rules, they are broadly similar in their administration of justice, which is subject to the scrutiny and superintendence of the Hon'ble Armed Forces Tribunal (AFT) and Hon'ble Supreme Court. The evolution and progress of Military legal System like any other legal system is a continuous process so as to be in tune with the changing environment, evolving jurisprudence and functional requirements. The existing laws

Human Rights of Armed Forces Personnel: The government has to ensure that the personnel of the armed forces enjoy basic human rights. It must replace the existing grievance redressal machinery with a vibrant system under which every person can take up his redressal for grievance without fear of higher authorities. Though such measures will draw tremendous opposition from the higher military authorities, the government must understand that respect for the human rights of members of armed forces would be helpful in remedying certain malaises like stress, suicides, fragging, and shortage of personnel, which the armed forces are facing today.

Rules of Engagement: Orders given to subordinates by military authorities for the use of force must be clear, precise, and lawful under military law, the laws of war and domestic law. The subordinates must be encouraged to report every violation to their superiors/ commanding officer, and every such incident must be investigated. The armed forces must train and re-train all their ranks on their obligations under the laws of war and human rights laws.[25]

Monitoring Compliance of Law: The chiefs of the army and paramilitary forces must put in place an effective monitoring mechanism to ensure that that the Do's and Don'ts issued for operations in disturbed areas and the guidelines of the Supreme Court in *Naga Peoples Movement case* are meticulously followed.

Arrests: The chiefs of the army and the paramilitary forces should also provide written guidelines to their forces who are likely to detain a suspect. The guidelines on questioning/ interrogation should be compatible with

---

are up to date and in synchronisation with human rights, humanitarian laws and the prevalent Criminal and Service jurisprudence." RAJYA SABHA Unstarred Question No. 2437, answered on 8 August 2017.

25 In J&K and certain parts of northeast, it is no longer unusual for women to encircle a security post and snatch a lone soldier's weapon; or for civilians to stall encounters with stones and slogans that throw a protective shield over the militants being hunted down. The armed forces need to devise innovative rules of engagement/ SOPs applicable in such circumstances as certain agitators are not afraid to get hurt or even die. See: Dutt Barkha, *Reimaging Kashmir*, ORF Special Report 38, August 2017.

international law, in particular, the Geneva Convention to minimize the dangers of a suspect being tortured or maltreated.[26]

Domestic Laws: Non-State actors have often taken advantage of the prevailing circumstances and used 'legal provisions' to their advantage. The armed forces must lay more emphasis on training its officers and men on domestic penal laws. They must understand important aspects relating to arrest, seizure, questing of a suspect, and the lodging of first information reports. They must also be trained to preserve evidence and other information necessary to 'prove' that actions taken in operations, and the decisions that led to them, were legal and authorized.

Investigations of Human Rights Violations: In order to ensure accountability and public confidence, the armed forces must maintain and publicly disclose the details of every investigation (court of inquiry) undertaken with relation to reported cases of human rights violations.

Lawfare: Lawfare must be integrated into military command structures to bring about the desired outcomes, and must be exploited to downsize insurgency and subdue non-state actors. The government must identify circumstances in which opponents may create legal facts that could give them an advantage in the future. While inducting new weapon systems for use in internal security situations, it must advance international legal rules which would not restrict the use of weapons. The government must identify insurgents' needs for material and resources, and attempt to block access within applicable law. Law is a good substitute for kinetic warfare; the government needs to exploit it for strategic advantages.

Media Management: The media has played an important role in many military campaigns including the 1971 war and the Kargil conflict. It is necessary for the military chain of command to understand the way the media functions. Since insurgency is a battle for the hearts and minds of the people, the media is the most potent weapon for conducting psychological initiatives. The armed forces must focus on balancing openness with security to exploit the power of the media. The military leadership must graduate from the outdated media policy of the ministry of defence. They

---

26 The armed forces, while arresting and questioning a suspect, must follow the guidelines laid down by the Supreme Court in *DK Basu v State of West Bengal*, AIR 1997 SC 610.

must be open about violations committed by the troops and apprise the media about the measures undertake to avoid the recurrence of such violation.

Armed conflict is today characterized by ambiguity, danger and complexity. In particular non-international conflicts will continue to be a contest of wills, characterized by danger, uncertainty and unpredictability. Many military personnel have made the ultimate sacrifice in these conflicts and many more have been seriously injured. Indian citizens must understand why the armed forces need additional powers under the AFSPA.

Every country in the world where the armed forces have been deployed to counter domestic disturbance, provides similar powers and protection to its armed forces.[27] The Australian defence forces (ADF) deployed in the aid to civil power have unprecedented powers such as to shoot down passenger aircraft, use lethal force, interrogate civilians and seize documents. It has been recently announced that the military will have sweeping powers[28] to deploy forces and even take charge during terrorists' attacks. The amended Australia's national security laws will give the military full legal authority to shoot and kill terrorists.[29]

---

27 The lethal capabilities of terrorists demonstrated by September/11 attacks have fundamentally changed the political and legal landscape. It has prompted the international community to examine international terrorism a new as the acts of terrorists was regarded as an act of war. Maogoto Jackson Nyamuya. 2005. *Battling Terrorism: Legal Perspectives on the Use of Force and the Law on Terror*, England: Ashgate, p. 151-152.

28 Under the current system, the ADF can only be deployed if state or territory police believe their capability or capacity to respond has been exceeded. That provision will be abolished, meaning states could request federal help even if they retained control of the situation.

29 On 17 July 2017, the Australian Prime Minister Malcolm Turnbull announced that the law is being amended to give more powers to the armed forces to managing domestic security. He stated that under the amended law, the state and territory governments would be able to call for military help any time a terror incident is declared. Previously, the military could only be called upon if police concluded they could no longer deal with an incident. In addition, the military's Special Forces will train state police teams and soldiers will be placed within law enforcement agencies to improve engagement between authorities. According to Malcolm Turnbull, the changes to domestic counterterrorism measures were made "to stay ahead of the evolving threat of terrorism" and to "ensure Australia has a coordinated and integrated response". The proposed changes, however, need parliament's approval.

The "right to kill" is not a drawback of the AFSPA. If the law and order situation has deteriorated to such an extent as to call for the deployment of the armed forces, the soldiers have to be allowed to use deadly force. Even a private citizen has the right to kill someone in self-defence. In fact, special legislation is necessary to protect the rights of soldiers. The legal machinery in the country has not shirked its responsibility in ensuring suitable action in cases where the law has been violated and successive judgments of the Supreme Court have held that the provisions of the AFSPA do not violate the Constitution. We must remember the inhumanity of the militants in killing innocent victims, abduction, rape and political assassination and consider the threat such acts pose to the integrity of our country. We must also remember that the armed forces personnel deployed in disturbed areas suffer casualties every day. We must honestly ask ourselves if a society is truly free when it needs to wrap layers of security blankets around its own national celebrations for fear of terrorists' attacks. Militants and non-State actors may wreak even greater damage, as the destructive power of their arsenal increases and they continue to get support from actors across the border. [30]

It is a fallacy to think that India's Constitution confers only rights and imposes no duties. The citizens have certain constitutional duties towards the state. They are to defend the country and are bound to uphold its sovereignty, unity, and integrity. They are also to safeguard public property and abjure violence. So when there is a high alert in a certain area and the forces have been tasked to protect their rights against violators, all citizens have a corresponding duty to help the security forces in their mission. A soldier on the ground cannot take a chance, particularly when the enemy remains faceless and fiercely lethal. While the death of every civilian is regrettable, the civil society has to understand its duty towards the country.

Our soldiers are human beings. We need to pay more attention and support for an expanded range of the rights of soldiers. In order to arrest and detain non-state actors in a conflict zone, a soldier should not be expected to comply with peace-time standards such as those exercised by

---

30 Today, more than 50 militants groups are active in South Asia. They are responsible for killing and maiming thousands of innocent civilians and creating instability in the region. Sharma Surinder K and Anshuman Behera. 2014. *Militant Groups in South Asia*, New Delhi: Pentagon Press.

a civilian police force. Many legal luminaries, human rights organisations and activists grant rights to an insurgent or to a fleeing bank robber than to soldiers who are trying to do their assigned task. With the terrorist camps operating across the line of control and attempting to destabilise our country,[31] it has become all the more necessary for the civil society to support the security forces.

---

31 Afghan- and Indian-focused militants continue to operate from Pakistan territory to the detriment of Afghan and regional stability. Pakistan uses these proxy forces to hedge against the loss of influence in Afghanistan and to counter India's superior military. *Progress Toward Security and Stability in Afghanistan*, The US Department of Defence, Report to Congress, October 2014, p. 95. In 2013, India was the sixth worst-affected country by terrorism, the other five being war zones at present. *Global Terrorism Index 2014*, The Institute for Economics and Peace, New York.

The Armed Forces (Special Powers) Ordinance, 1942

(Ordinance No XLI of 1942 of 15 August 1942)

An Ordinance to confer certain special powers upon certain officers of the armed forces

WHEREAS an emergency has arisen which makes it necessary to confer certain special powers upon certain officers of the armed forces:

Now therefore, in exercise of the powers conferred by section 72 of the Government of India Act, as set out in the Ninth Schedule of the Government of India Act, 1935, the Governor-General is pleased to make and promulgate the following Ordinance:-

1. **Short title, extent and commencement:-** (1) This Ordinance may be called THE ARMED FORCES (SPECIAL POWERS) ORDINACNCE, 1942.

   (2) It extends to the whole of India.

   (3) It shall come into force at once.

2. **Power to certain officers of the armed forces to order use of force in certain circumstances:-** (1) Any officer not below the rank of Captain in (the Indian) Military Forces and any officer holding equivalent rank either in (the Indian) Naval or Air Forces may, if in his opinion it is necessary for the proper performance of his duty so to do, by general or special order in writing require any personnel under his command to use such force as may be necessary, even to the causing death, against any person who—

   (a) fails to halt when challenged by a sentry, or

   (b) does, attempts to do, or appears to be about to do, any such act as would endanger or damage any property of any description whatsoever which is the duty of such officer to protect;

   and it shall be lawful for such personnel when so ordered, to use such force against such person.

(2) The use of force against any such person in obedience to an order under sub-section (1) shall include the power to arrest and take into custody such person, and the use of such force as may be necessary, even to the causing of death, in order to effect such arrest.

3. **Arrested persons to be made over to appropriate authority**:- Any person arrested and taken into custody under this Ordinance shall, as soon as practicable be made over, together with a report of the circumstances occasioning the arrest, to the officer in charge of the nearest police station, or where the said person is a person subject to the military law, to the appropriate military officer.

4. **Protection to persons acting under this Ordinance**:- No prosecution, suit or other legal proceedings for any order purporting to be mad under this ordinance or for any act purporting to be done in obedience to any such order shall be instituted in any Court except with the previous sanction of the Central Government, and notwithstanding anything contained in any other law for the time being in force, no person purporting in good faith to make such an order or to do any act in obedience thereto shall, whatever consequences ensure, be liable therefor.

The Ordinance was applied to the Darjeeling District with effect from 15 October 1942 vide Bengal Government Notification No. 20215-P dated 8 October 1942. Sections 2-4 were applied to members of the Armed Reserves, Special Emergency Forces, Vizianagram and Pallavaram and the Malabar Special Police, vide Madras Government Notification No. 220-Home, dated 29 January 1943. The Ordinance was extended to (a) the new provinces and merged States by Act LIX of 1949, S.3 (1-1-1950); (b) the States of Manipur, Tripura and Vindhya Pradesh by Act XXX of 1950, S.3 (16-4-1950); and (c) the Union Territories of Dadra and Nagar Haveli & Pondicherry by Regn. VI of 1965 (1-7-1965) and Regn. VII of 1963 (1-10-1963).

The Armed Forces (Special Powers) Act, 1958

(Act 28 of 1959)

An Act to enable certain special powers to be conferred upon members of the armed forces in disturbed areas in the States of Assam, Manipur, Meghalaya, Nagaland and Tripura and the Union Territories of Arunachal Pradesh and Mizoram.

BE it enacted by Parliament in the Ninth Year of the Republic of India as follows:-

1. Short title and extent.—(1) This Act may be called the Armed Forces (Special Powers) Act, 1958.

(2) It extends to the whole of the State of Assam, Manipur, Meghalaya, Nagaland and Tripura and the Union Territories of Arunachal Pradesh and Mizoram.

2. Definitions- In this Act, unless the context otherwise requires,

(a) "armed forces" means the military forces and the air forces operating as land forces, and includes any other armed forces of the Union so operating;

(b) "disturbed area" means an area which is for the time being declared by notification under section 3 to be a disturbed area;

(c) All other words and expressions used herein, but not defined and defined in the Air Force Act, 1950 or the Army Act 1950, shall have the meanings respectively attached to them in those Acts.

3. Power to declare areas to be disturbed areas- If, in relation to any State or Union Territory to which this Act extends, the Governor of that State or the Administrator of that Union Territory of the Central Government in either case, is of the opinion that the whole or any part of such State or Union Territory, as the case may be, is in such a disturbed or dangerous condition that the use of armed forces in aid of the civil power is necessary, the Governor of that State or the Administrator of that Union Territory or the Central Government, as the case may be, may, by notification in the Official Gazette, declare the whole or such part of such State or Union Territory to be a disturbed area.

4. Special powers of the armed forces- Any commissioned officer, warrant officer, non commissioned officer or any other person of equivalent rank in the armed forces may, in a disturbed area:-

(a) if he is of opinion that it is necessary so to do for the maintenance of public order, after giving such due warning as he may consider necessary, fire upon or otherwise use force; even to the causing of death, against any person who is acting in contravention of any law or order for the time being in force in the disturbed area prohibiting the assembly of five or more persons or the carrying of weapons or of things capable of being used as weapons or of fire-arms, ammunition or explosive substances;

(b) if he is of opinion that it is necessary so to do, destroy any arms dump, prepared or fortified position or shelter from which armed attacks are made or are likely to be made or are attempted to be made or any structure used as a training camp for armed volunteers or utilized as a hideout by armed gangs or absconders wanted for any offence:

(c) arrest without warrant, any person who has committed a cognizable offence or against whom a reasonable suspicion exists that he has committed or is about to commit a cognizable offence and may use such force as may be necessary to effect the arrest;

(d) enter and search without warrant any premises to make any such arrest as aforesaid or to recover any person believed to be wrongfully restrained and confined or any property reasonably suspected to be stolen property or any arms, ammunition or explosive substances believed to be unlawfully kept in such premises, and may for that purpose use such force as may be necessary.

5. Arrested persons to be made over to the police- Any person arrested and taken into custody under this Act shall be made over to the officer in charge of the nearest police station with the least possible delay, together with a report of the circumstances occasioning the arrest.

6. Protection to person acting under Act- No prosecution, suit or other legal proceeding shall be instituted, except with the previous sanction of the Central Government, against any person in respect of anything done or purported to be done in exercise of the powers conferred by this Act.

7. Repeal and Saving- (1) The Armed Forces (Assam and Manipur) Special Powers Ordinance, 1958, is here by repealed

(2) Not withstanding such repeal anything done or any action taken under the said ordinance shall be deemed to have been or taken under this Act, as if this had commenced on the 22nd day of May, 1958

The Armed Forces (Jammu & Kashmir) Special Power Act, 1990

(Act 21 of 1990)

An Act to enable certain special powers to be conferred upon members of the armed forces in the disturbed areas in the State of Jammu and Kashmir.

BE it enacted by Parliament in the Forty-first Year of the Republic of India as follows:-

1. Short title, extent and commencement- (1) This Act may be called the Armed Forces (Jammu and Kashmir) Special Powers Act, 1990.

(2) It extends to the whole of the State of Jammu and Kashmir.

(3) It shall be deemed to have come into force on the 5th day of July, 1990.

2. Definitions- In this Act, unless the context otherwise requires,-

(a) "armed forces" means the military forces and the air forces operating as land forces and includes any other armed forces of the Union so operating ;

(b) "disturbed area" means an area which is for the time being declared by notification under section 3 to be a disturbed areas;

(c) all other words and expressions used herein, but not defined and defined in the Air Force Act, 1950 (45 of 1950), or the Army Act, 1950 (46 of 1950), shall have the meanings respectively assigned to them in those Acts.

3. Power to declare areas to be disturbed areas- If, in relation to the State of Jammu and Kashmir, the Governor of the State or the Central Government, is of opinion that the whole or any part of the State is in such a disturbed and dangerous condition that the use of armed forces in aid of the civil power is necessary to prevent -

(a) activities involving terrorist acts directed towards overawing the Government as by law established or striking terror in the people or any section of the people of alienating any section of the people or adversely affecting the harmony amongst different sections of the people ;

(b) activities directed towards disclaiming, questioning or disrupting the sovereignty and territorial integrity of India or bringing about cession of a part of the territory of India or secession of a part of the territory of India from the Union or causing insult to the Indian National Flag, the Indian National Anthem and the Constitution of India,

the Governor of the State or the Central Government, may, by notification in the Official Gazette, declare the whole or any part of the State to be a disturbed area.

Explanation- In this section, "terrorist act" has the same meaning as in Explanation to Article 248 of the Constitution of India as applicable to the State of Jammu and Kashmir.

4. Special powers of the armed forces.- Any commissioned officer, warrant officer, non-commissioned officer or any other person of equivalent rank in the armed forces may, in a disturbed area:-

(a) if he is of opinion that it is necessary so to do for the maintenance of public order, after giving such due warning as he may consider necessary, fire upon or otherwise use force, even to the causing of death, against any person who is acting in contravention of any law or order for the time being in force in the disturbed area prohibiting the assembly of five or more persons or the carrying of weapons or of things capable of being used as weapons or of fire-arms, ammunition or explosive substances ;

(b) if he is of opinion that it is necessary so to do, destroy any arms dump, prepared or fortified position or shelter from which armed attacks are made or are likely to be made or are attempted to be made, or any structure used as a training camp for armed volunteers or utilised as a hide-out by armed gangs or absconders wanted for any offence;

(c) arrest, without warrant, any person who has committed a cognizable offence or against whom a reasonable suspicion exists that he has committed or is about to commit a cognizable offence and may use such force as may be necessary to effect the arrest;

(d) enter and search, without warrant, any premises to make any such arrest as aforesaid or to recover any person believed to be wrongfully restrained or confined or any property reasonably suspected to be stolen property or any arms, ammunition or explosive substances believed to be unlawfully kept in such premises, and may for that purpose use such force as may be necessary, and seize any such property, arms, ammunition or explosive substances;

(e) stop, search and seize any vehicle or vessel reasonably suspected to be carrying any person who is a proclaimed offender, or any person who has committed a non-cognizable offence, or against whom a reasonable suspicion exists that he has committed or is about to commit a non-cognizable offence, or any person who is carrying any arms, ammunition or explosive substance believed to be unlawfully held by him, and may, for that purpose, use such force as may be necessary to effect such stoppage, search or seizure, as the case may be.

5. Power of search to include powers to break open locks, etc - Every person making a search under this Act shall have the power to break open the lock of any door, almirah, safe, box, cupboard, drawer, package or other thing, if the key thereof is withheld.

6. Arrested persons and seized property to be made over to the police- Any person arrested and taken into custody under this Act and every property, arms, ammunition or explosive substance or any vehicle or vessel seized under this Act, shall be made over to the officer-in-charge of the nearest police station with the least possible delay, together with a report of the circumstances occasioning the arrest, or as the case may be, occasioning the seizure of such property, arms, ammunition or explosive substance or any vehicle or vessel, as the case may be.

7. Protection of persons acting in good faith under this Act- No prosecution, suit or other legal proceeding shall be instituted, except with the previous sanction of the Central Government, against any person in respect of anything done or purported to be done in exercise of the powers conferred by this Act.

8. Repeal and saving- (1) The Armed Forces (Jammu and Kashmir) Special Powers Ordinance, 1990 (Ord. 3 of 1990), is hereby repealed.

(2) Notwithstanding such repeal, anything done or any action taken under the said Ordinance shall be deemed to have been done or taken under the corresponding provisions of this Act.

Bibliography

Ackerman Bruce, The Emergency Constitution, *Yale Law Journal*, Vol. 113, (2004), p. 1029–91.

Agarwal A.K. 2013. *The Third Dimension: Air Power in Combating the Maoist Insurgency*, New Delhi: Vij Books India Pvt. Ltd.

Ahmed, Col Ali, Reconciling AFSPA with the Legal Spheres, *Journal of Defence Studies*, Vol. 5, No 2, April 2011, p. 109-121.

Aiyede, E R. "Democratic Security Sector Governance and Military Reform in Nigeria" in Bryden, A and Chappuis, F (eds.). 2015. *Learning from West African Experiences in Security Sector Governance*, London: Ubiquity Press, pp. 97–116.

Akbar M.J., Omar Must Know Army is not the enemy, *The Times of India*, 19 September 2010.

Albrecht Hans-Joerg, Terrorism, Risk, and Legislation, *USI Digest*, Vol. XI, No. 21, September 2008-February 2009, p. 1-51.

Alleged Perpetrators: Stories of Impunity in Jammu and Kashmir, International Peoples' Tribunal on Human Rights and Justice in Indian-Administered Kashmir, 2012.

Alley Roderic. 2004. *Internal Conflict and the International Community: Wars Without Ends?* Dartmouth: Ashgate.

Ana Maria Salinas De Frias, Katja Lh Samuel and Nigel D White (ed.). 2012. *Counter-Terrorism: International Law and Practice*, Oxford: Oxford University Press.

Annual Report 2012-13, Government of India, Ministry of Home Affairs.

Antonio Pablo and Fernandex Sanchez (ed.). 2005. *The New Challenges of International Humanitarian Law in Conflicts*, Leiden: Martinus Nijhoff Publishers.

Armed Forces Special Powers Act 1958: Manipur Experience, Campaign for Peace & Democracy (Manipur), 2010.

Army's Subversion of Justice, Editorial, *Economic and Political Weekly*, Vol. XLIX, No. 7, 15 February 2014, p. 7-8.

Arnold, Roberta, Military Criminal Procedure and Judicial Guarantees: The Example of Switzerland, Vol. 3 (3), *Journal of International Criminal Justice*, 2005, p. 749-777.

Art Robert J. And Louise Richardson (ed.). *Democracy and Counterinsurgency: Lessons from the Past*, Washington DC: United States Institute of Peace Press.

Ashworth Andrew. 2005. *Sentencing and Criminal Justice*, Cambridge: Cambridge University Press.

Austin Granville. 2003. *Working A Democratic Constitution: A History of the Indian experience*, New Delhi: Oxford India Paperback.

Bal Suryakant, The Human Element in Military Effectiveness: A Systems Approach, *Journal of Defence Studies*, Vol. 5, No. 1, January 2011, p. 134-146.

Balendra Natasha, Defining Armed Conflict, New York University Public Law and Legal Theory Working Papers, *Cardozo Law Review*, Vol. 29 (6), 2008, p. 2462-1516.

Barnes Catherine, Agents for Change: Civil Society Roles in Preventing War & Building Peace, Issue paper 2, European Centre for Conflict Prevention, 2006.

Bhaumik Subir, Counter to the Spirit of Counterinsurgency, *The Hindu*, 14 June 2014, p. 10.

Bilal Noor Mohammad, Implementation of Human Rights Norms: Violations and Impunity in Kashmir, *KULR*, Vol. XVI, No. XVI, 2009, p. 68-84.

Blaxland John C, Revisiting Counterinsurgency: A Manoeuvrist Response to the 'War on Terror' for Australian Army, Working Paper No. 131, Land Warfare Studies Centre Australia, 2006.

Blum Gabriella, The Crime and Punishment of States, *The Yale Journal of International Law*, Vol. 38, 2013, p. 57-122.

Bonner David, Responding to Crisis: Legislating Against Terrorism, *The Law Quarterly Review*, Vol. 122, p. 602-631.

Bonner David. 1985. *Emergency Powers in Peacetime*, London: Sweet & Maxwell.

Boothby, William H., Differences in the Law of Weaponry When Applied to Non-International Armed Conflicts, in Watkin Kenneth and Andrew J. Norris (eds.). 2011. *Non-International Armed Conflict in the Twenty-first Century*, International Law Series, Vol. 88, the US Naval War College, p. 197-210.

Brehm Maya. 2012. *Protecting Civilians from the Effects of Explosive Weapons: An Analysis of International Legal and Policy Standards*, United Nations Institute for Disarmament Research.

Brown Michael E. (ed). 1996. *The International Dimensions of Internal Conflict*, London: MIT Press.

Bukhari Shujaat, Defence Ministry ordered to pay compensation, *The Hindu*, 3 April 2011.

Call Out the Troops: an examination of the legal basis for Australian Defence Force involvement in 'non-defence' matters, Parliament of Australia; Parliamentary, Research Paper 8, 1997-1998.

Carswell, Andrew J., Classifying the conflict: a soldier's dilemma, *International Review of the Red Cross*, Vol. 91, No. 873, March 2009, p. 143-161.

Cerone, John, International Enforcement in Non-International Armed Conflict: Searching for Synergy among Legal Regimes in the Case of Libya, in Watkin Kenneth and Andrew J. Norris (eds.). 2011. *Non-International Armed Conflict in the Twenty-first Century*, International Law Series, Vol. 88, the US Naval War College, p. 369-395.

Chadha Vivek, *Armed Forces Special Powers Act: The Debate*, IDSA Monograph Series, No. 7, November 2012.

Chadha Vivek. 2005. *Low Intensity Conflicts in India*, New Delhi: Sage Publications.

Chandra Vishal, (ed.). 2013. *India's Neighbourhood: The Armies of South Asia*, New Delhi: Pentagon Press.

Chatterji, Angana P., et. al., *Buried Evidence: Unknown, Unmarked, and Mass Graves in Indian-administered Kashmir*, International Peoples' Tribunal on Human Rights and Justice in Indian-Administered Kashmir, November 2009.

Chaudhury Shweta, Extraordinary Military Powers and Right to Self Determination in Kashmir, Unpublished Thesis, University of Toronto, 2013.

Crawford Emily, Blurring the Lines between International and Non-International Armed Conflict – The Evolution of Customary International Law Applicable in Internal Armed Conflicts, *Australian International Law Journal*, Vol. 15, 2008, p. 29-54.

Clapham Andrew, Human rights obligations of non-state actors in conflict situations, *International Review of the Red Cross*, Vol. 88, No. 863, September 2006, p. 492-523.

Clode Charles M. 1869. *Military Forces of the Crown: Their Administration and Government*, London: John Murray, p. 125-180 & 353-365.

Cohen Amichai, Proportionality in Modern Asymmetrical Wars, Jerusalem Centre for Public Affairs, Israel, 2010.

Collier Kit, *The Armed Forces and Internal security in Asia: Preventing the Abuse of Power*, East-West Centre, Occasional Papers, Politics and Security Series, No. 2, December 1999.

Colonel Harvinder Singh Kohli v. Union of India, TA/254/09, in WP (C) No. 7827/2009 decided by the Armed Forces Tribunal, Principal Bench, New Delhi.

Combating terrorism: A Manual for Action. 2003. Amnesty International, AI Index ACT 40/001/2003.

Coracini Celso Eduardo Faria, The Lawful Sanctions Clause in the State Reporting Procedure before the Committee Against Torture, *Netherlands Quarterly of Human Rights*, Vol. 24/2, 2005, p. 305-318.

Corn, Geoffrey S., Self-defense Targeting: Blurring the Line between the Jus ad Belum and the Jus in Bello, in Watkin Kenneth and Andrew J. Norris (eds.). 2011. *Non-International Armed Conflict in the Twenty-first Century*, International Law Series, Vol. 88, the US Naval War College, p. 57-92.

Countering Insurgency, British Army Field Manual, Volume 1 Part 10, Army Code 71876, October 2009, UK: Ministry of Defence.

Criddle, Evan J. and Fox-Decent, Evan, Human Rights, Emergencies, and the Rule of Law, The William & Mary Law School Scholarship Repository, Faculty Publications, 2012, Paper 1531.

Criddle, Evan J., Proportionality in Counterinsurgency: A Relation Theory, *Notre Dame Law Review*, Vol. 87(3), p. 1073-1112.

Cullen Anthony. 2010. *The Concept of Non-International Armed Conflict in International Humanitarian Law*, Cambridge: Cambridge University Press.

Cullen Anthony, Kew developments Affecting the Scope of Internal Armed Conflict in International Humanitarian Law, *Military Law Review*, Vol. 183, Spring 2005, p. 66-109.

Cusack, Colin, We've Talked the Talk, Time to Walk the Walk: Meeting International Human Rights Law Standards for US Military Investigations, *Military Law Review*, Volume 217, Fall 2013, p. 48-90. S 108.

Henckaerts Jean-Marie and Louise Doswald-Beck. 2005. *Customary International Humanitarian Law*, Volume I: Rules, ICRC and Cambridge University Press.

Dahal, Shiva Hari, Haris Gazdar, S.I. Keethaponcalan and Padmaja Murthy, *Internal Conflict and Regional Security in South Asia: Approaches, Perspectives and Policies*, United Nations Institute for Disarmament Research (UNIDIR) Geneva, Switzerland, 2003.

Das Gautam. 2013. *Insurgencies in North-East India: Moving Towards Resolution*, New Delhi: Centre for Land Warfare and Pentagon Press, p. 46-57.

Defence Ministry must Respond Positively to Move to Amend AFSPA, Kashmir Interlocutors Report, *The Hindu*, 14 April 2012.

Detter Ingrid, The Law of War and Illegal Combatants, *The George Washington Law Review*, Vol. 75, (2007), p. 1049-1104.

Devasahyam M.G, Solution to Kashmir Problem—war or basic governance? *The Hindu*, 4 June 2002.

Dewar, M. 1997. *The British Army in Northern Ireland*, London: Arms and Armour Press.

Dill, Janina. 2010. *Applying Principle of Proportionality in Combat Operations*, Oxford Institute for Ethics, Law and Armed Conflict.

Dinstein Yoram, Concluding Remarks on Non-International Armed Conflicts, in Watkin Kenneth and Andrew J. Norris (eds.). 2011. *Non-International Armed Conflict in the Twenty-first Century*, International Law Series, Vol. 88, the US Naval War College, p. 399-321.

Dixit, K. C. 2012. *Building Army's Human Resource for Sub-Conventional Warfare*, New Delhi: Pentagon Press.

Dixit, K.C., Revoking AFSPA Blown out of Proportion, *Journal of Defence Studies*, Vol. 4, No. 4, October 2010, p.122-127.

Dormann Knut, Detention in Non-International Armed Conflicts, in Watkin Kenneth and Andrew J. Norris (eds.). 2011. *Non-International Armed Conflict in the Twenty-first Century*, International Law Series, Vol. 88, the US Naval War College, p. 347-366.

Drabik, Michal, Duty to Investigate Collateral Damage, *Minn. J. Int'l Law*, (Online), Vol. 15, (2013), p. 15-34.

Enforced or Involuntary Disappearances, Office of the United Nations High Commissioner for Human Rights, Fact Sheet No. 6/Rev.3, Geneva.

Engdahl David, Soldiers, Riots, and revolution: The Law and History of Military Troops in Civil Disorder, *Iowa Law Review*, Vol. 57, Number 1, October 1971, p. 1-73.

Everyone Lives in Fear: Patterns of Impunity in Jammy & Kashmir, Human Rights Watch, Vol. 18, No. 11 (C), September 2006.

Extra Judicial Execution Victim Families Association (EEVFAM) v. Union of India, (2013) 2 SCC 493.

Ferrer Raymundo B. and Rmldolph G. Cabangbang, Non-International Armed Conflicts in the Philippines, in Watkin Kenneth and Andrew J. Norris (eds.). 2011. *Non-International Armed Conflict in the Twenty-first Century*, International Law Series, Vol. 88, the US Naval War College, p. 263-278.

Ferstman Carla, Mariana Goetz, Alan Stephens (eds.). 2009. *Reparations for Victims of Genocide, War Crimes and Crimes Against Humanity: System in Place and System in Making*, Leiden: Martinus Nijhoff Publishers.

Fidell Eugene R. And Sullivan Dwight H (ed.). 2002. *Evolving Military Justice*, Annapolis: Naval Institute Press.

Fidell Eugene R., Accountability, Transparency and Public Confidence in the Administration of Military Justice, *The Green Bag*, Vol. 9, No. 4, Summer 2006, p. 361-166.

Finner, Samuel E. 2002. *The Man on Horseback: The Role of the Military in Politics*, USA: Transaction Publishers.

Finucane Brian, Enforced Disappearance as a Crime Under International Law: A Neglected Origin in the Laws of War, *The Yale Journal of International Law*, Vol. 35, 2010, p. 171-197.

Fletcher George P., Is Justice Relevant to the Law of War? *Washburn Law Review*, Winter 2009, Vol. 48, No. 2, Winter 2009. P. 407-415.

Frowe Helen. 2011. *The Ethics of War and Peace: An Introduction*, London: Routledge.

Ganguly Sumit and David P. Fidler (ed.). 2009. *India and Counterinsurgency: Lessons Learned*, London: Routledge.

Ganguly Sumit, 'Conflict and Crisis in South and Southwest Asia', in Brown Michael E. (ed). 1996. *The International Dimensions of Internal Conflict*, London: MIT Press, p. 141-172.

Gardam Judith and Charlesworth Hilary, Protection of Women in Armed Conflict, *Human Rights Quarterly*, Vol. 22, No. 1, February 2000, p. 148-166.

Garraway, C., Superior Orders and the International Criminal Court: Justice Delivered or Justice Denied', *International Review of the Red Cross*, No. 836, 1999, pp. 785–94.

Garraway Charles, War and Peace: Where Is the Divide? in Watkin Kenneth and Andrew J. Norris (eds.). 2011. *Non-International Armed Conflict in the Twenty-first Century*, International Law Series, Vol. 88, the US Naval War College, p. 93-118.

Gasser Hans-Peter, International Humanitarian Law and Human Rights Law in Non-international Armed Conflict: Joint Venture of Mutual Exclusion? Vol. 45, *German Yearbook of International Law*, 2002, p. 149.

Gayer Laurent and Jaffrelot Christophe. 2009. *Armed Militia of South Asia: Fundamentalists, Maoists and Separatists*, New Delhi: Foundation Books.

General Officer Commanding v Central Bureau of Investigation, [2012] 5 SCR 599.

Getting Away With Murder: 50 Years of the Armed Forces (Special Powers) Act, Human Rights Watch Report, August 2008.

Gibson Michael R., International Human Rights Law and the Administration of Justice through Military Tribunals: Preserving Utility while Precluding Impunity, *Journal of International Law and International Relations*, Vol. 4(1), 2008, p. 1-48.

Goodhand Jonathan. 2006. *Aiding Peace: The Role of NGOs in Armed Conflict*, London: Lynne Reinner Publishers.

Goswami Namrata, The Naga Narrative of Conflict: Envisioning a Resolution Roadmap, *Strategic Analysis*, Vol. 31, No. 2, March 2007, p. 287-313.

Graham, David E., 'Defining Non-International Armed Conflict: A Historically Difficult Task', in Watkin Kenneth and Andrew J. Norris (eds.). 2011. *Non-International Armed Conflict in the Twenty-first Century*, International Law Series, Vol. 88, the US Naval War College, p. 43-56.

Graham, David E., Counterinsurgency, The War on Terror, and the Laws of War: A Response, *Virginia Law Review In Brief*, Vol. 95, 2009, p. 79-86.

Grewal D.S. and Kamal Kinger, 'Role of Armed Forces in Internal Security Management in North Eastern States of India', in Adhikari Shekhar and Sanjeev Bhaduria (ed.). 2014. *India's National Security in the 21ˢᵗ Century*, New Delhi: Pentagon Press, p. 395-408.

Gross Oren and Fionnuala Ni Aolain. 2006. *Law in Time of Armed Conflict: Emergency Powers in Theory and Practice*, Cambridge: Cambridge University Press.

Gross, Oren, Providing for the Unexpected: Constitutional Emergency Provisions, *Israeli Yearbook on Human Rights*, Vol.13, 2005, p. 13–44.

Gross Oren, Chaos and Rules: Should Responses to Violent Crises Always Be Constitutional? *The Yale Law Journal*, Vol. 112, 2003, p. 1011-1134.

Gupta Shekhar, The Buck Starts Here, *Indian Express*, 10 April 2010.

Hancock, N., *Terrorism and the Law in Australia: Legislation, Commentary and Constraints*, Research Paper No. 12, 2001–2002, Canberra: Department of Parliamentary Library.

Handbook on Human Rights and Fundamental Freedoms of Armed Forces Personnel. 2008. Poland: OSCE/Office for democratic Institutions and Human Rights (ODIHR).

Hansen Victor, The Impact of Military Justice Reforms on the Law of Armed Conflict: How to Avoid Unintended Consequences, *Michigan State International Law Review*, Vol. 12 (2), 2013, p. 229-272.

Haque, Adil Ahmad, Killing in the Fog of War, *Southern California Law Review*, Vol. 86, 2012, p. 63-116.

Hartle Antony E. 2004. *Moral Issues in Military Decision Making*, USA: University of Kansas.

Hathaway, Oona A., Rebecca Crootof, Philip Levitz, Haley Nix, William Perdue, Chelsea Purvis, and Julia Spiegel, Which Law Governs During Armed Conflict? The Relationship between International Humanitarian Law and Human Rights Law, *Minnesota Law Review*, Vol. 96, 2012, p. 1883-1944.

Hathaway Oona, Samuel Adelsberg, Spencer Amdur, Philip Levitz, Freya Pitts & Sirine Shebaya, The Power To Detain: Detention of Terrorism

Suspects After 9/11, *The Yale Journal of International Law*, Vol. 38, 2013, p. 123-177.

Hayashi Nobuo (ed.), *National Military Manuals on the Law of Armed Conflict*, Forum for International Criminal and Humanitarian Law, International Peace Research Institute, Oslo (PRIO), 2008.

Haye Eve La. 2008. *War Crimes in Internal Armed Conflicts*, Cambridge: Cambridge University Press.

Haynes Jeff, 'The Principles of Good Governance', in Cleary Laura R. and Teri McConville (ed.). 2006. *Managing Democracy in Democracy*, Routledge, p. 17-31.

Head Michael, Calling out the Troops – Disturbing Trends and Unanswered Questions, *UNSW Law Journal*, Volume 28 (2), 2005, p. 479-506.

Head Michael and Scott Mann. 2009. *Domestic Deployment of the Armed Forces: Military Powers, Law and Human Rights*, USA: Ashgate.

How is the Term 'Armed Conflict' Defined in International Humanitarian Law? International Committee of the Red Cross (ICRC), Opinion Paper, March 2008.

Hughes Geraint, The Military's Role in Counterterrorism: Examples and Implications for Liberal Democracies, Strategic Studies Institute, The US Army War College, The Letort Papers, May 2011, pp. 228.

Ignoring Executions and Torture: Impunity for Bangladesh's Security Forces, Human Rights Watch, May 2009.

Inderjit Barua v. State of Assam, AIR 1983 Delhi 513.

India: Country Reports on Human Rights Practices for 2012, United States Department of State, Bureau of Democracy, Human Rights and Labour.

India: National Report Submitted in Accordance with Human Rights Council Resolution 5/1, UN General Assembly document, A/HRC/WG.6/1/IND/1 dated 6 March 2008.

International Legal Protection of Human Rights in Armed Conflict, United Nations, Office of the High Commissioner of Human Rights, 2011, HR/PUB/11/01.

Jackson Major Russel K., Lawlessness Within a Foreign State as a Legal Basis for United States Military Intervention to Restore the Rule of Law, *Military Law Review*, Vol. 187, Spring 2006, p. 1-42.

Jackson, Richard B., Perfidy in Non-International Armed Conflicts, in Watkin Kenneth and Andrew J. Norris (eds.). 2011. *Non-International Armed Conflict in the Twenty-first Century*, International Law Series, Vol. 88, the US Naval War College, p. 237-259.

Jamwal Anuradha Bhasin, Victory of Institutional Justice: Army's Pathribal Closure, *Economic and Political Weekly*, Vol. XLIX No. 9, March 1, 2014, p. 13-16.

Jamwal Anuradha Bhasin, Rapists in Uniform, *Economic and Political Weekly*, Vol. XLVIII, No. 8, 23 February 2013, p. 13-16.

Jha U.C., Terrorism and Human Rights: A Comment, *Economic and Political Weekly*, Vol. XLIV, No. 37, 12 September 2009, p. 70-71.

Jha U.C., International Humanitarian Law and the Doctrine of Command Responsibility, *ISIL Yearbook of International Humanitarian and Refugee Law*, Vol. II, 2007, p. 75-87.

Jinks Derek P., The Anatomy of an Institutionalized Emergency: Preventive detention and Personal Liberty in India, *Michigan Journal of International Law*, Vol. 22, Winter 2001, p. 311-370.

John Wilson, Kashmir: The Problem, and the Way Forward, *Strategic Analysis*, Vol. 35, No. 2, March 2011, p. 318-323.

Johnson Kermit D., 'Ethical issues of Military Leadership', in Matthews Lloyed J. and Dale E. Brown (ed.). 1989. *The Parameters of Military Ethics*, New York: Pergamon-Brassey, International Defence Publishers Inc., p. 73-78.

Kadyan Lt Gen Raj, The Armed Forces Special Powers Act—Need for review? *South Asia Defence & Strategic Review*, March-April 2013, p. 29-30.

Kalhan Anil, Gerald P. Conroy, Mamta Kaushal, Sam Scott Miller and Jed S. Rakoff, Colonial Continuities: Human Rights, Terrorism, and Human Security, *Columbia Journal of Asian Law*, Vol. 20 (1), 2006, p. 93-234.

Kanwal Gurmeet. 2008. *Indian Army Vision 2020*, New Delhi: Harper Collins India.

Kapoor Rajesh, Revolution in Military Affairs and Counterinsurgency in India, Working Paper 2, Centre for Land Warfare Studies, New Delhi, 2010.

Kasher Asa and Amos Yadlin, Determining Norms for Warfare in New Situations: Between Military Ethics and the Laws of War, *Military and Strategic Affairs*, Vol. 5, No. 1, May 2013, p.95-117.

Kasher Asa and Amos Yadlin, Military Ethics of Fighting Terror: Principles, *Philosophia*, Vol. 34, (2006), p. 75–84.

Kazi Seema, Law, Governance and Gender in India-Administered Kashmir, Working Paper Series, Centre for the Study of Law and Governance, Jawaharlal Nehru University, New Delhi, CSLG/WP/20, November 2012.

Kazi Seema, Rape, Impunity and Justice in Kashmir, *Socio-Legal Review*, Vol. 10, 2014, pp. 14-46.

Kerr Pauline, *The evolving dialectic between state-centric and human-centric security*, working Paper 2003/2, Department of International Relations RSPAS, Australian National University, Canberra, September 2003.

Khakee Anna, *Securing Democracy? A Comparative Analysis of Emergency Powers in Europe*, Geneva Centre for the Democratic Control of Armed Forces (DCAF), Policy Paper No. 30, 2009, Geneva.

Koh, Harold Hongju, International Criminal Justice 5.0, *The Yale Journal of International Law*, Vol. 38, 2013, p. 525-542.

Kohn, R., The Erosion of Civilian Control of the Military in the United States Today, *Naval War College Review*, Summer 2002.

Kretzmer David, Aviad Ben-Yehuda and Meirav Furth, 'Thou Shall Not Kill': The Use of Lethal Force in Non-International Armed Conflicts, *Israel Law Review*, Vol. 47 (2), 2014, p. 191-224.

Kretzmer David, Rethinking the Application of IHL in Non-International Armed Conflict, *Israel Law Review*, Vol. 42 (8), 2009, p. 8-42.

Krishna Rao V.K. 1997. *The Genesis of Insurgency in Jammu & Kashmir, and in the Northeast, and Future Prospects*, New Delhi: United Service Institution of India.

Law of Armed Conflict: Deskbook, The Judge Advocate General's Legal Centre and School, US Army, 2013.

Legras, F. Rubber Bullets, Tear Gas and Mass Arrests at the Summit of the Americas in Quebec City', *World Socialist Web Site*, 2 May 2001.

Lietzau, William K., Detention of Terrorists in the Twenty-first Century, in Watkin Kenneth and Andrew J. Norris (eds.). 2011. *Non-International Armed Conflict in the Twenty-first Century*, International Law Series, Vol. 88, the US Naval War College, p.323-345.

Lillich, Richard B., The Paris Minimum Standards of Human Rights Norms in a State of Emergency, *American Journal of International Law*, Vol. 79, 1985, p. 1072-81.

Longley, John R., Military Purpose Act: An Alternative to the Posse Comitatus Act—Accomplishing Congress's Intent with Clear Statutory Language, *Arizona Law Review*, Vol. 49, 2007, p. 717-743.

Lubell Noam, Challenges in applying human rights law to armed conflict, *International Review of the Red Cross*, Vol. 87, No. 860, December 2005, p. 737-754.

Maheshwari Anil. 1993. *Crescent Over Kashmir: Politics of Mullaism*, New Delhi: Rupa & Co, p. 148-166.

Malik, V P, Human Rights in the Armed Forces, *Journal of Human Rights*, Vol. 4, 2005.

Mallick, P.K., Role of the Armed Forces in Internal Security: Time for Review, *CLAWS Journal*, Winter 2007, p. 68-120.

Manipur: Perils of War and Womanhood, Memorandum submitted to Rashida Manjoo Special Rapporteur on Violence Against Women, its Causes and Consequences, Human Rights Council, 28 April 2013.

Manjoo Rashida and Calleigh Mcraith, Gender-Based Violence and Justice in Conflict and Post-Conflict Areas, *Cornell International Law Journal*, Vol. 44, 2011, p. 11-31.

Mann Michael. 1993. *The Sources of Social Power Vol. II, The Rise of Classes and Nation-States 1760-1914*, New York: Cambridge University Press, p. 403.

Marc Waring, The Domestic Deployment of the British Army: The Case for a Third Force, *The RUSI Journal*, Vol. 158, No. 3, 2013, pp. 62-69.

Marston Daniel P. And Chander S. Sundaram (ed.). 2007. *A Military History of India and South Asia: from the east India Company to the Nuclear Era*, London: Praeger Security International.

Marzek Josef, Armed Conflict and the Use of Force, *CYIL*, Vol 1, 2010, p. 87-119.

Mason, P. 1974. *A Matter of Honour: An Account of the Indian Army, Its Officers and Men*. London: Jonathan Cape.

Mattoo Amitabh, Kashmir After Shopian, *Economic and Political Weekly*, Vol. XLIV, No. 28, 11 July 2009, p. 39-43. HC 46.

McDonnell Thomas Michael. 2010. *The United States, International Law, and the Struggle Against Terrorism*, London and New York: Routledge.

McLaughlin, Rob, An Australian Perspective on Non-International Armed Conflict: Afghanistan and East Timor, in Watkin Kenneth and Andrew J. Norris (eds.). 2011. *Non-International Armed Conflict in the Twenty-first Century*, International Law Series, Vol. 88, the US Naval War College, p. 293-319.

Menezes S.L. 1999. *Fidelity and Honour: The India Army*, New Delhi: Oxford India Paperback.

Mettraux Guenael. 2009. *The Law of Command Responsibility*, Oxford: Oxford University Press.

Military Justice: Adjudication of Sexual Offences; Australia, Canada, Germany, Israel, and United Kingdom, July 2013, The Law Library of Congress, Global Legal Research Centre.

Mohamedou, Mohammad-Mahmoud Ould, *The Pitfalls of Lawlessness: Disorder, Emergencies, and Conflict*, Background Paper, Expert Seminar on Democracy and Rules of Law, UN Office of the High Commissioner for Human Rights, March 2005.

Moir Lindsay. 2002. *The Law of Internal Armed Conflict*, Cambridge: Cambridge University Press.

Moloto, Judge Bakone Justice, Command Responsibility in International Criminal Tribunals, *Berkeley Journal of International Law*, Vol. 3 (2009), p. 12-25.

Monitoring and Investigating Human rights abuses in armed conflict, Amnesty International and Council for the Development of Social Science Research in Africa, 2001.

Mullerson Rein, International Humanitarian Law in Internal Conflicts, *Journal of Conflict and Security Law*, Vol. 2 (2), 1997, p. 109-133.

Murphy, John F., Will-o'-the-Wisp? The Search for Law in Non-International Armed Conflicts, in Watkin Kenneth and Andrew J. Norris (eds.). 2011. *Non-International Armed Conflict in the Twenty-first Century*, International Law Series, Vol. 88, the US Naval War College, p. 15-39.

Murphy Ray, Contemporary Challenges to the Implementation of International Humanitarian Law, *The Quarterly Journal*, Vol. III, NO. 3, September 2004, p. 99-123.

Muttaqien, M., Japan in the Global War on Terrorism, *Global & Strategic Ph.*, Vol. 1, No. 2, July-December 2007, p. 151-169. S 53.

Naga People's Movement of Human Rights v Union of India, 1998 AIR SC 459.

Nachbar, Thomas B., The Use of Law in Counterinsurgency, *Military Law Review*, Vol. 213, 2011, p. 140-164.

Nair Ravi, The Unlawful Activities (Prevention) Amendment Act 2008: Repeating Past Mistakes, *Economic & Political Weekly*, 24 January 2009, p. 10-14.

Nanavatty Rostum K. 2013. *Internal Armed Conflict in India*, New Delhi: Pentagon Press.

Navlakha Gautam, A Force Stretched and Stressed, *Economic and Political Weekly*, 18 November 2006, p. 4722-23.

Nicholas Grono, Australia's Response to Terrorism, *Studies in Intelligence*, Vol. 48, No. 1, p. 27-38.

Nolte George (ed.). 2003. *European Military Law Systems*, Berlin: De Gruyter Recht.

Noorani A.G., Armed Forces (Special Powers) Act: Urgency of Review, *Economic and Political Weekly*, Vol. XLIV, No. 34, 22 August 2013, p. 8-11.

Odeku, kola O., Criminal Responsibility for Torture: A Human Rights Analysis, *Anthropologist*, Vol. 15(2), 2013, p. 125-135.

Olson Laura M., Practical Challenges of Implementing the Complementarity Between IHL and Human Rights Law—Demonstrated by the Procedural regulation of Internment in Non-International Armed Conflict, *Case Western Reserve Journal of International Law*, Vol. 40, 2009, p. 437-461.

Osiel, M. 1999, *Obeying Orders: Atrocity, Military Discipline and the Laws of War*, New Brunswick, NJ: Transaction Publishers.

Oudraat Chantal de jonge, 'The United Nations and Internal Conflict', in Brown Michael E. (ed). 1996. *The International Dimensions of Internal Conflict*, London: MIT Press, p. 489-536.

Padgaonkar Dileep, Radha Kumar and M.M. Ansari, A New Compact with the People of Jammu and Kashmir, Group for Interloculators for J&K, Final Report.

Perna, L. 2006. *The Formation of the Treaty Law of Non-international Armed Conflict*, Leiden, Boston: Martinus Nijhoff Publishers.

Penna, L. R., Written and customary provisions relating to the conduct of hostilities and treatment of victims of armed conflicts in ancient India, *International Review of the Red Cross*, 1989, p. 340-41.

Perry Robin, The Nature, Status and Future of Amnesties under International Criminal Law, *Australian International Law Journal*, 2011, p. 77-104.

Pervez Ayesha, Sexual Violence and Culture of Impunity in Kashmir: Need for a paradigm shift, *Economic and Political Weekly*, Vol. XLIX, No. 10, 8 March 2014, p. 10-13.

Petty Keith A., Humanity and National Security: The Law of Mass Atrocity Response Operations, *Michigan Journal of International Law*, Vol. 34 (4), 2013, p. 745-827.

Pomper Stephen, Toward a Limited Consensus on the Loss of Civilian Immunity in Non-International Armed Conflict: Making Progress through Practice, in Watkin Kenneth and Andrew J. Norris (eds.). 2011. *Non-International Armed Conflict in the Twenty-first Century*, International Law Series, Vol. 88, the US Naval War College, p.181-193.

Pradhan Sushil, Indian Army's Contribution to Internal Security, *CLAWS Journal*, Summer 2011, pp. 127-140.

Raguan Galit, Adjudicating Armed Conflict in Domestic Courts: The Experience of Israel's Supreme Court, *Yearbook of International Humanitarian Law*, Vol. 13, 2010, p. 61-95.

Ramakrishnan, Nitya. 2013. *In Custody: Law, Impunity and Prisoner Abuse in South Asia*, New Delhi: SAGE Publications India Pvt. Ltd.

Ramanathan Usha, India and the ICC, *Journal of International Criminal Justice*, Volume 3, 2005, pp. 627-634.

Ramraj Victor V., Hor Michael, Roach Kent and William George (eds.). 2012. *Global Anti-Terrorism Law and Policy*, Cambridge: Cambridge University Press.

Rasmussen, Moyano, *The Military Role in Internal Defence and Security: Some Problems*, Occasional Paper, The Center for Civil-Military Relations, Naval Post-Graduate School, California, October 1999.

Reinke Saundra J. and Randall Miller, 'The Profession of Arms and the Management of Violence', in Weber Jeffrey A. and Johan Eliasson (ed.). 2008. *Handbook of Military Administration*, New York: CRC Press, p. 301-316.

Report of the Committee to Review the Armed Forces (Special Powers) Act, 1958, Justice Reddy Committee Report, 2005.

Report of the Working Group on Enforced or Involuntary Disappearances, Human Rights Council, UN General Assembly, A/HRC/22/45, dated 28 January 2013.

Restricting Individual Liberty, *Commonwealth Human Rights Law Digest,* Winter 2008, p. 27-37.

Robertson, G. 2008, *Crimes Against Humanity,* Camberwell: Penguin Books.

Rowe P. 2006. *The Impact of Human Right Laws on Armed Forces.* UK: Cambridge University Press.

Rowe, P. and Whelan, C. (eds). 1985. *Military Intervention in Democratic Societies,* London: Croom Helm.

Rupesinghe, K. and K. Mumtaz (eds.). 1996. *Internal Conflicts in South Asia,* London: Sage.

Sabharwal Mukesh, The Armed Forces Special Powers Act (AFSPA), *Indian Defence Review,* Vol. 27 (2), April-June 2012, p. 134-139.

Sassoli, Marco, Taking Armed Groups Seriously: Ways to Improve their Compliance with International Humanitarian Law, *International Humanitarian Legal Studies,* Vol. 1, (2010), p. 5-51.

Sassoli Marco, Antoine A. Bouvier and Anne Quintin. 2011. *How Does Law Protect in War?* Vol. I, Geneva: ICRC.

Sato Hiromi, Modes of International Criminal Justice and General Principles of Criminal Responsibility, *Journal of International Law,* Vol. 4, No. 3, (2012) p. 765-807.

Saul Ben. 2006. *Defining Terrorism in International Law,* Oxford: Oxford University Press.

Sawhney Pravin & Ghazala Wahab, AFSPA Must Go, Force, November 2011, p. 10-19.

Schmitt, Michael N., Investigating Violations of International Law in Armed Conflict, *Harvard National Security Journal,* Vol. 2, 2011, p. 31-84.

Schmitt, Michael N., Charles H.B. Garraway and Yoram Dinstein, *The Manual on the Law of Non-International Armed Conflict,* San Remo, 2006.

Schmitt, Michael N., The Status of Opposition Fighters in a Non-International Armed Conflict, in Watkin Kenneth and Andrew J.

Norris (eds.). 2011. *Non-International Armed Conflict in the Twenty-first Century*, International Law Series, Vol. 88, the US Naval War College, p. 119-144.

Schmitt, Michael N., Human Shield in International Law, *Israel Yearbook on Human Rights*, Vol. 38, 2008. p. 17-59.

Schnabel Albrecht and Marc Krupanski, Mapping Evolving Internal Roles of the Armed Forces, The Geneva Centre for the Democratic Control of Armed Forces, SSR Paper 7, 2012, pp. 74.

Securing Australia: Protecting Our Community, Counter Terrorism: White Paper, The Department of the Prime Minister and Cabinet, Government of Australia, 2010.

Segall Anna. 2001. *Punishing Violations of IHL at the National Level*, Geneva: ICRC.

Shankar Shylashri. 2009. *Scaling Justice: India's Supreme Court, Anti-terror Laws and Social Rights*, New Delhi: Oxford University Press.

Sharma Surinder K. and Anshuman Behera. 2014. *Militant Groups in South Asia*, New Delhi: Pentagon Press.

Sharma V.N. 1996. *Threats to National security Dues to Internal Problems*, New Delhi: United Service Institution of India.

Shimpson A.W.B., Round up the Usual Suspects: The Legacy of British Colonialism and the European Convention on Human Rights, *Loyola Law Review*, Vol. 41, 1996. p. 629-711.

Silk, James J., International Criminal Justice and the Protection of Human Rights: The Rule of Law or the Hubris of Law? *The Yale Journal of International Law* (on line), Vol. 39, Spring 2014, p. 94-114.

Simons, Beth A. 2009. *Mobilizing for Human Rights: International Law in Domestic Politics*, Cambridge: Cambridge University Press.

Sitaraman Ganesh, Counterinsurgency, War on Terror, Laws of War, *Virginia Law Review* , Vol. 95, 2009, p. 1745-1839.

Smit Dirk van Zyl and Andrew Ashworth, Disproportionate sentences as Human Rights Violations, *The Modern Law Review*, Vol. 67, July 2004, No. 4, p. 541-560.

Smith Dan, Trends and Causes of Armed Conflict, Berghof Research Center for Constructive Conflict Management, 2004.

Snedden S.E., Northern Ireland; a British Military Success or a Purely Political Outcome? Defence Research Paper, Advanced Command and Staff Course, 2007.

Soldiers and Human Rights: Lawyers to right of them, lawyers to left of them, *The Economist*, 9 August 2015.

Steinhoff Dawn, Talking to the Enemy: State Legitimacy Concerns with Engaging Non-State Armed Groups, *Texas International Law Journal*, Vol. 45, No. 1, Fall 2009, p. 297-322.

Stevenson Jonathan, The Role of the Armed Forces of the United Kingdom in Securing the State Against Terrorism, *The Quarterly Journal*, Fall 2005, pp. 121-133.

Sundar Aparna and Sundar Nandini (ed.). 2014. *Civil Wars in South Asia: State Sovereignty, Development*, New Delhi: Sage Publications.

Teltumbde Anad, Criminalising People's Protests, *Economic and Political Weekly*, Vol. XLVIII, No. 14, 6 April 2013, p. 10-11.

Templeman D. and Bergin, A., *Taking a Punch: Building a More Resilient Australia*, ASPI Strategic Insights 39, May 2008.

The Armed Forces (Special Powers) Act, 1958 in Manipur and other States of the Northeast of India: Sanctioning repression in violation of India's human rights obligations, Asian Human Rights Commission, 18 August 2011.

The United Nations Global Counter-Terrorism Strategy, UN General Assembly Resolution A/RES/60/288, dated 20 September 2006.

The Use of Military Courts to Try Suspects, *International and Comparative Quarterly*, Vol. 51, October 2002, p. 967-980.

These Fellows Must be Eliminated: Relentless Violence and Impunity in Manipur, Human Rights Watch, September 2008.

Toney, Raymond J. and Shazia N. Anwar, International Human Rights Law and Military Personnel: A Look Behind the Barrack Walls, *American University International Law Review*, Vol. 14, No. 2, 1998, pp. 519-543.

Torture in Asia: The law and practice, *Article 2*, October 2013, Vol. 12, No. 3, Asian Legal Resource Centre, Asian Human Rights Commission.

Trechsel Stefan. 2005. *Human Rights in Criminal Proceedings*, Oxford: Oxford University Press.

Tripathy Sasmita and Saeed Ahmed Rid, *Democracy as a Conflict-Resolution Model for Terrorism: A Case Study of India and Pakistan*, Regional Centre for Strategic Studies, Colombo, Sri Lanka, 2010.

Upadhyay Archana, Terrorism in the North-east: Linkages and Implications, *Economic and Political Weekly*, 2 December 2006, p. 4993-4999.

Varadarajan Siddhartha, Official panel wants stringent safeguards on Army use, *The Hindu*, 6 October 2006.

Varin Caroline, The Role of Values in Counter-Insurgency and Stabilisation: Mil-Mil, Civ-Mil and 'Civ-Civ' Dialogue from the Balkans to South Asia, Chatham House London, September 2011.

Vimug Mukul, Lawfully Wedded to Democracy? India and the Armed Forces (Special Powers) Act, *Essex Human Rights Review*, Vol. 9, No. 1, June 2012, p. 1-28

Vladeck, Stephen I., Emergency Power and the Militia Acts, *The Yale Law Journal*, Vol. 114, 2004, p. 149-192.

Walzer Michael, 'Two Kinds of Military responsibility', in Matthews Lloyed J. and Dale E. Brown (ed.). 1989. *The Parameters of Military Ethics*, New York: Pergamon-Brassey, International Defence Publishers Inc., p. 67-72.

Wani Fayal, Feel-Good factor: Will revocation of AFSPA help Kashmir? *Force*, August 2009 p. 65-66.

Wardlaw Grant. 1989. *Political Terrorism: Theory, tactics, and counter-measures*, Cambridge: Cambridge University Press.

Watkin Kenneth and Andrew J. Norris. 2011. *Non-International Armed Conflict in the Twenty-first Century*, International Law Series, Vol. 88, the US Naval War College.

Watkin, Kenneth, "Small Wars": The Legal Challenges, in Watkin Kenneth and Andrew J. Norris (eds.). 2011. *Non-International Armed Conflict in the Twenty-first Century*, International Law Series, Vol. 88, the US Naval War College, p. 3-12.

Watkin Kenneth, Controlling the Use of Force: A Role for Human Rights Norms in Contemporary Armed Conflict, *The American Journal of International Law*, Vol. 98 (1), 2004, p. 1-34.

Watts Sean, Present and Future Conceptions of the Status of Government Forces in Non-International Armed Conflict, in Watkin Kenneth and Andrew J. Norris (eds.). 2011. *Non-International Armed Conflict in the Twenty-first Century*, International Law Series, Vol. 88, the US Naval War College, p. 145-180.

We Can Torture, Kill, or Keep You for Years, Enforced Disappearances by Pakistan Security Forces in Balochistan, Human Rights Watch, July 2011.

Webber Diane, Preventive Detention in the Law of Armed Conflict: Throwing Away the Key? *Journal of National Security Law & Policy*, Vol. 6, 2012, p. 166-205.

Weisman Elizabeth Sara, Learning to Win: An Examination of Counterterrorism in Northern Ireland, Unpublished Thesis, Wesleyan University, 2009.

Weiss Thomas G., 'Nongovernmental Organizations and Internal Conflict', in Brown Michael E. (ed). 1996. *The International Dimensions of Internal Conflict*, London: MIT Press, p. 435-460.

Wing Ian, *Refocusing Concepts of Security: The Convergence of Military and Non-military Tasks*, Land Warfare Studies Centre, Australia, Working Paper No. 111, November 2000.

World Report 2013, Human Rights Watch.

Zapalla Salvatore. 2003. *Human Rights in International Criminal Proceedings*, Oxford: Oxford University Press.

Zayas, Alfred de, Human Rights and Indefinite Detention, *International Review of the Red Cross*, Vol. 87, No. 857, March 2005, p. 15-38.

Index